# 199

# Children's Writer's & Illustrator's Market

*Edited by*
*Connie Wright Eidenier*

Writer's
Digest
Books

Cincinnati, Ohio

*Distributed in Canada by Prentice-Hall of
Canada Ltd., 1870 Birchmount Road,
Scarborough, Ontario M1P 2J7.*

*Managing Editor, Market Books Department:
Constance J. Achabal*

**Children's Writer's & Illustrator's Market.**
*Copyright © 1990
by Writer's Digest Books. Published by
F&W Publications, 1507 Dana Ave.,
Cincinnati, Ohio 45207. Printed and bound
in the United States of America. All rights
reserved. No part of this book may be repro-
duced in any manner whatsoever without
written permission from the publisher, except
by reviewers who may quote brief passages to
be printed in a magazine or newspaper.*

*International Standard Serial Number
0897-9790
International Standard Book Number
0-89879-382-3*

# Contents

## The Markets

# Resources

# _From the Editor_

"I was lucky enough," says Indianapolis children's writer (and "Close-up" personality, see page 65) Valiska Gregory, "to grow up in a Czech neighborhood in Chicago where children were treasured and where, always, my father told us stories. My brothers and I ate them with our daily bread, swallowed them whole, and begged for more. My father shaped his tales as carefully as he painted my name on my lunch box in Gothic letters; the black ink seemed to appear like angels on the penciled lines, a dimness made clear. It is this clarity of vision I wish to offer children—stories told with humor, charm and grace, stories that, like good soup, sustain the human spirit."

It is this love of stories—and reading—that so many writers and illustrators hope to instill in a new generation of readers. Certainly publishers are doing their part too. According to R.R. Bowker, the annual output of children's books has increased from 2,859 books in 1980 to 4,954 in 1988. As you read the Book Publishers' and Magazine Publishers' introductions in this book, pay attention to the other industry statistics—they are further proof that the market is indeed thriving with "story tellers" and "listeners."

## Book and magazine publishers

The growth of children's books is also reflected in the 50 additional book publishers included in this edition, plus the many changes in subject needs specified by the book publishers as they updated their listings for this second edition of _Children's Writer's & Illustrator's Market._

Children's magazines, as expected, are doing well also, and we've added many new publications geared to children and teens. You will notice that many of this year's children's magazine listings now include a special Poetry subsection which details the subject matter each editor wishes to review, poem length and maximum number of submissions allowed.

## New additions for 1990

In order to make this second edition more comprehensive and informative than our first, we have included two roundtable discussions—one for writers and another for illustrators. The Roundtable for Writers features Atheneum Editor Jean Karl, and children's writers Lois Duncan and Kathlyn Gay who discuss what it takes to be a successful writer. Our Roundtable for Illustrators showcases Harcourt Brace Jovanovich Art Director Michael Farmer and Ideals Publishing Corp. Children's Book Editor Peggy Schaefer along with illustrators (and sometimes writers) Ed Young and Robert Quackenbush who share the information necessary to compete as a professional illustrator today. To further provide you with tips detailing what it takes to thrive in children's book publishing, we have included eight "Close-up" interviews with professional children's book illustrators, Nancy Tafuri and John Stadler; children's book writer, Valiska Gregory; and Walker & Co. Editor-in-Chief of children's books, Amy Shields.

Magazine publishers are represented via two editors, Christine French Clark of _Humpty Dumpty's Magazine_ and Karle Dickerson of _'TEEN_ magazine who provide additional insights into selling to children's magazines.

## For students only

Because children who grow up with the love of reading can well become our famous authors and illustrators of tomorrow, we have included in our Young Writer's/Illustrator's Markets section an interview with the co-editor of *Stone Soup*. In this feature Gerry Mandel shares with 6 to 13 year old student writers and illustrators what she looks for in submitted work. Students will also want to read Elizabeth Haidle's interview in the Contests section for further proof that there is a place in publishing for them. Elizabeth, who at 13 was honored to have a book published through Landmark Editions annual student writing and illustrating contest, shares her experience in having her book published. There has been a surge in the growth of contest listings this year with 40 new responses—and many of these are geared for students as well as adults.

## New markets

This second edition of *Children's Writer's & Illustrator's Market* has grown from 192 to 272 pages because of the additional editorial matter, the many new listings in each market section and because of four new sections: Audiovisual, Audiotapes, Scripts and Special Markets. The latter section details those markets interested in producing children's greeting cards, puzzles, coloring books or games. You will also want to consult the Book Publishers listings for any additional references to "special market needs." Many times religious or educational—as well as trade—publishers carry separate lines of activity books the writer or illustrator could turn his creative energies to.

## Resources

As in last year's *Children's Writer's & Illustrator's Market*, we have included a current—and comprehensive—list of agents, organizations and workshops for your reference. I'm sure you will find this edition of *Children's Writer's & Illustrator's Market* to be a valuable marketing tool in your professional writing and illustrating endeavors. There is a burgeoning children's publishing market out there . . . and lots of competition. But if you—like Valiska Gregory—are sustained by the love of good books and are armed with the marketing know-how that can be gained from this book, you certainly have an edge on that competition.

Connie Eidenier

# How to Use Children's Writer's & Illustrator's Market

Take a few minutes to familiarize yourself with this sample listing before browsing through the book. Each component of the listing is numbered for your convenience and corresponds to an explanation following this sample.

When you see "SASE," it stands for self-addressed, stamped envelope and the acronym "SAE," possibly with "IRC," stands for self-addressed envelope and international reply coupon, respectively. If you are a foreigner marketing to a listing within the United States, or a United State's citizen marketing work abroad, send a SAE and the appropriate amount of IRCs (determined by the post office) in lieu of U.S. stamps. Also, a "ms" or "mss" refers to "manuscript" or "manuscripts" respectively.

Throughout many listings you will find four categories of children's writing/illustrating; they are defined as: "picture books," written/illustrated for pre-school-8 year olds; "young readers" for 5-8 year olds; "middle readers" for 9-11 year olds; and "young adults" for those 12 and older.

**(1) WATERFRONT BOOKS, (2)** 98 Brookes Ave., Burlington VT 05401. (802)658-7477. **(3)** Book publisher. **(4)** Publisher: Sherrill N. Musty. (Some listings specify the number of picture book, young reader, middle reader and/or young adult titles published per year.) **(5)** 100% of books by first-time authors. **(6)** (Some listings will provide information on the % of books subsidy published.)
**Fiction: (7)** Picture books, young readers, middle readers, young adults: mental health, family/parenting, health, special issues involving barriers to learning in children. **(8)** (Some listings specify a word or page length here.) **(9)** Recently published *JOSH: A Boy With Dyslexia*, by Caroline Janover (ages 8-12, paperback).
**Nonfiction: (10)** Picture books, young readers, middle readers, young adults: education, guidance, health, mental health, social issues. **(11)** (Some listings specify a word or page length here.) **(12)** Recently published *Changing Families*, by David Fassler, M.D., Michele Lash, A.T.R., Sally B. Ives, Ph.D. (ages 4-12, paper and plastic comb binding).
**How to Contact/Writers: (13)** Fiction/nonfiction: Query. **(14)** SASE (IRC) for answer to query. **(15)** Reports on queries in 2 weeks; on mss in 6 weeks. **(16)** Publishes a book 6 months after acceptance. **(17)** Will consider photocopied and computer printout submissions.
**Illustration: (18)** (Some listings specify the number of illustrations per type of book.) **(19)** Editorial will review ms/illustration packages submitted by authors/artists and ms/illustration packages submitted by authors with illustrations done by separate artists. **(20)** (Some listings will include information about the medium/style/size of artwork the editor or art director prefers to review.)
**How to Contact/Illustrators: (21)** Ms/illustration packages: Query first. Illustrations only: Résumé, tearsheets. **(22)** Reports on art samples only if interested. **(23)** (Some listings specify if artwork is returned after a job is completed.)
**Terms/Writers & Illustrators: (24)** Pays authors in royalties of 10-15% based on wholesale price. **(25)** (Some listings will give an average figure for advances paid

to authors.) **(26)** Pays illustrators by the job. Additional payment for ms/illustration packages: Negotiable. Factors used to determine final payment: Number of illustrations used. Pay for separate authors and illustrators: "amount is negotiable but it would be within industry standards." **(27)** Sends galleys to authors; dummies to illustrators. **(28)** Book catalog available for #10 SAE and 1 first class stamp. **(29)**(Some listings specify availability of manuscript and/or artist's guidelines.)

**Tips: (30)** "Have your manuscript thoroughly reviewed and copy edited, if necessary. If you are writing about a special subject, have a well-qualified professional in the field review it for accuracy and appropriateness. It always helps to get some testimonials before submitting it to a publisher. The publisher then knows she/ he is dealing with something worthwhile." (Some listings provide Tips to the illustrator, as well.) **(31)** (Some listings provide Tips about what type of manuscripts or illustrations the firm most needs.) **(32)** (Some listings provide information about industry trends.)

**(1)(2)** The full name, mailing address, and phone number of the book or magazine publishing company, agency, organization, workshop, or contest. A phone number in a listing does not mean the market accepts phone queries. Make a phone query only when your story's timeliness would be lost by following the usual procedures. As a rule, don't call unless you have been invited to do so.
**(3)** The type of business.
**(4)** Title and name of contact person. Address your query or submission to a specific name when possible. If no contact name is given consult a sample copy of the publication or catalog. As a last resort, you can address your query to "Editor" or "Art Director" or whatever is appropriate. The next series of information is a breakdown of the type and number of books published annually: picture books, young readers, middle readers, young adults. Use this breakdown to help you choose a company most receptive to your type of book.
**(5)** The percentage of books by first-time authors will give you an indication of how open a market is to new authors. Also given is the percentage of submissions accepted through agents.
**(6)** Information to let you know which companies subsidy publish.
**(7)** The specific fictional material desired is listed. Follow the guidelines. Do not submit a picture book about sports if it isn't what a market wants.
**(8)** Editors know the length of most material they buy; follow their word or page range. If your manuscript is longer or shorter by a large margin, submit to a more appropriate market.
**(9)** A list of recently published fiction is provided. Use this list to see what types of fiction a market publishes.
**(10)** Specific nonfiction material desired.
**(11)** The appropriate page or word length for nonfiction material is given.
**(12)** A list of recently published nonfiction.
**(13)** It is important to contact a market in the manner it states. If you send material (e.g., a complete manuscript) a market doesn't ask for, it shows a lack of adequate market research on your part.
**(14)** This states whether or not you should include a SASE for return of your manuscript. Submissions to foreign countries should include a self-addressed envelope (SAE) and International Reply Coupons (IRC) available at most major post offices.

**(15)** Reporting times indicate how soon a market will respond to your query or manuscript, but times listed are approximate. Wait four weeks beyond the stated reporting time before you send a polite inquiry.

**(16)** If your material is accepted this information gives you the approximate time it will take for your manuscript to be published.

**(17)** Submission requirements include the form of the submission (such as original typewritten copy preferred over a photocopied version) or if a computer printout is OK or the possibility of sending a manuscript via disk or modem. Send manuscripts or queries to one market at a time unless it indicates simultaneous submissions are OK. If you do send your manuscript to more than one market at a time, always mention in your cover letter that it is a simultaneous submission.

**(18)** The average number of illustrations required per type of book gives the illustrator an idea of how much work a project might entail.

**(19)** This information tells the illustrator if the company will see manuscripts with illustrations by the same person and/or manuscripts by an author with illustrations done by a separate artist. It also tells if the market is open to the use of freelance illustrators for the company's own book projects and provides a contact name if different from the contact at the beginning of the listing.

**(20)** Specific information regarding preferences in the medium/style/size of art submissions is provided here.

**(21)** Submit illustrations only in the manner an art director/editor asks.

**(22)** The approximate amount of time taken to report back on illustrations is provided. If an art director/editor doesn't respond within the stated time, wait four weeks before sending a polite inquiry.

**(23)** If it doesn't state that original artwork is returned, then it is not returned to the artist.

**(24)** Terms for payment of authors.

**(25)** If an advance is given, the average amount will be provided here.

**(26)** Payment information for ms/illustration packages and freelance illustration projects is provided here.

**(27)** If galleys are sent to authors and/or dummies to illustrators for review prior to publication, you will read the notification here.

**(28)(29)** If catalogs guidelines are available, it's important to send for them.

**(30)(31)(32)** Helpful suggestions for writers and illustrators are listed under the subhead, "Tips."

---

# Important Market Listing Information

- *Listings are based on questionnaires, phone calls and updated copy. They are not advertisements* nor *are markets reported here necessarily endorsed by the editor of this book.*
- *Information in the listings comes directly from the company and is as accurate as possible, but situations change and needs fluctuate between the publication of this directory and the time you use it.*
- **Children's Writer's & Illustrator's Market** *reserves the right to exclude any listing that does not meet its requirements.*

---

# A Roundtable for Writers

Writing for children is a creative and challenging profession. But even for many talented writers, the process of marketing their work is an anxiety-ridden experience. Often this frustration occurs because the writer is not familiar with the way the publishing profession works. We've brought together successful writers and a veteran editor to answer some of the frequently asked questions regarding the children's publishing industry.

Our two participating writers are Lois Duncan, Albuquerque, New Mexico-based author of 38 books for children and teenagers; and Kathlyn Gay, Elkhart, Indiana, a nonfiction writer of more than 40 books for children and teenagers. Jean Karl, founder and head of the Children's Book Department of Atheneum Books from 1964 to 1985, and current field editor for Atheneum's line of "Jean Karl Books" is our editorial voice. (For more indepth information about our roundtable personalities, refer to the biographies at the end of this question and answer article.) These professionals share their views about what it takes to succeed as a children's writer.

## In addition to using their Children's Writer's and Illustrator's Market, what other type of market research should writers conduct prior to querying and/or submitting a manuscript to a publisher?

*Jean Karl*: Get a general idea of the kinds of books we publish, which can be found from listings in *Writer's Market* or visit the public library and look at publishers' catalogs.

*Lois Duncan*: Study *Writer's Market*, plus plan a trip to the juvenile section of each bookstore in your area to study the types of books each house is currently publishing.

*Kathlyn Gay*: When submitting queries for articles or nonfiction books, I feel it is essential to first consult the *Reader's Guide to Periodical Literature* and *Books in Print* and, if possible, computer data banks with bibliographies on subjects one plans to write about. It is important also to consult the latest editions of *Publishers Weekly* and publishers' catalogs to see what is being published by particular houses. Also, browse through magazines in the periodical section of libraries — several libraries if possible — and check out the content of magazines. I don't think one can stress enough the need to continually research the content of magazines — if that is going to be the market for a person's writing. If a magazine stresses historical subjects, it hardly seems likely that publication would accept a manuscript about, say, video games or contemporary sports stars.

## What do you feel are the most common mistakes that appear in manuscripts?

*Jean Karl*: Such mistakes in manuscripts tend to be copy that is poorly thought out, poorly written and not truly literate.

*Lois Duncan*: Sometimes writers don't bother to outline their books before they start writing. A plot has three basic elements—(1) a sympathetic protagonist, who has (2) an important goal and (3) the obstacles that stand in the way of his or her reaching it. If one of these elements is missing, the story won't work. Many beginning writers are so eager to start putting words on paper that they don't take the time to plan what they're going to write about.

*Kathlyn Gay*: Although I have not published as much fiction as nonfiction, I believe from my own experience and after reading the works of adults in writing workshops I have conducted over the years that beginning writers have trouble finding a focus. If the work is nonfiction, I often ask, "What is the point you are trying to make?" If fiction, I wonder what a character is trying to accomplish/ overcome/solve. Characters often seem "wooden" or unbelievable. This can be true in beginning nonfiction also when anecdotes and scenes are used to dramatize a point; even real people can seem unbelievable if the writing does not show as well as tell what the people in the story/article are like. Dialogue that does not move a story or article along also seems to be a problem for beginners—small talk may be okay among friends, neighbors and relatives, but it gets boring very soon on paper unless a writer can use such dialogue in an artistic way to reveal character.

## What business and marketing skills (including negotiation abilities) do writers need to develop to compete in the marketplace?

*Lois Duncan*: Develop tenacity and a businesslike attitude; the ability to handle rejection and acceptance of the fact that creative material is a commodity that must be marketed like any other merchandise. You also need a willingness to consider making changes if an editor feels they're necessary and the strength to say "no" to those changes if you feel they are inappropriate and your story would suffer from them.

*Kathlyn Gay*: In my view, knowing what the markets are and what is the kind of material publishers want and need are perhaps the most important skills. Establishing friendly but business-like relationships with editors may not be a skill but I feel that is a sound basis for any type of negotiation. The most difficult part of marketing, I believe, is learning to see one's writing as a "product" during the time one is considering a fee or contract. A writer needs to learn as much as possible about the language of contracts or agreements and fortunately there are many articles and books on the subject—many of them from *Writer's Digest* magazine and Writer's Digest Books. This subject is also covered in many writing workshops and seminars.

**What would you "guesstimate" to be the ratio of manuscripts submitted to you versus the number actually accepted per year?**

*Jean Karl*: About one in 650. However, if you take away all books published by authors who have published with us before, it becomes about one in a 1,000 or one in 1,500.

**Describe your first book manuscript sale in terms of what qualities made it desirable to the publishing house that printed it. In other words, what did you do "right" with the story itself and with the way you marketed it to the acquisitions editor?**

*Lois Duncan*: I wrote my first young adult novel when I was 20 years old. The strength of that book was the fact that I was so close in age to my readers that the emotions, dialogue and subject matter couldn't help but ring true to them, even though the writing lacked professional polish. I submitted the manuscript to the "Seventeenth Summer Literary Competition." It won, and the sponsor of the contest offered me a contract.

*Kathlyn Gay*: My first book sale was a career-romance novel, a genre which required a girl-meets-boy story line with background information on a specific career. In my book, *Girl Pilot* (Messner), the heroine was trying to overcome the prejudices against women who chose to be pilots; at the same time, she was attempting to deal with a budding romance. Being able to weave these two aspects together helped make the book salable. In addition, I think the story developed characters as much as is possible within a set format and created suspense, as any story should, that carried the reader to the end. This particular book was sold through an agent, but I now market all of my own materials. In more recent nonfiction work, I try to determine what kind of books or magazine articles would fit a publisher's needs and send brief query letters to editors to determine whether I'm on target. Then, if I'm invited to submit, I send a book outline or magazine piece within 3-4 weeks or sooner if I can.

**How does a writer fine tune his text so it is easily understood by his targeted age group?**

*Jean Karl*: If plot, characters and background fit the age group; if the author knows that age group, then the language should follow. And if the language is not quite right but everything else is, the editors can help.

*Lois Duncan*: Read to a child while holding him on your lap. If he squirms to get down, you'll know the text is too wordy. With older kids, you can write as you would for adults. The question when writing for this older age group is how much slang to use. You want dialogue to sound natural, but since juvenile books stay in print a while—(I'm still gleaning royalties from some that are 20 years old)—you want to steer clear of terms that will be quickly outdated.

*Kathlyn Gay*: I make sure that concepts I'm writing about are explained with clear expository writing or by the use of brief but pertinent quotes from experts in the field. I also weave in background information if that is necessary for understanding new ideas. In other words, I try to provide some historical perspective that can be read easily and, I hope, with interest. I think a writer should be constantly aware, too, of her or his audience, creating scenes, using anecdotes, examples and quotes that readers can relate to and that are within their range of understanding.

### How do you, as a writer or editor, determine what type of book will be salable in each year's market? Are children ever used as a "test market" to help establish whether or not a book works?

*Jean Karl*: Salability is determined by the books that are already selling, and by reports of needs from librarians and book stores. No, children are not used (except maybe for books of humor) to test books. Children are not all the same. What works with one may not work with another. Are adult books–except for some obvious mass market books—test marketed? No. And for the same reasons children's books are not.

*Lois Duncan*: I have a multi-book contract with Dell for my young adult suspense novels, so I don't have to market those. I'm less secure about my books for younger children. I keep up on the trends in picture books by reading the catalogs from publishing houses to learn what's in current demand and where the holes in the market are. I don't "test market" my work before I submit it. My feedback comes from my editors

*Kathlyn Gay*: For nonfiction, I follow news events on a daily basis and often detect "trends" or feel that readers will be looking for information on a topic that's "in the news." For example, after living through the civil rights movement, I was hopeful that bigoted attitudes had begun to change in our country, but over the past decade I have read about an increasing number of violent acts based on bigotry and racism. As my file of materials kept getting larger and larger, I decided it was time to write about the effects of bigotry and racism and how these attitudes might be overcome. The result was *Bigotry*, published in 1989 by Enslow. In a lighter vein, I also collected story after story about various superstitious practices in sports—from baseball to wrestling, which led to *They Don't Wash Their Socks! (Sports Superstitions)* which Walker will publish in 1990. A number of environmental titles have come about because of my concern about the many ways we are "fouling our nest." Keeping up on information about the environment has helped me produce seven titles for Watts' Impact series, with another underway for 1991. I have never done any "test marketing" for my ideas or manuscripts.

### Is there any trend toward increasing use of photography, rather than illustration, in children's picture books?

*Jean Karl*: No, I think not. There are photographs in some kinds of books and for jackets on some books. But it is not something that is growing.

### How (in your opinion) are children's books different today than, say, a generation ago?

*Jean Karl*: There are more picture books. Books are shorter and many are more simply written. Also, they are less complex, faster moving, and in some ways, less varied. There is more fantasy and science fiction now than there was 25 or 30 years ago.

*Lois Duncan*: Today's young readers have been conditioned by TV to expect instant entertainment. They've developed a short attention span, and if their interest isn't caught immediately, they want to switch channels. For this reason, modern day authors are forced to compete with television by using the techniques of script writing — a lot of dialogue and action and almost no description. You have to grab their attention with your very first paragraph. When I wrote *Killing Mr. Griffin,* I started the book with the sentence, "It was a wild, windy, southwestern spring when the idea of killing Mr. Griffin occurred to them." Griffin wasn't slated to die until chapter eight, but I knew my readers wouldn't wade through seven chapters of build-up unless they knew they were headed for something dramatic.

*Kathlyn Gay*: In the case of nonfiction, many more books and articles are being published on important topics than were published a generation ago. Often controversial subjects were "wrapped" in a fictional story rather than presented as straight-forward factual information or in anecdotal form to show real people and events. Whether fiction or nonfiction, the preachiness of the past is not acceptable today. Few readers want a lecture. Readers want to be involved with the characters (in fiction) or with real people who are part of a nonfiction work, so I think it takes much more effort on the part of the writer to keep herself or himself out of the way and let the story (factual or fictional) unfold.

### What are some of your favorite children's books that you published or wrote? Why?

*Jean Karl*: When I think back, there are too many to name. The qualities that stand out are good writing, a sense of absolute unity in the work and a rightness that gives it stature and believability, warmth, humor, and a richness of experience that gives the book dimension and depth. A good book transcends its pages and becomes a living entity in the mind of the reader — not all readers, perhaps, but certainly those who are ready for the book.

*Lois Duncan*: *Songs From Dreamland* is special to me for personal reasons. I wrote these lullabies for my first grandchild, my daughter Kerry's baby, and my oldest daughter, Robin Arquette, set them to music. We recorded them together, with my doing the narration and Robin the singing, and, in June, 1989, Knopf brought them out as a book-cassette package. To my surprise, my youngest daughter, Kaitlyn, a sophisticated teenager, loved to fall asleep listening to them. In July, 1989, Kaitlyn was shot by an unknown assailant as she drove home from a friend's house. The music from *Songs From Dreamland* was played at her funeral. Those songs have become to me a symbol of family — the joy, the heartbreak, and most important, the love.

*Kathlyn Gay*: At this point, my favorite is *The Rainbow Effect: Interracial Families* (Watts, 1987). I had a chance to interview not only interracial and cross-cultural families, but also children of mixed-race/cultural ancestry. The subject for the most part had been taboo, unless it was treated as "exotic" or "erotic" in nature, and I believed that "ordinary people" of mixed heritage and interracial/interethnic families were being ignored. The book was written to show that "rainbow" families are as varied as any other group of families in our society.

## Is there any advice you wish to add that I haven't covered?

*Jean Karl*: Be yourself and give generously of that self.

*Kathlyn Gay*: I grew up with "If at first you don't succeed, try, try . . . etc." I don't know how many times I heard or read "The Little Engine That Could." Anyway, I think that philosophy stuck because I do believe that persistence pays off. Some manuscripts have been sent out 30-40 times before they finally found a "home." At times I've had to revise before material was accepted and I have learned to really like that part of writing. I think revision comes much easier when writers are able to get some distance from their work—put manuscripts away for awhile and read them later from a different perspective.

*In addition to editing her own line of books,* **Jean Karl** *has authored young adult novels, including* The Turning Place, Beloved Benjamin is Waiting, But We Are Not of Earth *and* The Strange Tomorrow.

*Among the 38 books that* **Lois Duncan** *has written are picture books, "first chapter" books, verse, nonfiction, mystery and suspense novels, teenage romances, "problem" novels and a series of audio recordings of children's songs. Duncan has received "Young Readers Awards" twice from California, Indiana and South Carolina as well as single citations from New Mexico, Colorado, Nevada, Massachusetts, Vermont, England and West Australia. Six of her books have been chosen as Junior Literary Guild selections, and she has received five "Special Awards" from the Mystery Writers of America.*

**Kathlyn Gay** *has authored a wide variety of trade books, educational booklets and guides, and major portions of textbooks as well as hundreds of magazine features, stories and plays. Some of her works deal with ozone pollution, bigotry, acid rain, interracial families and lighter topics such as sports superstitions and rituals, boxing and books for primary readers. Her book* Silent Killers, *which discusses the effects of indoor pollution from radon and other toxic hazards was chosen "one of the best science books for young people in 1988" by the National Science Teachers' Association. The National Council for Social Studies and National Science Teachers' Association also selected her book* Acid Rain *as the "outstanding book" in 1984.*

# A Roundtable for Illustrators

Illustrators, just like writers, need to know the children's book market. This roundtable discussion answers many of the most commonly asked questions. Sharing their professional advice are Michael Farmer, art director at Harcourt Brace Jovanovich; Peggy Schaefer, children's book editor at Ideals Publishing Corporation; Robert Quackenbush, New York City-based author and illustrator of more than 150 children's books; and Ed Young, New York-based illustrator and author with 40 children's books to his credit. They share with you their views about the state of publishing and marketing work, which may vary somewhat according to personal preference. Remember: some of these questions have more than one "right" answer. For more indepth information about our roundtable personalities, refer to the biographies at the end of this question and answer article.

## What type of market research should illustrators conduct prior to querying and/or submitting artwork to a publishing house?

*Michael Farmer*: First, an illustrator should make himself aware of what kinds of children's books are presently and historically successful. Second, an illustrator wishing to submit samples to HBJ should learn what types of books HBJ has chosen to publish. There are many publishers of children's books who choose, for various reasons, specific kinds of books to publish. All publishers are not alike.

*Peggy Schaefer*: It is essential for anyone submitting work to be familiar with the products and market of that particular publishing company. Write for guidelines and a catalog or do some research at your local bookstore or library. But find out beforehand whether the material you are offering is in sync with the needs of the publisher you are targeting.

*Robert Quackenbush*: Research is the most exciting part of my work. I keep in constant contact with children to find out their current interests and needs. I do this by conducting art classes for them at my studio/gallery twice a week, and by giving programs and setting up workshops at schools and libraries as a guest author anywhere in the United States and South America as my schedule permits. The children, teachers, librarians and parents I meet continually replenish me with a flow of new ideas.

*Ed Young*: I have not conducted any market research in any formal way. It is a good idea, however, to become familiar with the style and taste of each publishing house that one wishes to submit works to (by way of local public libraries).

## What type(s) of submission packages should be sent out when querying an art director or editor?

*Michael Farmer*: Unsolicited samples should consist of color copies, black and white copies, C-prints or printed samples. All materials submitted should be intended to be non-returnable. If a return is necessary, a self-addressed and stamped envelope is requested.

*Peggy Schaefer*: I prefer to receive a query letter with art samples, either color photocopies, slides or tearsheets, and a brief resume of any previously published works. If the submission relates to a particular project, thumbnails may also be appropriate. Never submit original artwork unless specifically requested to do so.

*Robert Quackenbush*: Since I now both write and illustrate my books, my queries are usually directed to publishing editors—not art directors. When I have been asked to make a submission it often is sent in one of two ways: One way is a story synopsis with thumbnail sketches or sketches of the main characters and the other way is a finished book dummy.

*Ed Young*: If you are in New York (or any big city) it is best to see the art director with a portfolio. If you are too far away, then submit some slides or color photocopies of a few of your favorite samples and a card. Then follow up with a phone call a week later for an appointment.

## What are the most common types of problems you see with artwork you reject?

*Michael Farmer*: Common problems are art that is inappropriate to a style and direction HBJ has chosen to pursue; art that is not unique, distinctive or expressive.

*Peggy Schaefer*: Actually not all that much artwork is rejected outright. In many cases, it's just a matter of a particular style or medium or use of colors not being needed at that time. Two problems that would keep me from following up on an artist's work are an inconsistency in quality of work and an inability to work well with figures.

## How do you select the appropriate illustrator for each children's book your company publishes? What qualities or skills do you look for in an artist and his artwork?

*Michael Farmer*: Illustrators are often selected by the editor of an accepted manuscript. Also, an illustrator can be recommended to an editor by another editor or the art director. We look for art, in any style, that cannot only tell a story but art that can react to a story. An illustrator should respond to what he or she feels about a story as well as to what they read literally. I like illustrations that express an appropriate emotion in addition to an accurate interpretation of the text.

*Peggy Shaefer*: Budget, target market and style are the main factors that are taken into consideration when looking for an appropriate illustrator. Consistency in art quality, dependability and promptness of delivery are among the most important qualities I look for once the field has been narrowed in terms of style.

## What would you "guesstimate" to be the ratio of artwork submitted to you versus the number actually accepted per year?

*Michael Farmer*: I receive unsolicited samples from at least 12-18 illustrators or representatives per week. Out of the hundreds of samples submitted annually, I would estimate that no more than two percent of these find themselves accepted in some form, either for a young adult or middle grade book jacket or for an illustrated picture book.

*Peggy Shaefer*: I would say that we pick up from four to six new illustrators a year. And generally, we go back to these illustrators more than once.

## Describe your first sale of illustrations or a manuscript/illustration package. What did you do "right" with the work itself and with the way you marketed it to the art director?

*Robert Quackenbush*: My first assignment, given to me one Friday afternoon by an art director, was to bring him a sample illustration on speculation the following Monday morning showing how I would illustrate Hans Christian Andersen's "Steadfast Tin Soldier." It was being published as a picture book. Other artists were competing for the assignment, so what I did, that the other artists did not, was to fully lay out the book in addition to doing the sample piece. There was no question how the published book would look; I won the commission. I have worked in this manner of delivering a finished book dummy to a publisher ever since.

*Ed Young*: Although children's illustration is no doubt a business, the illustrator is above all else an artist. If the training is thorough and the heart is there, one need not worry about how one markets one's work to any house.

## What business and marketing skills (including negotiation abilities) do illustrators need to compete in the marketplace?

*Robert Quackenbush*: I always admired the words of John F. Kennedy: "Ask not what your country can do for you, but what you can do for your country." I have adapted a similar philosophy when working with clients: To find out what I can do for them. And that means to find out their needs, to work cooperatively with them to help reach their goals, and to be paid appropriately for my services.

*Ed Young*; Join a writer's group locally (or a national group) or the Graphic Artists Guild, plus talk to other illustrators about contracts, royalties, rights, etc. Use your own sense about how it feels to work for any particular house. Discuss openly with the editor or art director anything that is bothersome.

**Do you work any differently with an author/illustrator doing his own picture book as compared to someone doing illustrations only? How much more does an author/illustrator make on a book? Also, if the artwork isn't up to your standards, does it hurt the manuscript's chance to be published?**

*Michael Farmer*: Working creatively with an author/illustrator is usually no different than working with only an illustrator. However, an author/illustrator will have two separate responsibilities that need creative direction, editorial direction and art direction. An author/illustrator needs to account for producing more work in a given time period than only an illustrator would. Regarding pay, advances and royalties for all HBJ authors and illustrators are confidential. Artwork and manuscripts are evaluated individually on their own merits. If art is not up to our standards, a good manuscript could certainly be considered for publication with another artist.

*Peggy Schaefer*: An author/illustrator may be given more freedom in design and subject matter of art, because he/she is so aware of the connection being sought between text and art. I generally work more closely with someone who is providing only illustrations in an effort to create that same wholeness of spirit of the book. While an author/illustrator normally works on a royalty basis for us, many of our illustrators work on a for-hire basis. Finally, a poor manuscript will generally hurt an artist's chance of being published more than vice versa. It is often easier to find an illustrator for a great manuscript than to find a manuscript for a great illustrator.

**How (if at all) does working with an art director differ when you're writing/illustrating a picture book package as opposed to illustrating another author's book? Do you feel you have more creative control with your own writing/illustration projects? Why or why not?**

*Robert Quackenbush*: No difference.

*Ed Young*: The relationship of any two people depends a great deal upon how eagerly both wish to produce an outstanding book and the mutual trust that can come about only with the help of the other. It's based on co-operation rather than power to override.

**How much does a book's budget affect color vs. black and white illustrations, number of images used and the medium? Does the artist determine the medium or does the art director based on the parameters of his budget?**

*Michael Farmer*: HBJ chooses primarily to publish full color picture books. Black and white art, when published, would primarily be used within the text of young adult and middle grade books, usually in a limited quantity. Obviously, a book's budget is affected by the use of color. More importantly, the number of pages in a book and the print run (quantity) are major determining factors in a book's budget. The medium used by an illustrator typically has little effect on a book's budget. Illustrators are given some requirements to follow regarding the size of their art and material used to illustrate on, all to more efficiently accommodate our separators' requirements.

*Peggy Schaefer*: Ideals mainly publishes picture books, almost all of which are four-color throughout, so the question of color versus black and white is not a big one for us. Budget would more likely affect the number of color images used and the book's specs and design. While I may express a preference for a particular medium, I have generally found that the medium in which the artist feels most comfortable at that time is the medium in which he/she will provide the best work.

*Robert Quackenbush*: An illustrator is like an actor performing on the stage: If the illustrator is "in character" with the story (even one the illustrator has written) then the selected medium will appear naturally right for the story. Being an artist is not just technique and design, it also requires that the artist be in touch with his feelings while he is creating.

*Ed Young*: The artist determines the style and medium used for any work, ideally. The art director can inspire or suggest the mood.

**If you started your career by illustrating children's books and are now writing and illustrating them, how (and why) did you make that switch?**

*Robert Quackenbush*: After illustrating 60 books by great authors both classical and contemporary, I felt ready. I had been analyzing a variety of writing styles as I interpreted words into pictures. Then when our son Piet was born in 1974, I was drawn to writing about him and for him—to tell about his experiences growing up and to tell him about my own experience when I was growing up. When Piet began walking and took a few nose dives off the couch because he thought he could fly, I decided it was time to tell him about the Wright brothers. *Take Me Out to the Airfield* launched a series of more than a dozen biographies. His natural childhood curiosity also led to the creation of a number of detective stories such as my Detective Mole, Miss Mallard and Sherlock Chick mystery series. Since 1974 I have written and illustrated over 100 books thanks to Piet, the children who have studied with me, and the children and adults I have met during my travels.

*Ed Young*: It's when one feels the need to write one's own story and to illustrate it. There is no great difference, only more involvement with the telling of the story.

## Is there any trend toward an increasing use of photography, rather than illustration, in children's picture books?

*Michael Farmer*: For HBJ there is not a trend toward using more photography than illustration. HBJ has published books for children using only photography. In the spring of 1989 we published *The American Family Farm*, a photo essay by George Ancona with text by Joan Anderson.

*Peggy Shaefer*: While there is a trend toward increased use of photography in children's books, I feel it is most apparent in nonfiction rather than fiction titles.

## How are children's books different today than say, a generation ago?

*Michael Farmer*: The quality of printing has advanced dramatically allowing much more accurate reproduction of original artwork. Design has come to play a more obvious role in children's books, focusing the design to be more commercial and less institutional looking. Publishers are more willing to take risks with new styles of illustration. Manuscripts that have some social relevance are finding their way into print as publishers respond to contemporary moral attitudes. Today, books can both educate and entertain children.

*Peggy Shaefer*: There is currently a much wider range to pick from in all age groups, and there is more experimentation in color and style of artwork. Subjects range from the imaginary to real issues and problems such as death, divorce and prejudice. The boundaries have been somewhat removed as long as the execution is in good taste.

*Robert Quackenbush*: Today's children have many more book subjects to choose from than they did a generation ago. The classics like "Snow White" and "Cinderella" still endure, but now children can also choose to read about realistic subjects that were once considered taboo. With all that children are exposed to today through the media about the events of the external world, they are not easily fooled. They are quick to recognize a false work—one that veils the truth from them. For this reason, I focus on humor in many of my books to let children know that as long as we keep our sense of humor, our spirits cannot be crushed.

*Ed Young*: Children's books are more creative, more open to anyone with a child's eye and attitude, and certainly more challenging because of the many talented and hard working people entering the field.

## What are some of your favorite books your company has published? What qualities stand out in your mind?

*Michael Farmer*: *The Little Prince,* by Antoine Saint-Exupery; *In the Beginning,* by Virginia Hamilton; *Rootabaga Stories,* by Carl Sandburg; *The Jolly Mon,* by Jimmy Buffett; *Tom Thumb,* retold by Richard Jesse Watson; *King Bidgood's in the Bathtub,* by Don and Audrey Wood; *The Witch Who Lives Down the Hall,* by Donna Guthrie; and *Bring Back the Deer,* by Jeffrey Prusski. These books stand out for a variety of reasons. Some because of memorable stories, some because of successful risk-taking with art, and others because I enjoy reading them to my children.

*Peggy Schaefer*: Obviously, I'm going to be biased in favor of the titles on which I've worked most closely. *Lullabies & Good Night* is a book/cassette package in which all the elements of the concept really came together—the art of Mary Cassatt combined with poetry of the masters and an outstanding tape. The art and design of *Beauty and the Beast* combine to make this a classic in presentation. And *Borrowed Black,* which is actually a co-publication, is a wonderful example of integration of text and art.

## Is there any advice you wish to include that I haven't covered?

*Robert Quackenbush*: I suggest sending for catalogs from the publishers each season to keep informed of the kinds of books each is doing, so that queries and materials being submitted are appropriate.

*Ed Young*: Regardless of any outward situation, the author/artist must continue to grow to improve his skill in the ability to tell stories and to work with teams of people who wish to produce something worthwhile for the world outside. The rest comes naturally and accordingly.

---

*Art Director* **Michael Farmer** *conducted his undergraduate studies at the California College of Arts and Crafts in Oakland, and completed his studies in design and printing at the California Polytechnic Institute, San Luis Obispo. He has been with Harcourt Brace Jovanovich since 1982.*

**Peggy Schaefer**, *children's book editor, has been with Ideals Publishing Corp. for four years. She earned an English degree from the University of Miami (Florida).*

**Robert Quackenbush** *graduated from the Art Center College of Design in Los Angeles. In addition to the 150 books he has written and/or illustrated, Quackenbush teaches art classes for children, hosts picture book workshops for adults and travels regularly to speak to school groups. He is a three time recipient of the American Flag Institute Award for outstanding contribution in the field of children's literature and winner of the Edgar Allen Poe Special Award for the best juvenile mystery of 1981.*

*Chinese-born* **Ed Young** *credits his upbringing for his ability to enhance text with simple, yet vibrant images. Young came to the U.S. to attend the Los Angeles Art Center, and upon graduation entered the commercial art field. His desire for creative growth was the reason he was drawn toward children's illustration. Young is the 1990 recipient of the Caldecott medal for the most distinguished American picture book—Lon Po Po: A Red Riding Hood Story from China—published in 1989.*

# The Business of Children's Writing & Illustrating

The market for children's books increases each year . . . along with the number of talented writers and illustrators who are submitting a variety of manuscripts, picture book packages and artwork to children's editors. A unique book proposal will always catch an editor's eye, but how do you know the package will even be opened? The odds are better when you send work that is professionally packaged and presented. The Business of Children's Writing & Illustrating is devoted to writers and artists who are adept at the craft of writing or illustrating, but may be a little unsure of the business techniques needed to successfully compete in the growing industry of children's publishing.

As a self-employed professional, you may also want to talk with other business people in your area, or in your professional writer's or artist's organization if you are a member of one (see the Organizations section of this book to decide which writing or art groups might be of interest to you). Talking to such people will help you to determine what day-to-day business techniques have worked best for each. Established business people can discuss setting up a bookkeeping system, advise you of any equipment you may need, and make you aware of any areas in which you may need legal assistance.

## Marketing your work

There is really no mystery to submitting your work successfully in the marketplace; the basic elements are good research and persistence. First, you need to familiarize yourself with the publications that interest you. Read through the listings of those markets in this book to determine what type of material is wanted, who the contact is, how the editor or art director wishes to be contacted initially, what types of rights they acquire to your work and how much they pay. (If a listing accepts unsolicited manuscripts, be sure you enclose a self-addressed, stamped envelope [SASE] for its return.)

Get copies of all these publications — or copies of their books — and study their writing and illustration styles and formats. Does the type of material they publish match the type of work you produce? Next you will want to request writer's or illustrator's guidelines to more carefully match work you will be submitting to their needs. If a particular market has changed its direction since *Children's Writer's & Illustrator's Market* has gone to press, these guidelines will reflect current needs. Also, many times throughout the year publishers will have special seasonal or holiday needs that will be explained in the guidelines.

## Format review for submitting work

Throughout these listings you will read editors' requests for a query letter, cover letter, book proposal, complete manuscript or resume as all or part of the initial contact procedure.

*Query letters.* A query letter should be no more than a one-page, well written, concise piece to arouse an editor's interest in your manuscript. Queries are usually required from writers submitting nonfiction material to a publisher. Such a letter should be single-spaced and include the editor's name, if available, though you will want to avoid using a first name during an initial contact until more familiarity is established. In the query letter you want to convince the editor that your idea is perfect for his readership and that you're the writer qualified to do the job. Include any previous writing experience in your letter plus published samples to prove your credentials, especially any samples that relate to the subject matter about which you're querying.

Many query letters start with a lead similar to the lead that would be used in the actual manuscript. Next, you want to briefly outline the work and include facts, anecdotes, interviews or any other pertinent information that give the editor a feel for the manuscript's premise. Your goal is to entice him to want to know more. End your letter with a straight-forward request to write the work, and include information on its approximate length, date it could be completed and the availability of accompanying photos or artwork.

Queries are rarely used for fiction manuscripts, but occasionally there are exceptions. For a fiction query you want to explain the story's plot, main characters, conflict and resolution. Just as in nonfiction queries, you want to make the editor eager to see more. For more information on writing good queries, consult *How to Write Irresistible Query Letters*, by Lisa Collier Cool (Writer's Digest Books).

*Cover letters.* Many editors prefer to review a complete manuscript, especially for fiction. In such a case, the cover letter will serve to introduce you and establish your credentials as a writer plus give the editor an overview of the manuscript. Unlike the query letter, a cover letter sent with a manuscript doesn't need to take a hard-sell orientation; the manuscript, at this point, will be the selling mechanism. Be sure to let the editor know whether the unsolicited manuscript is a simultaneous submission. However, if you're just sending a photocopy of your manuscript, and not a simultaneous submission, you might want to reassure him that he is the only one considering your work at this time. Some editors might assume a photocopied manuscript is being considered elsewhere. If you're sending the manuscript after a "go-ahead" from the editor, the cover letter should serve as a reminder of this commitment.

For an illustrator, the cover letter will also serve as your introduction to the art director and establish your credentials as a professional artist. Type the cover letter on your letterhead and, in addition to introducing yourself and your abilities, be sure to explain what services you can provide as well as what type of follow-up contact you plan to make, if any. If you are sending samples of your work, indicate whether they should be returned or filed. If you wish them returned include a self-addressed, stamped envelope (SASE) with your submission packet. Cover letters, like the query, should be no longer than one page.

*Resumes.* Often illustrators are asked to submit a resume with their cover letter and samples. A resume provides you with a vehicle to showcase your experience, education and awards. Resumes can be created in a variety of formats ranging from a single page listing information to color brochures featuring your art. Keep the resume brief, and focus on your artistic achievements, not your whole life. On your resume you want to include your name and address, your clients and the work you did for them. Also include your educational background and any awards you've won.

*Book proposals.* Throughout the listings in the Book Publishers section you will find references to submission of a synopsis, outline and sample chapters. Depending on an editor's preference, some or all of these components, as well as inclusion of a cover letter, comprise a book proposal.

A synopsis summarizes the book. Such a summary includes the basic plot of the book (including the ending), is easy to read and flows well.

An outline can also be used to set up fiction, but is more effective as a tool for nonfiction. The outline covers your book chapter by chapter and provides highlights of each. If you are developing an outline for fiction you will want to include major characters, plots and subplots, and length of the book. An outline can run 3 to 30 pages depending on the complexity of your manuscript.

Sample chapters give a more comprehensive idea of your writing skill. Some editors may request the first two or three chapters to see how your material is set up; others may request a beginning, middle and ending chapter to get a better feel for the entire plot. Be sure to determine what the editor needs to see before investing time in writing sample chapters.

Many picture book editors require an outline or synopsis, sample chapters and a variation of roughs or finished illustrations from the author/illustrator. Listings specifying an interest in picture books will detail what type of artwork should accompany manuscripts. You will also want to query the editor or art director prior to submitting material for more detailed information that will tailor your illustrations to their needs. If you want to know more about putting together a book proposal, read *How to Write a Book Proposal*, by Michael Larsen (Writer's Digest Books).

*Manuscript formats.* If an editor specifies that you should submit a complete manuscript for review, here is some format information to guide you. In the upper left corner type your legal name (not pseudonym), address, phone number and Social Security number (publishers must have this to file payment records with the government). In the upper right corner you should type the approximate word length, what rights are being offered for sale (this is not necessary for book manuscripts; rights will be covered in your contract) and your copyright notice, which should appear as © Joe Writer 1990 (a copyright notice is no longer necessary, though advisable; see "Rights for the Writer and Illustrator" for details). All material in the upper corners should be typed single-spaced, not double.

There is no need for a cover page or title page on a manuscript: The first page should include the title (centered) one-third of the way down. Two spaces under that type "by" and your name or pseudonym. To begin the body of your manuscript, drop down two double spaces and indent five spaces for each new paragraph. There should be 1¼ inch margins around all sides of a full typewritten page. Be sure to set your typewriter on "double-space" for the manuscript body. From page 2 to the end of your manuscript just include your last name followed by a dash and the page number in the upper left corner. You can include the title of your piece under your name if you wish. Drop down two double spaces to begin the body of the page and follow this format throughout the manuscript. If you're submitting a novel, type the chapter title one-third of the way down the page. On subsequent pages you again will want to include your name, dash symbol, page number and title of the manuscript.

On the last page of your manuscript skip down three double spaces after your last sentence and type "The End." Some nonfiction writers use the journalistic symbols "###" or "-30-." For more information on manuscript formats read *Manuscript Submission*, by Scott Edelstein (Writer's Digest Books).

To get an approximate word count for your manuscript, first count the number of characters and spaces in an average line, next count the number of lines on a representative page and multiply these two factors to get your average number of characters per page. Finally, count the number of pages in your manuscript, multiply by the characters per page, then divide by 6 (the average number of characters in a word). You will have your approximate word count.

## Packing and mailing submissions

Your primary concern in packaging material is to ensure that it arrives undamaged, although proper packaging also presents the image of an organized professional who takes pride in his work.

If your manuscript is fewer than six pages it is safe to simply fold it in thirds and send it out in a #10 (business-size) envelope. For a self-addressed, stamped envelope (SASE) you can then fold another #10 envelope in thirds or insert a #9 (reply) envelope which fits in a #10 neatly without any folding at all. Some editors appreciate receiving a manuscript folded in half into a 6x9 envelope. For larger manuscripts you will want to use a 9x12 envelope both for mailing the submission out and as a SASE for its return. The SASE envelope can be folded in half. Book manuscripts will require a sturdy box such as a typing paper or envelope box for mailing. Include a self-addressed mailing label and return postage so it can also double as your SASE.

Artwork requires a bit more packaging care to guarantee that it arrives in presentable form. Sandwich illustrations between heavy cardboard that is slightly larger than the work and tape it closed. You will want to write your name and address on each piece in case the inside material becomes separated from the outer envelope upon receipt. For the outer wrapping you can use either a manila envelope, foam-padded envelope, a mailer with plastic air bubbles as a liner or brown wrapping paper. Bind non-joined edges with reinforced mailing tape and clearly write your address.

Most often you will be mailing material first class. Mail sent within this classification is usually processed and delivered quickly. Also, first-class mail is forwarded for one year if the addressee has moved (which does happen with some magazine and book publishers), and can be returned if undeliverable. If you are mailing a package that weighs between one and 70 pounds it can go fourth class unless you specifically request first-class mail treatment. Fourth-class mail tends to be handled a bit more roughly so pack your material with this in mind. If you have enclosed a letter, write "first-class letter enclosed" on the package and add the correct amount of postage. Also write "return postage guaranteed" on your package so it can be returned to you if undeliverable.

If you are concerned about your material safely reaching its destination you may wish to send it certified mail. Material sent this way must be signed when it reaches its destination, and if you wish, a return receipt will be sent to you.

There is an 85¢ charge for this service, in addition to the postage which is determined by the weight, size and destination of your package. Material sent certified mail is also automatically insured for $100.

Your packages can also be sent UPS, though they aren't legally allowed to carry first-class mail so your letter will have to be mailed separately. UPS also has wrapping restrictions: packages must be in heavy, corrugated cardboard; no string or paper can be on the outside; and packages must be sealed with reinforced tape.

If material needs to reach your editor or art director quickly, you can elect to use overnight deliveries such as U.S. Priority Mail and Express Mail Next Day Services, UPS's Two-Day Blue Label Air Service, and dozens of privately owned overnight services such as Federal Express, Emery Worldwide or Purolater Courier. Fees and delivery destinations vary.

Occasionally throughout this book you will see the term International Reply Coupon (IRC). IRCs are used in lieu of U.S. postage when mailing packages abroad. The U.S. Post Office can help you determine, based on your package's weight, the correct number of IRCs to include to ensure its return. The current cost of an IRC is 95¢ per ounce traveling surface mail; two IRCs are recommended for packages being shipped via air.

If you're sending a photocopy of a manuscript or copies of artwork samples, you may wish to specify to the editor that the material doesn't need to be returned if not used. It may be cheaper in the long run on your postage bill. In the latter case you can track the status of your submissions by enclosing a postage-paid reply postcard listing "yes, I am interested" or "no, the material is not appropriate for my needs at this time" options. Some writers or illustrators simply set a deadline date after which the manuscript or artwork is withdrawn from consideration if nothing is heard from the editor or art director. Use a minimum deadline of 3 months, however, because many publishing houses are backed up that far in reading manuscripts.

## Pricing, negotiating and contracts

Negotiation is a two-way street on which, hopefully, both the author/artist and editor/art director will feel mutual satisfaction prior to signing a contract. Many book publishing companies have a predetermined range at which to negotiate with a writer. Such a range will usually only vary when negotiations are held with a top-name author who also has written the type of manuscript that is deemed marketable by a publisher "specializing" in his type of subject matter. Arriving at price structures for magazine work is much easier because many writer's guidelines provide a per-word rate or range for a specific length of article.

Artists, on the other hand, have a few more variables to contend with prior to contracting their services. Payment for illustrations can be set by such factors as whether the piece will be rendered in black and white or four-color, how many illustrations are to be purchased and the artist's prior experience. For a beginning illustrator, market research will be necessary to determine an hourly rate. Such a rate can be arrived at by using the annual salary of a staff artist doing similar work (try to find an artist willing to share this information), then dividing that salary by 52 (the number of weeks in a year) and again by 40 (the number of hours in a work week) to get the answer. You will want to add your overhead expenses such as rent, utilities, art supplies, etc. to this answer by multiplying your hourly rate by 2.5. Research, again, may have to come into play to be sure your rate is competitive within the marketplace.

Even though you may feel comfortable with the hourly rate you have set for your services, many art directors still will want to negotiate to be sure they are paying a good price for services rendered. The most important aspect of negotiating lies in your ability to listen to the other party; don't be so concerned with your needs that you miss what the other person is really saying he wants. On the other hand, take time to voice any questions or concerns you may have about the fee or other stipulations being offered; this is the only way you will be able to establish your needs to the art buyer. Negotiating is a process that can only be "perfected" by doing it often . . . if one meeting doesn't go well, use that experience to build your negotiating skills for the next "client."

Once you make a sale you will probably sign a contract. A contract is an agreement between two or more parties that specifies the fee to be paid, services to be rendered, deadlines, rights purchased and, for artists, return (or not) of original artwork. Be sure to get a contract in writing rather than agreeing to oral stipulations; written contracts protect both parties from misunderstandings and faulty memories. Also, look out for clauses that may not be in your best interest, such as "work-for-hire." If there are clauses that appear vague or confusing, get some legal advice. The time and money invested in counseling up front could protect you from more serious problems down the road. If you have an agent, he will review any contract.

## Business records

The only way to determine if you are making a profit as a writer or illustrator is to keep accurate business records. You will definitely want to keep a separate bank account and ledger apart from your personal finances. Also, if writing or illustrating is secondary to another freelance career, maintain separate business records from that career.

There are many ledgers available in office-supply stores. Look through some samples to decide what works best for your needs. Most ledgers use a single-entry system in which you list any business-related expenses as well as income. If you're just starting your career, you will most likely be accumulating some business expenses prior to showing any profit. To substantiate your income and expenses to the IRS be sure to keep all invoices, cash receipts, sales slips, bank statements, cancelled checks plus receipts related to entertaining clients such as for dinner and parking. For entertainment expenditures you also will want to record the date, place and purpose of the business meeting as well as gas mileage. Be sure to file all receipts in chronological order; if you maintain a separate file for each month of the year it will provide for easier retrieval of records at year's end. Keeping receipts is especially important for purchases of $25 or more.

When setting up a single-entry bookkeeping system you will want to record income and expenses separately. It may prove easier to use some of the subheads that appear on Schedule C of the 1040 tax form, this way you can transfer information more easily onto the tax form when filing your return. In your ledger you will want to include a description of each transaction — date, source of income (or debts from business purchases), description of what was purchased or sold; whether pay was by cash, check or credit card, and the amount of the transaction.

You don't have to wait until January 1 to start keeping records, either. The moment you first make a business-related purchase or sell an article, book manuscript or illustrations you will need to begin tracking your profits and losses. If you keep records from January 1 to December 31 you are using a calendar-year accounting method. Any other accounting period is known as a fiscal year. You also can choose between two types of accounting methods — the cash method and the accrual method. The cash method is used more often: You record income when it is received and expenses when they are disbursed. Under the accrual method you report income at the time you earn it rather than when it is actually received. Similarly, expenses are recorded at the time they are incurred rather than when you actually pay them. If you choose this method you will need to keep separate records for "accounts receivable" and "accounts payable."

## Recording submissions

An offshoot of recording income and expenses is keeping track of submissions under consideration in the marketplace. Many times writers and illustrators devote their attention to submitting material to editors or art directors, then fail to follow up on overdue responses because they feel the situation is out of their hands. By tracking those submissions still under consideration and then following up, you may be able to refresh a buyer's memory who temporarily forgot about your submission, or revise a troublesome point to make your work more enticing to him. At the very least you will receive a definite "no," thereby freeing you to send your material to another market.

When recording your submissions be sure to include the date they were sent, the business and contact name; and any enclosures that were inserted such as samples of writing, artwork or photography. Keep copies of the article or manuscript as well as related correspondence for easier follow up. When you sell rights to a manuscript or artwork you can "close" your file by noting the date the material was accepted, what rights were purchased, the publication date and payment.

## Rights for the writer and illustrator

The Copyright Law of 1976, which became effective January 1, 1978, was modified in 1989. So that the United States may have copyright relations with 80 other countries, Congress voted to amend our copyright law and ratify the Berne Convention. This means that it is no longer necessary to attach a copyright notice to works; material published after March 1, 1989 automatically carries copyright protection via this amendment.

The international recognition of copyright protection provided in the Berne Convention prevents foreign piracy of works copyrighted in the U.S. and allows prosecution of foreign copyright infringers in foreign courts. (Principal countries that haven't yet adopted the convention are China and the Soviet Union.)

In spite of this new protection, authors and artists who continue to display the copyright notice—© (your name) (year of work)—on their works benefit by the ability to more readily defeat an "innocent infringement" defense. Also, registration of a copyright notice doubles the payment an author or artist collects in a damage suit in comparison to the payment to the author or artist of a nonregistered work.

It's important to note also that the copyright owner of works created in the U.S. has to register his work with the Copyright Office before a suit in a foreign land can be initiated. However, authors or artists residing in other countries whose governments have joined the convention need not register their works to sue someone within the U.S.

In general, copyright protection ensures that you, the writer or illustrator, have the power to decide how the work is used and that you receive payment for each use. Not only does a copyright protect you, it essentially encourages you to create new works by guaranteeing you the power to sell rights to their use in the marketplace. As the copyright holder you can print, reprint or copy your work; sell or distribute copies of your work; or prepare derivative works such as plays, collages or recordings. The Copyright Law is designed to protect a writer's or illustrator's work for his lifetime plus 50 years. If you collaborate with someone else on a written or artistic project, the copyright will last for the lifetime of the last survivor plus 50 years. In addition, works created anonymously or under a pseudonym are protected for 100 years, or 75 years after publication, whichever is shorter. Incidentally, this latter rule is also true of work-for-hire agreements. Under work-for-hire you relinquish your copyright to your "employer." Try to avoid agreeing to such terms.

For more information about the proper procedure to register works, contact the Register of Copyrights, Library of Congress, Washington D.C. 20559. The registration fee is $10 per form, although you can register a group of articles or illustrations if:

- the group is assembled in order, such as in a notebook;
- the works bear a single title, such as "Works by (your name)";
- they are the work of one writer or artist;
- the material is the subject of a single claim to copyright.

The copyright law specifies that writers generally sell one-time rights to their work unless they and the buyer agree otherwise in writing. Be forewarned that many editors aren't aware of this. Many publications will want more exclusive rights from you than just one-time usage of your work; some will even require you to sell all rights to your work. Be sure that you are monetarily compensated for the additional rights you give up to your material. It is always to your benefit to retain as much control as possible over your work. Writers who give up limited rights to their work can then sell reprint rights to other publications, foreign rights to international publications, or even movie rights, should the opportunity arise. Likewise, artists can sell their illustrations to other book and magazine markets as well as to paper-product companies who may use an image on a calendar or greeting card. You can see that exercising more control over ownership of your work gives you a greater marketing edge for resale. If you do have to give up all rights to a work, think about the price you are being offered to determine whether it will compensate you for the loss of other sales.

Rights acquired through sale of a book manuscript are explained in each publisher's contract. Take the time to read through relevant clauses to be sure you understand what each contract is specifying prior to signing. The rights you will most often be selling to periodicals in the marketplace are:

● One-time rights—The buyer has no guarantee that he is the first to use a piece. One-time permission to run a written or illustrated work is acquired, then the rights revert back to the creator.

● First serial rights—The creator offers rights to use the work for the first time in any periodical. All other rights remain with the creator. When material is excerpted from a soon-to-be-published book for use in a newspaper or periodical, first serial rights are also purchased.

● First North American serial rights—This is similar to first serial rights, except that publishers who distribute both in the U.S. and Canada will stipulate these rights to ensure that a publication in the other country won't come out with simultaneous usage of the same work.

● Second serial (reprint) rights—In this case newspapers and magazines are granted the right to reproduce a work that already has appeared in another publication. These rights also are purchased by a newspaper or magazine editor who wants to publish part of a book after the book has been published. The proceeds from reprint rights are often split 50/50 between the author and his publishing company.

● Simultaneous rights—Use of such rights occurs among magazines with circulations that don't overlap, such as many religious publications. Many "moral guidance" stories or illustrations are appropriate for a variety of denominational publications. Be sure you submit to a publication that allows simultaneous submissions, and be sure to state in your cover letter to the editor that the submission is being considered elsewhere.

● All rights—Rights such as this are purchased by publishers who pay premium usage fees, have an exclusive format, or have other book or magazine interests from which the purchased work can generate more "mileage" for their interests. When the writer or illustrator sells all rights to a market he no longer has any say in who acquires rights to use his piece. Synonymous with purchase of all rights is the term "work-for-hire." Under such an agreement the creator of a work gives away all rights—and his copyright—to the company buying his work. Try to avoid such agreements; they're not in your best interest. If a market is insistent upon acquiring all rights to your work, see if you can negotiate for the rights to revert back to you after a reasonable period of time. It can't hurt to ask. If they're agreeable to such a proposal, be sure you get it in writing.

● Foreign serial rights—Be sure before you market to foreign publications that you have only sold North American—not worldwide—serial rights to previous markets. If not, you are free to market to publications you think may be interested in using material that has appeared in a U.S. or North American-based periodical.

● Syndication rights—This is a division of serial rights. For example, if a syndicate prints portions of a book in installments in its newspapers, it would be syndicating second serial rights. The syndicate would receive a commission and leave the remainder to be split between the author and publisher.

● Subsidiary rights—These are rights, other than book rights, and should be specified in a book contract. Subsidiary rights include serial rights, dramatic rights or translation rights. The contract should specify what percentage of

profits from sales of these rights go to the author and publisher.
● Dramatic, television and motion picture rights — Purchase of such rights usually begins with a one-year option (usually 10 percent of the total price). During this time the interested party tries to sell the story to a producer or director. Many times options are renewed because the selling process can be lengthy. Currently there is a good market for nonfiction as well as fiction; biographies of famous people are an example of nonfiction that has become salable for this market.

## Taxes

To successfully (and legally) compete in the business of writing or illustrating you must have knowledge of what income you should report and deductions you can claim. Before you can do this however, you must prove to the IRS that you are in business to make a profit, that your writing or illustrations are not merely a hobby. Under the Tax Reform Act of 1986 it was determined that you should show a profit for three years out of a five-year period to attain professional status. What does the IRS look for as proof of your professionalism? Keeping accurate financial records (see Business records), maintaining a business bank account separate from your personal account, the time you devote to your profession and whether it is your main or secondary source of income, and your history of profits and losses. The amount of training you have invested in your field also is a contributing factor to your professional status, as well as your expertise in the field.

If your business is unincorporated, you will fill out tax information on Schedule C of Form 1040. If you're unsure of what deductions you can take, request Publication 553 from the IRS. Under the Tax Reform Act only 80 percent (formerly it was 100 percent) of business meals, entertainment and related tips and parking charges are deductible. Other deductibles allowed on Schedule C include: capital expenditures (such as a computer), car expenses for business-related trips, professional courses and seminars, depreciation of office equipment, dues and publications and miscellaneous expenses, such as postage used for business needs, etc.

If you're working out of a home office, a portion of your mortgage (or rent), related utilities, property taxes, repair costs and depreciation can be deducted as business expenses. To qualify though, your office must be used only for business activities, it can't double as a family room during nonbusiness hours. To determine what portion of business deductions can be taken, simply divide the square footage of your business area into the total square footage of your house. You will want to keep a log of what business activities, and sales and business transactions occur each day; the IRS may want to see records to substantiate your home office deductions.

The method of paying taxes on income not subject to withholding is your "estimated tax." If you expect to owe more than $500 at year's end and if the total amount of income tax that will be withheld during the year will be less than 90% of the tax shown on the previous year's return, you will generally make estimated tax payments. Form 1040ES provides a worksheet to help you estimate how much will be owed to the IRS. Estimated tax payments are made in four equal installments due on April 15, June 15, September 15 and January

15. For more information, request Publication 505, Tax Withholding and Estimated Tax.

Depending on your net income you may be liable for a self-employment tax. This is a Social Security tax designed for those who don't have Social Security withheld from their paychecks. You're liable if your net income is $400 or more per year. Net income is the difference between your income and allowable business deductions. Request Schedule SE, Computation of Social Security Self-Employment Tax if you qualify.

If completing your income tax return proves to be a complex affair, call the IRS for assistance. In addition to walk-in centers, the IRS has 90 publications to instruct you in various facets of preparing a tax return.

# Insurance

As a self-employed professional you need to be aware of what health and business insurance coverage is available to you. Personal insurance needs to research include life, health and disability coverage. When looking for health insurance, you will want to consider the types of catastrophic illnesses and injuries the policy includes. Basic coverage protects you for a specified period of time that pays for most in-hospital costs. Major medical coverage, which picks up where basic coverage ends, covers long-term, major illnesses.

In addition to health insurance will be the need for some type of disability insurance. Such protection is offered through many private insurance companies and state governments, and pays a monthly fee that covers living and business expenses during periods of long-term recuperation from a health problem. The amount of money paid monthly is based on the writer's or artist's annual earnings.

Before contacting any insurance representative, talk to other writers or illustrators to find out about insurance companies they could recommend. If you belong to a writer's or artist's organization, be sure to contact them to determine if any insurance coverage for professionals is offered to members. Such group coverage may prove less expensive and yield more comprehensive coverage than an individual policy.

# Building business—and creative—skills

Now that you have an idea of what it takes to set up your freelance writing or illustrating practice, you may want to consult further publications to read in depth about business, writing or illustrating specialties you don't feel quite as comfortable with. Many of the publications recommended here incorporate business-oriented material with information about how to write or illustrate more creatively and skillfully.

## Books of interest

*The Artist's Friendly Legal Guide*. Conner, Floyd; Karlen, Peter; Perwin, Jean; Spatt, David M. North Light Books, 1988.
*Children's Media Marketplace*. Jones, Delores B., ed. Neal-Schuman, 1988.
*The Children's Picture Book: How to Write It, How to Sell It*. Roberts, Ellen E.M. Writer's Digest Books, 1984.
*How to Write a Children's Book & Get It Published*. Seuling, Barbara. Charles

Scribner's Sons, 1984.
*How to Write and Illustrate Children's Books*. Bicknell, Treld Pelkey; Trotman, Felicity, eds. North Light Books, 1988.
*Illustrating Children's Books*. Hands, Nancy S. Prentice Hall Press, 1986.
*Market Guide for Young Writers*. Henderson, Kathy. Shoe Tree Press, 1989.
*Nonfiction for Children: How to Write It, How to Sell It*. Roberts, Ellen E.M. Writer's Digest Books, 1986.
*Writing Books for Children.* Yolen, Jane. The Writer, Inc., 1983.
*Writing for Children & Teenagers*. Wyndham, Lee & Madison, Arnold. Writer's Digest Books, 1988.
*Writing Short Stories for Young People*. Stanley, George Edward. Writer's Digest Books, 1987.
*Writing Young Adult Novels*. Irwin, Ann; Hadley, Lee and Eyerly, Jeannette. Writer's Digest Books, 1988.

**Publications of interest**
*Children's Magazine Guide*. Sinclair, Patti, ed. 7 North Pinckney St., Madison WI 53703.
*The Horn Book*. Silvey, Anita, ed. The Horn Book, Inc., Park Square Building, 31 St. James Ave., Boston MA 02116.
*Society of Children's Book Writers Bulletin*. Mooser, Stephen; Oliver, Lin, eds. Society of Children's Book Writers, Box 296, Mar Vista Station, Los Angeles CA 90066.

---

## Important listing information

When using listings in the book and magazine sections, be aware that age categories can be found under the "Fiction" and "Nonfiction" headings for solicited material. They are given to aid you in targeting material for those age groups for which you write/illustrate. "Picture books" are geared toward the preschool-8-year-old group; "Young readers" to 5-8-year-olds; "Middle readers" to 9-11 year-olds; and "Young adults" to those 12 and up. These age breakdowns may vary slightly from publisher to publisher.

# The Markets

## _Book Publishers_

The volume of children's books being published—and sold—shows no sign of waning during the 1990s. According to the November 24, 1989 _Publishers Weekly_, 4,954 children's books were published in 1988 as compared to 2,859 books in 1980. This represents a growth of 73.3 percent in the last eight years. Add to these statistics the fact that more than $1.5 billion in children's books sales were realized in 1989, with projected sales figures of $2.3 billion in 1992, and it's clear that writers and illustrators can safely plan book projects for some time to come.

The reasons for the growth of children's books is explained by American Book Association president and bookseller, Ed Morrow, who (in the above-mentioned _Publishers Weekly_ article) says, "When you put it all together—the demographics of the population bulge (increased birth rate), and the fact that much more than in the past parents are oriented toward education—it's (the growth of children's books) one phenomenon reinforcing the other."

The growth of children's books also is reflected in the Book Publishers section of this book. We have received returns from 50 additional publishers this year who are eager to receive manuscripts and artwork. As in last year's edition of _Children's Writer's & Illustrator's Market_ we include a variety of subject needs, so study each listing carefully. Though fiction is always a mainstay of children's publishing, there is a surge in the popularity of nonfiction as well, partly due to increased uses of nonfiction trade books to supplement textbooks in the classroom. New nonfiction titles describe how things work, present a historical personality in a more contemporary light or teach us about other lands and cultures.

In a survey of booksellers, the picture book was named the over-all best seller, followed closely by the beginning reader. This should be heartening news for illustrators, because along with this information was the report that 90 percent of these booksellers scrutinize the quality of a book's illustrations—in addition to content and the author's/artist's reputation—prior to stocking a specific book. Books for pre-schoolers and younger readers, however, won't be the top sellers forever. Many publishers are keenly aware that there already is a large group of children ready for middle readers and that this age group will shift into the young-adult reading group as well—and they plan to be ready to service their needs.

## Determining publishers' needs

The listings in this section have been specially designed to help writers and illustrators determine each publisher's needs, methods of contact and pay specifications. Once you have read through the listings and decided what publishers' needs match your own abilities or interests, take the time to send for their catalog and writer's or artist's guidelines, if available. The guidelines may reflect needs that weren't available at *Children's Writer's & Illustrator's Market* press time.

## When you're ready to submit work

The "How to Contact/Writers" and "How to Contact/Illustrators" subheads in each listing will provide you with the preferred methods of approaching each editor or art director. Be sure to follow these guides to ensure that you—and your work—are perceived in a professional light. Some editors may prefer to receive a query letter only or sample chapters with a synopsis, still others may want to review the entire manuscript. (For fiction the latter request will be common.) Many publishers are open to reviewing the work of new writers and illustrators while others prefer to deal with you via an agent.

Information for submission of manuscript/illustration packages is included in the "Illustration" and "How to Contact/Illustrators" portions of most listings. In some cases, you will be working with the editor rather than just the art director. Your initial contact person, if different from the editor given at the beginning of each listing, will be specified in the "Illustration" paragraph. Publishers reviewing manuscript/illustration submissions generally will want to see the entire manuscript plus a sample of finished art and rough sketches to get a feel for the "plot" and "flow" of the book. If you're interested only in illustrating juvenile books, you will want to check those same subheads to determine what type of work each wishes to review. Many publishers express the desire to review manuscripts and illustrations separately so the artist whose style most closely matches the flavor of a specific manuscript can be assigned by the editor or art director.

In your query letter, or cover letter if you're sending a complete manuscript, be sure to include any publishing credits. Also, provide the editor with pertinent information such as the intended age group for your book, reasons why it is different from anything else on the market, and any competition you perceive from other books. Though a lot of this research will be done by the editor and marketing staff as well, your efforts will be appreciated in case they overlooked an important marketing point, plus your awareness of other books in the market will make you appear more professional.

When sending out queries or cover letters with manuscripts, be sure to check if an editor is open to simultaneous submissions. This is strictly a matter of personal preference, but if you are sending out simultaneous submissions, just let each editor know the material is being considered elsewhere.

Once you near contract negotiations with a book publisher you will be offered a somewhat standard range of royalties. Based on our listing statistics, royalties are fluctuating between 3-20 percent of the wholesale or retail price (you will want to negotiate for the retail price as your base, if possible). Illustrator's fees, on the other hand, come in a variety of arrangements such as a flat fee for artwork based on the number of drawings and color vs. black and white work, to a royalty breakdown similar to writer's percentages.

Occasionally, writers and illustrators will split a royalty, with varying percentages of breakdowns depending on the volume of writing or artwork each contributes to a collaborative project.

## Book packagers

Occasionally at the beginning of each listing you will notice markets that describe themselves as "book packagers" rather than "publishers." While the majority of packaged books for children have been nonfiction, there is currently an increase in the production of picture books. Book packagers, or "book producers" or "developers," work for publishers and offer services that range from hiring writers, photographers and/or illustrators to editing and producing the final book. What they don't do is market the book; you won't see a catalog of books a packager has produced since such publications will appear in the client/publisher's catalog instead. Book packagers can offer experienced manpower to a small publisher in which, for instance, the inhouse staff may not be skilled in a certain subject area or where experience in dealing with illustrations may be lacking.

What is the difference, besides marketing, between a book publisher and book packager? The book publisher reviews (and hopefully accepts) queries and/or manuscripts (mss) sent to them by writers. The book packager already has the book idea, they then go out to hire a writer and/or illustrator whose skills match their needs. It is often felt that this is a good outlet for the fledgling writer who wants to get started in book publishing. This isn't necessarily true . . . book packagers will ask to see a writer's credentials to ensure they are getting the best person for the job. Also, writing and/or illustrating for a book packager won't always give you credit for the work you have done. Many times you will labor under a work-for-hire arrangement, or will be offered a large advance with low royalty percentage.

## Subsidy publishing

You will notice that some of the listings in this section give percentages of subsidy-published material. Subsidy publishers ask writers to pay all or part of the costs of producing a book. There are different reasons people use subsidy publishers: they have had their material rejected by other publishers and believe they can't improve the work with further rewrites, or writing is more of a hobby and they want a book they can share with family and friends. Aspiring writers will want to strongly consider working only with publishers who pay. Paying publishers will more actively market your work because this is where they make their profit; subsidy publishers make their money from each writer who pays them to publish a book. If you are comfortable with the idea of working with a subsidy publisher, be sure you understand all points of a contract. If you're willing to underwrite the cost of producing a book, you should be willing to have an attorney look over your contract to clarify any unclear terms.

## Understanding your profession

Editors are often amazed at how novice writers and artists perceive children's books as easy and quick projects. The most successful writers and illustrators have had material rejected time after time before being published. Nobody knows better than professional writers and illustrators how truly difficult it can be to seek out the child in themselves and recall reactions to childhood events. Not every writer or artist has the instinct to tune in to today's children, and it is for this reason that editors and art directors are excited every time they find an outstanding manuscript or unique style of artwork.

**\*ACCENT BOOKS,** a div. of Accent Publications, Inc., Box 15337, Denver CO 80215. (303)988-5300. Book publisher. Executive Editor: Mary B. Nelson. "Picture books is a new category for us. We're just now soliciting first book for beginning readers." Publishes 1 young reader title/year.
**Fiction:** "We are an evangelical Christian publishing house. All books must reflect that." Picture books: animal, contemporary, easy-to-read and Christian books. Young readers: animal, contemporary, easy-to-read and Christian books. Average word length: picture books—1,000-1,500; young readers—1,500-2,000. "Now looking for first book to publish for beginning readers."
**Nonfiction:** Picture books: animal, religion. Young readers: animal, religion. "All books must be Christian in orientation and message—family, church, friends, etc." Average word length: Picture books—1,000-1,500. Young readers—1,500-2,000. "Now looking for first book to publish for beginning readers."
**How to Contact/Writers:** Fiction/Nonfiction: Submit complete ms, SASE (IRC) for answer to query and/or return of ms; include Social Security number with submission. Reports on queries/mss 10-12 weeks. Publishes a book 12 months after acceptance. Will consider simultaneous, photocopied and computer printout submissions.
**Illustration:** Editorial will review ms/illustration packages submitted by authors/artists and ms/illustration packages submitted by author with illustrations done by separate artists.
**How to Contact/Illustrators:** Ms/illustration packages: Submit "samples of final art with rest in roughs." Illustrations only: "No separate freelance artists yet. Artists can send samples of their work for us to hold as file reference." Reports on ms/art samples only if interested.
**Terms/Writers & Illustrators:** Pays authors in royalties. Additional payment for ms/illustration packages is "uncertain yet. May put both names on contract and split royalties." Book catalog for $1.05 and 9 × 12 SAE; manuscript guidelines for SASE.
**Tips:** "Be sure you understand children's interests, interest level, reading level and vocabulary as well as the doctrinal position of the company." Ms/illustration packages "need to be interesting to children as well as their parents, cute and easily illustrated. There are many more children's books coming into the bookstores, creating a broader, more competitive marketplace. In competing with the visual impact of television and other products, children's books must be top quality."

**\*ADDISON-WESLEY PUBLISHING CO.,** Trade Dept., Subsidiary of Pearson PLC, Route 128, Reading MA 01867. (617)944-3700. Book publisher. Assistant Editor: John Bell. Publishes 6 middle reader titles/year. 15% of books by first-time authors.

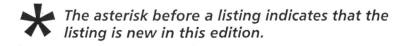

**\*** *The asterisk before a listing indicates that the listing is new in this edition.*

**Nonfiction:** Middle readers: history, hobbies, nature/environment. "All of our children's books are science activity books." Recently published *Sportworks*, by Ontario Science Center (ages 7-12, science activity); *Birdwise*, by Pamela M. Hickman (ages 7-12, science activity); *Science Sensations*, by Diane Willow and Emily Curran (age 7-12, science activity).

**How to Contact/Writers:** Nonfiction: Query. SASE (IRC) for return of ms. Reports on queries/mss in 6 weeks. Publishes a book 24 months after acceptance. Will consider simultaneous, photocopied and computer printout submissions.

**Illustration:** Number of illustrations used for fiction and nonfiction: middle readers— 90 full page. Editorial will review ms/illustration packages submitted by authors/artists; ms/illustration packages submitted by authors with illustrations done by separate artists; and an illustrator's work for possible use in authors' texts. Prefers "4-color representational art for covers and b&w for interior."

**How to Contact/Illustrators:** Ms/illustration packages: "Query first." Illustrations only: Send "résumé and tear sheets." Original artwork returned at job's completion.

**Terms/Writers & Illustrators:** Pays authors in royalties based on retail price. Factors used to determine payment for ms/illustration package include: "number of illustrations, technical nature of same." Pays for illustrators: by the project. Sends galleys to authors; dummies to illustrators. Book catalog for 7 × 10 SAE and 85¢ postage.

**Tips:** The writer and/or illustrator have the best chance of selling "science activity books *only*."

**ADVOCACY PRESS**, div. of The Girls Club of Santa Barbara, Box 236, Santa Barbara CA 93102. (805)962-2728. FAX: (805)963-3580. Book publisher. Editorial Contact: Kathy Araujo. Publishes 3-5 picture books/year; 2-4 young reader titles/year. 25% of books by first-time authors.

**Fiction:** "We are only allowed to publish books that are relevant to Equity (equal opportunity) issues." Two series: self-esteem concept stories and little known women in history "role models." Award winners: *My Way Sally*, by P. Paine and M. Bingham (ages 3-9, picture book); *Tonia the Tree*, by Sandy Stryker (ages 3-9, picture book); and newest release *Berta Benz and the Motorwagen*, by Mindy Bingham (ages 3-9, picture book).

**How to Contact/Writers:** Fiction/nonfiction: Submit outline/synopsis and sample chapters. Must SASE (IRC) for return of ms. Reports on queries/mss in 2 weeks. Publishes a book 6 months after acceptance. Will consider simultaneous, photocopied and computer printout submissions. Send for editorial policy.

**Illustration:** Number of illustrations used for fiction/nonfiction: picture books—30; middle readers—200; young adults—200. Editorial will review ms/illustration packages submitted by authors/artists and ms/illustration packages submitted by authors with illustrations done by separate artists. Marketing Director, Penny Paine, will review an illustrator's work for possible use in author's texts.

**How to Contact/Illustrators:** Ms/illustration packages: Query first. Reports on art samples in 4 weeks.

**Terms/Writers & Illustrators:** Illustrators paid by the project. Sends galleys to authors; dummies to illustrators. Book catalog/manuscript guidelines available for legal-size SAE.

**Tips:** "Make your package look as professional as possible."

**AEGINA PRESS/UNIVERSITY EDITIONS, INC.**, 59 Oak Lane, Spring Valley, Huntington WV 25704. (304)429-7204. Book publisher. Estab. 1983. Managing Editor: Ira Herman. Publishes 1 picture book/year; 1-2 young reader titles/year; 2 middle reader titles/year; 2-3 young adult titles/year. 50% of books by first-time authors; 5% of books from agented writers; 40% of books are subsidy published.

**Fiction:** Picture books: animal. Young readers: animal, easy-to-read, fantasy. Middle readers: history, sports. Young adults: problem novels, romance, science fiction. "Will consider most categories." Average word length: picture books—1,000; young readers—2,000; middle readers—10,000; young adults—20,000. Recently published *Oscar Crab and Rallo Car*, by Andrea Ross (picture book, easy-to-read); *The Sometimes Invisible Spaceship*, by Charles Bowles (middle readers, fantasy); *Boots, The Story of a Saint*, by Nancy Ball (young readers, animal).

**Nonfiction:** "We have not previously published any juvenile nonfiction. We may consider doing so in the future, however."

**How to Contact/Writers:** Fiction/nonfiction: Submit complete ms. SASE (IRC) for answer to query and/or return of ms. Reports on queries in 1 week; on mss in 1 month. Publishes a book 5-6 months after acceptance. Will consider simultaneous, photocopied, and computer printout submissions.

**Illustration:** Number of illustrations used for fiction: picture books—15-20; young readers—10; middle readers—5-6. Editorial will review ms/illustration packages submitted by authors/artists and ms/illustration packages submitted by authors with illustrations done by separate artists.

**How to Contact/Illustrators:** Ms/illustration packages: Query first. "We generally use our own artists. We will consider outside art only as a part of a complete ms/illustration package." Reports on art samples in 1 month. Original artwork returned at job's completion.

**Terms/Writers & Illustrators:** Pays authors in royalties of 10-15% based on retail price. Payment "negotiated individually for each book." Sends galleys to authors. Book catalog available for SAE + 4 first-class stamps; manuscript guidelines for #10 envelope and 1 first-class stamp.

**Tips:** "Focus your subject and plot-line. For younger readers, stress visual imagery and fantasy characterizations. A cover letter should accompany the manuscript, which states the approximate length (not necessary for poetry). A brief synopsis of the manuscript and a listing of the author's publishing credits (if any) should also be included. Queries, sample chapters, synopses and completed manuscripts are welcome."

**AFRICAN AMERICAN IMAGES**, 9204 Commercial, Chicago IL 60617. (312)375-9682. Book publisher. Editor: Jawanza Kunjufu. Publishes 2 picture books/year; 1 young reader title/year; 1 middle reader title/year; 1 young adult title/year. 90% of books by first-time authors.

**Fiction:** Picture books: contemporary, easy-to-read, history. Young readers, middle readers, young adults: contemporary, history.

**Nonfiction:** Picture books, young readers, middle readers, young adults: education, history.

**How to Contact/Writers:** Fiction/nonfiction: Submit complete ms. Reports on queries in 1 week; on mss in 3 weeks. Publishes a book 9 months after acceptance. Will consider simultaneous submissions.

**Illustration:** Number of illustrations used for fiction/nonfiction: picture books—20; young readers—15; middle readers—12; young adults—7. Editorial will review ms/illustration packages submitted by authors/artists; ms/illustration packages submitted by authors with illustrations done by separate artists; illustrator's work for possible use in author's texts.

**How to Contact/Illustrators:** Ms/illustration packages: Send 3 chapters of ms with 1 piece of final art. Illustrations only: Send tear sheets. Reports on art samples in 2 weeks. Original artwork returned at job's completion.

**Terms/Writers & Illustrators:** Buys ms outright. Factors to determine final payment: Color art vs. black-and-white and number of illustrations used. Pay for separate authors and illustrators: Authors get royalty; illustrator is paid for purchase of work outright.

Illustrator paid by the project. Book catalog, manuscript/artist's guidelines free on request.

**ALADDIN BOOKS/COLLIER BOOKS FOR YOUNG ADULTS,** imprint of Macmillan Children's Book Group, 24th floor, 866 Third Avenue, New York NY 10022. (212)702-9043. Book publisher. Estab. 1986. Associate Editor: Sharyn November. Publishes 30 picture books/year; 5 young reader titles/year; 15 middle reader titles/year; 15 young adult titles/year; 10 novelty titles/year. 20% of books by first-time authors; 40% of books from agented writers.
**Fiction:** Young readers: easy-to-read. Middle readers: contemporary, fantasy, problem novels, romance, science fiction, sports, spy/mystery/adventure. Young adults: contemporary, fantasy, problem novels, romance, science fiction, sports, spy/mystery/adventure. Recently published *Willie Bea and the Time the Martians Landed*, by Virginia Hamilton (9-12); *The Sword of the Spirits*, by John Christopher (12 and up, science fiction); and *Split Sisters*, by C.S. Adler (9-12).
**Nonfiction:** Middle readers, young adults: sports, self-help. Recently published *The Teenager's Survival Guide to Moving*, by Pat Nida (young adults); *What's Going to Happen to Me?*, by Eda LeShan (middle readers, self-help).
**How to Contact/Writers:** Fiction/nonfiction: Query; submit outline/synopsis and sample chapters. SASE (IRC) for answer to query and/or return of ms. Reports on queries in 2-6 weeks; on mss in 12-16 weeks. Publishes a book 1-2 years after acceptance. Will consider simultaneous, photocopied and computer printout submissions.
**Illustration:** Editorial will review ms/illustration package submitted by authors/artists and ms/illustration packages submitted by authors with illustrations done by separate artists.
**How to Contact/Illustrators:** Submit ms/illustration packages: 3 chapters of ms with 1 piece of final art. Illustrations only: submit résumé/tear sheets. Reports on art samples only if interested. Original artwork returned at job's completion. Pay for illustrators: by the project. Book catalog/manuscript guidelines available for SAE.
**Tips:** "We are currently concentrating on reprinting successful titles originally published by the hardcover imprints of the Macmillan Children's Book Group. However, we do occasionally publish original material. We prefer that longer manuscripts be preceded by a query letter and two or three sample chapters. We do not generally consider picture book manuscripts. Please do not submit more than two short (under 15 typed pages) or one longer manuscript at one time. If you wish to confirm that your manuscript has arrived safely, please include a self-addressed stamped postcard, or send the manuscript via registered mail. Read children's books—and talk to children, get a sense of their world. Learn something about the business of publishing—that way you can have an idea as to what editors are looking for and why they make the decisions that they do. Be clear-eyed and professional." Regarding illustrations: "Remember that what appeals to adults may not necessarily appeal to children." (See also Atheneum Publishers, Bradbury Press, Four Winds Press, Margaret K. McElderry Books.)

**\*ALBATROSS BOOKS PTY. LTD.,** Box 320 Sutherland, NSW Australia 2232. Book publisher. Publishes 1 picture book every 2 years; 2 young reader/middle reader titles/year. Editor: Ken Goodlet. 60% of books by first-time authors.

*"Picture books" are geared toward the preschool—8 year old group; "Young readers" to 5-8 year olds; "Middle readers" to 9-11 year olds; and "Young adults" to those 12 and up.*

**Fiction:** Recently published *Kirsty's Kite*, by Carol Curtis Stilz (ages 5-8, picture book); *Jo's Choice*, by Dorothy Dart (young adult).
**How to Contact/Writers:** Fiction: Submit outline/synopsis and sample chapters. SASE (IRC) for return of ms. Reports on queries in 2 weeks; mss in 6 weeks. Publishes a book 10 months after acceptance. Will consider simultaneous, photocopied, computer printout and electronic submissions via disk or modem.
**Illustration:** Will review ms/illustration packages submitted by authors/artists; ms/illustration packages submitted by authors with illustrations done by separate artists; illustrator's work for possible use in authors' text.
**How to Contact/Illustrators:** Ms/illustration packages: "Query first." Illustrations only: send "slides." Reports on ms/art samples in 6 weeks. Original art work returned at job's completion.
**Terms/Writers and Illustrators:** Pays authors in royalties of 10% (for Australian market) based on retail price. Other method of payment: "15% net receipts for overseas sales." Sends galleys to authors; dummies to illustrators. Book catalog, manuscript/artist's guidelines for standard size SAE.
**Tips:** Looking for "a Christian book for the general market."

**\*ALEGRA HOUSE PUBLISHERS**, Imprint of Kaya Books, Box 1443, Warren OH 44482. (216)372-2951. Book publisher. Managing Editor: Robert C. Peters. Publishes 2 picture books/year; 2 young reader titles/year; 2 middle reader titles/year. Subsidy publishes 50%.
**Fiction:** Picture books: contemporary, problem novels and sports. Young readers: animal, sports. Middle readers: contemporary, problem novels, sports. Young adults: contemporary, problem novels and sports. Average word length: picture books—3,000; young readers: 3,500; middle readers: 3,000; young adults: 5,000.
**Nonfiction:** Picture books/young readers/middle readers/young adult: animal, biography, education, history, hobbies, music/dance, nature/environment, religion, sports. Recently published *Divorce Happens to the Nicest Kids*, by M.S. Prokop (self-help problem solving); *Kids Divorce Workbook*, by M.S. Prokop (self-help problem solving); and *Kids Confidence and Creativity*, by M.S. Prokop (self-help problem solving).
**How to Contact/Writers:** Fiction: Submit complete ms. Reports on queries in 3 months; on mss in 4 months. Publishes a book 12 months after acceptance. Will consider simultaneous, photocopied and computer printout submissions.
**Illustration:** Number of illustrations used for fiction and nonfiction: picture books—20; young readers—30; middle readers—30; young adults—30. Editorial will review ms/illustration packages submitted by authors/artists; ms/illustration packages submitted by authors with illustrations done by separate artists; illustrator's work for possible use in authors' texts. Prefers to review "6″ × 9″ black line drawings."
**How to Contact/Illustrators:** Ms/illustrations packages: Submit 3 chapters and 3 pieces of final art. Illustrations only: send "résumé, tear sheets and sample black line drawings." Reports on ms/art samples in 1 month.
**Terms/Writers and Illustrators:** Pays authors in "negotiable" royalties. Average advance is negotiable. Additional payment for ms/illustration packages "negotiable." Illustrators paid a negotiable amount by the project when they work on authors' titles. Sends galleys to authors; dummies to illustrators. Book catalog free on request.
**Tips:** Writers/illustrators: "treat (publishing) it as a business; use an agent." Wants to see "more self-help books."

**\*AMERICAN BIBLE SOCIETY**, 1865 Broadway, New York NY 10023. (212)581-7400. Book publisher. Manager of Scripture Resource Development: Charles Houser. Publishes 2 picture books/year; 4 young reader titles /year; 4 young adult titles/year.

**Nonfiction:** Picture books, young readers, middle readers, young adults: religion. Recently published *A Book About Jesus*, (young readers, collection of scripture passages); *Good News Travels Fast*, (young readers, Book of Acts).
**How to Contact/Writers:** "All manuscripts developed in-house; unsolicited mss rejected."
**Illustration:** Number of illustrations used for nonfiction: picture book—5-10; young reader—5-60; middle reader—1-5 (cover); young adult—1-5 (cover). Editorial will review an illustrator's work for possible use in authors' texts.
**How to Contact/Illustrators:** Ms/illustration packages: "Query first." Illustrations only: send "résumés, tear sheets to keep; slides will be returned promptly." Reports back in 6 weeks. Factors used to determine payment for ms/illustration package include "nature and scope of project; complexity of illustration and continuity of work; number of illustrations." Pay for illustrators: pays $200-$30,000; based on fair market value. Sends dummies to illustrators. Book catalog free on request.
**Tips:** Illustrators must have the "ability to communicate traditional values about faith and worship in a fresh and modern way. Sensitivity to needs of children today and a realistic representation of their world (intergenerational, interracial, intercultural pictures are desireable)."

**\*ARCADE PUBLISHING,** Imprint of Little Brown & Co., 141 Fifth Ave., New York NY 10010. (212)475-2633. Book publisher. Editorial Director, Children's Books: Julie Amper. Publishes 7-10 picture books/year; 3-5 young reader titles/year; 5-8 middle reader titles/year; 3 young adult titles/year. 50% of books from agented writers.
**Fiction:** Young readers, middle readers, young adults: problem novels. "First juvenile list will appear fall 1989."
**Nonfiction:** Will consider general nonfiction—"all ages."
**How to Contact/Writers:** Fiction: Submit complete ms. Nonfiction: Query. SASE (IRC) for answer to query; return of ms. Reports on queries in 2 weeks. Publishes ms 12 months after acceptance. Will consider simultaneous and photocopied submissions.
**Illustration:** Number of illustrations used for fiction: picture books—30; young readers—12; middle readers 8-12. Number of illustrations used for nonfiction: picture books—30; young readers—25; middle readers—25. Will review ms/illustration packages submitted by authors/artists; with illustrations done by separate artists; illustrator's work for possible use in author's text.
**How to Contact/Illustrators:** "*No* original art—send slides or color photocopies." Illustrations only: Send tear sheets and slides. Reports on ms/art samples in 3 weeks. Original artwork returned at job's completion.
**Terms/Writers & Illustrators:** Pays authors in variable royalties; or buys ms outright for $400-$3,000; "also flat fees per b&w books and jackets." Offers average advance of $2,500. Additional payment for ms/illustration package is percentage of book. Sends galleys to authors; book catalog for 8×10 SAE; manuscript guidelines for legal-size SAE.

**ARCHWAY/MINSTREL BOOKS,** Pocket Books, 1230 Avenue of the Americas, New York NY 10020. (212)698-7000. Book publisher. Editorial contact: Patricia McDonald. Publishes originals and reprints. Minstrel Books (ages 7-11) and Archway Paperbacks (ages 12-16).
**Fiction:** Middle readers: animal. Young adults: contemporary, fantasy, romance, sports, suspense/mystery/adventure, humor, funny school stories.
**Nonfiction:** Middle readers: sports. Young adults: animal, sports.
**How to Contact/Writers:** Fiction/nonfiction: Query, submit outline/synopsis and sample chapters. SASE (IRC) for answer to query and/or return of ms is mandatory.
**Terms/Writers & Illustrators:** Pays authors in royalties.

# Close-up

**Nancy Tafuri**
*Children's Book Illustrator*
*Roxbury, Connecticut*

Established children's book illustrator, Nancy Tafuri, loves living a second childhood and not having to make excuses for it—after all, it's her job to think and feel like a child. Part of the ability to do this comes from her visualizing reading her story—or another author's story which she is illustrating—to a child. This imagery helps her to pace the "flow" of the story. "The page can talk to the child and the child can relate in the way that is most comfortable at that age," she explains.

Tafuri is thrilled picture books have experienced such growth during the past few years. Not only because it is her livelihood, but because she feels it's important for children to feel comfortable handling a book so they will continue to read for pleasure, not just when they have to later on in school. Many of Tafuri's picture books are actually "board books" which are printed on heavier cardboard stock so toddlers can handle them with more ease.

Many of the books she publishes through Greenwillow are projects she both writes and illustrates. "It just might be half and half," she explains of illustrating other authors' works versus her own. "I think I'm heading toward my own books now." Part of this transition, explains The New York City graduate of the School of Visual Arts, comes from illustrating other writers' works and developing a style that made her comfortable enough to venture into her own titles.

Also, illustrating other titles has provided her with story ideas for her own books. "When I worked on *Four Brave Sailors* (by Mirra Ginsburg, Greenwillow), I was working at the beginning with this cat. I enjoyed [drawing] that cat—it became a tiger cat—then I thought it would be fun to turn that tiger cat into a tiger, and that's sort of how *Jungle Walk* (one of her 1988 titles) started.

"If I have an idea and I don't know much about what I'm going to do yet, I just store it in the back of my mind and then something will trigger it off and I go 'That's it.' " It's at this point that Tafuri puts a dummy together to submit to Susan Hirschman, her editor. "When I show them a dummy, at first it's very rough and it's usually 24 or 32 pages. My audience is basically very young so most of my books are wordless. I have to give them (the editors) some idea of how it (the book) will look pictorially, and though it's not one bit exact (because the art is roughly drawn in black and white), it gives them the momentum of how the book is going to flow. They're so used to the way I'm going to handle [the artwork] that that's not a problem," she explains. "The concern is the story line and the pictures, and how it's going to flow."

Generally, Tafuri works in watercolor because she finds the bright colors appeal to her younger audience, though her art style has evolved somewhat into a "softer" tone. The complexity of Tafuri's artwork also changes a bit depending on the theme of a particular book and the general reading age.

"I find working on my own books very creative because I'm dealing with the story line and the illustrations and putting the whole thing together. That's a challenge," she says, though she is quick to point out that working on others' work and trying to put their feelings into her illustrations is rewarding also. "What happens, is that you forget someone else has written this. With *Four Brave Sailors* I reread and put so much of how I felt into it that now I feel it is almost my book. It becomes you, you forget that it is someone else's writing."

Aspiring writers and illustrators are reassured by Tafuri that they don't have to both write and illustrate the book if their expertise doesn't extend to crossing over. "Many people don't realize this and feel they have to be proficient in both areas." She encourages research prior to submitting a manuscript or dummy. "If they do their research in the library and the bookstores they can see where they would possibly fit in," she adds. She emphasizes the importance of looking at other books to see what art styles are compatible. Every publisher has a certain area they are strong in, she shares. If one's style needs don't match yours, another's might.

*— Connie Eidenier*

*This watercolor illustration is from Tafuri's 1984 book,* **Have You Seen My Duckling?,** *published by Greenwillow. Her use of colorful pictures and minimal text familiarizes pre-school and early elementary children with books and encourages their reading habits in later years.*

**ATHENEUM PUBLISHERS**, Macmillan Children's Book Group, 866 Third Ave., New York NY 10022. (212)702-2000. Book Publisher. Editorial Director: Jonathan Lanman. Editorial Contacts: Gail Paris, Marcia Marshall. Publishes 15-20 picture books/year; 4-5 young reader titles/year; 20-25 middle reader titles/year; 10-15 young adult titles/year. 15-25% of books by first-time authors; 50% of books from agented writers.
**Fiction:** Picture books: animal, contemporary, fantasy. Young readers: contemporary, fantasy. Middle readers: animal, contemporary, fantasy. Young adults: contemporary, fantasy. Recently published *One of the Third Grade Thonkers*, by Phyllis Reynolds Naylor (ages 8-12, middle grade fiction); *Coyote Dreams*, by Susan Nunes (ages 4-8, picture book); *The Changeling Sea*, by Patricia McKillip (ages 10 and up, young adult fantasy novel).
**Nonfiction:** Picture books: animal, biography, education, history. Young readers: animal, biography, education, history. Middle readers: animal, biography, education, history. Young adults: animal, biography, education, history. Recently published *Born Different*, by Frederick Drimmer (ages 10-14, biography); *The Smithsonian Book of Flight for Young People*, by Walter Boyne (ages 8-12, history); *Heads*, by Ron and Nancy Goor (ages 7-11, science photo essay).
**How to Contact/Writers:** Fiction/nonfiction: Query; will consider complete picture book manuscript; submit outline/synopsis and sample chapters for longer works. SASE (IRC) for answer to query and/or return of ms. Reports on queries 6-8 weeks; on mss 12 weeks. Publishes a book 18-24 months after acceptance. Will consider simultaneous, photocopied submissions from previously unpublished authors; "we request that the author let us know it is a simultaneous submission."
**Illustration:** Editorial will review ms/illustration packages submitted by authors/artists and ms/illustration packages submitted by authors with illustrations done by separate artists.
**How to Contact/Illustrators:** Ms/illustration packages: query first, 3 chapters of ms with 1 piece of final art. Illustrations only: résumé, tear sheets. Reports on art samples only if interested. Original artwork returned at job's completion.
**Terms/Writers & Illustrators:** Pays authors in royalties of 8-12½% based on retail price. Illustrators paid royalty or flat fee depending on the project. Sends galleys to authors; proofs to illustrators. Book catalog available for 9×12 SAE and 5 first-class stamps; manuscript guidelines for #10 SAE and 1 first-class stamp. (See also Aladdin Books/Collier Books for Young Adults, Bradbury Press, Four Winds Press, Margaret K. McElderry Books.)

**AVON BOOKS/BOOKS FOR YOUNG READERS (AVON FLARE AND AVON CAMELOT)**, div. of The Hearst Corporation, 105 Madison Ave., New York NY 10016. (212)481-5609. Book publisher. Editorial Director: Ellen Krieger. Editorial Contact: Gwen Montgomery. Editorial Assistant: Mary Bethscheider. Publishes 25-30 middle reader titles/year; 20-25 young adult titles/year. 10% of books by first-time authors; 20% of books from agented writers.
**Fiction:** Middle readers: contemporary, problem novels, sports, spy/mystery/adventure, comedy. Young adults: contemporary, problem novels, romance, spy/mystery/adventure. Average length: middle readers—100-150 pages; young adults—150-250 pages. Recently published *The Plant That Ate Dirty Socks*, by Nancy McArthur (middle readers, comedy); *Cross Your Heart*, by Bruce and Carole Hart (young adults, contemporary); *At the Edge*, by Michael Behrens (young adults, coming of age).

*Refer to the Business of Children's Writing & Illustrating for up-to-date marketing, tax and legal information.*

**Nonfiction:** Middle readers: hobbies, music/dance, sports. Young adults: "growing up." Average length: middle readers—100-150 pages; young adults pages. Recently published *Why Am I So Miserable If These Are the Best Years of My Life?*, by A. B. Eagan (young adults, growing up); *Dead Serious*, by Jane Mersky Leder (young adults, suicide); *Go Ask Alice*, Anonymous (young adults, drug abuse).

**How to Contact/Writers:** Fiction: Submit complete ms. Nonfiction: Submit outline/synopsis and sample chapters. SASE (IRC) for answer to query and/or return of ms. Reports on queries in 2 weeks; on mss in 4-8 weeks. Publishes book 18-24 months after acceptance. Will consider simultaneous, photocopied and computer printout submissions.

**Illustration:** Number of illustrations used for fiction: middle readers 6-8. Number of illustrations used for nonfiction: middle readers 8-10; young adults 6-8. Very rarely will review ms/illustration packages submitted by authors/artists and ms/illustration packages submitted by authors with illustrations done by separate artists.

**How to Contact/Illustrators:** "We prefer to use our own illustrators. Submit ms without art."

**Terms/Writers & Illustrators:** Pays authors in royalties of 6% based on retail price. Average advance payment is "very open." Sends galleys to authors; sometimes sends dummies to illustrators. Book catalog available for 9x12 SAE and 4 first-class stamps; manuscript guidelines for letter-size SAE and 1 first-class stamp.

**Tips:** "We have two Young Readers imprints, Avon Camelot books for the middle grades, and Avon Flare for young adults. Out list is weighted more to individual titles than to series, with the emphasis in our paperback originals on high quality recreational reading—a fresh and original writing style; identifiable, three dimensional characters; a strong, well-paced story that pulls readers in and keeps them interested." Writers: "Make sure that you really know what a company's list looks like before you submit work. Is your work in line with what they usually do? Is your work appropriate for the age group that this company publishes for? Most of all, make sure that you hand in something that is well done—check spelling, grammar, punctuation, etc. Keep aware of what's in your bookstore (but not what's in there for too long!)" Illustrators: "Submit work to art directors and people who are in charge of illustration at publishers. This is usually not handled entirely by the editorial department."

**BARRONS EDUCATIONAL SERIES**, 250 Wireless Blvd., Hauppauge NY 11788. (516)434-3311. FAX: (516)434-3723. Book publisher. Estab. 1945. Acquisitions Editor (picture books): Grace Freedson. Editorial contact (young/middle readers, young adult titles): Don Reis. Publishes 20 picture books/year; 20 young reader titles/year; 20 middle reader titles/year; 10 young adult titles/year. 25% of books by first-time authors; 25% of books from agented writers.

**Fiction:** Picture books: animal, easy-to-read, sports. Recently published *Stepping Stone Stories*, by Dr. Lawrence Balter (preschool, four storybooks dealing with children's problems).

**Nonfiction:** Picture books: animal. Young readers: biography, sports. Recently published *Playing It Smart*, by Tova Navarra (grades 1-7, tips for kids who spend time alone while parents are at work).

**How to Contact/Writers:** Fiction: Query. Nonfiction: Submit outline/synopsis and sample chapters. Reports on queries in 3-8 weeks; on mss in 3-12 weeks. Publishes a book 6 months after acceptance. Will consider simultaneous submissions.

**Illustration:** Number of illustrations used for fiction/nonfiction: picture books—16. Editorial will review ms/illustration packages submitted by authors/artists; ms/illustration packages submitted by authors with illustrations done by separate artists; and illustrator's work for possible use in author's texts.

**How to Contact/Illustrators:** Ms/illustration packages: Query first; 3 chapters of ms with 1 piece of final art, remainder roughs. Illustrations only: Tear sheets or slides plus résumé. Reports in 3-8 weeks.

**Terms/Writers & Illustrators:** Pays authors in royalties based on retail price. Illustrators paid by the project based on retail price. Sends galleys to authors; dummies to illustrators. Book catalog, manuscript/artist's guidelines free on request.

**Tips:** Writers: "We are predominately on the lookout for preschool storybooks and concept books." Illustrators: "We are happy to receive a sample illustration to keep on file for future consideration. Periodic notes reminding us of their work is acceptable." Children's book themes "are becoming much more contemporary and relevant to a child's day-to-day activities."

**\*BEACON PRESS**, 25 Beacon St., Boston MA 02108. (617)742-2110. Book publisher. Publishes 2 picture books/year; Editorial Contact: Anne Hollinshead. Publishes 2 young reader titles/year; 2 middle reader titles/year.

**Fiction:** Young reader: contemporary, easy-to-read. Middle reader: contemporary. Other: "folktales and multicultural stories." Average word length: picture books— 2,500; middle readers—7,000. Recently published *Ntombi's Song*, by Jenny Seed (picture books and young reader, multicultural picture book); *Tales of an Ashanti Father*, by Peggy Appiah (middle reader, African folktales); *Aditi and the One-Eyed Monkey*, by Suniti Namjoshi (middle reader, feminist multicultural fantasy).

**Nonfiction:** Young reader: biography, nature/environment, "handicaps." No nonfiction titles yet.

**How to Contact/Writers:** Fiction/nonfiction: Query, submit outline/synopsis and sample chapters. SASE (IRC) for return of ms. Reports on queries/mss in 2 months. Publishes a book 1 year after acceptance. Will consider simultaneous, photocopied (only clear copies) and computer printout submissions (pages must be separated and collated).

**Illustration:** Number of illustrations used for fiction: picture books—30; young reader—10; middle reader—10. Editorial will review ms/illustration packages submitted by authors/artists or ms/illustration packages submitted by authors with illustrations done by separate artists. Production and Design Manager, Pam Pokorney, will review illustrator's work for possible use in author's texts.

**How to Contact/Illustrators:** Reports in 1 month. Original art work returned at job's completion.

**Terms/Writers and Illustrators:** Pays authors in royalties based on wholesale price. Offers average advance payment of $2,000. Factors used to determine payment of ms/ illustration package include "color art vs. black-and-white, number of illustrations used, plus percentage of art to text." Pay for illustrators: by the project. Sends galleys to authors; dummies to illustrators. Book catalog, manuscript/artist's guidelines free on request.

**Tips:** "Do your homework. Find out what kind of books a publisher produces before you send in something that might be totally inappropriate." Looking for "feminist, multi-cultural, multi-racial (picture book, young reader, middle reader), folktales."

**\*BEHRMAN HOUSE INC.**, 235 Watchung Ave., West Orange NJ 07052. (201)669-0447. Book publisher. Vice President: Ruby G. Strauss. Publishes 2 young reader titles/year; 4 middle reader titles/year; 2 young adult titles/year. 20% of books by first-time authors; 5% of books from agented writers.

**Nonfiction:** Middle reader/young adult: history, religion, Jewish Educational textbooks. Young reader: religion. Other: "holidays—Israel ethics." Average word length: young reader—1,200; middle reader—2,000; young adult—4,000.

**How to Contact/Writers:** Nonfiction: Query. Reports on queries in 4 weeks; on mss in 6 weeks. Publishes a book 16 months after acceptance. Will consider simultaneous, photocopied and computer printout submissions.

**Illustration:** Number of illustrations used for nonfiction: young reader—50; middle reader—40; young adult—30. Editorial will review ms/illustration packages submitted by authors/artists; ms/illustration packages submitted by authors with illustrations done by separate artists; illustrator's work for possible use in authors' texts.

**How to Contact/Illustrators:** Ms/illustration packages: "Query first." Illustrations only: Send "tearsheets or photocopies." Reports only if interested. Original art work returned at job's completion.

**Terms/Writers and Illustrators:** Pays authors in royalties of 3-8% based on retail price or buys ms outright for $1,000-5,000. Offers average advance payment of $500. Factors used to determine payment for ms/illustration package include color art vs. black-and-white, number of illustrations. Pay for illustrators: by the project; $500-5,000. Sends galleys to authors; dummies to illustrators. Book catalog free on request.

**Tips:** Looking for "religious school texts."

**BOOKMAKER'S GUILD, INC.**, subsidiary of Dakota Graphics, Inc., 9655 W. Colfax Ave., Lakewood CO 80215. (303)235-0203. Book publisher. Publisher: Barbara J. Ciletti. Publishes 6 young reader titles/year; 2-4 middle reader titles/year. 5-10% of books by first-time authors; 5% of books from agented writers.

**Fiction:** Picture books: animal, fantasy "require strong myth and fable storylines," history. Young readers: animal, contemporary, history, adventure. Middle readers: history, adventure. Young adults: adventure. Average word length: picture books—5,000-10,000; young readers—30,000+; middle readers—30,000+; young adults—40,000+. Recently published *The Stolen Appaloosa*, by Levitt & Guralnick (ages 9-12, Northwest Indian legends); *Roxane, The Blue Dane*, by Alice LaChevre (ages 9-12, mini saga); *Orlanda & The Contest of Thieves* (Ages 6-10, Neopolitan folktale).

**Nonfiction:** Picture books: animal, biography, education, history, nature/environment. Young readers: animal, biography, education, history, nature/environment. Middle readers: animal, biography, education, history, nature/environment. Young adults: animal, biography, education, history, nature/environment. Average word length: picture books—5,000-10,000; young readers—30,000; middle readers—30,000; young adults—30,000+. Recently published *Call to Adventure*, by Hillary Hauser (ages 10 and up, adventure and biography).

**How to Contact/Writers:** Fiction/nonfiction: Query; submit outline/synopsis and sample chapters. SASE (IRC) for answer to query and/or return of mss; include Social Security number with submission. Reports on queries in 4 weeks; on mss 4-12 weeks. Publishes a book 12-18 months after acceptance. Will consider simultaneous, photocopied and computer printout submissions.

**Illustration:** Number of illustrations used for fiction: picture books—30; young readers—30. Number of illustrations used for nonfiction: picture books—30; young readers—30; middle readers—30-40; young adults—50+. Editorial will review ms/illustration packages submitted by authors/artists; ms/illustration packages submitted by authors with illustrations done by separate artists. Publisher, Barbara J. Ciletti will review an illustrator's work for possible use in author's texts.

**How to Contact/Illustrators:** Ms/illustration packages: Query first. Illustrations only: Résumé and tear sheets. Reports only if interested.

**Terms/Writers & Illustrators:** Pays authors in royalties on escalating scale from 10% based on wholesale price. Additional payment for ms/illustration packages: Illustrators receive their own contract or their own agreement of work for hire; final payment is made after final art is approved. We pay (illustrators working on author's titles) by project. The price ranges depending on the intended audience, number of illustrations and their complexity. Sends galleys to authors; dummies to illustrators. Books catalog free on request; manuscript guidelines/artist's guidelines available for #10 SAE and 1 first-class stamp.

**Tips:** Writers: "Research. Conduct a thorough study on what has been done and who has done it. Use Bowker's *Literary Marketplace* and read *Publishing: What It Is* by John Dessauer." Illustrators: "It's important to show versatility and personality in your images. Different books may have a combination of requirements." Looks for: "Fresh, wholesome stories and illustrations that reflect some educational value."

*All rights to this watercolor and colored pencil illustration by Cathy Morrison, Littleton, Colorado, were purchased for use in the book* Lions Tigers and Bears Go 'Round, *by Jo Anne Medler Bergeon, published by Bookmaker's Guild. According to Publisher Barbara J. Ciletti, "This artist's animation skills, experience and talent enable her to draw animals effectively, conveying movement."*

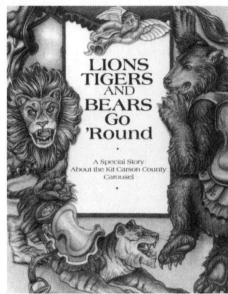

© Bookmaker's Guild 1989

**BRADBURY PRESS**, imprint of Macmillan Publishing Company, 866 Third Ave., New York NY 10022. (212)702-9809. Book publisher. Editorial Director: Barbara Lalicki. Publishes 15-20 picture books/year; 5 young reader titles/year; 5 middle reader titles/year; 3 young adult titles/year. 30% of books by first-time authors; 60% of books from previously published or agented writers.

**Fiction:** Picture books: animal, contemporary, history. Young readers: animal, contemporary, easy-to-read, history. Middle readers: contemporary, fantasy, history, science fiction, spy/mystery/adventure. Young adults: contemporary, fantasy, history, science fiction, spy/mystery/adventure. Average length: picture books—32-48 pages; young readers—48 pages; middle readers—128 pages; young adults—140-160 pages. Recently published *Hatchet*, by Gary Paulsen (ages 11-13, adventure/survival); *Her Seven Brothers*, by Paul Goble (all ages, picture book); *Henry and Mudge in the Sparkle Days*, by Cynthia Rylant (ages 6-8, easy-to-read).

**Nonfiction:** Picture books: animal, history, music/dance, nature/environment. Young readers: animal, biography, education, history, hobbies, music/dance, nature/environment, sports. Middle readers: animal, biography, education, history, hobbies, music/dance, nature/environment, sports. Average length: picture books—32-48 pages; young readers—48 pages; middle readers—128 pages; young adults—140-160 pages. *African Journey*, by John Chiasson (8 and up, photoessay); *Dinosaurs Walked Here*, by Patricia Lauber (8 and up, photoessay/nature/history); *When I See My Doctor*, by Susan Kuklin (ages 3-5, photoessay).

**How to Contact/Writers:** Fiction: Query. Nonfiction: Submit outline/synopsis and sample chapters. SASE (IRC) for answer to query and/or return of ms. Reports on queries in 2-3 weeks; on mss in 6-8 weeks. Publishes a book 18 months after acceptance. Will consider photocopied and computer printout submissions.
**Illustration:** Number of illustrations used for fiction and nonfiction: picture books— 30; young readers—1; middle readers—1; young adults—1. Art Director, Julie Quan, will review illustrator's work for possible use in author's texts.
**How to Contact/Illustrators:** Submit ms with color photocopies of art. Illustrations only: Portfolio drop off last Thursday of every month. Reports on art samples only if interested. Original artwork returned at job's completion.
**Terms/Writers & Illustrators:** Pays author in royalties based on retail price. Average advance: "% of estimated sales." Additional payment for ms/illustration packages. Pay for separate authors and illustrators: "advance, royalty." Sends galleys to authors; dummies to illustrators. Book catalog available for 8×10 SAE and 4 first-class stamps; manuscript and/or artist's guidelines for business-size SAE and 1 first-class stamp.
**Tips:** Writers: "Write about what you know about, think about pity, real conversations." Illustrators: "Know how to draw and paint children." Looks for "a strong story, nothing gimmicky, no pop-ups." Trends include "nonfiction for pre-schoolers." (See also Aladdin Books/Collier Books for Young Adults, Atheneum Publishers, Four Winds Press, Margaret K. McElderry Books.)

**BREAKWATER BOOKS**, Box 2188, St. John's Newfoundland, A1C 6E6 Canada. (709)722-6680. Book publisher. Marketing Manager: Caroline Vaughan. Publishes 3 middle reader titles/year; 2 young adult titles/year.
**Fiction:** Recently published *Smoke Over Grand Pré*, by Davison/Marsh (young adults, historical); *Fanny for Change*, by Jean Feather (middle reader); *Borrowed Black*, by Ellen B. Obed (young reader, fantasy).
**Nonfiction:** Recently published *A Viking Ship*, by Niels Neerso (young adults).
**How to Contact/Writers:** Fiction/nonfiction: Submit outline/synopsis and sample chapters; submit complete ms. Publishes a book 2 years after acceptance. Will consider simultaneous and photocopied submissions.
**Illustration:** Number of illustrations used per fiction/nonfiction title varies. Editorial will review ms/illustration packages submitted by authors/artists, ms/illustration packages submitted by authors with illustrations done by separate artists, and illustrator's work for possible use in author's text.
**How to Contact/Illustrators:** Submit 3 chapters of ms with 1 piece of final art, remainder roughs. Reports on art samples within weeks. Original artwork returned at job's completion.
**Terms/Writers & Illustrators:** Royalties are 10% based on retail price. "Amount varies" for mss purchased outright. Sends galleys to authors; dummies to illustrators. Book catalog free on request.

**\*BRIGHT RING PUBLISHING**, 1900 N. Shore Dr., Box 5768, Bellingham WA 98227-5768. (206)734-1601. Editor: Mary Ann Kohl. Publishes 1 young reader title/year. 50% of books by first-time authors.
**Nonfiction:** Picture books/young reader/middle reader: education and hobbies. Average word length: "about 125 ideas/book." Recently published *Mudworks* and *Scribble Cookies*, by Kohl (picture book, young reader, middle reader—art ideas).
**How to Contact/Writers:** Nonfiction: submit complete ms. SASE (IRC) for answer to query and/or return of ms; include social security number with submission. Reports in 1-6 weeks. Publishes a book 12 months after acceptance. Will consider simultaneous, photocopied and computer printout submissions.

**Illustration:** Editorial will review ms/illustration packages submitted by authors/artists; ms/illustration packages submitted by authors with illustrations done by separate artists; illustrator's work for possible use in authors' texts. Prefers to review "black line (drawings) for text."

**How to Contact/Illustrators:** Ms/illustration packages: "Query first." Illustrations only: send tearsheets and "sample of ideas I request after query." Reports in 6-8 weeks. Original art work returned at job's completion.

**Terms/Writers and Illustrators:** Pays authors in royalties of 5-10% based on wholesale or retail price. Pays illustrators $500-1,000. Also offers "free books and discounts for future books." Book catalog, ms/artist's guidelines for business-size SAE and 25¢ postage.

**Tips:** Writers: "Be neat, be yourself, don't expect fame and riches; be diligent and responsible." Illustrators: "Build your portfolio by taking a few jobs at lower pay—then grow." Looks for "creative ideas for children, recipe format, open-ended results" and for artists "black line drawings of children doing projects or project materials."

**CARNIVAL ENTERPRISES,** Box 19087, Minneapolis MN, 55419. (612)870-0169. Independent book producer/packager. Contact: Rosemary Wallner. Publishes 1-3 picture books/year; 1-3 young reader titles/year; 50 middle reader titles/year. 40% of books by first-time authors; no books from agented writers.

**Fiction:** Picture books: animal, easy-to-read. Young readers: history. Middle readers: animal, contemporary, history, sports, spy/mystery/adventure. Average word length: picture books—600; young readers—"varies"; middle readers—5,000. Recently published *Shy Charlene*, by C. Nobens (young readers); *All Through the Night*, illustrated by G. & S. Fasens (picture book); *Tracks in the Northwoods*, by Dana Brenford (middle readers, mystery).

**Nonfiction:** Middle readers: animal, biography, history, hobbies, music/dance, nature/environment. Average word length: middle readers—5,000. Recently published *Stuntpeople*, by G. Stewart (middle readers); *Yellowstone National Park*, by C. Marron (middle readers); *AIDS*, by M. Turck (middle readers).

**How to Contact/Writers:** Fiction/nonfiction: Submit query. SASE (IRC) for answer to query. Reports on queries in 3-4 weeks.

**Illustration:** Number of illustrations used for fiction: middle readers—10. Editorial will review ms/illustration packages submitted by authors/artists and ms/illustration packages submitted by authors with illustrations done by separate artists. Art director, Gloria Blockey, will review illustrator's work for possible use in author's texts.

**Terms/Writers & Illustrators:** Methods of payment: "Varies too much. Depends on the publisher who hires us and the writer." Sends galleys to authors; dummies to illustrators.

**CAROLINA WREN PRESS/LOLLIPOP POWER BOOKS,** Box 277, Carrboro NC 27510. (919) 560-2738 (office). (919)376-8152 (main editor). Book publisher. Carolina Wren estab. 1976; Lollipop Power estab. 1971. Editor-in-Chief: Judy Hogan. Regular children's editor: Elizabeth Core. Minority children's editor: Pauletta Bracy. Publishes 2 picture books/year; 1 young reader title in '89. 100% of books by first-time authors.

**Fiction:** Picture books: contemporary, easy-to-read, fantasy, history, problem novels, science fiction, black family, "especially interested in non-sexist, multi-racial." Average length: picture books—30 pages. Recently published *The Boy Toy*, by Phyllis Johnson (grade 1, picture book); *I Like You to Make Jokes*, by Ellen Bass (grades 1-2, picture book); *In Christina's Toolbox*, by Dianne Homan (grades 1-2, picture book).

**Nonfiction:** Picture books: biography, education, history, hobbies, music/dance, "children of divorce and lesbian homes and black families." Average length: picture books—30 pages.

**How to Contact/Writers:** Fiction/nonfiction: Query and request guidelines. SASE (IRC) for answer to query and/or return of ms. Reports on queries/ms in 12 weeks. Publishes a book 24-36 months after acceptance "at present."
**Illustration:** Number of illustrations used for fiction and nonfiction: picture books — 12. Editorial will review ms/illustration packages submitted by authors/artists and ms/illustration packages submitted by authors with illustrations done by separate artists. Designer, Martha Lange (215 Monmouth St., Durham NC 27701) will review illustrator's work for possible use in author's texts.
**How to Contact/Illustrators:** Query first to Martha Lange. Reports on art samples only if interested. Original artwork returned at job's completion.
**Terms/Writers & Illustrators:** Pays authors in royalties of 5% of print-run based on retail price, or cash, if available. Additional payment for ms/illustration packages: Author gets 5%; illustrator gets 5%. Pays illustrators in royalties of 5% "of print-run based on retail price, or cash, if available." Sends galleys to authors; dummies to illustrators. Book catalog, manuscript guidelines for business-size SASE.
**Tips:** "Our books aim to show children that girls and women are self-sufficient; boys and men can be emotional and nurturing; families may consist of one parent only, working parents, extended families; families may rely on daycare centers or alternative child care; all children, whatever their race, creed or color, are portrayed often and fairly in ways true to their own experience. We require that childhood be taken seriously. Children's lives can be no less complex than adults'; we expect that their problems are presented honestly and completely. The validity of their feelings must be recognized, as children will benefit from reading of others coping with emotions or conflicts and finding solutions to their own problems. Current publishing priorities: strong female protagonists, especially Black, Hispanic or Native-American girls and women; friendship and solidarity among girls; children working to change values and behavior; nontraditional family situations; stories with evident concern for the world around us." Writers: "Be sure you can hold the attention of a child. Practice stories on real children and become a good writer." Beginning illustrators: "Try to get classes with someone who understands illustration professionally. We are seeking new illustrators for our files. Please send us your name and current address and we will notify you when we have a manuscript ready for illustration. Keep us notified of any address change, as it may be a while before we contact you."

**CAROLRHODA BOOKS, INC.,** Lerner Publications, 241 First Ave. N., Minneapolis MN 55401. (612)332-3344. Book publisher. Estab. 1969. Submissions Editor: Rebecca Poole. Publishes 5 picture books/year; 2 young reader titles/year; 20 middle reader titles/year. 20% of books by first-time authors; 10% of books from agented writers.
**Fiction:** Picture books: general. Young readers: historical. Average word length: picture books — 1,000-1,500; young readers — 2,000. Recently published *Porker Finds a Chair*, by Sven Nordqvist (ages 4-8, story book); *A Christmas Guest*, by David LaRochelle (ages 4-8, story book); and *The Stingy Baker*, by Janet Greeson (ages 4-8, historical).
**Nonfiction:** Young readers: history, hobbies, music/dance, nature/environment. Middle readers: animal, biography, history, music/dance, nature/environment. Average word length: young readers — 2,000; middle readers — 6,000. Recently published *Arctic Explorer*, by Jeri Ferris (8-11, biography); *Tule Elk*, by Caroline Arnold (7-10, nature/science); and *Trash!*, by Charlotte Wilcox (5-9, photo essay).
**How to Contact/Writers:** Fiction/nonfiction: Submit complete ms. SASE (IRC) for return of ms. Reports on queries in 3 weeks; on mss in 12 weeks. Publishes a book 18 months after acceptance. Will consider simultaneous and photocopied submissions.
**Illustration:** Number of illustrations used for fiction: picture books — 15-20; young readers — 20. Number of illustrations used for nonfiction: young readers — 15-20; middle readers — 10-12. Editorial will review ms/illustration packages submitted by authors/artists; ms/illustration packages submitted by authors with illustrations done by separate

artists and illustrator's work for possible use in author's texts.

**How to Contact/Illustrators:** Ms/illustration packages: At least one sample illustration (in form of photocopy, slide, duplicate photo) with full ms. Illustrations only: résumé/slides. Reports on art samples only if interested.

**Terms/Writers & Illustrators:** Buys ms outright for variable amount. Factors used to determine final payment: color vs. black-and-white, number of illustrations, quality of work. Sends galleys to authors; dummies to illustrators. Book catalog available for 9 × 12 SAE and 2 first-class stamps; manuscript guidelines for letter-size SAE and 1 first-class stamp.

**Tips:** Writers: "Research the publishing company to be sure it is in the market for the type of book you're interested in writing. Familiarize yourself with the company's list. We specialize in beginning readers, photo essays, and books published in series. We do very few single-title picture books, and no novels. For more detailed information about our publishing program, consult our catalog. We do not publish any of the following: textbooks, workbooks, songbooks, puzzles, plays and religious material. In general, we suggest that you steer clear of alphabet books; preachy stories with a moral to convey; stories featuring anthropomorphic protagonists ('Amanda the Amoeba,' 'Frankie the Fire Engine,' 'Tonie the Tornado'); and stories that revolve around trite, hackneyed plots: Johnny moves to a new neighborhood and is miserable because he can't make any new friends; Steve and Jane find a sick bird with a broken wing, and they nurse it back to health; lonely protagonist is rejected by his peers—usually because he's 'different' from them in some way—until he saves the day by rescuing them from some terrible calamity; and so on. You should also avoid racial and sexual stereotypes in your writing, as well as sexist language." Illustrators: "Research each company and send appropriate samples for their files." (See also Lerner Publications.)

**\*CHARLESBRIDGE**, Subsidiary of Mastery Education, 85 Main St., Watertown MA 02172. (617)926-0329. Book publisher. Publishes 5 picture books/year. Managing Editor: Elena Wright. 50% of books by first-time authors; 50% of books from agented writers.

**Fiction:** "We are interested in very interesting story books all categories," e.g., animal, contemporary, easy-to-read, fantasy, history, problem novels, romance, science fiction, sports, spy/mystery/adventure. "We are just starting to plan our fiction list."

**Nonfiction:** Recently published *The Yucky Reptile Book*, by Jerry Pelota (ages 6-9, nonfiction).

**How to Contact/Writers:** Fiction/nonfiction: Submit complete ms. SASE (IRC) for return of ms. Reports on queries in 3 months. Publishes a book 6 months after acceptance. Will consider computer printout submissions.

**Illustration:** Editorial will review ms/illustration packages submitted by authors/artists; ms/illustration packages submitted by authors with illustrations done by separate artists; illustrator's work for possible use in authors' texts.

**How to Contact/Illustrators:** Ms/illustration packages: Send "as much as possible—complete." Illustrations only: Send résumé, tearsheets. Reports only when interested. Will keep on file.

**Terms/Writers and Illustrators:** Buys ms outright. Factors used to determine payment for ms/illustration package include color art vs. black-and-white and number of illustrations used. Pay for separate authors and illustrators: "They split royalties as per their agreement." Pay for illustrators: by the project per contract.

**THE CHILD'S WORLD, INC.**, Box 989, Elgin IL 60121. (708)741- 7591. Book publisher. Estab. 1968. Contact: Editorial Department. Publishes 50 picture books/year. 5% of books by first time authors.

**Fiction:** Picture books: animal, easy-to-read, history, sports, spy/mystery/adventure. Recently published *Thank You*, by Janet Riehecky (preschool-2, Manners Matter Series); *Word Bird's School Words*, by Jane Belk Moncure (preschool-2, Word Bird Books); *Understanding*, by Sandra Ziegler (preschool-2, Values to Live By).

**Nonfiction:** Picture books: animal, biography, nature/environment. Recently published *Bigfoot*, by Janet Riehecky (grades 3-7, Great Mysteries Series); *Animal Migration*, by Janet McDonnell (grades 2-6, Amazing Animal Facts); and *A Visit to the Post Office*, by Sandra Ziegler (grades K-3, Field Trip Books).

**How to Contact/Writers:** Fiction/nonfiction: Query. SASE (IRC) for answer to query and/or return of ms. Reports on queries in 3-4 weeks; on mss in 4-12 weeks. Publishes a book 6 months after acceptance. Will consider simultaneous and photocopied submissions.

**Illustration:** Number of illustrations used for fiction and nonfiction: picture books—16+. Will review ms/illustration packages submitted by authors/artists.

**How to Contact/Illustrators:** Ms/illustration packages: Query first. Reports on art samples up to 3 months.

**Terms/Writers & Illustrators:** "Price differs on job" for outright purchases. Factors used to determine final payment for ms/illustration package includes "number of illustrations used." Pay for illustrators: "sometimes" by the project. Book catalog/manuscript guidelines/artist's guidelines free on request.

**Tips:** Looks for "preschool-grade 2—easy-to-read or 'read-to-me' 32 pages."

**CHINA BOOKS,** 2929 24th St., San Francisco CA 94110. (415)282-2994. Book publisher. Independent book producer/packager. Managing Editor: Bob Schildgen. 10% of books by first-time authors; 10% of books from agented writers.

**Nonfiction:** Young readers, middle readers: hobbies, nature/environment. Average word length: young readers—2,000; middle readers—4,000. Recently published *Paper Pandas and Jumping Frogs*, by Florence Temko (young adults, hobby).

**How to Contact/Writers:** Fiction/nonfiction: Query; submit outline/synopsis and sample chapters. SASE for answer to query and/or return of ms. Publishes a book 9 months after acceptance. Will consider simultaneous, photocopied, computer printout and electronic submissions via disk or modem.

**Illustration:** Editorial will review ms/illustration packages submitted by authors/artists; ms/illustration packages submitted by authors with illustrations done by separate artists; and illustrator's work for possible use in author's texts.

**Terms/Writers & Illustrators:** Pays authors in royalties of 8-10% based on retail price; buys ms outright for $100-$500. Offers average advance payment of "1/3 of total royalty." Pay for illustrators: by the project $100-$500; royalties of 8% based on retail price. Sends galleys to authors; dummies to illustrators. Book catalog free on request; manuscript/artist's guidelines for SAE.

**Tips:** Looks for "something related to China or to Chinese-Americans."

**CHRONICLE BOOKS,** 275 Fifth St., San Francisco CA 94103. (415)777-7240. Book publisher. Editor: Victoria Rock. Publishes 12-16 picture books/year; 0-6 young reader titles/year; 0-4 middle reader titles/year; 0- 2 young adult titles/year.

**Fiction:** Picture books: animal, contemporary, fantasy, history. Young readers: animal, contemporary, easy-to-read, fantasy, history, sports, adventure. Middle readers: animal, contemporary, fantasy, history, problem novels, sports, adventure. Young adults: contemporary, fantasy, history, adventure.

**Nonfiction:** Picture books: animal, biography, history, nature/environment. Young readers: animal, biography, history, nature/environment. Middle readers: animal, biography, history, music/dance, nature/environment. Young adults: biography, history, nature/environment.

**How to Contact/Writers:** Fiction/nonfiction: Query; submit outline synopsis and sample chapters; submit complete ms. SASE (IRC) for answer to query and/or return of ms. Reports on queries in 2 weeks; on mss in 6 weeks. Publishes a book 1-2 years after acceptance. Will consider simultaneous and photocopied submissions.

**Illustration:** Number of illustrations used for fiction and nonfiction: picture books—12-20; young readers—10-20; middle readers—5-10; young adults—jacket illustrations. Editorial will review ms/illustration packages submitted by authors/artists and ms/illustration packages submitted by authors with illustrations done by separate artists. Editor, Victoria Rock, will review illustrator's work for possible use in author's texts.

**How to Contact/Illustrators:** Picture book, young readers: complete ms and sample finished art (need not be from book itself as long as it is representative of style), slides of varied work. Middle readers/young adults: sample chapters and sample art. Illustrations only: résumé and tear sheets and/or slides and/or photocopies. Reports on art samples only if interested or if artist requests response. Original artwork returned at job's completion.

**Terms/Writers & Illustrators:** In most cases, pays author in royalties . . . although there are instances when work is commissioned on a flat-fee basis. Pays authors in royalties based on retail price. Average advance payment "varies." Additional payment for ms/illustration packages. Factors used to determine final payment "vary according to type of book." Sends galleys to authors. Book catalog available for SAE.

**Tips:** Writers: "Try to write a story that is your story—not the story you think you should be writing. Try not to be condescending to your readers." Illustrators: "Send samples that vary in style. The wider range you demonstrate, the more likely you are to strike a note with an editor or art director. Again, as with writing, imbue your work with individual personality. Artwork must be graphically outstanding."

**CLARION BOOKS,** Houghton Mifflin Company, 215 Park Ave. South, New York NY 10003. (212)420-5800. Book publisher. Editor and Publisher: Dorothy Briley. Publishes 10 picture books/year; 7 young reader titles/year; 14 middle reader titles/year; 4 young adult titles/year. 10% of books by first-time authors; 15% of books from agented writers.

**Fiction:** Picture books: animal, contemporary, fantasy, history, problem novels. Young readers: animal, contemporary, fantasy, history, problem novels. Middle readers: animal, contemporary, fantasy, history, problem novels, sports, spy/mystery/adventure. Young adults: history, problem novels, spy/mystery/adventure. Average word length: picture books—50-1,000; young readers—1,000-2,500; middle readers—10,000-30,000; young adults—20,000—30,000. Recently published *Beauty and the Beast*, by Jan Brett (6-12, picture book).

**Nonfiction:** Picture books: animal. Young readers: animal, history, nature/environment. Middle readers: biography, history, nature/environment. Average word length: picture books—750-1,000; young readers—1,000-2,500; middle readers—10,000-30,000. Recently published *Klondike Fever*, by Michael Corper (9 and up).

**How to Contact/Writers:** Fiction: Query on all ms over 50 pages. Nonfiction: Query. SASE (IRC) for answer to query and/or return of ms. Reports on queries in 4 weeks; mss in 8-12 weeks. Publishes a book 18 months after acceptance. Will consider photocopied and computer printout submissions.

**Illustration:** Number of illustrations used for fiction: picture books—20; young readers—15. Number of illustrations used for nonfiction: picture books—20; young readers—40; middle readers—20-50. Editorial will review ms/illustration packages submitted by authors/artists and ms/illustration packages submitted by authors with illustrations done by separate artists. Art Director, Carol Goldenberg, will review illustrator's work for possible use in author's texts.

**How to Contact/Illustrators:** Ms/illustration packages: "query first." Illustrations only: "tear sheets, photos or photocopies of samples." Reports on art samples only if interested. Original artwork returned at job's completion.

**Terms/Writers & Illustrators:** Pays authors in royalties of 10-12½% based on retail price. Offers average advance payment of $2,500-$5,000. Pay for separate authors and illustrators: "Separately, on an advance and royalty basis." Sends galleys to authors; dummies to illustrators. Book catalog, manuscript/artist's guidelines free on request.
**Tips:** Writers: "Discover the unique things that you have to say, and say them in the most effective way possible." Illustrators: "Discover the unique things that you have to draw/paint, and say them in the most effective way possible." Looks for: "A fresh, imaginative story or nonfiction text, written and/or illustrated in a distinctive voice and style." There is "a growing book store market for quality books, especially at the younger age levels."

**\*COBBLEHILL BOOKS,** affiliate of Dutton Children's Books, a division of Penguin Books USA Inc., 2 Park Ave., New York NY 10016. (212)725-1818. Book publisher. Editorial Director: Joe Ann Daly. Sr. Editor: Rosanne Lauer.
**Fiction/Nonfiction:** Will review manuscripts for picture books, young readers, middle readers and young adults. "All manuscripts submitted will be read and considered."
**How to Contact/Writers:** Fiction/nonfiction: Query for mss longer than picture book length; submit complete ms (for picture books). Reports on queries/mss in 1 month. Will consider simlutaneous submissions "if we are informed about them."
**How to Contact/Illustrators:** Illustrations only: send samples to keep on file, no original art work. Original art work returned at job's completion.
**Terms/Writers and Illustrators:** Pays authors in royalties. Illustrators paid in a flat fee or by royalty.

**\*COLORMORE, INC.,** Box 111249, Carrollton TX 75011-1249. (214)245-1059. Book publisher. President: Susan Koch. Publishes 4-6 young reader titles/year. 25% of books by first-time authors.
**Nonfiction:** Young readers: history, travel and world cultures. Average word length: 3,000. Recently published *Colormore Travels—Fort Worth, Texas—The Travel Guide for Kids* and *Colormore Travels—Austin, Texas—The Travel Guide for Kids,* by Susan Koch (young reader, travel guide/activity book); and *Colormore Travels—San Diego, California—The Travel Guide for Kids,* by Mary Stack (young reader, travel guide/activity book).
**How to Contact/Writers:** Nonfiction: Submit outline/synopsis and sample chapters; submit complete ms. SASE (IRC) for answer to query and/or return of ms. Reports on queries/mss in 2-4 weeks. Publishes a book 9 months after acceptance. Will consider photocopied and computer printout submissions.
**Illustration:** Number of illustrations used for nonfiction: young readers—25. Editorial will review ms/illustration packages submitted by authors/artists, ms/illustration packages submitted by authors with illustrations done by separate artists, and illustrator's work for possible use in authors' texts. Preference for "8½×11 format books, mainly black and white, coloring-type pictures and activities."
**How to Contact/Illustrators:** Ms/illustration packages: Send "complete ms with 1 piece of final art." Illustrations only: Send "example(s) of black line drawing suitable for coloring." Reports in 2-4 weeks. Original art work returned at job's completion.
**Terms/Writers and Illustrators:** Authors paid a 5% royalty based on wholesale price. Ms/illustration packages: 5% royalty. Pay for separate authors and illustrators: "separate royalty percentage." Pay for illustrators: 5% royalty based on wholesale price. Sends galleys to authors; dummies to illustrators. Ms/artist's guidelines for legal SAE.
**Tips:** Looking for "a regional/local travel guide with lively, interesting illustrations and activities specifically for kids."

**CONSUMER REPORT BOOKS,** Consumer Union, 51 East 42nd St., New York NY 10017. (212)983-8250. Book publisher. Editorial Contact: Sarah Uman. Publishes 2 young adult titles/year. 50% of books from agented writers.

**Nonfiction:** Young adults: education, nature/environment, health. Average word length: young adults—50,000. Recently published *How and Why?*, by Catherine O'Neill (young adults, health); *AIDS: Trading Fears for Facts*, by Karen Hein, M.D. and Theresa DiGeronimo (young adults, health).

**How to Contact/Writers:** Nonfiction: Submit outline/synopsis and sample chapters; submit complete ms; submit table of contents. SASE (IRC) for answer to query. Reports on queries/mss in 6 weeks. Publishes a book 24 months after acceptance. Will consider simultaneous, photocopied and computer printout submissions.

**Illustrations:** Number of illustrations used for nonfiction: young adults—50. Editorial will review ms/illustration packages submitted by authors/artists and ms/illustration packages submitted by authors with illustrations done by separate artists.

**How to Contact/Illustrators:** Ms/illustration packages: Query first.

**Terms/Writers & Illustrators:** Pays authors in royalties based on retail price. Factors used to determine payment for ms/illustration packages include "number of illustrations." Pay for separate authors and illustrators: Pay for "author—advance against royalty; illustrator—flat fee by the project." Sends galleys to authors. Book catalog/manuscript guidelines free on request.

**COTEAU BOOKS LTD.**, Thunder Creek Publishing Co-op Ltd., 209-1945 Scarth St., Regina SK, S4P 2H2 Canada. (306)352-5346. Book publisher. Managing Editor: Shelley Sopher. Publishes 1 picture book/year, 9-11 books/year. 85% of books by first-time authors.

**Fiction:** Picture books: animal, contemporary, fantasy, spy/mystery/adventure. Average word length: picture books—500. Recently published *Milford & Me*, by Patrick Lane (ages 3-8, rhyming poem); *Jumbo Gumbo*, anthology (ages 6-12, songs, poems, stories).

**How to Contact/Writers:** Fiction: Submit complete ms. SASE (IRC) for answer to query and/or return of ms. Reports on queries in 2 weeks; on mss in 3 months. Publishes a book 12-24 months after acceptance. Will consider photocopied and computer print-out submissions. Coteau Books publishes Canadian writers only.

**Illustration:** Number of illustrations used for fiction: picture books—30. Editorial will review ms/illustration packages submitted by authors/artists and ms/illustration packages submitted by authors with illustrations done by separate artists. Managing Editor, Shelley Sopher, will review illustrator's work for possible use in author's texts.

**How to Contact/Illustrators:** Ms/illustration packages "roughs." Reports on art samples within 6 weeks. Original artwork returned at job's completion.

**Terms/Writers & Illustrators:** Pays authors in royalties of 5-12% based on retail price. Other method of payment: "signing bonus." Pay for illustrators: by the project $500-$2,000; royalty 5% maximum based on retail price. Sends galleys to authors; dummies to illustrators. Book catalog free on request.

**COUNCIL FOR INDIAN EDUCATION**, 517 Rimrock Rd., Billings MT 59102. (406)252-7451. Book publisher. Estab. 1968. Editor: Hap Gilliland. Publishes 1 picture book/year; 1 young reader title/year; 3 middle reader titles/year; 1 young adult title/year. "Have done only one shared expense book but may do one a year—larger books that we can't afford alone."

**Fiction:** Picture books: animal, easy-to-read. Young readers: animal, easy-to-read, history. Middle readers: animal, history. Young adults: animal, history. All must relate to Native American life, past and present. Recently published *The Vision of the Spokane Prophet*, by Egbert (grade 5-10, Indian legend); *Chief Stephen's Party*, by Chardonnet (grade 4-12, Alaskan Indian life); and *Sacajawea*, by Martha Bryant (grade 6-adult, biography).

**Nonfiction:** Picture books: animal, nature/environment. Young readers: animal, biography, history, hobbies, nature/environment. Middle readers: animal, biography, history, hobbies, music/dance, nature/environment. Young adults: animal, biography, history, hobbies, music/dance, nature/environment, sports. All of above must be related to American Indian life and culture, past and present. Recently published *Havasupai Years*, by Knobloch (high school-adult, journal of reservation teacher); *Red Power on the Rio Grande*, by Folsom (grade 9-adult, history of Pueblo Indians).

**How to Contact/Writers:** Fiction: Submit complete ms. Nonfiction: Submit outline/synopsis and sample chapters, or submit complete ms. SASE (IRC) for return of ms. Reports on queries in 2 months; mss in 3 months. "We accept ⅓ to ⅙ of the manuscripts received. Those with potential must be evaluated by all the members of our Indian Editorial Board, who make the final selection. This board makes sure the material is true to the Indian way of life and is the kind of material they want their children to read." Publishes a book 4 months after acceptance. Will consider simultaneous, photocopied, and computer printout submissions.

**Illustration:** Number of illustrations used for fiction: picture books—25; young readers—12; middle readers—10; young adults—10. Number of illustrations used for nonfiction: picture books—20; young readers—10; middle readers—10; young adults—10. Editorial will review ms/illustration packages submitted by authors/artists and ms/illustration packages submitted by authors with illustrations done by separate artists. Editor, Hap Gilliland, will review illustrator's work for possible use in author's texts. "Black and white art work only."

**How to Contact/Illustrators:** Ms/illustration packages: "samples sent with manuscript." Illustrations only: "samples." Reports on art samples in 3 months "when we report back to author on ms." Original artwork returned "if requested."

**Terms/Writers & Illustrators:** Pays authors in royalties of 10% based on wholesale price. Buys ms outright for "1½¢ per word." Additional payment for ms/illustration packages "sometimes." Factors used to determine payment for ms/illustration package include "number of illustrations used." Sends galleys to authors. Book catalog/manuscript guidelines available for SAE and 1 first-class stamp.

**Tips:** "For our publications write about one specific tribe or group and be sure actions portrayed are culturally correct for the group and time period portrayed. What kind of material can we use? These are our preferences, in the order listed: Contemporary Indian Life—exciting stories that could happen to Indian children now. (Be sure the children act like present-day Indians, not like some other culture.) Indians of the old days—authentically portrayed. Be specific about who, where, and when. How-to—Indian arts, crafts, and activities. Biography—Indians past and present. History and culture—factual material of high interest only. If you are Indian express your ideas and ideals. Folk stories and legends—high interest expressing Indian ideas. Name the specific tribe. Poetry—possibly—if it expresses real Indian ideals. Instructional material and information for teachers of Indian children."

**\*CROCODILE BOOKS, USA**, Imprint of Interlink Publishing Group, Inc., 99 Seventh Ave., Brooklyn NY 11215. (718)797-4292. Book publisher. Vice President: Ruth Moushabeck. Publishes 16 picture books/year. 30% of books by first-time authors.

**Fiction:** Picture books: animal, contemporary, history, spy/mystery/adventure. Recently published *Crocodile Crocodile*, by Binette Schroeder (illustrated children's book); and *The Elephant's Child*, by Kipling/Mogensen (illustrated children's book).

**Nonfiction:** Picture book: history, nature/environment.

**How to Contact/Writers:** Fiction/nonfiction: Submit outline/synopsis and sample chapters. SASE (IRC) for return of ms. Reports on queries in 2-3 weeks; on ms in 8 weeks. Publishes a book 12 months after acceptance. Will consider photocopied and computer printout submissions.

**Illustration:** Editorial will review ms/illustration packages submitted by authors/artists, and ms/illustration packages submitted by authors with illustrations done by separate artists.

**How to Contact/Illustrators:** Ms/illustration packages: Send "2-3 sample chapters (whole ms if less than 48 pages) and sample art." Original art work returned at job's completion.

**Terms/Writers and Illustrators:** Pays authors in royalties. If ms/illustration package is the work of a writer and a separate illustrator, "royalties will be shared equally." Sends galleys to author; dummies to illustrator. Book catalog free on request.

**\*THOMAS Y. CROWELL JUNIOR BOOKS**, Harper Junior Books Group, 10 E. 53rd St., New York NY 10022. (212)207-7044. Executive Editor: Barbara Fenton. Book publisher.

**Fiction:** Picture books: animal, sports. Young readers: easy-to-read, sports. Middle readers: adventure, fantasy, history, sports. Young adult titles: contemporary, history, problem novels, sports.

**Nonfiction:** Picture books, young readers, middle readers, young adult titles: animal, biography, history, music/dance, nature/environment, sports.

**How to Contact/Writers:** Fiction/nonfiction: query, submit outline/synopsis and sample chapters. SASE for answer to query. Will consider photocopied or computer printout submissions.

**Illustration:** Will review ms/illustration packages submitted by authors/artists (preferable to see picture books without art); ms/illustration packages submitted by authors with illustrations done by separate artists; illustrator's work for possible use in authors' texts (no original art, please).

**How to Contact/Illustrators:** Ms/illustrations packages: query first.

**Terms/Writers & Illustrators:** Pays authors in royalties based on retail price. Additional payment for ms/illustration packages: if the work is done by one person, he/she will get the full amount of royalty; otherwise it is split between the two.

**MAY DAVENPORT, PUBLISHERS**, 26313 Purissima Rd., Los Altos Hills CA 94022. (415)948-6499. Book publisher. Estab. 1976. Independent book producer/packager. Editor: May Davenport. Publishes 1-2 picture books/year; 2-3 young adult titles/year. 99% of books by first-time authors. Subsidy publishes 20% of books.

**Fiction:** Young adults: fantasy, plays for teens. Average length: plays—30 minutes stage or TV performance; young adult fantasy—20,000-30,000 words. Recently published *Pompey Poems*, by Ellen Langill (grades 7-12, paper and hardcover); *Creeps*, by Shelly Fredman, (grades 7-12 hardcover); *The Chase of the Sorceress*, by Philip R. Johnson (grades 7-12 hardcover).

**Nonfiction:** Picture books: animal. Recently published *Willie, Zilly and the Bantams*, by Grace Collins (preschool-1, hardcover); *Turtles*, by Andrea Ross (preschool-2, paper).

**How to Contact/Writers:** Fiction/nonfiction: Query. SASE for answer to query. Reports on queries in 2-3 weeks. Publishes a book 6-12 months after acceptance.

**Illustration:** "If illustrators send samples, I keep those on file and get in touch with them if I need extra help."

**How to Contact/Illustrators:** Ms/illustration packages: Query first with SASE and Sample spontaneous art; thumbnail sketches.

**Terms/Writers & Illustrators:** Pays authors in royalties based on retail price. Pays "by mutual agreement, no advances." Usually my illustrators are paid as work-for-hire, so there is no writer-illustrator problem." Pay for illustrators: By the project $4.50-$7.50 per line drawing—3½×4. Book listing, manuscript guidelines free on request with SASE.

**Tips:** "If you are a writer—write humorously. Don't preach; If you are an illustrator—be an artist and draw your thumbnail sketches spontaneously. The lines will communicate your thoughts and feelings."

**DIAL BOOKS FOR YOUNG READERS**, Penguin Books USA Inc., 375 Hudson St., New York NY 10014. (212)725-1818. Editor-in-Chief: Phyllis J. Fogelman. Publishes 40-50 picture books/year; 10 young reader titles/year; 5 middle reader titles/year; 10 young adult titles/year.

**Fiction:** Picture books: animal, contemporary, fantasy, history, sports, spy/mystery/adventure. Young readers: animal, contemporary, easy-to-read, fantasy, history, sports, spy/mystery/adventure. Middle readers, young adults: contemporary, fantasy, history, problem novels, science fiction, sports, spy/mystery/adventure. Recently published *Nora and the Great Bear*, by Ute Krause (ages 4-8, picture book); *The Christmas Fox*, by John Bush (ages 4-8, poetry picture book); and *Bailey's Bones*, by Victor Kelleher (YA novel).

**Nonfiction:** Uses very little nonfiction but will consider submissions of outstanding artistic and literary merit. Recently published *A Flower Grows*, by Ken Robbins (ages 4-8, picture book); *How Animals See*, by Sandra Sinclair (middle readers).

**How to Contact/Writers:** Fiction: Query, submit outline/synopsis and sample chapters for longer work, submit complete ms for short material. SASE (IRC) for answer to query and/or return of ms. SASE must be able to hold your ms if returned.

**Illustration:** Editorial will review ms/illustration packages submitted by author/artist (i.e. a single individual who does both art and text). Prefers to use own artists for mss submitted by authors. Will review an illustrator's work for possible use in author's texts.

**How to Contact/Illustrators:** Ms/illustration packages: Query first or 1 piece of final color art and sketches. Illustrations only: Résumé, tear sheets.

**Terms/Writers & Illustrators:** Pays authors and illustrators in royalties based on retail price. Average advance payment "varies." Manuscript guidelines for SAE.

**DILLON PRESS, INC.**, 242 Portland Ave. S., Minneapolis MN 55415. (612)333-2691. Book publisher. Nonfiction: Tom Schneider. Fiction: Shelley Sateren. Publishes 15-20 young reader titles/year; 15-20 middle reader titles/year. 30% of books by first-time authors; 10% of books from agented writers.

**Fiction:** Young readers: history—refers to a specific series of books titled *It Really Happened*. Average word length: young readers—3,000-4,000. Recently published *The Camel Express*, by Ann Shaffer; *Day of Darkness, Night of Light*, by C.L.G. Martin; *Patrick and the Great Molasses Explosion*, by Marjorie Stover (all for grades 2-4, historical fiction).

**Nonfiction:** Young readers and middle readers: animal, biography, U.S. cities, foreign countries, citeies and festivals, nature/environment, contemporary issues. Average word length: young readers—2,000; middle readers—5,000-7,000. Recently published *St. Louis*, by Barbara Ford (grades 3-6, Downtown America series); *The Pileated Woodpecker*, by Seliesa Pembleton (grades 3-6, Remarkable Animals series); and *Making Headlines: A Biography of Nellie Bly*, by Kathy Emerson (grades 5-8, People in Focus series).

**How to Contact/Writers:** Nonfiction: Query, with writing sample (refers to *It Really Happened* series). SASE (IRC) for answer to query and/or return of ms. Reports on queries in 2-3 weeks; on mss in 6-8 weeks. Publishes a book 12-18 months after acceptance. Will consider simultaneous, photocopied and computer printout submissions.

**Illustration:** Number of illustrations used for fiction: young readers—6-8 (refers to *It Really Happened* books). Number of illustrations used for nonfiction: young readers—20; middle readers—25. Editorial will review ms/illustration packages submitted by authors/artists and ms/illustration packages submitted by authors with illustrations done by separate artists. Editorial Director, Uva Dillon, will review an illustrator's work for possible use in author's texts.

**How to Contact/Illustrators:** Ms/illustration packages: Query with sample chapters and art sample. Illustrations only: Slides and/or samples. Reports on art samples only if interested.

**Terms/Writers & Illustrators:** Pays authors in royalties of 5-10%. Outright purchase "negotiated." Average advance: "negotiated." Additional payment for ms/illustration packages: "negotiated." Factors to determine final payment: number of illustrations or photos—quality. Pay for separate authors and illustrators: "negotiated." Illustrators paid by the project via negotiation. Sends galleys to authors. Book catalog for 9x12 SAE; manuscript guidelines for 4x9 SAE.

**Tips:** Writers: "Research competitive books and ideas and submit a complete well-organized proposal with sample chapters or complete manuscript." Illustrators: "Provide evidence of artistic ability and knowledge of book publishing." Looks for a book: "that matches our current publishing plans for existing or new series of educational books (nonfiction) for young readers K-12, with an emphasis on 2nd grade through 7th grade."

**DOUBLE M PRESS,** 16455 Tuba St., Sepulveda CA 91343. (818)360-3166. Book publisher. Publisher: Charlotte Markman Stein. Publishes young reader titles, middle reader titles, and young adult titles. 50% of books by first-time authors.

**Fiction:** Middle readers: contemporary, fantasy, historical. Young readers: contemporary. Young adults: contemporary, problem novels. Average word length: young adults—40,000-60,000. "We are trade publishers, who, starting in 1989, are concentrating on children's books, all ages." Recently published *The Stained Glass Window*, by Stein (young adult, historical/love).

**Nonfiction:** Young readers: biography, education, history, mythology. Middle readers: biography, education, history, mythology. Young adults: biography, education, history, mythology. Distributes *Greek Mythology* (Series A, B, C and D), by Stephanides Brothers (middle reader, mythology).

**How to Contact/Writers:** Fiction/nonfiction: Query. SASE (IRC) for answer to query and/or return of mss. Reports on queries in 2 weeks; on mss in 4-6 weeks. Publishes a book 12 months after acceptance. Will consider photocopied submissions.

**Illustration:** Number of illustrations used for fiction/nonfiction: middle readers—3-4; young adults—3-4. Editorial will review ms/illustration packages submitted by authors/artists and ms/illustration packages submitted by authors with illustrations done by separate artists "query first." Michele P. Bodenheimer, will review an illustrator's work for possible use in author's texts.

**How to Contact/Illustrators:** Ms/illustration packages: Query first. Illustrations only: Tear sheets, slides. Reports on art samples in 4 weeks.

**Terms/Writers & Illustrators:** Pays authors in royalties based on retail price. Buys ms outright "based on work." Additional payment for ms/illustration packages. Factors used to determine final payment include color art, number of illustrations. Pay for separate authors and illustrators: "royalties to each." Pay for illustrators: by the project; "we also pay royalties, depends on work." Sends galleys to authors; dummies to illustrators.

**Tips:** In writing looks for: "Stories that pertain and are relevant to children's and young adult's lives. They must be well written. Imaginative handling of contemporary problems and a constructive outlook." Looks for: "Illustrations that appeal to the imaginative, or fantasy in children. Good technique."

**DOUBLEDAY,** div. of Bantam Doubleday Dell, 666 Fifth Ave., New York NY 10103. (212)492-9772. Book publisher. Publisher: Wendy Barish. Publishes 10-20 picture books/year; 20 young reader titles/year; 20 middle reader titles/year. 10% of books by first-time authors; 30% of books from agented writers.

**How to Contact/Writers:** Fiction/nonfiction: Query. SASE (IRC) for answer to query. Reports on queries in 5 weeks; on mss in 12 weeks. Publishes a book 24 months after acceptance. Will consider simultaneous, photocopied and computer printout submissions.

**Illustration:** Editorial will review ms/illustration packages submitted by authors/artists; ms/illustration packages submitted by authors with illustrations done by separate artists and an illustrator's work for possible use in author's texts.

**How to Contact/Illustrators:** Ms/illustration packages: Query. Illustrations only: "Previous books, slides, tear sheets." Reports on art samples only if interested. Original art work returned at job's completion.

**Terms/Writers & Illustrators:** Pays authors in royalties based on retail price. Buys ms outright. Additional payment for ms/illustration packages. Separate writers and illustrators paid separately. Illustrators paid by the project. Sends galleys to authors; dummies to illustrators. Book catalog, manuscript guidelines free on request.

**Tips:** Writers: "Learn the marketplace and fill a need." Illustrators: "Do a sample dummy and sample art for an available, well-known text to show ability."

**\*DUNDURN PRESS LTD.**, #301, 2181 Queen Street, Toronto ON M4L 1E5 Canada. (416)698-0454. President: Kirk Howard. 20% of books by first-time authors; 10% of books from agented writers.

**Fiction:** Young adults: history. Average word length: 40,000. Recently published *Beginning Again*, by M.B. Fryer (young adult, history).

**Nonfiction:** Young adult: history. Average word length: 40,000.

**How to Contact/Writers:** Fiction/nonfiction: Submit outline/synopsis and sample chapters. SASE (IRC) for return of ms. Reports on queries in 3 months. Publishes a book 12 months after acceptance. Will consider simultaneous, photocopied, computer printout and electronic submissions via disk or modem.

**Illustration:** Number of illustrations used for fiction and nonfiction: young adult—12. Will review ms/illustration packages submitted by authors/artists; ms/illustration packages submitted by authors with illustrations done by separate artists.

**Terms/Writers and Illustrators:** Pays authors in royalties or 10% based on retail price. Offers average advance payment of $500. Pay for separate authors and illustrators: "author's responsibility." Sends galleys to authors. Book catalog free on request.

**DUTTON CHILDREN'S BOOKS**, NAL-Penguin, 2 Park Ave., New York NY 10016. (212)725-1818. Book publisher. Editor-in-Chief: Lucia Monfried. Publishes approximately 40 picture books/year; 4 young reader titles/year; 10 middle reader titles/year; 8 young adult titles/year. 15% of books by first-time authors.

**Fiction:** Picture books: animal, fantasy, spy/mystery/adventure. Young readers: easy-to-read, fantasy, science fiction. Middle readers: animal, contemporary, fantasy, history, science fiction, spy/mystery/adventure. Young adults: animal, contemporary, fantasy, history, romance, science fiction, spy/mystery/adventure. Recently published *Digby and Kate*, by Barbara Baker (young readers, easy-to-read); *The Jedera Adventure*, by Lloyd Alexander (middle readers/young adults, fantasy); *Almost Fifteen*, by Marilyn Sachs (young adults, contemporary).

**Nonfiction:** Picture books: animal, nature/environment. Young readers: nature/environment. Middle readers and young adults: animal, nature/environment. Recently published *Animal Faces*, by Pierre Marie Valat (all levels, punch-out novelty); *Sir Dana, A Knight*, by Dana Fradon (picture book, historical); *Blimps*, by Roxie Munro (picture book, science/aviation).

**How to Contact/Writers:** Fiction/nonfiction: query. SASE (IRC) for answer to query and/or return of ms. Reports on queries in 2 months; on mss in 2-3 months. Publishes a book 12-18 months after acceptance. Will consider simultaneous, photocopied, computer printout and electronic submissions via disk or modem.

**Illustration:** Number of illustrations used for fiction: picture books—14-28; easy readers—30; middle readers—15. Editorial will review ms/illustration packages submitted by authors/artists and ms/illustration packages submitted by authors with illustrations done by separate artists. Design department will review illustrator's work for possible use in author's texts.

**How to Contact/Illustrators:** Ms/illustration packages: Query first. Illustrations only: Resume, tear sheets, slides — no original art please. Reports on art samples in 2 months. Original artwork returned at job's completion.

**Terms/Writers & Illustrators:** Pays authors in royalties based on retail price. Book catalog, manuscript guidelines for SAE.

**Tips:** Writers: "We publish high-quality trade books and are interested in well-written manuscripts with fresh ideas and child appeal. We recommend spending time in bookstores and libraries to get an idea of the books on the market. Find out what topics have been treated again and again and should thus be avoided. Dutton has a complete publishing program — we are looking for good writing and strong quality in all categories of fiction. We would be interested in nonfiction including preschool and middle-grade nonfiction, including U.S. history, general biography (ages 7-10), science and photo essays." Illustrators: "Spend time in bookstores and libraries to familiarize yourself with the market. Be aware of which style of illustration would be of interest to which publishing house — is your work best suited for mass market or trade? We're interested in seeing samples or portfolios from potential illustrators of picture books (full color), young novels (black and white), and jacket artists."

**EAKIN PUBLICATIONS, INC.,** Box 90159, Austin TX 78709. (512)288-1771 FAX: (512)288-1813. Book publisher. President: Ed Eakin. Publishes 2 picture books/year; 3 young reader titles/year; 10 middle reader titles/year; 2 young adult titles/year. 50% of books by first-time authors; 5% of books from agented writers.

**Fiction:** Picture books: animal. Middle readers: history, sports. Young adults: history, sports. Average word length: picture books — 3,000; young readers — 10,000; middle readers — 15,000-20,000; young adults — 20,000-30,000. Recently published *The Canary Who Sailed With Columbus*, (ages 3-7, picture book); *My Mom Your Dad*, (ages 10-14, young adult).

**Nonfiction:** Picture books: animal. Middle readers: history, sports. Young adults: history, sports. Recently published *Build the Alamo*, (ages 4-10, picture book).

**How to Contact/Writers:** Fiction/nonfiction: Query. SASE (IRC) for answer to query. Reports on queries in 2 weeks; on mss in 6 weeks. Publishes a book 1 year after acceptance. Will consider simultaneous, photocopied, computer printout and electronic submissions via disk or modem.

**Illustration:** Number of illustrations used for fiction/nonfiction: picture books — 40; young readers — 40; middle readers — 5; young adults — 5. Editorial will review ms/illustration packages submitted by authors/artists; ms/illustration packages submitted by authors with illustrations done by separate artists; and an illustrator's work for possible use in author's texts.

**How to Contact/Illustrators:** Ms/illustration packages: Query. Illustrations only: Tear sheets. Reports on art samples in 2 weeks.

**Terms/Writers & Illustrators:** Pays authors in royalties of 10-15% based on wholesale price. Pay for separate authors and illustrators: "Usually share royalty." Pay for illustrators: Royalty 10-15% based on wholesale price. Sends galleys to authors. Book catalog, manuscript/artist's guidelines for SAE.

**Tips:** Writers: "Always include SASE — be sure all elements of manuscript are included — include vitae of author or illustrator." Illustrators: "Team up with good writer." Looks for: "books relating to Texas and the Southwest or ethnic groups." (Eakin Press has a new imprint — Panda Books.)

**ENSLOW PUBLISHERS INC.,** Bloy St. & Ramsey Ave., Box 777, Hillside NJ 07205. (201)964-4116. Vice President: Mark Enslow. Estab. 1978. Publishes 15 middle reader titles/year; 15 young adult titles/year. 30% of books by first-time authors; 10% of books from agented writers.

**Nonfiction:** Middle readers: biography, history, sports. Young adults: biography, history, sports. Average word length: middle readers—10,000; young adults—20,000. Recently published *Learning about AIDS*, by Alvin Silverstein (grades 4-6, health); *Archbishop Tutu*, by Judith Bentley (grades 7-9, biography).

**How to Contact/Writers:** Nonfiction: Query. SASE (IRC) for answer to query. Reports on queries/mss in 2 weeks. Publishes a book 12 months after acceptance. Will consider simultaneous and photocopied submissions.

**Illustration:** Number of illustrations used for nonfiction: middle readers—28; young adults—28.

**Terms/Writers & Illustrators:** Pays authors in royalties of 6-10% based on retail price. Sends galleys to authors. Book catalog/manuscript guidelines available for SAE.

**Tips:** "Know about competing books already published."

**EXPOSITION PHOENIX PRESS**, 1620 South Federal Highway, Pompano FL 33062. (305)943-7165. Chief Executive Officer/Vice President: Dr. Mallick. Publishes 12-20 picture books/year; 12-20 young reader titles/year; 50 middle reader titles/year; 50 young adult titles/year. 90% of books by first-time authors; 1% of books from agented writers. Subsidy publishes 99%.

**Fiction:** Picture books: animal. Young readers: easy-to-read, fantasy, sports. Middle readers: contemporary, history, romance, science fiction, sports. Average length: "64 page minimum."

**How to Contact/Writers:** Fiction/nonfiction: Submit through agent only. SASE (IRC) for answer to query. Publishes a book 7 months after acceptance. Will consider simultaneous, photocopied and computer printout submissions.

**Illustration:** Editorial will review ms/illustration packages submitted by authors/artists; ms/illustration packages submitted by authors with illustrations done by separate artists; and an illustrator's work for possible use in author's texts.

**How to Contact/Illustrators:** Original artwork returned at job's completion.

**Terms/Writers & Illustrators:** Pays authors in royalties of 40% based on wholesale price. Illustrators "usually" paid by the project. Sends galleys to authors. Book catalog, manuscript/artist's guidelines free on request.

**Tips:** "The 'PPP' plan—Publish, Present & Push plus the PAG plan—Personal Attention Guaranteed!" Looks for "children's and how-to books."

**\*FABER AND FABER, INC.**, Faber and Faber, Ltd. (London), 50 Cross Street, Winchester MA 01890. (617)721-1427. Book publisher. Editor: Betsy Uhrig. Publishes 5 middle reader titles/year; 5 young adult titles/year. 20% of books by first-time authors; 50% of books from agented writers.

**Fiction:** Middle readers: animal, contemporary, fantasy, spy/mystery/adventure. Young adults: contemporary and spy/mystery/adventure. Recently published *Stories for 7 year-olds*, by Corrin (ages 7-9, story collection); *Jonah's Mirror*, by Lillington (ages 9-12, fantasy); *Pet Poems*, by Fisher (ages 7-9, poetry collection).

**How to Contact/Writers:** Fiction: Submit outline/synopsis and sample chapters. SASE (IRC) for answer to query and/or return of ms. Reports on queries 6 weeks; mss 2 months. Publishes a book 6-12 months after acceptance. Will consider simultaneous, photocopied and computer printout submissions.

**Illustration:** Number of illustrations used for fiction and nonfiction: Middle readers—12. Editorial will review ms/illustration packages submitted by authors/artists and ms/illustration packages submitted by authors with illustrations done by separate artists.

**How to Contact/Illustrators;** Ms/illustration packages: "Query first." Illustrations only: "Send résumé, samples—not slides, not originals." Reports only if interested. Original art work returned at job's completion.

**Terms/Writers and Illustrators:** Pays authors in royalties. Pay for illustrators: by the project. Sends galleys to authors; dummies to illustrators. Book catalog for 8 ½ × 11 SAE; manuscript guidelines free on request.
**Tips:** "Timeless novels of fantasy and adventure for mid-older readers, simple pen-and-ink illustrations."

**FACTS ON FILE**, 460 Park Ave. S., New York NY 10016. (212)683-2244. Book publisher. Editorial Contacts: James Warren and Helen Flynn. Publishes 8-10 middle reader titles/year; 18-20 young adult titles/year. 5% of books by first-time authors; 45% of books from agented writers. Subsidy publishes 35%.
**Nonfiction:** Middle readers: animal, biography, education, science, history, music/dance, nature/environment, religion, sports. Young adults: animal, biography, science, education, history, music/dance, nature/environment, religion, sports. Recently published *Martin Luther King, Jr.*, by Lillie Patterson; *The CIA*, by Graham Yost; *Opening the Space Frontier*, by Drake Moser and Ray Spangenburg. (All-ages 11-16).
**How to Contact/Writers:** Nonfiction: Submit outline/synopsis and sample chapters. Reports on queries in 4 weeks. Publishes a book 10 months after acceptance. Will consider simultaneous, photocopied and computer printout submissions. Sends galleys to authors. Book catalog free on request.
**Tips:** "Nothing too cutesy. Prepare a very thorough, carefully written proposal. We do a lot of series books."

**FARRAR, STRAUS & GIROUX**, 19 Union Square West, New York NY 10003. (212)741-6934. Book publisher. Children's books Editor-in-Chief: Margaret Ferguson. Estab. 1946. Publishes 21 picture books/year; 6 middle reader titles/year; 5 young adult titles/year. 5% of books by first-time authors; 5% of books from agented writers.
**Fiction:** "Original and well-written material for all ages." Recently published *Valentine & Orson*, by Nancy Ekholm Burkert (all ages); *Carl Goes Shopping*, by Alexandra Day (ages 3 up); *An Acceptable Time*, by Madeleine L'Engle (young adult).
**How to Contact/Writers:** Fiction/nonfiction: Query; submit outline/synopsis and sample chapters. SASE (IRC) for answer to query and/or return of mss. Reports on queries in 6 weeks; on mss in 12 weeks. Publishes a book 18 months after acceptance. Will consider simultaneous, photocopied and computer printout submissions.
**Illustration:** Number of illustrations used for fiction: picture books—32; middle readers—10. Number of illustrations used for nonfiction: middle readers—15. Will review ms/illustration packages submitted by authors/artists and an illustrator's work for possible use in author's texts.
**How to Contact/Illustrators:** Ms/illustration packages: Ms with 1 piece of final art, remainder roughs. Illustrations only: Tear sheets. Reports on art samples only if interested. Original artwork returned at job's completion.
**Terms/Writers & Illustrators:** "We offer an advance against royalties for both authors and illustrators." Sends galleys to authors; dummies to illustrators. Book catalog available for 6½ × 9½ SAE and 56¢ postage; manuscript guidelines for 1 first-class stamp.
**Tips:** "Study our catalog before submitting. We will see illustrator's portfolios by appointment."

**\*FIESTA CITY PUBLISHERS**, Box 5861, Santa Barbara CA 93150-5861. (805)733-1984. Book publisher. Editorial contact: Ann Cooke. Publishes 1 middle reader title/year; 1 young adult title/year. 25% of books by first-time authors.

**Nonfiction:** Young adult: music/dance, self-help. Average word length: 30,000. Recently published *Kids Can Write Songs, Too*, by Eddie Franck, (12-18, self-help).
**How to Contact/Writers:** Fiction/nonfiction: Query. SASE (IRC) for answer to query and/or return of ms. Reports on queries in 2 weeks; on ms in 4 weeks. Publishes a book 12 months after acceptance. Will consider simultaneous, photocopied and computer printout submissions.
**Illustration:** Number of illustrations used for nonfiction: young adult—12.
**How to Contact/Illustrators:** "We use our own."
**Tips:** "Write clearly and simply. Do not write 'down' to young adults (or children). Always query. Always submit clean, double-spaced material." Looking for "self-help books on current subjects."

**FOUR WINDS PRESS,** imprint of Macmillan Publishing Co., 866 Third Ave., New York NY 10022. Book publisher. Editor-in-Chief: Cindy Kane. 15-20% of books by first-time authors; 80% of books from agented writers.
**Fiction:** Picture books: animal. Young readers: animal, contemporary, easy-to-read. Middle readers: animal, history, sports, spy/mystery/adventure. Average word length: picture books—750-1,500; young readers—5,000-6,000; middle readers—10,000-30,000. Recently published *Sarah Bear and Sweet Sidney*, by Nancy Patz (picture book); *Pig and Bear*, by Vit Hořejš, illustrated by Friso Henstra (picture book); and *Parchment House*, by Casa Lockhart Smith (novel). "YA books are no longer being considered."
**Nonfiction:** Picture books: animal, nature/environment. Young readers: animal, nature/environment. Middle readers: animal, biography, history, hobbies, music/dance, nature/environment, sports. Average word length: picture books—750-1,500; young readers—5,000-6,000; middle readers—10,000-30,000.
**How to Contact/Writers:** Fiction: Submit outline/synopsis and sample chapters (middle readers); submit complete ms (picture books). Nonfiction: Query. SASE (IRC) for answer to query and/or return of ms. Reports on queries/mss in 6-8 weeks. Publishes a book 18-24 months after acceptance. Will consider photocopied and computer printout submissions. "We are *not* reviewing simultaneous submissions." SASE a must for return of ms.
**Illustration:** Number of illustrations used for fiction and nonfiction: picture books—24-40 full page illustrations; young readers—15-20 mostly full page illustrations; middle readers—10-20 ¼, ½ and full page illustrations. Editorial will review ms/illustration packages submitted by authors/artists and ms/illustration packages submitted by authors with illustrations done by separate artists. Art Director, Cecilia Yung, will review illustrator's work for possible use in author's texts.
**How to Contact/Illustrators:** Picture books: Submit full ms with art samples (not originals!). Illustrations only: "Illustration portfolios are reviewed every Thursday on a drop-off basis. If you cannot drop off your portfolio, you should mail tear sheets. Your portfolio should contain samples of work that best reflect your technical and creative ability to illustrate a text for children. These samples should include two or three different scenes of animals and/or children rendered in a setting. These should show your ability to handle composition, create interesting characters, and maintain consistency between scenes. Use whatever medium is best suited to your technique. Generally, still life, three dimensional artwork and abstract compositions do not translate well to children's book illustrations." Reports on ms/art samples in 4-6 weeks; art samples only if interested. Original artwork returned at job's completion.
**Terms/Writers & Illustrators:** Pays authors in royalties of 5-10% based on retail price (depends on whether artist is sharing royalties). Factors used to determine payment for ms/illustration package include "complexity of artwork, number of pieces, color vs. black-and-white." Pay for separate authors and illustrators: "Each has separate contract and is paid by royalty or flat fee." Pay for illustrators: by the project; royalties range

from 2-5%; "fees and royalties vary widely according to budget for book." Sends galleys to authors; dummies to illustrators. Manuscript and/or artist's guidelines for 1 first-class stamp and a business-size envelope.

**Tips:** The length of your story depends on the age of the child for whom it is intended. There are no fixed lengths. A good story is almost always the right length or can easily be made so. (See also Aladdin Books/Collier Books for Young Adults, Atheneum Publishers, Bradbury Press, Margaret K. McElderry Books.)

**FREE SPIRIT PUBLISHING**, Ste. 716, 123 N. 3rd St., Minneapolis MN 55401. (612)338-2068. Book publisher. Publisher/President: Judy Galbraith. Publishes 1-2 middle reader titles/year; 1-2 young adult titles/year. 80% of books by first-time authors.

**Nonfiction:** Young readers: education, psychology/self-help, reference. Middle readers: education, psychology/self-help, reference. Young adults: education, psychology/self-help, reference. Recently published *Directory of American Youth Organizations*, by Judith Erickson (grades 3-12, reference); *Perfectionism: What's Bad About Being Too Good*, by Miriam Adderholdt-Elliott (young adults, psychology/self-help).

**How to Contact/Writers:** Nonfiction: Submit outline/synopsis and sample chapters. SASE (IRC) for return of mss. Reports on queries in 3 months. Publishes a book 12-18 months after acceptance. Will consider photocopied and computer submissions.

**Illustration:** Number of illustrations for nonfiction: young readers—15; middle readers—15; young adults—10. Editorial will review ms/illustration packages submitted by authors/artists; ms/illustration packages submitted by authors with illustrations done by separate artists; illustrator's work for possible use in author's title.

**How to Contact/Illustrators:** Submit 3 chapters of ms with 1 piece of final art. Prefers to see: "B&w cartoon illustrations, graphic treatments." Illustrations only: résumé, tear sheets. Reports on art samples only if interested. Original artwork returned at job's completion if requested.

**Terms/Writers & Illustrators:** Pays authors in royalties of 8-12% based on wholesale price. Offers advance payment of $500-$1,000. Factors used to determine final payment for ms/illustration is color art vs. black-and-white and number of illustrations used. Pay for illustrations: by the project, $50-$500. Sends galleys to authors; dummies to illustrators. Book catalog free on request.

**Tips:** Writers: "Research publisher interests *before* sending anything." Illustrations: "Hustle your work as much as possible. I've hired illustrators 'off the street.' " Looks for: "A truly helpful, informative, pro-kid, and good-humored book."

**\*FRIENDSHIP PRESS**, National Council of Churches of Christ in the USA, Rm. 772, 475 Riverside Dr., New York NY 10469. (212)870-2585. Book publisher. Publishes 2 picture books/year. Editorial Contact (picture books/young readers): Carol Ames. Publishes 1 young reader title/year; 1 middle reader title/year; Editorial Contact (middle reader/young adult titles): Nadine Hundertmark. Publishes 1 young adult title/year. 90% of books by first-time authors.

**Fiction:** Picture books, young readers, middle readers, young adults: mission and religion. Average word length: young adults—20,000-40,000. Recently published *It's Hard Not to Worry,* by John M. Barrett (grades 1-6, stories for children about poverty); *Courage for a Cross,* by Leslie Merlin (Grades 1-6, stories about USSR); *Silver Ships/Green Fields,* by Sara Covin Juengst (Grades 1-6, story about technology in Bangladesh).

**Nonfiction:** Picture books, young readers, middle readers, young adults: mission and religion. Average word length: middle readers—10,000; young adults—10,000.

**How to Contact/Writers:** Fiction and nonfiction: Query. SASE (IRC) for answer to query/return of ms. Reports on queries/mss in 3-6 weeks. Publishes a book 18 months after acceptance. Will consider simultaneous and clear photocopied submissions.

# Close-up

## Valiska Gregory
*Writer*
*Indianapolis, Indiana*

Will am C. Lutholtz

"I think the biggest difference between children's books now and a generation ago is their wonderful variety," says Valiska Gregory. "In format, in subject matter, in illustrations, children's books offer writers a delightful challenge to do original and important work."

As an author of four books for children, she is familiar with the unique challenge that writing for a young audience provides. Currently a Fellow at the Butler University Writers' Studio she cites the influence of storytelling in her childhood as instrumental in the development of her interest in writing for children.

"I was lucky enough to grow up in a Czech neighborhood in Chicago where children were treasured and where, always, my father told us stories. My brothers and I ate them with our daily bread, swallowed them whole, and begged for more. My father shaped his tales as carefully as he painted my name on my lunch box in Gothic letters. The black ink seemed to appear like angels on the penciled lines, a dimness made clear. It is this clarity of vision I wish to offer children—stories told with humor, charm and grace, stories that, like good soup, sustain the human spirit."

She received her M.A. from the University of Chicago on a Ford Foundation Fellowship and has received awards for both poetry and children's books, including a grant from the Indiana Arts Commission and the National Endowment for the Arts for "artistic excellence." Her children's books include *Terribly Wonderful*, *Sunny Side Up*, *The Oatmeal Cookie Giant* and *Riddle Soup*.

Gregory finds writing for children to be thoroughly enjoyable, but challenging. "To write for children, I must cultivate an insouciant playfulness that allows me to see the world always with new eyes. I must write with wit and elegance, but without artifice. I must avoid didacticism, yet love justice. And if it is a children's picture book, I must do all of that in four to six typed pages, in addition, of course, to creating characters, plot, setting and theme that will appeal to the sensibilities of a child as well as possess lasting literary merit."

She encourages aspiring children's writers to develop "discipline, patience and absolute commitment. My advice to aspiring children's writers is to make sure you love writing as much as you love the idea of being a published writer. Take as many years as you need to develop your talent—read, study, experience life widely."

*—Roseann Shaughnessy*

**Illustration:** Number of illustrations used for fiction and nonfiction—8. Editorial will review ms/illustration packages submitted by authors/artists and ms/illustration packages submitted by authors with illustrations done by separate artists. Art Director, Paul Lansdale, will review an illustrator's work for possible use in author's texts.

**How to Contact/Illustrators:** Ms/illustration packages: send 3 chapters of ms with 1 piece of final art. Illustrations only: send résumé and tear sheets. Reports only if interested. Original artwork returned at job's completion.

**Terms/Writers and Illustrators:** Buys ms outright for $25-1200. Factor used to determine payment includes number of illustrations used. If the ms/illustration package is the work of a writer and a separate illustrator, "one payment will be divided." Sends galleys to authors; dummies to illustrators. Book catalog and ms guidelines free on request.

**DAVID R. GODINE, PUBLISHER**, 300 Massachusetts, Boston MA 02115. (617)536-0761. Book publisher. Estab. 1970. Editor: Audrey Bryant. Publishes 3-4 picture books/year; 2 young reader titles/year; 3-4 middle reader titles/year. 10% of books by first-time authors; 20% of books from agented writers.

**Fiction:** Picture books: animal. Young readers: animal, easy-to-read, fantasy, mystery/adventure, folk or fairy tales. Middle readers: animal, fantasy, folk or fairy tales. Recently published *Cuckoo Clock*, by Mary Stolz (ages 9-11, middle readers); *Sea Gifts*, by George Shannon (ages 8-10, early readers); *A Natural Man*, by Steve Sanfield (ages 8-10, early reader).

**How to Contact/Writers:** Fiction: Submit complete ms. Reports on queries in 2 weeks; on mss in 3 weeks. Publishes a book 18 months after acceptance. Will consider simultaneous, photocopied and computer printout submissions.

**Illustration:** Number of illustrations used for fiction: picture books—16; young readers—12; middle readers—10. Editorial will review ms/illustration packages submitted by authors/artists; ms/illustration packages submitted by authors with illustrations done by separate artists and illustrator's work for possible use in author's texts.

**How to Contact/Illustrators:** Ms/illustration packages: "roughs and 1 finished art plus either sample chapters for very long works or whole ms for short works." Illustrations only: "slides, with one full-size blow-up of art." Reports on art samples in 3 weeks. Original artwork returned at job's completion.

**Terms/Writers & Illustrators:** Pays authors in royalties based on retail price. Factor used to determine final payment: number of illustrations. Pay for separate authors and illustrators: "differs with each collaboration." Illustrators paid by the project. Sends galleys to authors; dummies to illustrators. Book catalog/manuscript guidelines free on request.

**\*GOLDEN BOOKS**, Western Publishing Co., 850 Third Ave., New York NY 10022. (212)753-8500. Editor-in-Chief: Eric Suben. Book publisher.

**Fiction:** Picture books: animal, easy-to-read. Young readers: easy-to-read. Middle readers: history, sports. Young adult titles: contemporary, sports.

**Nonfiction:** Picture books: education, history, nature/environment, sports. Young readers: animal, education, history, nature/environment, sports. Middle readers: animal, education, history, nature/environment, sports.

**How to Contact/Writers:** "Not accepting any solicitations for at least a year." Fiction/nonfiction: query. SASE for answer to query. Will consider photocopied or computer printout submissions.

**Illustration:** Will "sometimes" review ms/illustration packages submitted by authors/artists or ms/illustration packages submitted by authors with illustrations done by separate artists; will review an illustrator's work for possible use in authors' texts.

**How to Contact/Illustrators:** Ms/illustration packages: query first.

**Terms/Writers & Illustrators:** Pays authors in royalties based on retail price.

**\*GREEN TIGER PRESS, INC.**, 435 E. Carmel St., San Marcos CA 92069. (619)744-7575. Book, calendar and card publisher. Publishes 10-15 picture books/year. Also publishes 2-4 calendars and assorted notecards annually.

**Fiction:** Juvenile and adult picture books. Average word length: 250. Recently published *My Secret Sunrise*, by Tomkins (5 and up, picture book); *Tinker's Journey*, by Bryant (4 and up, picture book); and *7 Ages of Childhood*, by Wells (all ages, picture book).

**How to Contact/Writers:** Fiction: Submit complete ms. SASE (IRC) for answer to query and/or return of ms. Reports on queries/mss in 3 months. Publishes a book 12 months after acceptance. Will consider photocopied and computer submissions.

**Illustration:** Number of illustrations used for fiction: picture book—12-20. Editorial will review ms/illustration packages submitted by authors/artists; ms/illustration packages submitted by authors with illustrations done by separate artists; illustrator's work for possible use in authors' texts.

**How to Contact/Illustrators:** Ms/illustration packages: Send "entire ms, prints, slides or color Xeroxes of illustrations and dummy." Illustrations only: Send prints, slides or color Xeroxes. Do not send originals of art work. Reports only if interested. Original art work returned at job's completion.

**Terms/Writers and Illustrators:** Usually pays authors and illustrators a royalty based on retail price. Royalty percentages vary. Book catalog, ms/artist's guidelines free on request.

**Tips:** "Study the publisher's catalog before submitting." Looking for "32-60 page—one illustration and one concise paragraph per spread. 'Dreams, visions and fantasies'—not religious or necessarily educational material."

**GREENHAVEN PRESS**, 10907 Technology Place, San Diego CA 92127. (619)485-7424. Book publisher. Senior Editors: Terry O'Neill and Bonnie Szumski. Greenhaven Press, 573 Shoreview Park Rd., St. Paul MN 55126. Publishes 8 young adult titles/year. 25% of books by first-time authors.

**Nonfiction:** Middle readers: biography, history, controversial topics, issues. Young adults: animal, biography, history, nature/environment. Other titles "to fit our specific series." Average word length: young adults—15,000-18,000. Recently published Great Mysteries: Opposing Viewpoints *Pearl Harbor*; Great Mysteries: Opposing Viewpoints *The Bermuda Triangle*; Great Mysteries: Opposing Viewpoints *Animal Communication* (young adults). Explores multiple views of the topic.

**How to Contact/Writers:** Nonfiction: Query; submit outline/synopsis and sample chapters. SASE (IRC) for answer to query and/or return of mss. Reports on queries (with SASE) generally in 1-2 weeks. Publishes a book 12-15 months after acceptance.

**Illustration:** Number of illustrations used for nonfiction: young adults—50-75. Senior Editors, Terry O'Neill and Bonnie Szumski, will accept query letters with a couple of examples of illustrations to keep on file—no portfolios. Preference: photos; line art.

**How to Contact/Illustrators:** Ms/illustration packages: Query first. Illustrations only: Resume, tear sheets, 1 or 2 samples we can keep. Reports on art samples only if interested. Original artwork returned at job's completion, "varies."

**Terms/Writers & Illustrators:** Buys ms outright for $1,500-$2,500. Offers average advance payment of ⅓-½. Factors used to determine final payment include number of illustrations used. Sends galleys to authors. Books catalog available for 9×12 SAE and 65¢ postage.

**Tips:** "Always send SASE; find out about publishers before submitting—don't waste their time and your time by submitting inappropriate material; submit material in proofread, clean, legible copies."

**HARBINGER HOUSE, INC.,** Ste. 106, 3131 N. Country Club, Tucson AZ 85716. (602)326-9595. Publisher: Laurel Gregory. Editor, Children's Books: Jeffrey H. Lockridge. Publishes 4 picture books/year; 2 young reader titles/year; 2-3 middle reader titles/year. 40% of books by first-time authors; 10% of books from agented writers.
**Fiction:** Picture books: "all kinds." Young readers: adventure, fantasy, history. Middle readers: animal, fantasy, problem novels, science fiction, sports, spy/mystery/adventure. Recently published *The Marsh King's Daughter*, by Andersen/Gentry (all ages, classic fantasy); *One Green Mesquite Tree*, by Jernigan (ages 3-5, counting rhyme); *Mystery on Mackinac Island*, (ages 8-11).
**Nonfiction:** Picture books: "all kinds." Young readers: animal, history, nature/environment, geography. Middle readers: animal, biography, history, music/dance, nature/environment, space science, geography. Recently published *The Reef & the Wrasse*, by Steere & Ring (ages 8-11, natural history); *Out in the Night*, by Liptak (ages 8-11, natural history); *Zoot Zoot Zaggle Splot or, What to Do With A Scary Dream*, (ages 4-8).
**How to Contact/Writers:** Fiction/nonfiction: Submit outline/synopsis and sample chapters. SASE (IRC) for answer to query. Reports on queries in 3-4 weeks; on mss in 6-8 weeks. Publishes a book 12-18 months after acceptance. Will consider simultaneous, photocopied, and computer printout submissions.
**Illustration:** Average number of illustrations used for fiction: picture books—14; young readers—12; middle readers—12. Number of illustrations used for nonfiction: picture books—14; young readers—20; middle readers—18. Editorial will review ms/illustration packages submitted by authors/artists; ms/illustration packages submitted by authors with illustrations done by separate artists and illustrator's work for possible use in author's texts.
**How to Contact/Illustrators:** "For picture books and young readers only: Minimum of 3 pieces of finished art." Illustrations only: "Tear sheets and slides." Reports on art samples in 4 weeks. Original artwork returned at job's completion.
**Terms/Writers & Illustrators:** Pays authors in royalties based on net receipts. Average advance payment $800-$1,000. Factors used to determine final payment for ms/illustration package include "color art vs. black-and-white, and number of illustrations for outright purchase of illustrations for middle titles." Pay for separate authors and illustrators: "royalties split between author and artist." Pay for illustrators: "royalties based on net receipts." Sends galleys to authors; "sometimes" sends dummies to illustrators. Book catalog free on request.
**Tips:** Writers: "Study writing and the field of children's literature beforehand." Looks for "manuscripts with a particular, well-articulated message or purpose." Illustrators: "Study illustration and the field of children's literature beforehand." Looks for "art of imagination and skill that has something special." In children's book publishing there has been "a gradual improvement in the standards of quality in both the ideas and their presentation."

**HARCOURT BRACE JOVANOVICH,** Children's Books Division which includes: HBJ Children's Books, Gulliver Books, Voyager Paperbacks, Odyssey Paperbacks, Jane Yolen Books, 1250 Sixth Ave., San Diego CA 92101. (619)699-6810. Book publisher. Attention: Manuscript Submissions, Children's Books Division. Publishes 40-45 picture books/year; 15-20 middle reader titles/year; 8-12 young adult titles/year. 20% of books by first-time authors; 50% of books from agented writers.
**Fiction:** Picture books: animal, contemporary, fantasy, history. Young readers: animal, contemporary, fantasy, history. Middle readers: animal, contemporary, fantasy, history, problem novels, romance, science fiction, sports, spy/mystery/adventure. Young adults: animal, contemporary, fantasy, history, problem novels, romance, science fiction, sports, spy/mystery/adventure. Average word length: picture books—"varies greatly;" middle readers—20,000-50,000; young adults—35,000-65,000.

**Nonfiction:** Picture books, young readers: animal, biography, history, hobbies, music/dance, nature/environment, religion, sports. Middle readers, young adults: animal, biography, education, history, hobbies, music/dance, nature/environment, religion, sports. Average word length: picture books—"varies greatly;" middle readers—20,000-50,000; young adults—35,000-65,000.

**How to Contact/Writers:** Fiction/nonfiction: Query; submit outline/synopsis and sample chapters; submit complete ms for picture books only. "Only HBJ Children's Books accepts unsolicited manuscripts." SASE (IRC) for answer to query and/or return of mss. Reports on queries/mss in 6-8 weeks. Will consider photocopied and computer printout submissions.

**Illustration:** Number of illustrations used for fiction and nonfiction: picture books—25-30; middle readers—6-12; young adults—jacket. Editorial will review ms/illustration packages submitted by authors/artists and ms/illustration packages submitted by authors with illustrations done by separate artists. Art Director, Children's Books, Michael Farmer, will review an illustrator's work for possible use in author's texts.

**How to Contact/Illustrators:** Ms/illustration packages: picture books ms—complete ms acceptable. Longer books—outline and 2-4 sample chapters. Send several samples of art; no original art. Illustrations only: Resume, tear sheets, color xeroxes, color stats all accepted. Please DO NOT send original artwork or transparencies. Include SASE for return, please. Reports on art samples in 6-10 weeks. Original artwork returned at job's completion.

**Terms/Writers & Illustrators:** Pays authors in royalties based on retail price. Pay for separate writers and illustrators: "separately, usually on advance/royalty basis. Situations vary according to individual projects." Pay for illustrators: by the project. Sends galleys to authors; dummies to illustrators. Book catalog available for 8½×11 SASE; manuscript/artist's guidelines for business-size SASE.

**Tips:** "Study the field of children's books—go to your local library and book stores. Become acquainted with HBJ's books in particular if you are interested in submitting proposals to us. Our current needs include young adult fiction, nonfiction for all ages, and picture books for the very young."

**HARVEST HOUSE PUBLISHERS**, 1075 Arrowsmith, Eugene OR 97402. (503)343-0123. Book publisher. Manuscript Coordinator: LaRae Weikert. Publishes 5-6 picture books/year; 3 young reader titles/year; 3 young adult titles/year. 25% of books by first-time authors.

**Fiction:** Christian theme. Picture books: animal, easy-to-read. Young readers: contemporary, easy-to-read. Middle readers: contemporary, fantasy. Young adults: fantasy, problem novels, romance. Recently published *The Rumpoles and the Barleys*, by Karen Mezek (ages 2-8, picture book); *Grumbleweeds*, by Gil Beers (ages 3-6, picture book); *Bedtime Hugs*, by Debby Boone (ages 2-6, picture book).

**Nonfiction:** Religion: picture books, young readers, middle readers, young adults.

**How to Contact/Writers:** Fiction/nonfiction: Query; submit outline/synopsis and sample chapters; submit complete ms. SASE (IRC) for return of mss. Publishes a book 12 months after acceptance. Will consider simultaneous, photocopied and computer printout submissions.

**Illustration:** Number of illustrations used for fiction: picture books—32. Editorial will review ms/illustration packages submitted by authors/artists; ms/illustration packages submitted by authors with illustrations done by separate artists and illustrator's work for possible use in author's texts.

**How to Contact/Illustrators:** Ms/illustration packages: "3 chapters of ms with 1 piece of final art and any approximate rough sketches." Illustrations only: "résumé, tear sheets." Reports on art samples in 2 months. Original artwork returned at job's completion.

**Terms/Writers & Illustrators:** Pays authors in royalties of 10-15%. Average advance payment: "negotiable." Additional payment for ms/illustration packages. Factors used to determine final payment for ms/illustration package include "color art vs. black-and-white, number of illustrations used, experience of the illustrator, time-frame for completion of work." Pay for separate authors and illustrators: "Shared royalty with illustrator oftentimes receiving an advance." Pay for illustrators: "Sometimes paid by project." Sends galleys to authors; sometimes dummies to illustrators. Book catalog, manuscript/artist's guidelines free on request.

*HERALD PRESS, Mennonite Publishing House, 616 Walnut Ave., Scottdale PA 15683. (412)887-8500. Publishes 1-2 young reader titles/year; 3-4 middle reader titles/year; 2-3 young adult titles/year. Editorial Contact: S. David Garber. 25% of books by first-time authors; 10% of books from agented writers.
**Fiction:** Picture books: religious, social problems. Young readers: religious, social problems. Middle readers: religious, social problems. Young adults: religious, social problems. Recently published *The White Feather,* by Ruth Eitzen (young readers, peace with Indians—historical); *The Christmas Surprise,* by Ruth Nulton Moore, (middle readers, Moravian peace story); *A Life in Her Hands,* by Shirlee Evans, (young adults, pregnant 15-year-old faces options).
**Nonfiction:** Picture books: religious, social concerns. Young readers: religious, social concerns. Middle readers: religious, social concerns. Young adults: religious, social concerns. Recently published *How to Survive as a Teen,* by Atanasoff, (young adults, facing youth issues); *Junior High's a Jungle, Lord,* by Clair Cosby, (middle reader), prayers—contemporary).
**How to Contact/Writers:** Fiction/nonfiction: Submit outline/synopsis and sample chapters. SASE (IRC) for answer to query/ms. Reports on queries in 3 weeks; ms in 2 months. Publishes a book in 12 months. Will consider photocopied submissions and computer printout submissions.
**Illustration:** Will review ms/illustration packages submitted by authors/artists and ms/illustration packages submitted by authors with illustrations done by separate artists. Art Director, Jim Butti, will review an illustrator's work for possible use in authors' texts.
**How to Contact/Illustrators:** Illustrations only: Send tear sheets and slides.
**Terms/Writers and Illustrators:** Pays authors in royalties of 10-15% based on retail price. Pay for illustrators: by the project; $220-600. Sends galleys to authors. Book catalog for 3 first-class stamps; manuscript guidelines free on request.

*HOLIDAY HOUSE INC., 40 East 49th St., New York NY 10017. (212)688-0085. Book publisher. Editorial contacts: Shannon Maughan, Margery Cuyler. Publishes 30 picture books/year; 7 young reader titles/year; 7 middle reader titles/year; 3 young adult titles/year. 20% of books by first-time authors; 10% from agented writers.
**Fiction:** Picture book: animal, sports. Young reader: contemporary, easy-to-read, history, sports, spy/mystery/adventure. Middle reader: contemporary, fantasy, history, sports, spy/mystery/adventure. Recently published *Ma and Pa Dracula*, by Ann M. Martin (middle reader, novel); *No Bean Sprouts, Please!*, by Connie Hiser (young reader,

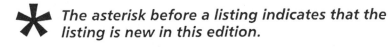

**The asterisk before a listing indicates that the listing is new in this edition.**

# Close-up

### John Stadler
*Illustrator/Writer*
*Etna, New Hampshire*

John Stadler says successfully writing and illustrating children's picture books takes a maximum amount of effort, but it's not beyond the abilities of anyone who possesses the appropriate talents. "It's a lot of work, though brain surgery is more difficult," he chuckles.

In addition to picture books, Stadler illustrates posters and magazines. He says his original intention was to be a cartoonist specializing in adult humor. "I'm not so sure I went into children's books on purpose, but because of the circumstances I was drawn that way.

"I was very worked up about it," Stadler says about his first book, *Cat at Bat*. The then 25-year-old hit a home run with *Cat at Bat* without ever leaving home base. He attributes being in the right place at the right time as the reason why it was published in 1979. He sold the book to his employer at the time, E.P. Dutton. Now a full-time freelance writer and illustrator, Stadler has little difficulty keeping busy. 1989's *The Ballad of Wilbur and the Moose* was a *People Magazine* "pick." His latest endeavor is *Lucy and the Gift-Wrapped Guests*.

According to Stadler, obtaining a business degree from Harvard may be a bit extreme, but it is essential for writers and illustrators to be aware of the actual business of producing picture books. "Writers and illustrators have to know it's ultimately a business, and it's getting to be more of a business." A recommended source of information regarding contract negotiations and other business and legal issues is the Author's Guild.

"Whatever your book is about, if you can put it into a phenomenal dummy book, it's the best thing you can do," says Stadler. "The more to the point you can be the better. A really tight dummy can save you and everybody else time."

Stadler considers himself an artist more than a writer, and says the picture book business consists primarily of artists who also happen to write. Though he has collaborated with children's writers in the past, for the most part, Stadler both writes and illustrates the majority of his projects. He prefers it that way. "If I do both, then I have access to myself if I want to change something. I don't have to get in touch with the editor in order to contact the author." He also cites financial incentives as a reason why illustrators do their own writing.

Non-cliché material, Stadler emphasizes, is most likely to attract an editor's second glance. "My impression is that [editors] look for something fresh. Don't necessarily do something to fit in with what you *think* children's books should be. Do something you really feel strongly about. That will eventually work out better for the children."

*—Lisa Carpenter*

chapter book); and *Awfully Short for the 4th Grade*, by Elvira Woodruff (young reader/ middle reader, short novel).
**Nonfiction:** Picture books: biography, history, sports. Young reader: biography, history, nature/environment, sports. Middle reader: biography, history, nature/environment, sports. Recently published *The White House*, by Leonard E. Fisher (middle reader, historical); *Buffalo Hunt*, by Russell Freedman (middle reader, historical).
**How to Contact/Writers:** Fiction/nonfiction: Submit complete ms. SASE for answer to query and/or return of ms. Reports on queries in 4-6 weeks; on mss in 8-10 weeks. Publishes a book 10 months after acceptance. Will consider simultaneous, photocopied and computer printout submissions.
**Illustration:** Editorial will review ms/illustration packages submitted by authors/artists; ms/illustration packages submitted by authors with illustrations done by separate artists. David Rogers, art director, will review an illustrator's work for possible use in authors' texts.
**How to Contact/Illustrators:** Ms/illustration packages: Query first. Illustrations only: send résumé, and tear sheets. Reports within 6 weeks with SASE or only if interested (if no SASE). Original art work returned at job's completion.
**Terms/Writers and Illustrators:** Manuscript/artist's guidelines for #10 SAE and 25¢ postage.
**Tips:** "Be patient. Keep trying. We look for highly original story ideas and interesting characters."

**HENRY HOLT & CO., INC.**, 115 W. 18th St., New York NY 10011. (212)886-9200. Book publisher. Editor-in-Chief: Brenda Bowen. Publishes 15-20 picture books/year; 40-60 young reader titles/year; 6 middle reader titles/year; 6 young adult titles/year. 5% of books by first-time authors; 40% of books from agented writers.
**Fiction:** Recently published *Here Are My Hands*, by Bill Martin, illustrated by Ted Rand (ages 4-7, picture book); *Moon Tiger*, by Phyllis Root/Ed Young (ages 4-7, picture book).
**How to Contact/Writers:** Fiction/nonfiction: Submit complete ms. SASE (IRC) necessary for answer to query and/or return of mss. Reports on queries/mss in 2 months. Publishes a book 12-18 months after acceptance. Will consider simultaneous, photocopied, and readable computer printout submissions.
**Illustration:** Editorial will review ms/illustration packages submitted by authors/artists; ms/illustration packages submitted by authors with illustrations done by separate artists; and illustrator's work for possible use in author's texts.
**How to Contact/Illustrators:** Ms/illustration packages: "Random samples OK." Illustrations only: Tear sheets, slides. Reports on art samples only if interested. Original art work returned at job's completion.
**Terms/Writers & Illustrators:** Pays authors in royalties based on retail price. Pay for illustrators: royalties based on retail price. Sends galleys to authors; dummies to illustrators.

**HOMESTEAD PUBLISHING**, Box 193, Moose WY 83012. Book publisher. Editor: Carl Schreier. Publishes 8 picture books/year; 2 young reader titles/year; 2 middle reader titles/year; 2 young adult titles/year. 30% of books by first-time authors; 1% of books from agented writers.
**Fiction:** Picture books: animal. Young readers: animal. Middle readers: animal. Average word length: young readers—1,000; middle readers—5,000; young adults—5,000. Recently published *The Great Plains: A Young Reader's Journal*, by Bullock (ages 1-8, nature).
**Nonfiction:** Picture books: animal, biography, history, nature/environment. Young readers: animal, nature/environment. Middle readers: animal, biography, history, nature/environment. Young adults: animal, history, nature/environment. Average word length: young readers—1,000; middle readers—5,000; young adults—5,000. Recently

published *Yellowstone: Selected Photographs 1870-1960*, by Simpson (ages 1-adult, history); *Looking at Flowers*, by O'Connor (ages 1-adult, nature) ; *Yellowstone's Geyser's Hot Springs and Fumaroles*, by Schreier (ages 1-adult, nature).

**How to Contact/Writers:** Fiction/nonfiction: Query; submit outline/synopsis and sample chapters. SASE (IRC) for answer to query and/or return of ms. Reports on queries/mss in 4 weeks. Publishes a book 1 year after acceptance. Will consider simultaneous and photocopied submissions.

**Illustration:** Number of illustrations used for fiction: picture books—70; young readers—50; middle readers—50; young adults—50. Number of illustrations used for nonfiction: picture books—150; young readers—50; middle readers—50; young adults—50. Editorial will review ms/illustration packages submitted by authors/artists; ms/illustration packages submitted by authors with illustrations done by separate artists and illustrator's work for possible use in author's texts. Prefers to see "watercolor, opaque, oil" illustrations.

**How to Contact/Illustrators:** Ms/illustration packages: "Query first with sample writing and art style." Illustrations only: "Resumes, style samples." Reports on art samples in 4 weeks. Original artwork returned at job's completion.

**Terms/Writers & Illustrators:** Pays authors in royalties of 5-10% based on wholesale price. Outright purchase: "depends on project." Average advance payment: "depends on project." Factors used to determine final payment: "quality and price." Pay for separate authors and illustrators: "split." Pay for illustrators: $50-$10,000/project; 3-10% royalty based on wholesale price. Sends galleys to authors; dummies to illustrators.

**Tips:** Provide "good quality, top rate, original idea, thought out."

**HOUGHTON MIFFLIN CO.**, Children's Trade Books, 2 Park St., Boston MA 02108. Book publisher. VP/Director: Walter Lorraine. Senior Editor: Matilda Welter; Editor: Mary Lee Donovan. Averages 50-55 titles/year. Publishes hardcover originals and trade paperback reprints (some simultaneous hard/soft).

**Fiction:** Recently published *The Lost Lake*, by Allen Say (ages 4-8, picture book); *Angel's Mother's Baby*, by Judy Delton (ages 7-10, middle-grade novel, illustrated); *My Name is not Angelica*, by Scott O'Dell (ages 10-14, young adult novel).

**Nonfiction:** Recently published *Big Friend, Little Friend*, by Susan Sussman and Robert James (ages 7-10, science, illustrated with photos); *At Home In Two Worlds*, by Aylette Jenness and Alice Rivers (ages 10-14, social studies, illustrated with photos); *The Way Things Work*, by David Macaulay (all ages, reference, illustrated).

**How to Contact/Writers:** Fiction: Submit complete ms. Nonfiction: Submit outline/synopsis and sample chapters. SASE (IRC) for answer to query and/or return of mss. Reports on queries in 1 month; on mss in 2 months. Will consider computer printout submissions (no dot matrix).

**How to Contact/Illustrators:** Review artwork/photos as part of ms package.

**Terms/Writers & Illustrators:** Pays standard royalty; offers advance. Book catalog free on request.

**Tips:** "The growing independant-retail book market will no doubt affect the number and kinds of books we publish in the near future. Booksellers are more informed about children's books today than ever before."

**HUMANICS CHILDREN'S HOUSE**, Humanics Limited, 1389 Peachtree St., Atlanta GA 30309. (404)874-1930. Book publisher. Acquisitions Editor: Robert Grayson Hall. Publishes 4 picture books/year; 4 young reader titles/year. 85% of books by first-time authors; 30% subsidy published.

**Fiction:** Picture books: contemporary, easy-to-read, fantasy, spy/mystery/adventure, self-image concentration. Average word length: picture books—250-350. Recently published *Home at Last*, by Mauro Magellan (ages 1-7, fantasy/fiction); *Max the Apt. Cat*, by Mauro Magellan (ages 1-7, self-image); *Creatures of an Exceptional Kind*, by Dorothy

Whitney (ages 1-7).

**Nonfiction:** "Educational materials, Author-Ph.D, M.A. level, activities, project books." Average word length: picture books—500-600. Recently published *Lessons From Mother Goose*, by E. Commins (grades 1-6, teacher's aid); *Learning Through Color*, by Penn and Peacock, (grades 1-6, teacher's aid).

**How to Contact/Writers:** Fiction: Submit outline/synopsis and sample chapters or submit complete ms. Nonfiction: Query; submit outline/synopsis and sample chapters or submit complete ms. SASE (IRC) for answer to query and/or return of mss. Reports on queries/mss in 6 months. Publishes a book 12-18 months after acceptance. Will consider simultaneous, photocopied, computer printout and electronic submissions via disk or modem.

**Illustration:** Number of illustrations used for fiction: picture books—16. Number of illustrations used for nonfiction: picture books—25-80. Editorial will review ms/illustration packages submitted by authors/artists; ms/illustration packages submitted by authors with illustrations done by separate artists; and illustrator's work for possible use in author's texts.

**How to Contact/Illustrators:** Ms/illustration packages: Preferably complete ms with 3-4 illustrations. Illustrations only: Résumé, tear sheets. Original artwork returned at job's completion "depending on contract."

**Terms/Writers & Illustrators:** Pays authors in royalties of 3-10% based on wholesale price. Outright purchase "dependent on ms, previous work." Factors used to determine final payment: "overall ms quality." Pay for separate authors and illustrators: "equally, or through prior agreement between the two. Ideally, prefer authors to be the illustrator for the work." Sends galleys to authors; dummies to illustrators. Book catalog free on request; manuscript/artist's guidelines for regular SAE and 1 first-class stamp.

**Tips:** Writers: "Have some academic educational background. Ms should be creative, innovative, and have an approach geared toward self-image social, and intellectual development." Illustrators: "Take chances! I like abstract, thought provoking illustrations as well as simple line drawings. (Actually, we prefer the more fantastic, abstract illustrations)." Trends in children's book publishing includes "a general movement toward self-image, holism, creativity and anti-ethnocentrism."

**IDEALS PUBLISHING CORPORATION**, Box 140300, Nashville TN 37214. (615)885-8270. Book publisher. Children's Book Editor: Peggy Schaefer. Publishes 50-60 picture books/year; 15-20 young reader titles/year. 5-10% of books by first-time authors; 5-10% of books from agented writers.

**Fiction:** Picture books: adventure, animal, contemporary, easy-to-read, fantasy, history, problem novels, sports. Young readers: animal, contemporary, easy-to-read, history, sports, spy/mystery/adventure. Average word length: picture books—200-1,200; young readers—1,200-2,400. Recently published *A Star in the Pasture*, by Zwers/Tobin Heyer (ages 4-7, 10×9 hardcover with dust jacket); *Chores*, by Cosgrove (ages 3-6, 10×9 hardcover with dust jacket); *Snarly Snuffin*, by Cosgrove (ages 3-8, 8½×11 softcover).

**Nonfiction:** Picture books: animal, biography, history, hobbies, music/dance, nature/environment, religion, sports. Young readers: animal, biography, history, hobbies, music/dance, nature/environment, religion, sports. Average word length: picture books—200-1,000; young readers—1,000-2,400. Recently published *Daniel Boone*, by Gleiter/Thompson (ages 5-8, 8×9 softcover); *Trucks*, by Stickland (ages 3-5, 6×6 hardcover); *The Deer*, by Royston (ages 5-8, 8×8 softcover).

**How to Contact/Writers:** Fiction/nonfiction: Submit complete ms. SASE (IRC) for answer to query and/or return of ms. Report on queries/mss in 6-8 weeks. Publishes a book 18-24 months after acceptance. Will consider photocopied and computer printout submissions.

**Illustration:** Number of illustrations used for fiction and nonfiction: picture books—12-18; young readers—12-18. Editorial will review ms/illustration packages submitted by authors/artists; ms/illustration packages submitted by authors with illustrations done by separate artists; and an illustrator's work for possible use in author's texts. Preference: No cartoon—tight or loose, but realistic watercolors, acrylics.
**How to Contact/Illustrators:** Ms/illustration packages: Ms with 1 piece final art and remainder roughs. Illustrations only: Resume and tear sheets showing variety of styles. Reports on art samples only if interested.
**Terms/Writers & Illustrators:** "All terms vary according to individual projects and authors/artists."
**Tips:** Writers: "Know the type of book the publisher you are approaching is interested in. Trend is placing more value on nonfiction and packaging." (i.e., We are not interested in young adult romances.) Illustrators: "Be flexible in contract terms—and be able to show as much final artwork as possible."

**\*INCENTIVE PUBLICATIONS, INC.**, 3835 Cleghorn Ave., Nashville TN 37215. (615)385-2934. Editor: Sherri Y. Lewis. 20% of books by first-time authors.
**Nonfiction:** Young reader/middle reader/young adult: education.
**How to Contact/Writers:** Nonfiction: Submit outline/synopsis and sample chapters. SASE (IRC) for return of ms. Reports on queries/mss in 4 weeks. Publishes a book 18 months after acceptance. Will consider simultaneous submissions.
**Illustration:** Editorial will review ms/illustration packages submitted by authors/artists; ms/illustration pakcages submitted by authors with illustrations done by separate artists. Susan Eaddy, art director, will review an illustrator's work for possible use in authors' texts.
**How to Contact/Illustrators:** Ms/illustration packages: "Query first." Illustrations only: send "résumé." Reports on ms/art samples in 4 weeks.
**Terms/Writers and Illustrators:** Pays in royalties or outright purchase. Illustrators paid by the project. Book catalog for SAE and .90 postage; ms/artist's guidelines for legal-size SAE.

**\*JALMAR PRESS**, Subsidiary of B.L. Winch and Associates, 45 Hitching Post Dr., Rolling Hills Estates CA 90274. (213)547-1240. Book publisher. President: B.L. Winch. Publishes 3 picture books and young reader titles/year. 25% of books by first-time authors.
**Fiction:** Picture book/young reader: animal, fantasy. Average text length: picture book/young reader—80 pages. Recently published *Do I Have To Go To School Today*, *Aliens in My Nest* and *Hoots and Toots and Hairy Brutes*, by L. Shles (picture books/young readers, self-esteem).
**How to Contact/Writers:** Fiction/nonfiction: Query or submit outline/synopsis and sample chapters. SASE (IRC) for return of ms. Reports on queries in 4 weeks; on mss in 3 months. Publishes a book 12 months after acceptance. Will consider simultaneous, photocopied and computer printout submissions.
**Illustration:** Editorial will review ms/illustration packages submitted by authors/artists; ms/illustration packages submitted by authors with illustrations done by separate artists; illustrator's work for possible use in authors' texts.

*"Picture books" are geared toward the preschool—8 year old group; "Young readers" to 5-8 year olds; "Middle readers" to 9-11 year olds; and "Young adults" to those 12 and up.*

**How to Contact/Illustrators:** Ms/illustration packages: Query first. Illustrations only: Send résumé.

**Terms/Writers and Illustrators:** Pays authors 7-15% royalty based on a combination of wholesale and retail prices. Average advance "varies." Pay for separate authors and illustrators: "split royalty." Pay for illustrators: 7-15% royalty based on combination of wholesale and retail prices. Book catalog free on request.

**Tips:** Looks for a "positive self-esteem type of book that deals with feelings."

**\*JEWISH PUBLICATION SOCIETY,** Room 1339, 60 E. 42 St., New York NY 10165. (212)687-0809. Editor: Alice Belgray. Book publisher.

**Fiction:** "All must have Jewish content." Picture books: animal, contemporary, easy-to-read. Young readers: contemporary, easy-to-read, problem novels. Middle readers: contemporary, history, problem novels, sports. Young adult titles: contemporary, history, romance (occasionally).

**Nonfiction:** "All must have Jewish theme." Picture books: history, religion. Young readers: biography, history, religion. Middle readers: biography, history, religion, sports. Young adult titles: biography, history, music/dance, religion.

**How to Contact/Writers:** Fiction/nonfiction: query, submit outline/synopsis and sample chapters. SASE for answer to query/return of ms. Will consider simultaneous submissions (please advise), photocopied or computer printout submissions.

**Illustration:** Will review ms/illustration packages submitted by authors/artists; ms/illustration packages submitted by authors with illustrations done by separate artists; illustrator's work for possible use in authors' texts.

**How to Contact/Illustrators:** Ms/illustration packages: query first or send three chapters of ms with one piece of final art, remainder roughs. Illustrations only: prefers photocopies of art.

**Terms/Writers & Illustrators:** Pays authors in royalties based on retail price.

**\*JOY STREET BOOKS,** Imprint of Little, Brown and Company, 34 Beacon St., Boston MA 02108. (617)227-0730. Editor in Chief: Melanie Kroupa. Publishes 20-25 picture books/year; 5-10 young reader/middle reader/young adult titles/year.

**How to Contact/Writers:** Fiction/nonfiction: Submit outline/synopsis and sample chapters or submit complete ms. SASE (IRC) for answer to query and/or return of ms. Reports on queries in 2-4 weeks; on mss in 4-8 weeks. Publishes a book 18 months after acceptance. Will consider simultaneous, photocopied and computer submissions.

**Terms/Writers:** Pays authors in royalties or outright purchase. Book catalog for 8 × 10 SAE; ms guidelines for legal-size SAE.

**\*JUST US BOOKS, INC.,** Imprint of Afro-Bets Series, Suite 22-24, 301 Main St., Orange NJ 07050. (201)672-7701. Book publisher; "for selected titles" book packager. Vice President/Publisher: Cheryl Willis Hudson. Publishes 3-4 picture books/year; "projected 4" young reader/middle reader titles/year. 33% books by first-time authors.

**Fiction:** Picture books: easy-to-read, African-American themes. Young readers: contemporary, history, African-American themes. Middle reader: history, sports. Average word length: "varies" per picture book; young reader—500-2,000; middle reader—5,000. Recently published *Afro-Bets ABC Book* and *Afro-Bets 123 Book*, by Cheryl Willis Hudson (pre-kindergarten-3rd, picture/concept).

**Nonfiction:** Picture book: African-American themes; young reader: biography, history, African-American themes; middle reader: biography, history, African-American themes. Recently published *Book of Black Heroes from A to Z*, by Wade Hudson and Valerie Wilson Wesley (biography for young and middle readers); (forthcoming) *Afro-Bets First Book About Africa*, by Veronica Freeman Ellis (young readers, ©1990, combination history/storybook format).

**How to Contact/Writers:** Fiction/nonfiction: Query or submit outline/synopsis and sample chapters. SASE (IRC) for answer to query; include social security number with submission. Reports on queries in 2-3 weeks; on ms in 8 weeks "or as soon as possible." Publishes a book 12-18 months after acceptance. Will consider simultaneous and photo-copied submissions.

**Illustration:** Number of illustrations used for fiction: picture book—12-24; for nonfiction: young reader—25-30. Editorial will review ms/illustration packages submitted by authors/artists and illustrator's work for possible use in authors' texts.

**How to Contact/Illustrators:** Ms/illustration packages: "Query first." Illustrations only: Send "résumé, tear sheets, and slides." Reports in 2-3 weeks. Original art work returned at job's completion "depending on project."

**Terms/Writers and Illustrators:** Pays authors a "flat fee and royalty depending on project." Royalties based on retail price. Factors to determine final payment include color art vs. black-and-white and number of illustrations used. Separate authors and illustrators are paid via "negotiated fees." Sends galleys to author; dummies to illustrator. Book catalog for business-size SAE and 25¢-65¢ postage; ms/artist's guidelines for business-size SAE and 25¢ postage.

**Tips:** Writers: "Keep the subject matter fresh and lively. Avoid "preachy" stories with stereotyped characters. Rely more on authentic stories with sensitive three-dimensional characters." Illustrators: "Submit 5-10 good, neat samples. Be willing to work with an art director for the type of illustration desired by a specific house and grow into larger projects."

**KAR-BEN COPIES, INC.**, 6800 Tildenwood Lane, Rockville MD 20852. (301)984-8733. Book publisher. Editor: Madeline Wikler. Publishes 10 picture books/year. 20% of books by first-time authors.

**Fiction:** Picture books: Jewish Holiday, Jewish storybook. Average word length: picture books—1,500. Recently published *Grandma's Soup*, by Nancy Karkowsky (grades K-3); *Mommy Never Went to Hebrew School*, by Mindy Avra Portnoy (grades K-3).

**Nonfiction:** Picture books: religion-Jewish interest. Average word length: picture books—1,500. Recently published *All About Hanukkah*, by Groner/Wikler (grades K-5, picture book); *Kids Love Israel*, by Barbara Sofer (adult, family travel guide); *Alef Is One*, by Katherine Kahn (grades K-3, a Hebrew counting book).

**How to Contact/Writers:** Fiction/nonfiction: Submit complete ms. SASE (IRC) for answer to query and/or return of mss. Reports on queries in 6 weeks. Publishes a book 6 months after acceptance. Will consider simultaneous, photocopied and computer printout submissions.

**Illustration:** Number of illustrations used for fiction: picture books—15. Number of illustrations used for nonfiction: picture books—10. Editorial will review ms/illustration packages submitted by authors/artists; ms/illustration packages submitted by authors with illustrations done by separate artists; and illustrator's work for possible use in author's texts.

**How to Contact/Illustrators:** Ms illustration packages: Query first. Illustrations only: Tear sheets. Reports on art samples in 6 weeks. Original artwork returned at job's completion.

**Terms/Writers & Illustrators:** Pays authors in royalties of 4-8% based on net sales. Buys ms outright for $250-$2,500. Offers average advance payment of $1,000. Pay for separate authors and illustrators: "both get advance and royalty." Sends galleys to authors; dummies to illustrators. Book catalog/manuscript guidelines free on request.

**Tips:** Looks for "books for young children with Jewish interest and content, modern, non-sexist, not didactic."

**KENDALL GREEN PUBLICATIONS**, imprint of Gallaudet University Press, 800 Florida Ave. NE, Washington DC 20002. (202)651-5488. Book publisher. Editor, Children's Books: Robyn D. Twito. Publishes 2-3 picture books/year; 2-3 young reader titles/year; 1-2 middle reader titles/year; 1-2 young adult titles/year. 75% of books by first-time authors. All titles deal with hearing loss or deafness.

**Fiction:** Picture books, young readers: contemporary. Middle readers, young adults: contemporary, problem novels, spy/mystery/adventure. Average word length: picture books—50; young readers—1,300; middle readers—26,000; young adults—52,000. Recently published *A Very Special Friend*, by Dorothy Hoffman Levi (picture book); *The Secret in the Dorm Attic*, by Jean Andrews, forthcoming (middle readers, mystery); *Annie's World*, by Nancy Smiler Levinson, forthcoming (young adults, problem).

**Nonfiction:** Picture books; young readers: sign language. Middle readers; young adults: biography, history, sign language. Average word length: picture books—50; young readers—1,300; middle readers—26,000; young adults—52,000. Recently published *My Signing Book of Numbers*, by Patricia Bellan Gillen (picture book, sign language); *Buffy's Orange Leash*, by Stephen Golder and Lise Memling (young readers, informational); *In Another Voice: The Story of Laurent Clerc*, by Cathryn Carroll, forthcoming (young adults, biography).

**How to Contact/Writers:** Fiction/nonfiction: submit outline/synopsis and sample chapters; submit complete ms. Reports on queries/mss in 4-8 weeks. Publishes a book 10-12 months after acceptance. Will consider simultaneous and photocopied submissions.

**Illustration:** Number of illustrations used for fiction: young readers—32; middle readers—1-5; young adults—1-5. Number of illustrations used for nonfiction: picture books—30-40; young readers—32; middle readers—20; young adults—5. Editorial will review ms/illustration packages submitted by authors/artists; ms/illustration packages submitted by authors with illustrations done by separate artists; and illustrator's work for possible use in author's texts.

**How to Contact/Illustrators:** Ms/illustration packages: Full ms with 2 finished pieces, remainder roughs. Illustrations only: Tear sheets, finished art, résumé. Reports on art samples in 4 weeks. Original artwork returned at job's completion.

**Terms/Writers & Illustrators:** Pays authors in royalties of 10-15% based on net price. Factors used to determine final payment: number of illustrations, color vs. black and white. Pay for separate authors and illustrators: Split royalty. Pay for illustrators: by the project; royalties of 5% based on net price. Sends galleys to authors; sometimes dummies to illustrators. Book catalog, manuscript guidelines free on request.

**Tips:** "All books published by Kendall Green Publications have to be related to hearing loss. This includes sign language books, books explaining hearing loss, and fiction with hearing-impaired character(s)."

**\*KINGSWAY PUBLICATIONS**, 1 St. Anne's Rd., Eastbourne, E. Sussex BN21 3UN England. (011-44)323-410930. Book publisher. Managing Editor: Elizabeth Gibson. Editorial contact (picture books): T. Collins. Editorial contact (young reader titles): R. Herkes. Editorial contacts (middle reader/young adult titles): R. Herkes/E. Gibson. Publishes 4-6 picture books/year; 1-2 young reader titles/year; 6 middle reader titles/year; 2-4 young adult titles/year. 25% of books by first-time authors; very few through agents.

**Fiction:** Picture book: contemporary, easy-to-read, "religious content." Young reader: animal, contemporary, easy-to-read, "religious content." Middle reader: animal, contemporary, easy-to-read, fantasy, science fiction, "religious content." Young adult: contemporary, easy-to-read, fantasy, problem novels, romance, science fiction, spy/mystery/adventure, "religious content." Average word length: picture book—700; young reader—20,000-60,000; middle reader—20,000-60,000; young adult—60,000. Recently published *The Will of Dargan*, by Phil Allcock (middle reader/young adult, fantasy—UK orig.); *Summer Promise*, by Robin Gunn (young adult, romance—US orig.); *The Book*

& *the Phoenix*, by Cherith Baldry (middle reader/young adult, fantasy—UK orig.).
**Nonfiction:** Picture book/young reader/middle reader/young adult: religion. Young adult: biography, music/dance. Recently published *AIDS and Young People*, by P. Dixon (young adult, medical/ethics/faith); *Knowing God's Will*, by P. Miller (young adult, faith journey); *When Your Rope Breaks*, by S. Brown (young adult, self-help/psych/humor).
**How to Contact/Writers:** Fiction/nonfiction: Submit outline/synopsis and sample chapters. Reports on queries/mss in 2-8 weeks. Publishes a book 12-24 months after acceptance. Will consider photocopied and computer printout submissions.
**Illustration:** Number of illustrations used for fiction: young readers—8+; middle readers—8+; young adult—0-6. Editorial will review ms/illustration packages submitted by authors with illustrations done by separate artists.

**\*ALFRED A. KNOPF BOOKS FOR YOUNG READERS**, Random House, Inc., 8th Floor, 225 Park Ave. S., New York NY 10003. (212)254-1600. Book publisher. Publisher: J. Schulman; Associate Publisher: S. Spinner. 90% of books published through agents.
**Fiction:** Picture books: animal, easy-to-read. Young readers: easy-to-read, spy/mystery/adventure., Middle readers: fantasy, science, science fiction, sports, spy/mystery/adventure. Young adult titles: fantasy, history, problem novels, romance, science, science fiction, spy/mystery/adventure. Recently published titles: *Baby Time*, by L. Brown; *The Boy Who Lost His Face*, by L. Sachar (novel); *Eyewitness Books*, by various authors (nonfiction).
**Nonfiction:** Picture books: animal. Young readers: animal, sports. Middle readers: animal, history, hobbies, nature/environment, sports. Recently published titles: *My First Cookbook*, by Angela Wilkes; *A Gallery of Dinosaurs*, by D. Peters (with gatefolds).
**How to Contact/Writers:** Fiction/nonfiction: submit through agent only. SASE for answer to query/return of ms. Publishes a book in 12-18 months. Will consider simultaneous, photocopied or computer printout submissions.
**Illustration:** Will review ms/illustration packages submitted by authors/artists (through agent only); ms/illustration packages submitted by authors with illustrations done by separate artists (through agent only). Executive Art Director, Denise Cronin, will review an illustrator's work for possible use in authors' texts.
**Terms/Writers & Illustrators:** Pays authors in royalties; sometimes buys mss outright. Sends galleys to authors. Book catalog free on request.

**KRUZA KALEIDOSCOPIX, INC.**, Box 389, Franklin MA 02038. (508)528-6211. Book publisher. Picture Books Editor: Jay Kruza. Young/middle readers editorial contact: Russ Burbank. Publishes 8 picture books/year; 1 young reader title/year; 1 middle reader title/year. 50% of books by first-time authors.
**Fiction:** Picture books: animal, fantasy, history. Young readers: animal, fantasy, history. Average word length: picture books—200-500; young readers—500-2,000; middle readers—1,000-10,000. Recently published *Petey the Pelican*, by Cox (ages 4-8, picture book); *Long Sleep*, by Blackman (ages 4-8, picture book); *ABC's Sports*, by Carole Iverson (ages 4-8, picture book).
**Nonfiction:** Picture books: animal, history, nature/environment. Young readers: animal, history, nature/environment, religion. Middle readers: biography, sports.
**How to Contact/Writers:** Fiction/nonfiction: Query; submit outline/synopsis and sample chapters; submit complete ms. SASE (IRC) for answer to query and/or return of mss. Reports on queries/mss in 2-8 weeks. Publishes a book 15 months after acceptance.
**Illustration:** Number of illustrations used for fiction: picture books—20-36; young readers—20-36; middle readers—20-36. Number of illustrations used for nonfiction: picture books—20; young readers—36; middle readers—20. Editorial will review ms/illustration packages submitted by authors/artists and ms/illustration packages submitted by authors with illustrations done by separate artists. Art Editor, Brian Sawyer, will review an

illustrator's work for possible use in author's texts. Prefers to see "realistic" illustrations.
**How to Contact/Illustrators:** Illustrations only: "actual work sample and photos."
Reports on art samples only if interested.
**Terms/Writers & Illustrators:** Pays authors in royalties of 3-5% based on wholesale
price; buys ms outright for $250-$500. Additional payment for ms/illustrations package.
Pay for illustrators: $25-$200/illustration. Manuscript/artist's guidelines available for
#10 SASE.
**Tips:** Writers: "Rework your story several times before submitting it without grammati-
cal or spelling mistakes. Our company charges a $3 reading fee per manuscript to reduce
unprepared manuscripts." Illustrators: "Submit professional looking samples for file.
The correct manuscript may come along." Wants ms/illustrations "that teach a moral.
Smooth prose that flows like poetry is preferred. The story will be read aloud. Vocabulary and language should fit actions. Short staccato words connote fast action; avoid
stories that solve problems by the "wave of a wand" or that condone improper behavior.
Jack of Beanstalk fame was a dullard, a thief and even a murderer. We seek to purchase
all rights to the story and artwork. Payment may be a lump sum in cash. For stronger
mss., a royalty arrangement based on actual books sold for a period of seven years may
be the payment."

**LERNER PUBLICATIONS CO.**, 241 First Ave. N., Minneapolis MN 55401. (612)332-
3344. Book publisher. Editor: Jennifer Martin. Publishes 15 young reader titles/year; 25
middle reader titles/year; 30 young adult titles/year. 20% of books by first-time authors;
5% of books from agented writers.
**Fiction:** Middle readers: contemporary, history, science fiction, sports, mystery. Young
adults: contemporary, history, science fiction, sports, mystery. Recently published *Earth-
change*, by Clare Cooper (grades 4-8, science fiction); *Hot Like the Sun*, by Mel Cebulash
(grades 5 and up, mystery).
**Nonfiction:** Young readers: animal, biography, history, nature/environment, sports,
science, social studies, geography, social issues. Middle readers: animal, biography, history, nature/environment, sports, science, social studies, geography, social issues. Young
adults: animal, biography, history, nature/environment, sports, science, social studies,
geography, social issues. Average word length: young readers – 3,000; middle readers –
7,000; young adults – 12,000. Recently published *Understanding AIDS*, by Ethan Lerner
(grades 3-6, social issues); *Be A Dinosaur Detective*, by Dougal Dixon (grades K-4, science); *Dwight Gooden-Strikeout King*, by Nate Aaseng (grades 4-9, sports).
**How to Contact/Writers:** Fiction: Submit outline/synopsis and sample chapters. Nonfiction: Query; submit outline/synopsis and sample chapters. SASE (IRC) for return of
mss. Reports on queries in 1 month; on mss in 2 months. Publishes a book 12 months
after acceptance. Will consider simultaneous, photocopied, and computer printout submissions.
**Terms/Writers & Illustrators:** Sends galleys to authors. Book catalog available for
9 × 12 SAE and $1 postage; manuscript guidelines for 4 × 9 SAE and 1 first-class stamp.
**Tips:** "Before you send your manuscript to us, you might first take a look at the kinds of
books that our company publishes. We specialize in publishing high-quality educational
books for children from preschool through high school. Avoid sex stereotypes (e.g.,
strong, aggressive, unemotional males/weak, submissive, emotional females) in your
writing, as well as sexist language." (See also Carolrhoda Books, Inc.)

*Refer to the Business of Children's Writing & Illustrating*
*for up-to-date marketing, tax and legal information.*

**LIGUORI PUBLICATIONS**, 1 Liguori Dr., Liguori MO 63057-9999. (314)464-2500. Book publisher. Editor-in-Chief: Rev. David Polek, C.SS.R. Managing Editor: Audrey Vest. Publishes 1 middle reader title/year; 3 young adult titles/year. 15% of books by first-time authors.
**Nonfiction:** Young readers, Middle readers, Young adults: religion. Average word length: young readers—10,000; young adults—15,000. Recently published *Advent is for Children*, by Julie Kelemen (middle grades, religion); *10 Good Reasons to be Catholic*, by Jim Auer (young adults, religion); *ABC's of the Old Testament*, by Francine O'Connor (ages 3-6, religion).
**How to Contact/Writers:** Nonfiction: Query; submit outline/synopsis and sample chapters. SASE (IRC) for return of ms; include Social Security number with submission. Reports on queries in 6 weeks; on mss in 6-8 weeks. Publishes a book 12 months after acceptance. Will consider photocopied, computer printout and electronic submissions via disk or modem.
**Illustration:** Number of illustrations used for nonfiction: young readers—40. Editorial will review ms/illustration packages submitted by authors/artists and ms/illustration packages submitted by authors with illustrations done by separate artists.
**How to Contact/Illustrators:** Ms/illustration packages: Query first.
**Terms/Writers & Illustrators:** Pays authors in royalties of 9-11% based on retail price. Book catalog available for 9×12 SAE and 3 first-class stamps; manuscript guidelines for #10 SAE and 1 first-class stamp.
**Tips:** Ms/illustrations "must be religious and suitable to a Roman Catholic audience. Writers should note that children's/teen's books are a very small part of Liguori's book publishing endeavors."

**\*LION BOOKS, PUBLISHER**, Imprint of Sayre Ross Co., Suite B, 210 Nelson, Scarsdale NY 10583. (914)725-2280. Book publisher. Editorial contact: Harriet Ross. Publishes 2 picture books/year; 5 middle reader titles/year; 10 young adult titles/year. 50-70% of books by first-time authors.
**Fiction:** History, sports. Average word length: middle reader—30,000-35,000; young adult—40,000-50,000.
**Nonfiction:** Biography, history, sports, black nonfiction. Average word length: young adult—50,000. Recently published *Phillis Wheatley*, by Jensen; *Great Black Women*, by Liss; *Great Black Americans*, by Liss.
**How to Contact/Writers:** Fiction/nonfiction: Query, submit complete ms. SASE (IRC) for answer to query and/or return of ms. Reports on queries in 1 month; on ms in 2 months.
**How to Contact/Illustrators:** Reports in 2 weeks.
**Terms/Writers and Illustrators:** Pays in outright purchase—$250-5,000. Average advance: $750-4,000. Separate authors and illustrators work "for hire or paid a royalty arrangement, unless contracted independent of each other." Illustrators paid $250-5,000. Sends galleys to author. Book catalog is free on request.
**Tips:** Looks for "nonfiction, well-written, notwithstanding the subject matter providing the writer knows our requirements of subjects."

**\*LION PUBLISHING CORPORATION**, 1705 Hubbard Ave., Batavia IL 60510. (708)879-0707. Book publisher. Editorial Contact: Bob Bittner. Publishes 3-6 picture books/year; 2-4 young reader titles/year; 2-4 middle reader titles/year; 2-4 young adult titles. 5% of books by first-time authors.
**Fiction:** Picture books: animal, contemporary, fantasy. Young readers: animal, contemporary fantasy. Middle readers: contemporary, fantasy, history. Young adults: contemporary, fantasy, history, problem novels, science fiction. Average word length: picture books and young readers—1,000; middle readers—25,000; young adults—40,000. Recently published *The Tale of Three Trees*, by Angela Hunt, (4 and up, picture book:

folktale); *Nothing Ever Stays the Same,* by Peggy Burns, (10-16, young adults: contemporary problems); *Shape-Shifter: The Naming of Pangur Ban,* by Fay Sampson, (9-14, middle readers: fantasy).

**Nonfiction:** Picture books: animal, nature/environment, religion. Middle readers: biography, history, nature/environment, religion. Young readers: nature/environment, religion. Young adults: nature/environment, religion. Average word length: picture books and young readers—1,000; middle readers and young adults—"varies." Recently published *When the Dinosaurs Lived,* by Jonathan Shelly, (4-8, picture book: humor); *Our World,* by Ernest and Hazel Lucas, (8-14, middle readers: nature); *The Trouble with Josh,* by Carolyn Nystrom, (8-12, middle readers: self-help).

**How to Contact/Writers:** Fiction: Submit complete ms. Nonfiction: Submit outline/synopsis and sample chapters. SASE (IRC) for return of ms. Reports on queries in 4 weeks; mss in 8 weeks. Publishes a book 12-18 months after acceptance. Will consider computer printout submissions (if letter quality).

**Illustration:** Editorial will review ms/illustration packages submitted by authors/artists and ms/illustration packages submitted by authors with illustrations done by separate artists.

**How to Contact/Illustrators:** Ms/illustration packages: "Query first."

**Terms/Writers and Illustrators:** Pays authors in variable royalties based on wholesale price. Sometimes buys ms outright. Book catalog/manuscript guidelines for 2 first-class stamps.

**Tips:** "Lion publishes Christian books for the general reader. A writer should carefully study our guidelines before submitting manuscripts or querying."

**\*JB LIPPINCOTT JUNIOR BOOKS,** Harper Junior Books Group, 10 E. 53rd St., New York NY 10022. (212)207-7044. Editorial assistant: Katharine Rigby. Book publisher.

**Fiction:** Middle readers: contemporary, history, science fiction, sports, spy/mystery/adventure. Young adult titles: contemporary, history, problem novels, romance, science fiction, sports, spy/mystery/adventure.

**Nonfiction:** Middle readers/young adult titles: biography, history.

**How to Contact/Writers:** Fiction/nonfiction: submit outline/synopsis and sample chapters, (for younger books) submit complete ms. SASE for answer to query/return of ms. Will consider simultaneous submissions (please advise), photocopied or computer printout submissions.

**Illustration:** Will review ms/illustration packages submitted by authors/artists; ms/illustration packages submitted by authors with illustrations done by separate artists; illustrator's work for possible use in authors' texts.

**How to Contact/Illustrators:** Ms/illustration packages: send three chapters of ms with one piece of final art, remainder roughs. Illustrations only: color photocopies preferred.

**Terms/Writers & Illustrators:** Pays authors in royalties based on retail price.

**LITTLE, BROWN AND COMPANY,** 34 Beacon St., Boston MA 02108. (617)227-0730. Book publisher. Editor-in-Chief: Maria Modugno. Editor: Stephanie O. Lurie. Estab. 1837. Publishes 30% picture books/year; 10% young reader titles/year; 30% middle reader titles/year; 10% young adult titles/year. 10% of books by first-time authors; 50% of books from agented writers.

**Fiction:** Picture books: animal, contemporary, fantasy, history, problem novels, sports, spy/mystery/adventure. Young readers: contemporary, fantasy, history, problem novels, sports, spy/mystery/adventure. Middle readers: animal, contemporary, fantasy, history, problem novels, sports, spy/mystery/adventure. Young adults: animal, contemporary, fantasy, history, problem novels, sports, spy/mystery/adventure. Average word length: picture books—1,000; young readers—6,000; middle readers—15,000-25,000; young adults—20,000-40,000. Recently published *My Father,* by Judy Collins/Jane Dyer (ages 4-8, picture book); *Angel and Me and the Boys, de Bombers,* by M.J. Arch (ages 7-9,

younger reader); *Just a Little Ham*, by Joan Carris (ages 8-12, middle grade novel).
**Nonfiction:** Average word length: picture books—2,000; young readers—4,000-6,000; middle readers—15,000-25,000; young adults—20,000-40,000. Recently published *Catch the Wind!*, by Gail Gibbons (ages 4-8, nonfiction picture book); *Ed Emburley's Christmas Tree Kit*, by Ed Emburley (all ages, crafts book); *The Strength of the Hills*, by Nancy Graff/Richard Howard (ages 8-12, photo essay).
**How to Contact/Writers:** Fiction: Submit complete ms. Nonfiction: Submit outline/synopsis and 3 sample chapters. SASE (IRC) for return of ms. Reports on queries in 6 weeks; on mss in 6-8 weeks. Publishes a book 18 months after acceptance. Will consider photocopied, computer printout and electronic submissions via disk or modem.
**Illustration:** Number of illustrations used for fiction: picture books—32; young readers—8-10; middle readers—1; young adults—1. Number of illustrations used for nonfiction: picture books—32; young readers—32-48; middle readers—1; young adults—1. Editorial will review ms/illustration packages submitted by authors/artists and ms/illustration packages submitted by authors with illustrations done by separate artists. Editor-in-Chief, Maria Modugno, will review illustrator's work for possible use in author's texts.
**How to Contact/Illustrators:** Ms/illustration packages: complete ms with 1 piece of final art. Illustrations only: Slides. Reports on art samples in 6-8 weeks. Original art work returned at job's completion.
**Terms/Writers & Illustrators:** Pays authors in royalties based on retail price. Offers average advance payment of $2,000-$10,000. Sends galleys to authors; dummies to illustrators. Book catalog, manuscript/artist's guidelines free on request.

**\*LODESTAR BOOKS**, Affiliate of Dutton Children's Books, an imprint of Penguin Books, USA, 2 Park Ave., New York NY 10016. (212)725-1818. Editorial Director: Virginia Buckley. Senior Editor: Rosemary Brosnan. Publishes 5 picture books/year; 15-20 middle reader titles/year; 5 young adult titles/year (25-30 books a year). 5-10% of books by first-time authors; 50% through agents.
**Fiction:** Picture books: animal, contemporary, history. Middle reader: contemporary, fantasy, history, science fiction, sports, spy/mystery/adventure. Young adult: contemporary, fantasy, history, science fiction, sports, spy/mystery/adventure. Recently published *Beyond Safe Boundaries*, by Sacks (young adult, novel); *Park's Quest*, by Paterson (young adult, novel); and *The Best Bet Gazette*, by Gondosch (middle reader, novel).
**Nonfiction:** Picture books: animal, history, nature/environment. Young reader: animal, history, nature/environment, sports. Middle reader: biography, history, nature/environment, sports. Young adult: biography, history, nature/environment, sports. Recently published *Gold! The Klondike Adventure*, by Ray (10-14, photo illustrated middle grade history); *Where Butterflies Grow*, by Ryder/Cherry (picture book, nonfiction); and *Wild Animals of Africa ABC*, by Ryden (picture book, photographic).
**How to Contact/Writers:** Fiction: submit outline/synopsis and sample chapters or submit complete ms. Nonfiction: Query or submit outline/synopsis and sample chapters. SASE (IRC) for answer to query and/or return of ms. Reports on queries in 4 weeks; on mss in 8-12 weeks. Publishes a book 12 months after acceptance. Will consider simultaneous, photocopied and computer printout submissions.
**Illustration:** Number of illustrations used for fiction: picture book—16-20; middle reader—10. Number of illustrations (photographs) used for nonfiction: 30-50. Editorial will review ms/illustration packages submitted by authors with illustrations done by separate artists; illustrator's work for possible use in author's texts.
**How to Contact/Illustrators:** Ms/illustration packages: Send "manuscript and copies of art (no original art, please)." Illustrations only: Send tear sheets. Reports back only if interested. Original art work returned at job's completion.

**Terms/Writers and Illustrators:** Pays authors and illustrators in royalties of 5% each for picture books; 8% to author, 2 % to illustrator for illustrated novel; and 10% for novel based on retail price. Factors used to determine final payment forms/illustration package include "color art vs. black-and-white and number of illustrations used." Pays for separate authors and illustrators: separate advances and royalties. Sends galleys to author. Book catalog for SAE; manuscript guidelines for #10 SAE and 1 first class stamp.

*"We hired Patricia [Henderson Lincoln, Longmeadow, Massachusetts] to illustrate the jacket," Lodestar Books Senior Editor Rosemary Brosnan explains, "based on samples she sent. This [The Best Bet Gazette, by Linda Gondosch] is a period piece set in the 50s, and I felt she would be good at this. She does very appealing work." Lincoln's next assignment is to illustrate a Lodestar book which has a plot set in the 40s.*

©Patricia Henderson Lincoln 1989

**LOTHROP, LEE & SHEPARD BOOKS**, div. and imprint of William Morrow Co. Inc., Children's Fiction and Nonfiction, 105 Madison Ave., New York NY 10016. (212)889-3050. Editor-in-Chief: Susan Pearson. Publishes 60 total titles/year.
**Fiction:** Picture books: across the board. Young and middle readers: contemporary, easy-to-read, fantasy, history, mystery, humor. Young adults: contemporary, fantasy, history, mystery, humor.
**Nonfiction:** Picture books, young readers, middle readers, young adults: animal, biography, science, history, music/dance, nature/environment.
**How to Contact/Writers:** Nonfiction: Query, submit outline/synopsis and sample chapters. Fiction and picture books: Submit entire ms. SASE (IRC) for answer to query and/or return of ms.
**Illustration:** Editorial will review ms/illustration packages submitted by authors/artists and ms/illustration packages submitted by authors with illustrations done by separate artists.
**How to Contact/Illustrators:** Ms/illustration packages: Write for guidelines first.
**Terms/Writers & Illustrators:** Methods of payment: "varies." Manuscript/artist's guidelines free for SASE.

**\*LUCAS/EVANS BOOKS**, 1123 Broadway, New York NY 10010. (212)929-2583. Executive Director: Barbara Lucas. Book packager specializing in children's books, preschool to high school age. Books prepared from inception to camera-ready point for all major publishers.

**Fiction/Nonfiction:** Particularly interested in series ideas, especially for middle grades and beginning readers. Recently published fiction titles: *Time for School, Nathan*, by Lulu Dulacre (preschool, fiction—Scholastic); *The Glass Salamander*, by Ann Downer (young adult, fantasy—Atheneum); *Dinosaur Beach*, by Liza Donnelly (preschool, fantasy—Scholastic). Recently published nonfiction titles: *Partners for Life* (series), by Margery Facklam (middle, nonfiction—Sierra Club); *Arroz con Leche*, by Lulu Dulacre (preschool, nonfiction—Scholastic).
**How to Contact/Writers:** Query. SASE for return of ms.
**Illustration:** Portfolios reviewed (bring, do not mail, original art). Color photo copies of art welcome for our file. Art not necessary to accompany mss unless artist professionally trained.
**Terms/Writers & Illustrators:** Royalty-based contracts with advance.
**Tips:** Prefer experienced authors and artists but will consider unpublished work.

**LUCENT BOOKS, (formerly New Day Books)**, Sister Company to Greenhaven Press, Box 289011, San Diego CA 92128-9009. (619)485-7424. Book publisher. Editor: Carol O'Sullivan. We are new. "We published 16 books in 1989 and are projecting 32 for 1990." 50% of books by first-time authors; 10% of books from agented writers.
**Nonfiction:** Middle readers (grades 5-8): education, topical histories, nature/environment, sports, "any overviews of specific topics—i.e., political, social, cultural, economic, criminal, moral issues." Average word length: 15,000-20,000. Recently published *Garbage*, by Karen O'Connor (grades 5-8, overview); *Special Effects in the Movies*, by Tom Powers (grades 5-8, overview); *Smoking*, by Lila Gano.
**How to Contact/Writers:** Nonfiction: Query. Reports on queries in 2 weeks. Publishes a book 6 months after acceptance. Will consider simultaneous, photocopied and computer printout submissions.
**Illustration:** "We use photos, mostly." Will review ms/illustration packages submitted by authors with illustrations done by separate artists. Preference: "7×9 format—4-color cover."
**How to Contact/Illustrators:** Ms/illustration packages: Query first.
**Terms/Writers & Illustrators:** "Fee negotiated upon review of manuscript." Sends galleys to authors. Manuscript guidelines free on request.
**Tips:** "Know the publisher's needs and requirements. Books must be written at a 7-8 grade reading level. There's a growing market for quality nonfiction. Tentative titles: Free Speech, Tobacco, Alcohol, Discrimination, Immigration, Poverty, The Homeless in America, Space Weapons, Drug Abuse, Terrorism, MAD (Arms Race), Animal Experimentation, etc. We are currently working on books addressing endangered species, AIDS, pollution, gun control, etc. Both the above lists are presented to give writers an example of the kinds of titles we seek. If you are interested in writing about a specific topic, please query us by mail before you begin writing to be sure we have not assigned a particular topic to another author. The author should strive for objectivity. There obviously will be many issues on which a position should be taken—e.g. discrimination, tobacco, alcoholism, etc. However, moralizing, self-righteous condemnations, maligning, lamenting, mocking, etc. should be avoided. Moreover, where a pro/con position is taken, contrasting viewpoints should be presented. Certain moral issues such as abortion and euthanasia, if dealt with at all, should be presented with strict objectivity."

**MARGARET K. McELDERRY BOOKS**, imprint of Macmillan Publishing Co., 866 Third Ave., New York NY 10022. (212)702-7855. Book publisher. Publisher: Margaret K. McElderry. Publishes 10-12 picture books/year; 2-4 young reader titles/year; 8-10 middle reader titles/year; 3-5 young adult titles/year. 33% of books by first-time authors; 33% of books from agented writers.

**Fiction:** Picture books: contemporary, traditional. Young readers: contemporary, beginning chapter books. Middle readers: contemporary, fantasy, science fiction, mystery/adventure. Young adults: contemporary, fantasy, science fiction. Average word length: picture books—500; young readers—2,000; middle readers—10,000-20,000; young adults—45,000-50,000. Recently published *Who Said Red?*, by Mary Gerforo, illustrated by Keiko Harahashi (ages 3-6, an unusual concept book about colors); *False Face*, by Welwyn Katz (ages 10-14 a contemporary fantasy involving an Iroquois god); *Another Shore*, by Nancy Bond (ages 12 and up, time travel story).

**Nonfiction:** Picture books: animal, history, nature/environment, science. Young readers: animal, history, nature/environment, science, sports. Middle readers: animal, biography, history, music/dance, nature/environment, science, sports. Young adults: biography, music/dance, nature/environment. Average word length: picture books—500-1,000; young readers—1,500-3,000; middle readers—10,000-20,000; young adults—30,000-45,000. Recently published *Searches in the American Desert*, by Sheila Cowing (ages 10 and up); *Dilly Dilly Piccalilli*, edited by Myra Cohn Livingston (ages 8-12, poetry); *Story of The Seashore*, by John S. Goodall (all ages, pictorial social history).

**How to Contact/Writers:** Fiction/nonfiction: Submit complete ms. SASE (IRC) for return of ms. Reports on queries in 2-3 weeks; on mss in 8 weeks. Publishes a book 12-18 months after acceptance. Will consider simultaneous (only if indicated as such) and computer printout submissions.

**Illustration:** Number of illustrations used for fiction: picture books—"every page"; young readers—15-20; middle readers—15-20. Number of illustrations used for nonfiction: picture books—"every page"; young readers—20-30; middle readers—20-30. Editorial will review ms/illustration packages submitted by authors/artists; ms/illustration packages submitted by authors with illustrations done by separate artist (2 or 3 samples only); and an illustrator's work for possible use in author's text (2 or 3 samples only).

**How to Contact/Illustrators:** Ms/illustration packages: Ms (complete) and 2 or 3 pieces of finished art. Illustrations only: Résumé and slides or sketches. Reports on art samples in 6-8 weeks. Original artwork returned at job's completion.

**Terms/Writers & Illustrators:** Pays authors in royalties based on retail price. Pay for separate authors and illustrators: "50-50 as a rule for picture books." Pay for illustrators: by the project. Sends galleys to authors; dummies to illustrators, "they make the dummies for picture books." Book catalog, manuscript/artist's guidelines free on request.

**Tips:** Writers: "Read widely in the field and write constantly." Illustrators: "Look at books already published and go to exhibitions of all sorts; sketch constantly." There is an "emphasis on books for babies and young children; on nonfiction." (See also Aladdin Books/Collier Books for Young Adults, Atheneum Publishers, Bradbury Press, Four Winds Press.)

**\*MAGE PUBLISHERS INC.**, 1032-29th St. NW, Washington DC 20007. (202)342-1642. Book publisher. Editorial contact: A. Sepehri. Publishes 2-3 picture books/year. 100% of books by first-time authors.

**Fiction:** Contemporary/myth, Persian heritage. Average word length: 5,000.

**Nonfiction:** Persian heritage. Average word length: 5,000.

**How to Contact/Writers:** Fiction/nonfiction: Query. SASE (IRC) for answer to query; include social security number with submission. Reports on queries/ms in 3 months. Will consider simultaneous, photocopied and computer printout submissions.

**Illustration:** Number of illustrations used in fiction/nonfiction: picture book—12. Editorial will review ms/illustration packages submitted by authors/artists; ms/illustration packages submitted by authors with illustrations done by separate artists; illustrator's work for possible use in authors' texts.

**How to Contact/Illustrators:** Illustrations only: Send résumé and slides. Reports in 3 months. Original art work returned at job's completion.
**Terms/Writers and Illustrators:** Pays authors in royalties. Sends galleys to authors. Book catalog free on request.

**\*MARCH MEDIA, INC.,** #256, 7003 Chadwick, Brentwood TN 37027. (615)370-3148. FAX: (615)370-0530. Independent book producer/agency. President: Etta G. Wilson. 35% of books by first-time authors.
**Fiction:** Recently produced *Five Hanna/Barbera Family Favorites*, (young reader, trade).
**Nonfiction:** Young reader: religion. Middle reader: social studies and values.
**How to Contact/Writers:** Fiction: Submit outline/synopsis and sample chapters. Nonfiction: submit complete ms. SASE (IRC) for answer to query. Reports on queries in 2 weeks, on ms in 8 weeks. Will consider simultaneous submissions.
**Illustration:** Editorial will review ms/illustration packages submitted by authors'/artists' or illustrators' work for possible use in author's texts.
**How to Contact/Illustrators:** Ms/illustration packages: "query first." Illustrations only: send "résumé and samples." Reports back only if interested. Original art work returned at job's completion.
**Terms/Writers and Illustrators:** Method of payment: "Either royalty or fee, depending on project and publisher's requirements."
**Tips:** Writers: "Study children's literature and play with children." Illustrators: "Be certain you can draw children and study book design." Looking for a "series of board books or middle-grade titles, either fiction or nonfiction." There is "more need for nonfiction and middle-grade fiction."

**MARYLAND HISTORICAL PRESS,** 9205 Tuckerman St., Lanham MD 20706. (301)577-5308. Book publisher. Independent book producer/packager. Publisher: Mrs. Vera Rollo. Publishes 1 picture book/year; 1 young reader title/year; 1 middle reader title/year; 1 young adult title/year. 30% of books by first-time authors.
**Nonfiction:** Picture books, young readers, middle readers, young adults: biography, history. Recently published *The American Flag*, by Vera F. Rollo (young adults); *Indians of the Tidewater Country of Maryland, Virginia, North Carolina, and Delaware*, by Thelma G. Ruskin (elementary students); *Maryland: Its Past and Present*, by Dr. Richard Wilson and Dr. E. L. Bridner, Jr. (4th-grade level).
**How to Contact/Writers:** Nonfiction: Query. Reports on queries in 1 month. Publishes a book 9 months after acceptance. Will consider simultaneous submissions.
**Terms/Writers & Illustrators:** Pays authors in royalties, buys artwork outright. Factors used to determine final payment: Time spent. Pay for illustrators: By the project. Sends galley to authors. Book catalog free on request.
**Tips:** "See what niche is not filled, ask: 'What do libraries and teachers need?' "

**\*MEADOWBROOK PRESS,** 18318 Minnetonka Blvd., Deephaven MN 55391. (612)473-5400. Book publisher. Editorial Contact: Cassandra McCullough. Publishes 7 young reader titles/year; 4 middle reader titles/year; 2 young adult titles/year. 25% of books by first-time authors; 8% of books from agented writers.
**Nonfiction:** Young readers: education, hobbies, activity books. Middle readers: education, hobbies, activity books. Young adults/teens: education, hobbies, activity books. Average word length: Young readers—8,200; Middle readers—8,200. Recently published *Free Stuff for Kids*, by Free Stuff Eds. (6 and older, activity); *Science in the Tub*, by James Lewis (5 and older, activity); *Almost Grown Up*, by Claire Patterson (11 and up, nonfiction).

**How to Contact/Writers:** Nonfiction: Query, submit outline/synopsis and sample chapters or submit complete ms. SASE (IRC) for return of ms. Reports on queries/mss in 4 weeks. Publishes a book 9 months after acceptance. Will consider simultaneous, photocopied and computer printout submissions.

**Illustration:** Number of illustrations used for nonfiction: young readers—100; middle readers—100. Editorial will review ms/illustration packages submitted by authors/artists; ms/illustration packages submitted by authors with illustrations done by separate artists; Kevin Bowen, art director, will review an illustrator's work for possible use in authors' texts.

**How to Contact/Illustrators:** Ms/illustration packages: Send "three sample chapters of ms with 1 piece of final art." Illustrations only: Send résumé and samples. Reports back in 6 weeks. Original art work returned at job's completion.

**Terms/Writers & Illustrators:** Pays authors in royalties of 5-7.5% based on retail price. Offers average advance payment of $1,000-5,000. Factors used to determine final payment for ms/illustration package include sales potential and number and type of illustrations. Pay for separate authors and illustrators: "either they can split the advance/royalty, or if there are few illustrations, the illustrator might receive a fee." Pay for illustrators: $100-10,000; ¼%-¾% of total royalties. Sends galleys for review to authors "sometimes." Book catalog, manuscript/artist's guidelines free on request.

**Tips:** Writers: "Ignore the advice of all the 'How to Write' books and start with a strong idea that you have reason to believe is marketable." Illustrators: "Develop a commercial style—compare your style to that of published authors, and submit your work when it is judged 'in the ball park.'" Looking for: "A children's book by objective observers, aimed at early elementary aged kids which explains how to get into, e.g., science, astronomy, magic, collecting, hobbies." Trends in book publishing: "The baby boom babies of 5-10 years ago are now in elementary school. Soon they'll be in junior high and high school."

**MERIWETHER PUBLISHING LTD.**, 885 Elkton Dr., Colorado Springs CO 80907. Book publisher. "We do most of our artwork in house; we do not publish for the children's elementary market." 85% of books by first-time authors; 5% of books from agented writers.

**Nonfiction:** Young adults: how-to, how-to church activities. Average length: 200 pages. Recently published *Theatre Games for Young Performers* (junior high); *Winning Monologues for Young Actors*, by Litherland (junior and senior high, theatrical); *You Can Do Christian Puppets* (elementary and teens, church market).

**How to Contact/Writers:** Nonfiction: Query or submit outline/synopsis and sample chapters. SASE (IRC) for answer to query and/or return of mss; include Social Security number with submission. Reports on queries in 4 weeks. Publishes a book 6-12 months after acceptance. Will consider simultaneous, photocopied, and computer printout submissions.

**Illustration:** Number of illustrations used for nonfiction: young adults—15. Art Director, Michelle Zapel, will review an illustrator's work for possible use in author's texts.

**How to Contact/Illustrators:** Ms/illustration packages: Query first. Illustrations only: Slides. Reports on art samples in 4 weeks.

**Terms/Writers & Illustrators:** Pays authors in royalties based on retail or wholesale price. Pay for illustrators: by the project; royalties based on retail or wholesale price. Sends galleys to authors. Book catalog for SAE and $1 postage; manuscript guidelines for SAE and 1 first-class stamp.

**Tips:** Plans "more nonfiction on communication arts subjects."

**JULIAN MESSNER,** imprint of Simon & Schuster, Prentice Hall Bldg., Englewood Cliffs NJ 07632. Book publisher. Editorial Director: Jane Steltenpohl. Publishes 4 young reader titles/year; 15 middle reader titles/year; 6 young adult titles/year. 25% of books by first-time authors; 50% of books from agented writers.
**Nonfiction:** Middle readers: animal, biography, history, hobbies, nature/environment, general science. Young adults: animal, biography, history, nature/environment, general science. Average word length: middle readers—30,000; young adults—40,000-45,000. Recently published *The Starry Sky*, Rose Wyler (5-7 years, science); *The Homeless*, by Elaine Landau (11-13 years, teenage nonfiction); *George Bush*, by George Sullivan (12-14 years, biography).
**How to Contact/Writers:** Nonfiction: Query. Reports on queries in 2 months; on mss in 3 months. Publishes a book 8 months after acceptance. Will consider simultaneous inquiries.
**Illustration:** Number of illustrations used for nonfiction: middle readers—20; young adults—12. Editorial will review ms/illustration inquiries submitted by authors with illustrations done by separate artists. Art Director, Carol Kuchta, will review an illustrator's work for possible use in author's texts.
**How to Contact/Illustrators:** Ms/illustration packages: Query first. Illustrations only: "Résumé and Xeroxes." Reports on art samples only if interested. Original artwork returned at job's completion.
**Terms/Writers & Illustrators:** Pays authors in royalties. Additional payment for ms/illustration packages. Sends galleys to authors.

**METAMORPHOUS PRESS,** Box 10616, Portland OR 97210. (503) 228-4972. Book publisher. Editorial Contact: Anita Sullivan. Estab. 1982. Publishes 1 picture book/year; 1 young reader title/year; 1 middle reader title/year; 1 young adult title/year. 90% of books by first-time authors; 10% of books from agented writers. Subsidy publishes 10%.
**Fiction:** "Metaphors for positive change."
**Nonfiction:** Picture books: education. Young readers: education, music/dance. Middle readers: education, music/dance, self help/esteem. Young adults: education, music/dance, self-help/esteem. Recently published *Thinking, Changing, Rearranging*, by Anderson (ages 10 and up, workbook to improve self-esteem); *Classroom Magic*, by Lloyd (lesson plans for elementary grades).
**How to Contact/Writers:** Fiction: Query. Nonfiction: Query; Submit outline/synopsis and sample chapters. SASE (IRC) for return of mss. Reports on queries in 3-4 months; on mss in 4-6 months. Publishes a book 12-24 months after acceptance. Will consider simultaneous, photocopied, computer printout and electronic submissions via disk or modem.
**Illustration:** Number of illustrations used for fiction/nonfiction: "varies." Editorial will review ms/illustration packages submitted by authors/artists and ms/illustration packages submitted by authors with illustrations done by separate artists. Children's Editor, Janele Gantt, will review an illustrator's work for possible use in author's texts.
**How to Contact/Illustrators:** Ms/illustrations: Query. Illustrations only: "vitae with samples of range and style." Reports on art samples only if interested.
**Terms/Writers & Illustrators:** Other methods of pay: "varies, negotiable." Pay for separate authors and illustrators: "Individually negotiated usually between author and illustrator." Sends galleys to authors; dummies to illustrators. Book catalog free on request.
**Tips:** Looks for "Books that relate and illustrate the notion that we create our own realities, self-reliance and positive outlooks work best for us—creative metaphors and personal development guides given preference."

**MISTY HILL PRESS**, 5024 Turner Rd., Sebastopol CA 95472. (707)823-7437. Book publisher. Editor-in-Chief: Sally Karste. Publishes 2 middle reader titles/year. 100% of books by first-time authors.
**Fiction:** Middle readers: history. Young adults: history.
**Nonfiction:** Middle readers: history. Young adults: history. Recently published *Trails to Poosey*, by Olive Cooke (young adults, historical fiction).
**How to Contact/Writers:** Fiction/nonfiction: Submit outline/synopsis and sample chapters. SASE (IRC) for answer to query and/or return of ms. Reports on queries in 1 week; on mss in 4 weeks. Publishes a book 8 months after acceptance. Will consider simultaneous submissions.
**Terms/Writers & Illustrators:** Illustrators paid by the project. Sends galleys to authors.
**Tips:** "Historical fiction: substantial research, good adventure or action against the historical setting. Historical fiction only."

**MOREHOUSE PUBLISHING CO.**, 78 Danbury Rd., Wilton CT 06897. (203)762-0721. FAX: (203)762-0727. Book publisher. Juvenile Books Editor: Stephanie Oda. Publishes 10 picture books/year. 75% of books by first-time authors. Subsidy publishes 25%.
**Fiction:** Picture book, young readers, middle readers, young adults: religion.
**Nonfiction:** Picture books: religion, moral message, family values. Young readers: religion, moral message, family values. Middle readers: religion, moral message, family values. Young adults: moral message, family values.
**How to Contact/Writers:** Fiction/nonfiction: Submit outline/synopsis and sample chapters. Include Social Security number with submission. Reports on queries in 4-6 weeks. Publishes a book 12 months after acceptance. Will consider computer printout and electronic submissions via disk or modem. Editorial will review ms/illustration packages submitted by authors/artists; ms/illustration packages submitted by authors with illustrations done by separate artists; and illustrator's work for possible use in author's texts.
**How to Contact/Illustrators:** Ms/illustration packages: 3 chapters of ms with 1 piece of final art. Illustrations only: Résumé, tear sheets. Reports on art samples in 4-6 weeks. Original artwork returned at job's completion.
**Terms/Writers & Illustrators:** Pays authors "both royalties and outright." Offers average advance payment of $500. Additional payment for ms/illustration packages. Sends galleys to authors. Book catalog free on request.
**Tips:** Writers: "Prefer authors who can do own illustrations. Be fresh, be fun, not pedantic, but let your work have a message." Currently expanding juvenile list. Illustrators: "Work hard to develop original style." Looks for ms/illustrations "with a religious or moral value while remaining fun and entertaining."

**MOSAIC PRESS**, 358 Oliver Rd., Cincinnati OH 45215. (513)761-5977. Miniature book publisher. Publisher: Miriam Irwin. Publishes less than 1 young reader title/year. 50% of books by first-time authors.
**Fiction:** Middle readers: animal, contemporary, history, problem novels, sports, spy/mystery/adventure. Average word length: middle readers—under 2,000.
**Nonfiction:** Middle readers: animal, biography, education, history, hobbies, music/dance, nature/environment, religion, sports. Average word length: middle readers—2,000. Recently published *Plain Jane Vanilla*, by Missy McConnell (10-11 year olds, story-poem); *Miriam Mouse's Survival Manual*, by Miriam Irwin (ages 6-10, story); *The Grandparent Book*, by Christopher Irwin (ages 8-10, story). "We have done 4 children's books in 10 years. None of our recent books were for children (out of 87 titles)."
**How to Contact/Writers:** Fiction: Query; submit complete ms. Nonfiction: Submit complete ms. SASE (IRC) for answer to query and/or return of mss. Reports on queries/mss in 2 weeks. Publishes a book 4 years after acceptance. Will consider simultaneous, photocopied, and computer printout submissions.

**Illustration:** Number of illustrations used for fiction: middle readers—12. Number of illustrations used for nonfiction: middle readers—8. Editorial will review ms/illustration packages submitted by authors/artists; ms/illustration packages submitted by authors with illustrations done by separate artists; and illustrator's work for possible use in author's texts. Prefers to see "pen and ink under 5″ tall."

**How to Contact/Illustrators:** Illustrations only: "photocopies of pen and ink work with SASE." Reports on art samples in 2 weeks. Original artwork returned at job's completion "after several years if requested."

**Terms/Writers & Illustrators:** Buys ms outright for $50 and 5 copies of book. Additional payment for ms/illustration package is $50 and 5 copies of book. Factors used to determine final payment: "flat fee." Pay for separate authors and illustrators: "by check when the book goes to press. The first completed copies are sent to artist and author." Pay for illustrators: $50 and 5 copies. Book catalog is available for $3. Manuscript/artist's guidelines for business-size SAE and 45¢.

**Tips:** Looks for "any type of writing that has something to say worth preserving in the form of a miniature book; that says it beautifully in very few words. Most of our children's books are bought by adults for *themselves*. Most of our books are in the $24 range, and people won't pay that much for a little book for children."

**\*MULTNOMAH PRESS,** 10209 SE Division, Portland OR 97266. (503)257-0526. Book publisher. Editor: Deena Davis. Publishes 1-2 picture books/year/ 1-2 young reader titles/year; 1-2 middle reader titles/year. 60% of books by first-time authors.

**Fiction:** Picture books: animal. Young readers: animal, contemporary, easy-to-read, spy/mystery/adventure. Middle readers: contemporary, fantasy, history, sports, spy/mystery/adventure. Average word length: picture books—2,000-3,000; young readers—5,000-6,000; middle readers 15,000-25,000. Recently published *T. J. Flopp*, by Stephen Cosgrove, (5-9, picture book); *Brown Ears*, by Stephen Lawhead, (5-9, young reader); *I Know the World's Worst Secret*, by Doris Sanford, (5-9, picture book/young reader).

**Nonfiction:** Picture books: animal, nature/environment, religion. Young readers: animal, biography, nature/environment, religion, sports. Middle readers: animal, biography, history nature/environment, sports. Average word length: picture books—2,000-3,000; young readers—5,000-6,000; middle readers—15,000-25,000. Recently published *Destination: Moon*, by Jim Irwin, (8-12, middle readers).

**How to Contact/Writers:** Fiction: Submit complete ms. Nonfiction: Submit outline/synopsis and sample chapters. SASE (IRC) for return of ms. Reports on queries in 2-3 weeks; on mss in 6 weeks. Publishes a book 9-12 months after acceptance. Will consider simultaneous, photocopied and computer printout submissions (if it is letter quality so scanner machine can read the manuscripts).

**Illustration:** Number of illustrations used for fiction: picture books—16; young readers—7-10; middle readers—7-10. Nonfiction: picture books—16. Editorial will review an illustrator's work for possible use in authors' texts.

**How to Contact/Illustrators:** Ms/illustration packages: "Send 3 chapters with 1 finished piece of art; pencil sketches of rest." Illustrations only: Send "résumé and either tear sheets, slides or photographs. Also, need to see that artist can follow a story line. So, if possible, submit illustrations of a well-known story, such as a fairy tale, etc." Original artwork returned at job's completion.

**Terms/Writers and Illustrators:** Pays author in royalty; percentage "depends on type of book; first time or well known author." Factors used to determine final payment are "type of illustration and number of illustrations." "Split royalty if well-known or work is equal. Generally the illustrator receives a flat fee." Pay for illustrators: by the project-negotiable fee. Sends galleys to authors. Book catalog/manuscript guidelines are free on request.

**Tips:** Writers: "Read as many books as you can so that you can recognize quality writing. Be aware of the kind of books a publisher publishes before you submit a manuscript." Illustrators: "Put only the work that you do well in your portfolio. Be willing to concept an entire story (well-known fairy tale) so editor can see how you follow a story and the kind of creativity you would bring to the story." Looking for "series format for both fiction and nonfiction. In fiction a well-developed main character. Multnomah is an evangelical publishing house, so we desire wholesome fiction with a Christian world view, although not necessarily an overt one."

**NATIONAL PRESS INC.**, 7201 Wisconsin Ave., Bethesda MD 20814. (301)657-1616. Book publisher. Contact: Submissions Editor. Publishes 3 picture books/year. "We are currently building up our children's market in all categories." 75% of books by first-time authors; 25% of books from agented writers.
**Fiction:** Picture books: animal, contemporary, easy-to-read, fantasy, history, problem novels, romance, science fiction, sports, spy/mystery/adventure. Young readers: animal, contemporary easy-to-read, fantasy, history, problem novels, romance, science fiction, sports, spy/mystery/adventure. Middle readers: animal, contemporary easy-to-read, fantasy, history, problem novels, romance, science fiction, sports, spy/mystery/adventure. Young adults: animal, contemporary easy-to-read, fantasy, history, problem novels, romance, science fiction, sports, spy/mystery/adventure. Recently published *Planet of Trash*, by Poppel (young readers, picture book); *Battle of the Dinos*, by Poppel (young readers, picture book); *Winnie the Blue Whale*, (young readers, picture book).
**Nonfiction:** Picture books: animal, biography, history, sports. Young readers: animal, biography, history, sports. Middle readers: animal, biography, history, sports. Young adults: animal, biography, history, sports.
**How to Contact/Writers:** Fiction/nonfiction: Submit outline/synopsis and sample chapters. SASE (IRC) for answer to query and/or return of mss. Reports on queries in 6 weeks; on mss in 8 weeks. Publishes a book 12 months after acceptance. Will consider simultaneous, photocopied, computer printout and electronic submissions via disk or modem.
**Illustration:** Editorial will review ms/illustration packages submitted by authors/artists and ms/illustration packages submitted by authors with illustrations done by separate artists. Editor, K. McComas, will review an illustrator's work for possible use in author's texts.
**How to Contact/Illustrators:** Reports on art samples in 6 weeks.
**Terms/Writers & Illustrators:** Factors used to determine final payment: color art vs. black-and-white and number of illustrations used. Sends dummies to illustrators. Book catalog, manuscript guidelines free on request.
**Tips:** "Well-conceived submissions are extremely rare. Good ideas fall through the cracks of meandering query letters and amateurish material. Writers' naïveté, in most cases, is astonishing—and unproductive. However, good material will always filter through." Trends in children's book publishing include: "Return to the classics, which hopefully means more discriminating parents."

**NEW DAY PRESS**, 2355 E. 89, Cleveland OH 44106. (216)795-7070. Book publisher. Editorial Contact: Carolyn Gordon. Publishes 1 middle reader title/year; 1 young adult title/year. 75% of books by first-time authors.
**Fiction:** Middle readers, young adults: history. Recently published *Fireside Tales*, by Mary S. Moore (5th grade to adult, stories from the oral traditional folk tales).
**Nonfiction:** Middle readers, young adults: biography, history. Recently published *Black Image Makers*, E. Gaines et al. (middle readers-young adults, biographical narratives).
**How to Contact/Writers:** Fiction/nonfiction: Query. SASE (IRC) for return of mss. Reports on queries in 4 weeks; on mss in 12 weeks. Publishes a book a year or more after acceptance.

**Illustration:** Number of illustrations used for fiction and nonfiction: middle readers — 5; young adults — 5. Editorial will review ms/illustration packages submitted by authors/ artists and ms/illustration packages submitted by authors with illustrations done by separate artists.

**How to Contact/Illustrators:** Reports on art samples in 3 months. Buys ms outright for $100. Book catalog free on request.

**Tips:** "Next project will be picture/story book for children 3-6 years — with African-American heritage emphasis."

**NEW SEED PRESS,** Box 9488, Berkeley CA 94709. (415)540-7576. Book publisher. Editor: Helen Chetin. Published 1 young adult title in 1982; 1 in 1986; 2 in 1989. 90% of books by first-time authors.

**Fiction:** Picture books, young readers: contemporary. Middle readers, young adults: contemporary, history. Recently published *The Girls of Summer*, by Anita Corwell (ages 10-16, young adult); *The Good Bad Wolf*, by Lynn Rosengarten Horowitz (preschool-grade 2, picture book).

**How to Contact/Writers:** Fiction/nonfiction: Query. SASE (IRC) for answer to query and/or return of mss. Reports on queries in 2 weeks; on mss in 8 weeks. Will consider simultaneous, photocopied and computer printout submissions.

**Illustration:** Editorial will review ms/illustration packages submitted by authors/artists; ms/illustration packages submitted by authors with illustrations done by separate artists; and an illustrator's work for possible use in author's texts.

**How to Contact/Illustrators:** Ms/illustration packages: Query with sample. Illustrations only: Tear sheets. Reports on art samples only if interested. Original artwork returned at job's completion.

**Terms/Writers & Illustrators:** Pays authors in royalties of 10% based on retail price. Buys ms outright for "negotiable" price. Average advance payment "varies." Sends galleys to authors; dummies to illustrators. Book catalog free on request; manuscript guidelines for legal-size SAE and 1 first-class stamp.

**Tips:** "Know your publisher before submitting."

**ODDO PUBLISHING, INC.,** Box 68, Fayetteville GA 30214. (404)461-7627. Book publisher. Contact: Editor. Publishes 3-6 picture books/year; 1-2 young reader titles/year; 1-2 middle reader titles/year. 25% of books by first-time authors.

**Fiction:** Picture books: animal, contemporary, easy-to-read, science fiction, sports, spy/ mystery/adventure. Young readers: animal, contemporary, easy-to-read, fantasy, science fiction, sports, spy/mystery/adventure. Middle readers: animal, contemporary, fantasy, science fiction, sports, spy/mystery/adventure. Average word length: picture books — 500; young readers — 1,000; middle readers — 2,000. Recently published *Bobby Bear's Treasure Hunt*, by Marilue Johnson (grade 1, children's storybook); *Bobby Bear at the Fair*, by Marilue Johnson (grade 1, children's storybook); *Timmy Tiger and Too Many Twins*, by Alvin Westcott (grade 2, children's storybook).

**Nonfiction:** Picture books: animal, nature/environment, sports. Young readers: animal, biography, hobbies, nature/environment, sports. Middle readers: animal, biography, hobbies, nature/environment, sports. Average word length: picture books — 500; young readers — 1,000; middle readers — 2,000.

**How to Contact/Writers:** Fiction/nonfiction: Query; submit outline/synopsis and sample chapters. SASE (IRC) for answer to query and/or return of mss. Reports on queries 1-2 weeks; on mss 8-12 weeks. Publishes a book 24 months after acceptance. Will consider simultaneous, photocopied, and computer (excluding dot matrix) submissions.

**Illustration:** Number of illustrations used for fiction and nonfiction: picture books — 33; young readers — 33; middle readers — 33. Editorial will review ms/illustration packages submitted by authors/artists; ms/illustration packages submitted by authors with illustrations done by separate artists; and an illustrator's work for possible use in author's texts.

**How to Contact/Illustrators:** Ms/illustration packages: Query first. Illustrations only: Sample art or slides. Reports on art samples only if interested, or if required to review slides.
**Terms/Writers & Illustrators:** Buys ms outright, "negotiable" price. Additional payment for ms/illustration packages "negotiable." Factors used to determine final payment include number of illustrations. Pay for separate authors and illustrators: separate contracts. Illustrators paid by the project. Sends galleys to authors "only if necessary." Book catalog available for 9 × 12 SAE and $2.25.
**Tips:** "Send simultaneous submissions. Do not be discouraged by 'no.' Keep sending to publishers." Looks for: "Books/art with a 'positive' tone. No immorality or risque subjects. Books must have an underlying theme or concept. 'Coping' subjects are accepted. We want children who read our books to learn something and feel good when they are finished."

**\*ODYSSEY PRESS**, Imprint of Lawyers and Judges Publishing Co., Box 181676, Coronado CA 92118. Book publisher. Publisher: Steve Weintraub. Publishes 6 picture books/year. 10% of books by first-time authors; 5% through agents.
**Fiction:** Picture books: animal, fantasy, science fiction, spy/mystery/adventure. Average word length: 0-400. "Company is a new start-up by former sales and marketing manager of Green Tiger Press."
**How to Contact/Writers:** Fiction: Submit complete ms. SASE (IRC) for answer to query and/or return of ms. Reports on queries in 4 weeks. Publishes a book 6 months after acceptance. Will consider simultaneous, photocopied and computer printout submissions.
**Illustration:** Number of illustrations used in fiction: picture book—16. Editorial will review ms/illustration packages submitted by authors/artists; ms/illustration packages submitted by authors with illustrations done by separate artists; illustrator's work for possible use in authors' texts.
**How to Contact/Illustrators:** Ms/illustration packages: Send "ms with sample art with SASE." Illustrations only: send "tear sheets, samples, slides with SASE." Reports back in 6 weeks. Original art work returned at job's completion.
**Terms/Writers and Illustrators:** Authors paid 5-10% royalty based on retail price; buys ms outright for $25-2,500. Additional payment for ms/illustration packages: 7½%-10% royalty. Pay for illustrators: 3-6% royalty based on retail price. Sends galleys to authors; dummies to illustrators. Ms/artist's guidelines for #10 SAE and 25¢ postage.
**Tips:** Writers/illustrators: "Develop your ideas from your own experiences." Looking for "picture books which are futuristic and stress dreams, fantasy, odysseys, successes/triumphs/victories and challenge the imagintion. The children's book market is soaring. More than $1 billion worth of children's books are being purchased annually—about 4,200 books split the reward."

**ORCHARD BOOKS**, div. and imprint of Franklin Watts, Inc., 387 Park Ave. S., New York NY 10016. (212)686-7070. Book publisher. Publisher and Editor-in-Chief: Norma Jean Sawicki. "We publish between 50 and 60 books, fiction, poetry, picture books, and photo essays." 10-25% of books by first-time authors.
**Nonfiction:** "We publish very selective nonfiction."
**How to Contact/Writers:** Fiction: Submit outline/synopsis and sample chapters; submit complete ms. Nonfiction: Submit outline/synopsis and sample chapters. SASE (IRC) for answer to query and/or return of mss. Reports on queries in 4 weeks; on mss in 4-8 weeks. Average length of time between acceptance of a book-length ms and publication of work "depends on the editorial work necessary. If none, about 8 months." Will consider simultaneous, photocopied, and computer printout submissions.

**Illustration:** Editorial will review ms/illustration packages submitted by authors/artists and ms/illustration packages submitted by authors with illustrations done by separate artists. "But it is better to submit ms and illustration separately unless they are by the same person, or a pairing that is part of the project such as husband and wife."

**How to Contact/Illustrators:** Ms/illustration packages: 3 chapters of ms with 1 piece of final art, remainder roughs. Illustrations only: "tear sheets or xerox copies or photostats of the work." Reports on art samples in 4 weeks. Original artwork returned at job's completion.

**Terms/Writers & Illustrators:** Pays authors in royalties "industry standard" based on retail price. Additional payment for ms/illustration packages. Factors used to determine final payment for ms/illustration package include number of illustrations, and experience. "We never buy manuscripts outright. An author/illustrator gets the whole royalty. An author who needs the illustrator shares the royalty." Sends galleys to authors; dummies to illustrators. Book catalog free on request.

**Tips:** "Master your craft, be true to your highest aspirations, and persevere."

**PANDO PUBLICATIONS,** 540 Longleaf Dr., Roswell GA 30075. (404)587-3363. Book publisher. Owner: Andrew Bernstein. Publishes 2-6 middle reader titles/year; 2-6 young adult titles/year. 20% of books by first-time authors.

**Fiction:** Middle readers: animal, contemporary, easy-to-read, fantasy, history, problem novels, science fiction, sports, spy/mystery/adventure. Young adults: animal, contemporary, easy-to-read, fantasy, history, problem novels, science fiction, sports, spy/mystery/adventure. Average length: middle readers—175 pages; young adults—200 pages. "New company, no children's fiction yet."

**Nonfiction:** Middle readers: animal, biography, education, history, hobbies, music/dance, nature/environment, sports. Young adults: animal, biography, education, history, hobbies, music/dance, nature/environment, sports. Average length: middle readers—175 pages; young adults—200 pages. Recently published *Teach Me to Play: A First Bridge Book*, by Jude Goodwin (ages 8-14, how-to, about card game of bridge).

**How to Contact/Writers:** Fiction/nonfiction: Prefers full ms. SASE (IRC) for return of ms. Reports on queries in 4 weeks; on mss in 6 weeks. Publishes a book 9 months after acceptance. Will consider simultaneous, photocopied, computer printout but "prefers" electronic submissions via disk or modem.

**Illustration:** Number of illustrations used for nonfiction: middle readers—125; young adults—125. Editorial will review ms/illustration packages submitted by authors/artists; ms/illustration packages submitted by authors with illustrations done by separate artists; and illustrator's work for possible use in author's texts.

**How to Contact/Illustrators:** Ms/illustrations: Query first. Illustrations only: Tear sheets. Reports on art samples in 1 month. Original artwork returned at job's completion.

**Terms/Writers & Illustrators:** Method(s) of payment: "Whatever we agree on." Offers average advance payment of "⅓ royalty due on first run." Factors used to determine final payment: "Our agreement (contract)." Pay for separate authors and illustrators is "according to contract." Illustrators paid "according to contract." Sends galleys to authors; dummies to illustrators. "Book descriptions available on request." Manuscript/artist's guidelines are free on request.

**Tips:** Writers: "Find an untapped market then write to fill the need." Illustrators: "Find an author with a good idea and writing ability. Develop the book with the author. Join a professional group to meet people—ABA, publisher's groups, as well as writer's groups and publishing auxiliary groups. Talk to printers." Looks for "how-to books, but will consider anything."

**\*PARENTING PRESS, INC.**, Box 15163, Seattle WA 98115. (206)527-2900. Book publisher. Editorial Director: Shari Steelsmith. Publishes 2-3 picture books/year; 1-2 young reader titles/year; 1-2 middle reader titles /year. 40% of books by first-time authors.
**Fiction:** "We rarely publish straight fiction." Recently published *A Horse's Tale,* by Nancy Luenn (ed), (middle readers, collection of 10 short stories on children in history). "No other fiction titles on our list."
**Nonfiction:** Picture books: biography, education, social skills building. Young readers: education, nature/environment, social skills building books. Middle readers: social skills building. Average word length: picture books—500-800; young readers—1,000-2,000; middle readers—up to 10,000. Recently published *Bully on the Bus,* by Carl Bosch, (middle readers, how to deal with bullies); *Ellie's Day,* by Conlin/Friedman, (picture book); *Harriet Tubman,* by Linda Meyer, (picture book, biography).
**How to Contact/Writers:** Fiction: Query. "We rarely publish fiction, unless it has a very clear educational component." Nonfiction: Query. SASE (IRC) for answer to query and/or return of ms. Reports on queries 4-6 weeks; mss in 1-2 months, "after requested." Publishes a book 10-11 months after acceptance. Will consider simultaneous, photocopied and computer printout submissions.
**Illustrations:** Number of illustrations used for fiction and nonfiction: picture books—14; young readers—50. Will review ms/illustration packages submitted by authors/artists, "we do reserve the right to find our own illustrator, however." Editorial will review an illustrator's work for possible use in authors' texts.
**How to Contact/Illustrators:** Ms/illustration packages: "query." Illustrations only: Send "résumé, samples of art/drawings (no original art); photocopies or color Xerox okay." Original art work returned at job's completion for illustrators under contract.
**Terms/Writers and Illustrators:** Pays authors in royalties of 4% based on retail price. Outright purchase of ms, "negotiated on a case-by-case basis. Not common for us." Offers average advance of $150. Additional payment for ms/illustration package: "We offer an 8% royalty on list price. This royalty is split 50/50 with the illustrator and author." Pay for separate authors and illustrators: "split royalty." Pay for illustrators: by the project; 4% royalty based on retail price. Sends galleys to authors; dummies to illustrators. Book catalog/manuscript guidelines for #10 SAE and 1 first-class stamp.
**Tips:** Writers: "Query publishers who already market to the same audience. We often get manuscripts (good ones) totally unsuitable to our market." Illustrators: "We pay attention to artists who are willing to submit an illustration on speculation." Looking for "social skills building books for children, books that empower children, books that encourage decision making, books that are balanced ethnically and in gender. Since 1983 there has been a proliferation of children's-only bookstores. Publishers are producing more children's titles."

**PAULIST PRESS**, 997 Macarthur Blvd., Mahwah NJ 07430. (201)825-7300. FAX: (201)825-8345. Book publisher. Editor: Georgia J. Christo. Publishes 6 picture books/year; 2 young reader titles/year; 3 middle reader title/year; 1 young adult title/year. 70% of books by first-time authors; 30% of books from agented writers.
**Fiction:** Picture books, young readers, middle readers, young adults: religious/moral. Average length: picture books—24 pages; young readers—24-32 pages; middle readers—64 pages; young adults—64-80 pages. Recently published *A Season for Giving*, by Susan Heyboer O'Keefe (ages 8-12, "Jewish-Christian dialogue," Hanukah and Christmas are explained); *Pablo and the Miracle of St. Anton*, by Robin Hansen-Cole (ages 8-10, picture-story book); *Jesus' Stocking*, by Patricia Crump (ages 3-8, Christmas picture story).
**Nonfiction:** Picture books, young readers, middle readers, young adults: religion. Recently published *Junipero Serra: God's Pioneer*, by Teri Martini; *Thomas More*, by Dorothy Smith; *Joan of Arc*, by Dorothy Smith (all ages 9-12, biographies of saints).

**How to Contact/Writers:** Fiction/nonfiction: Submit complete ms. SASE (IRC) for return of ms. Reports on queries in 1-2 weeks; on mss in 4 weeks. Publishes a book 12-16 months after acceptance. Will consider simultaneous, photocopied, and computer printout submissions, "prefer original, typed, double-spaced ms."

**Illustration:** Number of illustrations used for fiction and nonfiction: picture books—12-16; young readers—12; middle readers—6-8; young adults—6. Editorial will review ms/illustration packages submitted by authors/artists; ms/illustration packages submitted by authors with illustrations done by separate artists; and an illustrator's work for possible use in author's texts.

**How to Contact/Illustrators:** Ms/illustration packages: Complete ms with 1 piece of final art, remainder roughs. Illustrations only: Résumé, tear sheets. Reports on art samples in 2-3 weeks. Original artwork returned at job's completion, "if requested by illustrator."

**Terms/Writers & Illustrators:** Outright purchase: $25-$40/illustration. Offers average advance payment of $350-$500. Factors used to determine final payment: Color art, b&w, number of illustrations, complexity of work. Pay for separate authors and illustrators: Author paid by royalty rate; illustrator paid by flat fee. Sends galleys to authors; dummies to illustrators. Book catalog available for SAE.

**Tips:** "Television has made children aware of almost everything, from mental health illnesses to drug abuse to sexual abuse, etc. I would be interested in reviewing manuscripts that sensitively treat the above subjects for children (ages 8-12)."

*All rights to this, and other, watercolor pieces by Kevin Novack, Savannah, Georgia, were purchased for use as inside Illustrations in a Paulist Press book, Junipero Serra: God's Pioneer. Novack was paid $60 per illustration. Editor Georgia Christo feels that the artist, with his familiarity of the missions in California, succeeds at depicting this scene with honesty. "In addition," says Christo, "he has conveyed a sense of trust."*

© Paulist Press 1989

**\*PELICAN PUBLISHING CO. INC.**, 1101 Monroe St., Gretna LA 70053. (504)368-1175. Book publisher. Associate Editor: Dean M. Shapiro. Publishes 3-4 picture books/year; 2-3 young reader titles/year; 1-2 middle reader titles/year; 1-2 young adult titles/year. 30% of books by first-time authors; 5% of books from agented writers.

**Fiction:** Picture books, young readers, middle readers, young adult titles: animal, contemporary, fantasy, history, problem novels, sports. Average word length: picture books, young readers, middle readers—32 pages; young adults—96-128 pages. Recently published *Texas Jack at the Alamo*, by James Rice (picture book, young reader, middle reader—32 pg. picture book); *The Over-the-Hill Witch*, by Ruth Calif (young adult, adventure).

**Nonfiction:** Picture books, young readers, middle readers, young adult titles: biography, education, hobbies, music/dance, nature/environment, religion. Plans to publish several nonfiction titles in 1990; none published yet.

**How to Contact/Writers:** Fiction/Nonfiction: Query. SASE for answer to query; return of ms. Reports on queries in 4-6 weeks; mss in 12-16 weeks. Publishes a book 12-18 months after acceptance. Will consider photocopied and computer printout submissions "only on contracted works."

**Illustration:** Number of illustrations used for fiction and nonfiction: picture books—16-32; young readers—16-32; middle readers—16-32; young adult titles—1 per chapter. Will review ms/illustration packages submitted by authors/artists and ms/illustration packages submitted by authors with illustrations done by separate artists. Production Manager, Dana Bilbray, will review an illustrator's work for possible use in author's texts.

**How to Contact/Illustrators:** Ms/illustration packages: Query first. Illustrations only: Send resume, samples (preferably photocopies). Reports on ms/art samples/art samples only if interested. Original artwork returned at job's completion "on request."

**Terms/Writers & Illustrators:** Pays authors in royalties; buys ms outright "rarely." Pays for separate authors and illustrators: "By arrangement; can either be through contract or between author and artist." Sends galleys to authors; dummies to illustrators.

**Tips:** Writers: "Be as original as possible. Develop characters that lend themselves to series and always be thinking of new and interesting situations for those series." Illustrators: "Familiarize yourselves with the company, then query and submit samples that reflect themes consistent with the company's line." Looks for: "Series, preferably with anthropomorphic animals or other humorous characters. Stories that reflect moral values."

**PERSPECTIVES PRESS**, Box 90318, Indianapolis IN 46290. (317)872-3055. Book publisher. Publisher: Pat Johnston. Publishes total 2-6 children's titles of all ages. 95% of books by first-time authors.

**Fiction:** Picture books, young readers, middle readers, young adults: adoption, foster care. Recently published *Real For Sure Sister*, by Angel (middle readers); *Where the Sun Kisses the Sea*, by Gabel (young/middle readers).

**Nonfiction:** Picture books, young readers, middle readers, young adults: adoption, foster care. Recently published *Filling in the Blanks*, by Gabel (middle/young adults, self-help).

**How to Contact/Writers:** Fiction/nonfiction: Query. SASE (IRC) for answer to query and/or return of mss. Reports on queries in 2 weeks; on mss in 6 weeks. Publishes a book 6-9 months after acceptance. Will consider simultaneous and photocopied submissions.

**Terms/Writers & Illustrators:** Pays authors in royalties of 5-15% based on net sales. Sends galleys to authors; dummies to illustrators. Book catalog, manuscript guidelines available for #10 SAE and 2 first-class stamps.

**Tips:** "Do your homework! I'm amazed at the number of authors who don't bother to check that we have a very limited interest area and subsequently submit unsolicited material that is completely inappropriate for us. For children, we focus exclusively on issues of adoption and interim (foster) care; for adults we also include infertility issues."

**PHILOMEL BOOKS**, imprint of The Putnam & Grosset Group, 200 Madison Ave., New York NY 10016. (212)951-8700. Book publisher. Editor-in-Chief: Patricia Lee Gauch (picture books). Editorial Contact: Paula Wiseman (young reader titles). Publishes 20 picture books/year; 5-10 young reader titles/year. 50% of books by first-time authors; 20% of books from agented writers.

**Fiction:** Picture books: animal, fantasy, history. Young readers: animal, fantasy, history. Middle readers: fantasy, history. Young adults: contemporary, fantasy, history. "Any well written book." Average word length: "Books of quality varying length." Recently published *The Broccolli Tapes*, by Jan Shepard (middle reader).

**Nonfiction:** Picture books, young readers, middle readers, young adults: animal, biography, history. "Creative nonfiction on any subject." Average length: "not to exceed 150 pages." Recently published *Elephant Crossing*, by Yoshida (middle reader).

**How to Contact/Writers:** Fiction/nonfiction: Query; submit outline/synopsis and sample chapters; all other unsolicited mss returned unopened. SASE (IRC) for answer to query. Reports on queries/mss in 3 months. Publishes a book 2 years after acceptance. "Prefer type or daisy wheel electronic submissions."

**Illustration:** Number of illustrations used for fiction: picture books—24. Will review ms/illustration packages submitted by authors/artists "if requested." Art Director, Nanette Stevenson, will review an illustrator's work for possible use in author's texts.

**How to Contact/Illustrators:** Ms/illustration packages: Query first. Illustrations only: "appointment to show portfolio." Reports on art samples in 2 months. Original art work returned at job's completion.

**Terms/Writers & Illustrators:** Pays authors in advance royalties. Average advance payment "varies." Illustrators paid by advance and in royalties. Sends galleys to authors; dummies to illustrators. Books catalog, manuscript/artist's guidelines free on request.

**Tips:** "Discover your own voice and own story—and persevere." Looks for "something unusual, original, well-written. Fine art. Our needs change, but at this time, we are interested in receiving young fiction for the 4- to 10-year-old child. The genre (fantasy, contemporary, or historical fiction) is not so important as the story itself, and the spirited life the story allows its main character. We are also interested in receiving adolescent novels, particularly novels that contain regional spirit, such as a story about a young boy or girl written from a southern, southwestern, or northwestern perspective."

**PIPPIN PRESS**, 229 E. 85th St., Gracie Station, Box 92, New York NY 10028. (212)288-4920. Children's book publisher. Publisher/President: Barbara Francis. Publishes 6-8 picture books/year; 3 young reader titles/year. "Not interested in young adult books.

**Fiction:** Picture books: animal, fantasy, humorous. Young readers: fantasy, spy/mystery/adventure, humorous. Middle readers: fantasy, spy/mystery/adventure, humorous. Average word length: picture books—750-1,500; young readers—2,000-3,000; middle readers—3,000+. Recently published *A Spring Story*, by David Updike, illustrated by Robert Andrew Parker (ages 7-10, fantasy, picture book); *Nanny Noony and the Magic Spell*, written and illustrated by Edward Frascino (ages 4-8, humor, picture book); *Danger in Tibet! A Miss Mallard Mystery*, written and illustrated by Robert Quackenbush.

**Nonfiction:** Picture books: animal. Young readers: biography, humorous. Recently published *I Did it With My Hatchet: A Story of George Washington* and *Pass the Quill, I'll Write a Draft: A Story of Thomas Jefferson*, both by Robert Quackenbush.

**How to Contact/Writers:** Fiction/nonfiction: Query. SASE (IRC) for answer to query; Include Social Security number with submission. Reports on queries in 2-3 weeks; on mss in 6-8 weeks. Publishes a book 9-18 months after acceptance. Will consider simultaneous and photocopied submissions.

**Illustration:** Number of illustrations used for fiction: picture books—25-30; young readers—15-20; middle readers—8-10. Number of illustrations used for nonfiction: picture books—25-30; young readers—15-20; middle readers—15-20. Editorial will review an illustrator's work for possible use in author's texts.

**How to Contact/Illustrators:** Illustrations only: "Tear sheets or Xeroxes would be fine. I see illustrations by appointment." Reports on art samples only if interested. Original artwork returned at job's completion.

**Terms/Writers & Illustrators:** Pays authors in royalties. Pay for illustrators: Royalty. Sends galleys to authors; dummies to illustrators. "The illustrator prepares the dummy on picture books; dummies for longer books prepared by the designer are submitted to the illustrator." Book catalog available for 6 × 9 SAE; manuscript/artist's guidelines for #10 SAE.
**Tips:** "Be thoroughly familiar with the market, what is being published and what sells. Visits to children's room at local libraries and to children's bookstores would be helpful. Read reviews in *The New York Times Book Review, The Booklist, Publishers Weekly, School Library Journal*." Looks for "humorous picture book story, humorous fiction for young readers, middle group. Children's books almost across the board are the fastest growing segment of the publishing industry. Exceptions include young adult problem novels, historical fiction."

**PLAYERS PRESS, INC.,** Box 1132, Studio City CA 91614. (818)789-4980. Book publisher. Vice President/Editorial: R. W. Gordon. Publishes 2-10 young readers dramatic plays and musicals titles/year; 2-10 middle readers dramatic plays and musicals titles/year; 4-20 young adults dramatic plays and musicals titles/year. 12% of books by first-time authors; 1% of books from agented writers.
**Fiction:** "We use all categories (young readers, middle readers, young adults) but only for dramatic plays and/or musicals." Recently published *Rhyme Time*, by William-Alan Landes (grades 3-6, musical play).
**Nonfiction:** "Any children's nonfiction all pertaining to the entertainment industry, performing arts and how-to for the theatrical arts only." Recently published *Clown Makeup*, by C. Strutter, (ages 5-15, theater).
**How to Contact/Writers:** Fiction/nonfiction: Submit plays or outline/synopsis and sample chapters of entertainment books. SASE (IRC) for answer or return of mss. Reports on queries in 2-4 weeks; on mss in 12-16 weeks. Publishes a book 10 months after acceptance. No simultaneous submissions.
**Illustration:** Number of illustrations used for fiction: young readers — 1-10; middle readers — 1-8. Number of illustrations used for nonfiction: young readers — 15; middle readers — 2; young adults — 20. Associate Editor, M.E. Clapper, will review an illustrator's work for possible use in author's texts.
**How to Contact/Illustrators:** Ms/illustration packages: Query first. Illustrations only: Resume, tear sheets, slides, "SASE." Reports on art samples only if interested.
**Terms/Writers & Illustrators:** Pays authors in royalties of 2-20% based on retail price. Other method(s) of payment: "Negotiable." Factors used to determine final payment include color art, number of illustrations used. Pay for illustrators: by the project; royalties range from 2-5%. Sends galleys to authors; dummies to illustrators. Book catalog available for $1.
**Tips:** Looks for "plays/musicals and books pertaining to the performing arts only."

**\*CLARKSON N. POTTER INC.,** Random House, 201 E. 50th St., New York NY 10022. (212) 572-6166. Editor: Shirley Wohl. Book publisher.
**Fiction:** "We do nature and picture books for children through age 11."
**Nonfiction:** "We rarely do nonfiction for children."
**How to Contact/Writers:** Fiction/nonfiction: query. SASE for return of ms. Will consider simultaneous, photocopied or computer printout submissions.
**Illustration:** Will review ms/illustration packages by authors/artists; ms/illustration packages submitted by authors with illustrations done by separate artists; illustrator's work for possible use in authors' texts.
**How to Contact/Illustrators:** Ms/illustration packages: query first with one piece of photocopied art.
**Terms/Writers & Illustrators:** Pays authors in royalties based on retail price.

**THE PRESS OF MACDONALD & REINECKE,** imprint of Padre Productions, Box 840, Arroyo Grande CA 93420-0840. (805)473-1947. Book publisher. Editor: Lachlan P. MacDonald. 80% of books by first-time authors; 5% of books from agented writers.
**Fiction:** Middle readers: fantasy, history, nature. Average length: middle reader—120-140 pages. Recently published *Joel in Tananar*, by Robert M. Walton (ages 8-14, fantasy adventure).
**Nonfiction:** Middle readers: biography, history, hobbies, nature/environment. Average length: middle readers—120 pages. Recently published *Pioneer California*, by Margaret Roberts (grades 4-9, history).
**How to Contact/Writers:** Fiction: Submit outline/synopsis and sample chapters. Nonfiction: Submit complete ms. SASE (IRC) for answer to query and/or return of mss. Reports on queries in 2 weeks; on mss in 16 weeks. Publishes a book 36 months after acceptance. Will consider simultaneous submissions.
**Illustration:** Number of illustrations used for fiction: middle readers—8. Number of illustrations used for nonfiction: middle readers—12. Editorial will review ms/illustration packages submitted by authors/artists; ms/illustration packages submitted by authors with illustrations done by separate artists; and illustrator's work for possible use in author's texts.
**How to Contact/Illustrators:** Illustrations only: Tear sheets. Reports on art samples only if interested.
**Terms/Writers & Illustrators:** Pays authors in royalties based on retail price. Other method(s) of payment: "Advance plus royalty." Average advance payment "varies." Additional payment for ms/illustration packages. Factors used to determine final payment include color art vs. black-and-white. Pay for separate authors and illustrators: "Separate contracts." Illustrators paid by the project. Sends galleys to authors; dummies to illustrators. Book catalogs for 9 × 12 SAE and 45¢ in first-class stamps. Manuscript guidelines/artist's guidelines for #10 SASE.
**Tips:** Writers: "Concentrate on nonfiction that recognizes changes in today's audience and includes minority and gender considerations without tokenism. The Press of Mac-Donald & Reinecke is devoted to highly selected works of drama, fiction, poetry and literary nonfiction. Juveniles must be suitable for 140-page books appealing to both boys and girls in the 8-14 year range of readers." Illustrators: "There is a desperate lack of realism by illustrators who can depict proportionate bodies and anatomy. The flood of torn-paper and poster junk is appalling." Looks for: "A book of historical nonfiction of U.S. regional interest with illustrations that have 19th Century elegance and realistic character representations, about topics that still matter today."

**PRICE STERN SLOAN,** 360 N. LaCienega Blvd., Los Angeles CA 90048. (213)657-6100. Book publisher. Publishes 6 picture books/year; 10 young reader titles/year; 15 middle reader titles/year. 65-70% of books by first-time authors; 35% of books from agented writers.
**Fiction:** Picture books: animal, contemporary, easy-to-read, spy/mystery/adventure. Young readers: animal, contemporary, easy-to-read, spy/mystery/adventure. Middle readers: animal, contemporary, easy-to-read, spy/mystery/adventure. Recently published *Adventures in the Solar System*, by Geoffrey Williams (ages 7-12, space adventure book and cassette); *Elephant Ann & How the First Circus Began*, by Jon Madian (ages 0-7, storybook); *Good Night Sleep Tight*, by Mary Cron (ages 0-7, storybook).
**Nonfiction:** Picture books, young readers, middle readers: animal, educational, history, hobbies, nature/environment, sports. Young adults: biography. Recently published *Since 1776*, by Paul C. Murphy (ages 11 and up, history); *Collecting Bugs & Things*, by Julia Moutran (ages 5 and up, science activities).
**How to Contact/Writers:** Fiction/nonfiction: Query. SASE (IRC) for answer to query. Reports on queries/mss in 3 months. Publishes a book 6-8 months after acceptance. Will consider simultaneous, photocopied, and computer printout submissions.

**Illustration:** Editorial will review ms/illustration packages submitted by authors/artists and ms/illustration packages submitted by authors with illustrations done by separate artists. Art Director, John Beach, will review an illustrator's work for possible use in author's texts.

**How to Contact/Illustrators:** Ms/illustration: Query first. Illustrations only: Resume, tear sheets, slides. Reports on art samples only if interested.

**Terms/Writers & Illustrators:** Pays authors in royalties based on net price. Sends galleys to authors; dummies to illustrators. Book catalog available for 9×12 SAE and 6 first-class stamps; manuscript guidelines for legal-size SAE; artist's guidelines for letter-size SAE and 1 first-class stamp.

**Tips:** "Avoid writing stories with themes that have been done over and over again. We are looking for books that teach as well as entertain. Subject areas include nature, science, how-to, wordplay for early readers, book and cassette ideas, activity books, and original storybooks."

**PROFORMA BOOKS,** Q.E.D. Press of Ann Arbor, Inc., #112, 1008 Island Ct., Ann Arbor MI 48105. (313)994-0371. Book publisher. Marketing Manager: Dan Fox. Publishes 1 young adult title/year. 80% of books by first-time authors. Subsidy publishes 15%.

**Fiction:** Young readers: fairy tale. Young adults: contemporary, history, problem novels, fairy tale. Average word length: young readers—2,000-5,000; young adults—5,000-10,000. Recently published *The Princess and the Unicorn*, by Michele Gallatin (young readers, young adults, fairy tale).

**Nonfiction:** Average word length: young readers—5,000-10,000; young adults—10,000-15,000.

**How to Contact/Writers:** Fiction/nonfiction: Query; submit outline/synopsis. Report on queries in 10 weeks. Publishes a book 6 months after acceptance. Will consider simultaneous, photocopied, computer printout submissions and electronic submissions via disk or modem (Macintosh format).

**Illustration:** Number of illustrations used for fiction: Young adults—6. Editorial will review ms/illustration packages submitted by authors/artists; ms/illustration packages submitted by authors with illustrations done by separate artists; and an illustrator's work for possible use in author's texts.

**How to Contact/Illustrators:** Ms/illustration packages: Query. Reports on art samples in 6 weeks. Original artwork returned at job's completion.

**Terms/Writers & Illustrators:** Pays authors in royalties of 6-15% based on retail price. Sends galleys to authors; dummies to illustrators.

**Tips:** Looks for: "Fairy tales for young children to adult allegory types."

**\*RANDOM HOUSE BOOKS FOR YOUNG READERS,** Random House, Inc., 8th Floor, 225 Park Ave. S., New York NY 10003. (212)254-1600. Book publisher. Editor-in-Chief: Jane O'Connor. 100% of books published through agents.

**Fiction:** Picture books: animal, easy-to-read, history, sports. Young readers: animal, easy-to-read, history sports, spy/mystery/adventure. Middle readers: history, science, sports, spy/mystery/adventure. Recently published titles: *Hello Baby*, by Charlotte Doyle (ages 3 & 4, Just Right Books); *New at the Zoo*, by Kees Moerbeek (mix-and-match pop-up—Random House doesn't do many pop-up books); *Machines as Tall as Giants*, by Paul Strickland (8×8 picture book).

**Nonfiction:** Picture books: animal. Young readers: animal, biography, hobbies. Middle readers: biography, history, hobbies, sports.

**How to Contact/Writers:** Fiction/nonfiction: submit through agent only. SASE for answer to query/return of ms. Publishes a book in 12-18 months. Will consider simultaneous, photocopied and computer printout submissions.

**Illustration:** Will review ms/illustration packages submitted by authors/artists (through agent only); ms/illustration packages submitted by authors with illustrations done by separate artists (through agent only). Executive Art Director, Cathy Goldsmith, will review an illustrator's work for possible use in author's texts.

**Terms/Writers and Illustrators:** Pays authors in royalties; sometimes buys mss outright. Sends galleys to authors. Book catalog free on request.

**Tips:** There is a "trend away from licensed characters" in book publishing.

**\*THE ROCKRIMMON PRESS, INC.,** Imprint of Industrial Printers of Colorado, Inc., 110 E. Enterprise, Colorado Springs CO 80918. (719)594-6337. Book publisher. Editor: Toni Knapp. Publishes 2 young reader titles/year; 2 middle reader titles/year.

**Fiction:** "If an idea is good, we'll consider it."

**Nonfiction:** Young reader/middle reader: animal, history, nature/environment.

**How to Contact/Writers:** Query or submit outline/synopsis and sample chapters. SASE (IRC) necessary for return of ms. Reports on queries in 1 month; on ms in 2 months. Publishes a book 1 year after acceptance. Will consider simultaneous, photocopied and computer printout submissions (letter quality only).

**Illustration:** Number of illustrations used in fiction: young reader—10-15; middle reader—8-10. Editorial will review ms/illustration packages submitted by authors/artists. Editor, Toni Knapp, will review illustrator's work for possible use in authors' texts.

**How to Contact/Illustrators:** "Query first except for picture books." Illustrations only: submit résumé, tear sheets. Reports in 2 months. Originals sometimes returned to artist at job's completion.

**Terms/Writers and Illustrators:** Pays authors in royalties based on wholesale price. Advance payment varies. Pay for illustrators: by the project; royalties based on wholesale price. Sends galleys to author; dummies to illustrator. Book catalog and ms/artists guidelines free on request.

**Tips:** Illustrators should "have an excellent professional portfolio as well as outstanding examples for queries. Try the major trade houses, but don't overlook the small, high quality presses. The trend is toward nonfiction, a higher language level, excellence in illustration and writing."

**\*ROSEBRIER PUBLISHING CO.,** Box 1725, Ransom St., Blowing Rock NC 28605. Independent book producer/packager. Editorial contact: Beverly Donadio. Publishes 1 picture book/year. 50% of books by first-time authors.

**Fiction:** Picture books: animal, fantasy. Recently published *The Rosebrier Collection, Mis' Luci, The Rabbit Family, Montgomery Mole* and *Quincy Quail,* by Beverly Rose (K-5th grades, fantasy).

**How to Contact/Writers:** Fiction: submit complete ms. SASE (IRC) for return of ms: include social security number with submission. Reports on queries/ms in 6 months. Publishes a book 6 months after acceptance.

**Illustration:** Number of illustrations used in fiction: picture book—20. Editorial will review ms/illustration packages submitted by authors/artists; ms/illustration packages submitted by authors with illustrations done by separate artists.

**How to Contact/Illustrators:** Submit 3 chapters of ms with 1 piece of art.

**Terms/Writers and Illustrators:** Pays authors in royalties.

**Tips:** Looking for "positive literature."

**THE ROSEN PUBLISHING GROUP,** 29 E. 21st St., New York NY 10010. (212)777-3017. Book publisher. Editorial Contact: Ruth Rosen. Publisher: Roger Rosen. Publishes 8 middle reader titles/year; 50 young adult titles/year. 50% of books by first-time authors; 3% of books from agented writers.

**Nonfiction:** Young readers: contemporary, easy-to-read, sports. Middle readers: contemporary, easy-to-read, sports, psychological self-help. Young adults: contemporary, easy-to-read, sports, careers, psychological self-help. Average word length: young readers—8,000; middle readers—10,000; young adults—40,000. Recently published *Careers in Trucking*, by Donald Schauer (grade 8, vocational guidance); *Coping with Date Rape*, by Andrea Parrot (grade 8, psychology, self-help); *Everything You Need to Know About Teen Suicide*, by Jay Schliefer (grade 4, psychology, self-help).
**How to Contact/Writers:** Nonfiction: Submit outline/synopsis and sample chapters. SASE (IRC) necessary for answer to query. Publishes a book 9 months after acceptance. Will consider simultaneous, photocopied and computer printout submissions.
**Illustration:** Number of illustrations used for nonfiction: young readers—20; middle readers—10. Editorial will review ms/illustration packages submitted by authors/artists and ms/illustration packages submitted by authors with illustrations done by separate artists. Roger Rosen will review an illustrator's work for possible use in author's texts.
**How to Contact/Illustrators:** Ms/illustration packages: 3 chapters of ms with 1 piece of final art. Illustrations only: Résumé, tear sheets. Original artwork returned at job's completion.
**Terms/Writers & Illustrators:** Pays authors in royalties. Sends galleys to authors. Book catalog free on request.
**Tips:** "Target your manuscript to a specific age group and reading level and write for established series published by the house you are approaching."

**\*ST. ANTHONY MESSENGER PRESS**, 1615 Republic St., Cincinnati OH 45210. (513)241-5615. Book publisher. Managing Editor: Lisa Biedenbach. Publishes 1 middle reader title/year; 1 young adult title/year. 25% of books by first-time authors.
**Fiction:** Middle readers and young adults: religious. Recently published *Saints of the Seasons for Children*, by Ethel Pochocki Marbach, (middle readers, lives of saints with illustrations).
**Nonfiction:** Young readers, middle readers and young adults: religion. Recently published *What's A Kid to Do? Practicing Moral Decision-Making with 10- to 13-year-olds*, by John A. Flanagan, (middle readers, 39 exercises for moral development); *What's a Teen to Do? Developing Helping Skills With 14- to 16-year-olds*, by John A. Flanagan, (young adults, 40 stories with discussion questions to lead teens to growth in awareness of needs and to satisfaction of helping others).
**How to Contact/Writers:** Fiction/nonfiction: Query, submit outline/synopsis and sample chapters. SASE (IRC) for return of ms. Reports on queries in 2-4 weeks; mss in 4-6 weeks. Publishes a book 12-18 months after acceptance. Will consider photocopied and computer printout submissions (not dot matrix; laser OK).
**Illustration:** Editorial will review ms/illustration packages submitted by authors/artists. "We design all covers and do most illustrations in house."
**Terms/Writers and Illustrators:** Pays authors in royalties of 10-12% based on retail price. Offers average advance payment of $600. Sends galleys to authors. Book catalog, manuscript guidelines free on request.
**Tips:** "We're looking for programs to be used in Catholic schools and parishes, programs that have a successful track record."

**ST. PAUL BOOKS AND MEDIA**, Daughters of St. Paul, 50 St. Paul's Ave., Jamaica Plain, Boston MA 02130. (617)522-8911. Book publisher. Editor: Sister Anne Joan, fsp. Publishes 4 picture books/year; 2 young reader titles/year; 2-3 middle reader titles/year; 2 young adult titles/year. 25% of books by first-time authors.
**Fiction:** Picture books: animal, contemporary. Young readers: contemporary, history. Middle readers: contemporary, fantasy, history, problem novels. Young adults: contemporary, fantasy, history, problem novels. Average word length: picture books—500; young readers—1,500-3,000; middle readers—12,000; young adults—21,000. Recently

published *Hoover Wants to Help*, by Price (picture book, animal/toys); *Best Gift of All*, by Wilkeshvis (young reader, religion).

**Nonfiction:** Picture books: religion. Young readers, middle readers, young adults: religious biography, religion. Average word length: picture books—500-750; young readers—1,800-3,000; middle readers—14,000; young adults—21,000. Recently published *That's Me in Here*, by Darby (picture book-young reader, contemporary).

**How to Contact/Writers:** Fiction/nonfiction: Submit outline/synopsis and sample chapters. SASE (IRC) for return of ms. Reports on queries in 3-4 weeks; on mss in 4-8 weeks. Publishes a book 1-2 years after acceptance. Will consider computer printout submissions. No simultaneous submissions.

**Illustration:** Number of illustrations used for fiction: picture books—14; young readers—10; middle readers—8; young adults—6. Number of illustrations used for nonfiction: picture books—14; young readers—10; middle readers—8; young adults—8. Editorial will review ms/illustration packages submitted by authors/artists; ms/illustration packages submitted by authors with illustrations done by separate artists; and illustrator's work for possible use in author's texts. Style/size of illustration "varies according to the title. Re: colors, our scanner will not take fluorescents."

**How to Contact/Illustrators:** Ms/illustration packages: "Outline, sample chapters, one piece finished art, remainder roughs." Illustrations only: "Résumé and tear sheets." Reports on art samples in 2 weeks.

**Terms/Writers & Illustrators:** Pays authors in royalties of 8-12% based on gross sales. Additional payment for ms/illustrations packages: "negotiable." Pay for separate authors and illustrators: "Royalties (based on gross sales) are divided. Usually does not" send galleys to authors or dummies to illustrators. Manuscript guidelines for legal-size SAE.

**Tips:** "We are a Roman Catholic publishing house looking for manuscripts (whether fiction or nonfiction) that communicate high moral, religious and family values. Lives of saints, Bible stories welcome, as well as historical or contemporary novels for children. In Catholic circles, a renewed interest in saints. In general, high interest in allegorical fantasy, as well as stories that reflect attitudes and life situations children are deeply familiar with."

**SANDLAPPER PUBLISHING CO., INC.**, 281 Amelia St., Box 1932, Orangeburg SC 29116. (803)531-1658. Book publisher. Editor: Frank Handal. 10% of books by first-time authors.

**Fiction:** Middle readers: easy-to-read, spy/mystery/adventure. Young adults: contemporary, history. Recently published *Whopper!*, by Idella Bodie (middle readers).

**Nonfiction:** Young adults: biography, education, history, hobbies, nature/environment, sports. Recently published *The South Carolina Story*, by Anne Osborne (young adults to adults, history); *SC's Lowcountry: A Past Preserved*, by Halcomb/Messmer (adults, pictorial/history); *Dorn: Of the People*, by Dorn/Derks (adults, political/history).

**How to Contact/Writers:** Fiction/nonfiction: Submit outline/synopsis and sample chapters. SASE (IRC) for answer to query. Reports on queries in 1 week; on mss in 24 weeks. Publishes a book 24 months after acceptance. Will consider simultaneous and photocopied submissions.

**Illustration:** Number of illustrations used for fiction: picture books, young readers, middle readers, young adults—6/category. Number of illustrations used for nonfiction: picture books, young readers, middle readers, young adults—20/category. Editorial will review ms/illustration packages submitted by authors/artists; ms/illustration packages submitted by authors with illustrations done by separate artists; and an illustrator's work for possible use in author's texts.

**How to Contact/Illustrators:** Illustrations only: Resume, tear sheets, slides. Reports on art samples in 2 weeks. Original artwork returned at job's completion.
**Terms/Writers & Illustrators:** Pays authors in royalties. Illustrator paid by the project. Sends galleys to authors. Book catalog, manuscript guidelines free on request.
**Tips:** Looks for: "regional works on the south; history, literature, cuisine and culture."

*SCHOLASTIC HARDCOVER, Imprint of Scholastic Inc., 730 Broadway, New York NY 10003. (212)505-3223. Book publisher. Editorial Director, Jean Feiwel. Senior Editor (picture books): Dianne Hess; Editorial contacts (young readers): Eva Moore and Dianne Hess; Editorial contact (middle readers): Regina Griffin; Editorial contact (young adult tales): Jean Feiwel and Regina Griffin. Publishes 40+ (in hardcover) picture books/year; 20+ young reader titles/year; 20+ middle reader titles/year; 20+ young adult titles/year. 5% of books by first-time authors; 50% of books through agents.
**Fiction:** Picture books/young readers/middle readers/young adult: animal, contemporary, humor, easy-to-read, fantasy, history, problem novels, romance, science fiction, sports, spy/mystery/adventure, etc. Recently published *Fallen Angels*, by Walter Dean Meyers (young adult, Vietnam War, historic fiction); *The Trouble with the Johnsons*, by Mark Teague (picture book, humor/fantasy); and *Time for School, Nathan*, by Lulu Delaune (picture book, friendship/contemporary fantasy).
**Nonfiction:** Picture books/young readers/middle readers/young adult: animal, biography, education, history, hobbies, music/dance, nature/environment, religion, sports. Recently published *Sarah Morton's Day: A Day in the Life of a Pilgrim Girl*, by Kate Waters (picture book/young reader, historic nonfiction); *The Magic School Bus*, by Joanna Cole (picture book/young reader, humorous science-fantasy); *Exploring the Titanic*, by Robert D. Ballard (middle reader/young adult, history/social studies).
**How to Contact/Writers:** Fiction (for picture book and young reader): Submit complete mss with SASE; (for young adult and middle reader): Query or submit outline/synopsis and sample chapters. Nonfiction: Query or submit outline/synopsis and sample chapters. SASE (IRC) for answer to query and/or return of ms. Reports on queries in 2-4 weeks; on mss in 6-8 weeks. Publishes a book 1 year after acceptance. Will consider photocopied or computer printout submissions.
**Illustrations:** Editorial will review ms/illustration packages submitted by authors/artists; ms/illustration packages submitted by authors with illustrations done by separate artists. Dianne Hess, senior editor, or Claire Counihan, Art Director, will review an illustrator's work for possible use in authors' texts.
**How to Contact/Illustrators:** Illustrations only: Send tear sheets or slides. Reports in 1-8 weeks. Original art work returned at job's completion.
**Terms/Writers and Illustrators:** Pays authors in royalties of 10% (5% if split with artist) based on retail price. Sends galleys to author; dummies to illustrator. Book catalog for postage and mailing label.
**Tips:** Writers: "Attend writing workshops, learn your craft, don't be afraid to revise. Study the field and learn which company is suitable to your style of work." Illustrators: "Learn your craft. Create a finished dummy of any story and one piece of finished art to show an editor how you work."

*SCHOLASTIC, INC., 730 Broadway, New York NY 10003. (212)505-3000. Book publisher. Editorial Contact: Dianne Hess (picture books); Eva Moore (young readers). Executive Editor: Ann Reit (middle readers/young adult titles). 25% of books by first-time authors; 75% of books from agented writers.
**Fiction:** Middle readers: contemporary, mystery/adventure. Young adults/teens: contemporary, romance, mystery/adventure. Average word length: middle readers—35,000; young adult/teens—45,000. Recently published *Tell Me How the Wind Sounds*, by Leslie Guccione (young adult, hard/paper).

**Nonfiction:** Middle readers: biography, nature/environment. Recently published *Jesse Jackson*, by Patricia McKissack (middle reader, hard/paper).
**How to Contact/Writers:** Fiction/nonfiction: Submit outline/synopsis and sample chapters or submit complete ms. SASE (IRC) for return of ms. Reports on queries 1 month; mss 3 months. Publishes a book 12-18 months after acceptance. Will consider computer printout submissions.
**Terms/Writers & Illustrators:** Pays in royalties.
**Tips:** Writers: "Know the firm you are sending a submission to—what they publish, what they don't publish." Trends in book publishing: "Emphasis is on middle readers, young readers and picture books."

**SCOJTIA, PUBLISHING CO., INC.,** The Lion, 6457 Wilcox Station, Box 38002, Los Angeles CA 90038. Book publisher. Managing Editor: Patrique Quintahlen. Publishes 2 picture books/year; 1 young reader title/year; 1 middle reader title/year; 1 young adult title/year. 90% of books by first-time authors; 50% of books from agented writers.
**Fiction:** Picture books: animal, contemporary, easy-to-read. Young adults: history, problem novels, romance, science fiction, sports, spy/mystery/adventure. Average word length: picture books—2,000; young readers—3,000; middle readers—2,500; young adults—20,000. Recently published *The Boy Who Opened Doors*, by Prentiss Van Daves (musical and picture book).
**How to Contact/Writers:** Fiction/nonfiction: Query; submit outline/synopsis and sample chapters. SASE (IRC) for answer to query and/or return of ms. Reports on queries/mss in 4 months. Publishes a book 12 months after acceptance. Will consider simultaneous, photocopied and electronic submissions via disk or modem.
**Illustration:** Number of illustrations used for fiction and nonfiction: picture books—25; young readers—25; middle readers—8; young adults—8. Editorial will review ms/illustration packages submitted by authors/artists; ms/illustration packages submitted by authors with illustrations done by separate artists; and an illustrator's work for possible use in author's texts.
**How to Contact/Illustrators:** Ms/illustration packages: Query first. Illustrations only: Résumé, tear sheets. Reports on art samples in 4 months. Original artwork returned at job's completion.
**Terms/Writers & Illustrators:** Pays authors in royalties of 4-8% based on retail price. Buys ms outright for $20-$200. Offers average advance payment of $500. Factors used to determine final payment include number of illustrations. Pay for separate authors and illustrators: According to the terms of contract for each, author's contract, illustrator's contract, for project. Pay for illustrators: By the project, $60-$600. Sends galleys to authors; dummies to illustrators.
**Tips:** Writers: "Children love action, characters that touch on emotions that they feel but cannot explain, except by play; and by pretending to be, for a moment, such likeable characters. Create realistic characters that children will love, even the child in all of us. There is a growing need for children's books for 12 and up that deal more with acceptable roles for children in the new American family, which children in movies—morally—don't always exemplify." Illustrators: "Be original, here it is necessary to remember that with your imagination you can do anything; but it is also important to be organized with a stock of your best work that you perfect and keep in a portfolio, work from strength, your best of your work (drawings/illustrations). Originality will spring best from here."

**\*CHARLES SCRIBNER'S SONS,** imprint of Macmillan Publishing Co., 866 Third Ave., New York NY 10940. (212)702-7885. Book publisher. Senior Vice President/Editorial Director: Clare Costello. 30% of books from agented writers.
**Fiction:** Picture books: animal, contemporary. Young readers: animal, contemporary. Middle readers: animal, contemporary, fantasy, history, science fiction, spy/mystery/adventure. Young adults/teens: animal, contemporary, fantasy, history, science fiction,

spy/mystery/adventure. Recently published *Lisa's War*, by Matas (young adult, period WW II); *Billy Boone*, by Smith (ages 9-13, contemporary); *Murder at the Spaniel Show*, by Hall (young adult, mystery).
**Nonfiction:** Picture books: animal. Young readers: animal, nature/environment. Middle readers: animal, biography, history, nature/environment. Young adults/teens: animal, biography, history, nature/environment. Recently published *Making a Difference*, by Hodges (young adult, biography); *Digging to the Past*, by Hackevell (middle readers, archaeology); *Bearman*, by Pringle (middle readers, animals).
**How to Contact/Writers:** Fiction: Submit outline/synopsis and sample chapters. Nonfiction: Query. SASE (IRC) for answer to query and/or return of ms. Reports on queries in 4 weeks; mss in 8-12 weeks. Publishes a book 12-18 months after acceptance, "picture books longer." Will consider simultaneous (if specified when submitted), photocopied and computer printout submissions.
**Illustrations:** Editorial will review ms/illustration packages submitted by authors/artists; art director, Vikki Sheatsley, will "sometimes" review an illustrator's work for possible use in authors' texts.
**How to Contact/Illustrators:** Ms/illustration packages: "Query first." Illustrations only: Send tearsheets. Reports back only if interested. Original artwork returned at job's completion.
**Terms/Writers & Illustrators:** Pays authors in royalties based on retail price. Sends galleys to authors; dummies to illustrators. Book catalog for 8×10 SAE; manuscript guidelines are for legal-size SAE.

**HAROLD SHAW PUBLISHERS**, 388 Gundersen Dr., Box 567, Wheaton IL 60189. (312)665-6700. Book publisher. Dir. of Editorial Services: Ramona Cramer Tucker. Publishes 4 young adult titles/year. 10% of books by first-time authors; 5% of books from agented writers.
**Nonfiction:** Middle readers: religion, Bible studies. Young adults: religion, Bible studies, teen devotionals. Average length: middle readers—32-46 pages.; young adults—64-120 pages. Recently published *Keeping Cool in a Crazy World*, by Jim Plueddemann (middle readers, camp study guide); *No Artificial Flavors*, by Jeff and Ramona Tucker; and *Not a Hollywood Family*, by Annette Heinrich (young adults, teen devotionals).
**How to Contact/Writers:** Nonfiction: Query. SASE (IRC) necessary for answer to query and/or return of ms. Reports on queries in 2-4 weeks; on mss in 4-6 weeks. Publishes a book 12 months after acceptance. Will consider simultaneous and photocopied submissions.
**Illustration:** Number of illustrations used for nonfiction: middle readers—12; young adults—12. Editorial will review ms/illustration packages submitted by authors/artists; ms/illustration packages submitted by authors with illustrations done by separate artists and an illustrator's work for possible use in author's texts.
**How to Contact/Writers:** Ms/illustration packages: Query first. Illustrations only: Résumé, sample of work (2-3). Reports on art samples in 4 weeks. Original artwork returned at job's completion.
**Terms/Writers & Illustrators:** Pays authors in royalties of 5-10% based on retail price. Buys ms outright for $500-$1,500. Factors used to determine final payment include color art vs. b&w and number of illustrations used. Pay for separate authors and illustrators: royalty or ms payment is split. Illustrators paid by the project. Sends galleys to authors. Book catalog available for SAE and $1.25; manuscript guidelines for SAE and 1 first-class stamp.
**Tips:** Writers: "Visit your bookstore. Read what is out on the market, and focus on doing it better! Read your stories to children and to adults. (You'll find children are the most honest)." Illustrators: "Visit bookstores and see what illustrations are on the market. Show your illustrations to children and see if they appeal to them first before contacting a publisher." Looks for "a study guide or a very unusual story which would

make us change our minds about not picking up any more children's books! It (the children's book market) is growing bigger, but at the same time the quality has been going down (quality of writing and illustrations). Lasting books are being replaced by more chapbook-flimsy paperbooks."

**SHOE TREE PRESS**, Imprint of Betterway Publications, Inc., Box 219, Crozet VA 22932. (201)496-4441. Book publisher. Editor: Joyce McDonald. Published 3 middle reader titles in 1989. 25% of books by first-time authors; 25% of books from agented writers.
**Fiction:** Young readers: easy-to-read. Middle readers: history, problems novels, humor. Average word length: young readers—1,500-7,500; middle readers—20,000-35,000; young adults—50,000-75,000. Recently published *Melvil and Dewey in the Fast Lane*, by Pamela Curtis Swallow (middle readers, contemporary fiction); *Summer Captive*, by Penny Pollock (young adults, contemporary); *By George Bloomers!*, by Judith St. George (easy reader for young readers).
**Nonfiction:** Young readers: animal, history. Middle readers: animal, biography, history, hobbies, music/dance, nature/environment, reference. Young adults: reference. Average word length: young readers—1,500-7,500; middle readers—30,000-45,000; young adults—35,000-75,000. Recently published *Market Guide for Young Writers*, by Kathy Henderson (ages 10 and up, reference).
**How to Contact/Writers:** Fiction/nonfiction: Query; all unsolicited mss returned unopened. SASE (IRC) for answer to query. Reports on queries in 4 weeks; on mss in 12 weeks. Publishes a book 12-18 months after acceptance. Will consider simultaneous and photocopied submissions.
**Illustration:** Number of illustrations used for fiction and nonfiction: young readers—12-30; middle readers—12-30. Editorial will review ms/illustration packages submitted by authors/artists; ms/illustration packages submitted by authors with illustrations done by separate artists; and an illustrator's work for possible use in author's texts.
**How to Contact/Illustrators:** Ms/illustration packages: Query first. Illustrations only: Resume/tear sheets. Reports on art samples only if interested. Original artwork returned at job's completion.
**Terms/Writers & Illustrators:** Pays authors in royalties, "sometimes retail, sometimes wholesale, it varies with author." Pay for illustrators: By the project or on a royalty basis; Sends galleys to authors; dummies to illustrators.
**Tips:** "Avoid getting caught up in market trends." Looks for "middle years and young adult nonfiction. We do *not* publish picture books. Our focus has shifted to mainly nonfiction."

**SKYLARK/BOOKS FOR YOUNG READERS**, imprint of Bantam Books Inc., 666 Fifth Ave., New York NY 10103. Editorial Contact: Judy Gitenstein.
**Fiction:** Middle readers: contemporary, fantasy, historical, spy/mystery/adventure.
**How to Contact/Writers:** Fiction: Submit outline/synopsis and sample chapters; "You will get a form rejection if your ms is not for us. It isn't you; we don't have time to comment on them all." SASE (IRC) for answer to query and/or return of mss.
**Terms/Writers & Illustrators:** Pays authors in royalties of 6-8% based on retail price.

**\*SRI RAMA PUBLISHING**, Box 2550, Santa Cruz CA 95063. (408)426-5098. Book publisher. Secretary/Manager: Karuna K. Ault. Publishes 1 or fewer young reader titles/year.

**Fiction:** Recently published *Mystic Monkey*, Hari Dass (ages 7-13, story book).
**Nonfiction:** Recently published *A Child's Garden of Yoga*, by Hari Dass (ages 3-12, Yoga instruction).
**Illustration:** 40 illustrations used for fiction. Graphic Design Director, Josh Gitomer, will review illustrators' work for possible use in authors' texts.
**How to Contact/Illustrators:** Submit several samples. Reports on art samples in 2 months. Original art work returned at job's completion.
**Terms/Writers & Illustrators:** "We are a nonprofit organization. Proceeds from our sales support an orphanage in India, so we encourage donated labor, but each case is worked out individually." Pay for illustrators: $200 minimum, $1,000 maximum. Sends galleys to authors; dummies to illustrators. Book catalog and manuscript guidelines free on request.

*"This particular piece (rendered in colored pencil and dye) happened to be a landmark for me," begins Heidi Petach, Cincinnati, Ohio in explaining her book Bird Alphabet, published by Standard Publishing. "The book caught the eye of New York agent (Evelyne Johnson, Evelyne Johnson Associates) who subsequently signed me on. My income has increased and she also insists on retaining future copyright in my name and other rights as much as possible," Petach says.*

© Standard Publishing 1988

**STANDARD PUBLISHING**, 8121 Hamilton Ave., Cincinnati OH 45231. (513)931-4050. Book publisher. Director: Mark Plunkett. Publishes 25 picture books/year; 4 young reader titles/year; 8 middle reader titles/year; 4 young adult titles/year. 25% of books by first-time authors; 1% of books from agented writers.
**Fiction:** Picture books: animal. Young readers: easy-to-read. Middle readers: contemporary, sports. Young adults: contemporary, problem novels. Average word length: picture books—400; young readers—1,000; middle readers—25,000; young adults—40,000. Recently published *Summer's Quest*, by Susanne Elliott (young adults, contemporary); *Wheeler's Big Break*, by Daniel Schantz (middle readers, contemporary); *Runaway*, by Janet Willig (ages 12-15, fiction).
**Nonfiction:** Picture books: animal, religion. Young readers, middle readers, young adults: religion. Average word length: picture books—400; young readers—1,000; middle readers—25,000; young adults—40,000. Recently published *The Little Lost Sheep*, by Marilyn Lindsay (picture book, religious); *Thank You God, for Christmas*, by Henrietta

Gambill (picture book, religious); *Seven Special Days*, by Henrietta Gambill (picture book, religious).

**How to Contact/Writers:** Fiction/nonfiction: Query. SASE (IRC) for return of ms. Reports on queries in 3 weeks; on mss in 12 weeks. Publishes a book 18 months after acceptance. Will consider simultaneous, photocopied, computer printout and electronic submissions via disk or modem.

**Illustration:** Number of illustrations used for fiction: picture books — 24; young readers — 24; middle readers — 12; young adults — 12. Number of illustrations used for nonfiction: picture books — 24. Editorial will review ms/illustration packages submitted by authors/artists and ms/illustration packages submitted by authors with illustrations done by separate artists. Art Director, Frank Sutton, will review an illustrator's work for possible use in author's texts.

**How to Contact/Illustrators:** Ms/illustration packages: "Query." Illustrations only: "Tear sheets and résumé." Reports on art samples in 3 weeks.

**Terms/Writers & Illustrators:** Pays authors in royalties of 5-12% based on wholesale price. Buys ms outright for $250-$1,000. Offers average advance payment of $250. Sends galleys to authors. Books catalog available for 8½ × 11 SAE; manuscript guidelines for letter-size SAE.

**Tips:** "When writing children's books, make the vocabulary level correct for the age you plan to reach. Watch spelling and sentence structure. Keep your material true to the Bible. Be accurate in quoting Scriptures and references." Looks for: "picture books."

**STAR BOOKS, INC.,** 408 Pearson St., Wilson NC 27893. (919)237-1591. Editorial Contact: Irene Burk Harrell. "We are still a new and growing company."

**Fiction/Nonfiction:** "Manuscripts must be somehow strongly related to the good news of Jesus Christ." Recently published *The Cat That Barked* (legend, for all ages); *The Unsilent Angel*, by Douglas F. Johnson (fiction, ages 8-12).

**How to Contact/Writers:** Submit complete ms. SASE for return of ms; include Social Security number. Reports on queries in 1-2 weeks; mss in 4-8 weeks. Publishes a book 6 months after acceptance ("longer if extensive editing needed"). Will consider photocopied, computer printout submissions "if readily legible, nice dark ribbon." *No* simultaneous submissions.

**Illustration:** Editorial will review ms/illustration packages submitted by authors/artists; ms/illustration packages submitted by authors with illustrations done by separate artists; and illustrator's work for possible use in author's texts. "At present, we prefer informal black and white line art. As finances improve, we'll be interested in color."

**How to Contact/Illustrators:** Ms/illustration packages: send whole ms, 1-3 roughs of art. Reports on art samples within a month. Original artwork returned at job's completion.

**Terms/Writers & Illustrators:** Pay: "We issue contract for the whole (ms/illustration) package." Sends galleys to authors. Book catalog/guidelines available for #10 SAE and 2 first-class stamps.

**Tips:** "We want biblical values, conversation that sounds real, characters that come alive, stories with 'behavior modification' strengths. We want illustrations that are 'appealing.' "

**STARFIRE,** imprint of Bantam Books Inc., 666 Fifth Ave., New York NY 10103. (212)765-6500. Editorial Director: Beverly Horowitz. Publishes 48-60 adult titles/year.

**Fiction:** Young adults: contemporary, fantasy, historical novels, problem novels, romance, science fiction, spy/mystery/adventure.

**How to Contact/Writers:** Fiction: Query, submit outline/synopsis and sample chapters, cover letter. SASE (IRC) for answer to query and/or return of ms.

**Terms/Writers & Illustrators:** Pays authors in royalties of 6-8% based on retail price. Manuscript guidelines free on request.

**\*STEMMER HOUSE PUBLISHERS, INC.**, 2627 Caves Rd., Owings Mills MD 21117. (301)363-3690. Book publisher. President: Barbara Holdridge. Publishes 1-3 picture books/year. "Sporadic" numbers of young reader/middle reader/young adult titles/year. 50% of books by first-time authors.
**Fiction:** Picture books: animal, ecology. Young reader/middle reader: history. Recently published *Dooley's Lion*, by Gudrun Alcock (middle reader, novel); *Grey Neck*, by Marguerita Rudolph (4-8 years old, picture book); *Grandma's Band*, by Brad Bowles (4-8 years old, picture book).
**Nonfiction:** Picture book: animal, music/dance. Young reader: music/dance.
**How to Contact/Writers:** Fiction/nonfiction: query, submit outline/synopsis and sample chapters. SASE (IRC) for return of ms. Reports on queries in 6 weeks. Publishes a book 18 months after acceptance. Will consider simultaneous, photocopied and computer printout submissions.
**Illustration:** Number of illustrations used for fiction: picture books—48; young readers—24; middle readers—12. Number of illustrations used for nonfiction: picture book—48; young reader—24; middle reader—24. Will review ms/illustration packages submitted by authors/artists; ms/illustration packages submitted by authors with illustrations done by separate artists; illustrator's work for possible use in authors' texts.
**How to Contact/Illustrators:** Ms/illustration packages: "Query first, with several photocopied illustrations." Illustrations only: Send "tearsheets and/or slides (with SASE for return)." Reports in 2 weeks.
**Terms/Writers and Illustrators:** Pays authors in royalties of 4-6% based on wholesale price. Offers average advance payment of $300. Additional payment for ms/illlustration packages is 6-10% royalty. Factors used to determine payment for ms/illustration package include "permissions fees and/or other authors." Pay for illustrators: 4-5% royalty based on wholesale price. Sends galleys to authors. Book catalog for 9×12 SAE and 1 first-class stamp.
**Tips:** Writers: "simplicity and originality are the keys." Illustrators: "submit illustrations for children's books, not adult material."

**STERLING PUBLISHING CO., INC.**, 2 Park Ave., New York NY 10016. (212)532-7160. Book publisher. Acquisitions Editor: Sheila Anne Barry. Publishes 2 picture books/year; 30 middle reader titles/year. 15% of books by first-time authors.
**Nonfiction:** Middle readers: animal, hobbies, nature/environment, sports, humor. "Since our books are highly illustrated, word length is seldom the point. Most are 96-128 pages." Recently published *World's Best Sports Riddles and Jokes*, by Joseph Rosenbloom (middle readers, humor); *World's Best True Ghost Stories*, by C.B. Colby (middle readers-young adults, very short anecdotes); *Amazing Pranks and Blunders*, by Peter Eldin (middle readers, humor).
**How to Contact/Writers:** SASE (IRC) for answer to query and/or return of mss. Reports on queries in 2 weeks; on mss in 6-8 weeks. Publishes a book 6-12 months after acceptance. Will consider simultaneous and photocopied submissions.
**Illustration:** Number of illustrations used for nonfiction: middle readers—approximately 60. Editorial will review ms/illustration packages submitted by authors/artists; ms/illustration packages submitted by authors with illustrations done by separate artists; and an illustrator's work for possible use in author's texts.
**How to Contact/Illustrators:** Ms/illustration packages: "Query first." Illustrations only: "Send sample photocopies of line drawings." Original artwork returned at job's completion "if desired, but usually held for future needs."
**Terms/Writers & Illustrators:** Pays authors in royalties of up to 10% "standard terms, no sliding scale, varies according to edition." Sends galleys to authors; dummies to illustrators. Manuscript guidelines for SAE.
**Tips:** Looks for: "Humor, hobbies, science books for middle-school children." Also, "mysterious occurrences, fun and games books."

**TRILLIUM PRESS**, Box 209, Monroe NY 10950. (914)783-2999. Book publisher. Editorial Contact: William Neumann. Publishes 70 picture books, young readers, middle readers, young adult titles/year. 50% of books by first-time authors.
**How to Contact/Writers:** Fiction: Submit complete ms. Nonfiction: Query; submit complete ms. SASE (IRC) for answer to query and/or return of mss. Reports on queries in 1 week; on mss in 8 weeks. Publishes a book 6 months after acceptance. Will consider photocopied and computer printout submissions.
**Illustration:** Editorial will review ms/illustration packages submitted by authors/artists; ms/illustration packages submitted by authors with illustrations done by separate artists; and illustrator's work for possible use in author's texts.
**Terms/Writers & Illustrators:** Pays authors in royalties. Buys ms outright. Sends galleys to authors; dummies to illustrators. Book catalog available for 9 × 12 SAE and 65¢ first-class stamp; manuscript guidelines for #10 SAE and 1 first-class stamp.

**\*TSM BOOKS, INC.**, 535 Broad Hollow Rd., Ste A-11, Melville NY 11747 (516)420-0961. President: Thomas V. Melodia. Publishes 1 picture book/year. 100% of books by first-time authors.
**Fiction:** Picture books: easy-to-read, fantasy. Average word length: 500. Recently published *The Easter Bunny Comes to Forgottenville*, by Melodia and Malinowskie (preschoool-age 8, picture book); *Forgottenville, The Town That Arrested Santa Claus*, by McQuilken (preschool-age 8, picture book).
**Nonfiction:** Picture book: juvenile. Average word length: 500.
**Illustration:** Number of illustrations used for fiction: 48. Thomas V. Melodia, president, will review illustrator's work for possible use in authors' texts. Looking for "animatible characters."

**\*TYNDALE HOUSE PUBLISHERS**, 336 Gendersen Dr., Wheaton IL 60187. (312)668-8300. Book publisher. Children's Editorial Contact: Kenneth Taylor. Publishes 3 picture books/year. 10% of books by first-time authors.
**Fiction:** Picture books: animal, contemporary, easy-to-read.
**How to Contact/Writers:** Fiction: Query, submit outline/synopsis and sample chapters. SASE (IRC) for return of ms. Reports on queries/mss in 3 weeks. Publishes a book 12 months after acceptance. Will consider simultaneous, photocopied and computer printout submissions.
**Illustration:** Number of illustrations used for fiction and nonfiction: picture books— 15. Will review ms/illustration packages submitted by authors/artists; ms/illustration packages submitted by authors with illustrations done by separate artists; an illustrator's work for possible use in authors' texts.
**How to Contact/Illustrators:** Ms/illustration packages: Send 3 chapters of ms with 1 piece of final art. Illustrations only: Send tear sheets.
**Terms/Writers and Illustrators:** Pays authors in royalties of 10-15% for manuscript with illustrations, based on net receipts. Pay for illustrators: by the project; $500-1,500. Book catalog free on request.
**Tips:** Looking for religious material only.

**\*VOLCANO PRESS**, Box 270, Volcano CA 95689. (209)296-3345. FAX: (209)296-4515. Book publisher. President: Ruth Gottstein. Published 1 picture book 1989; 3 in 1990.
**Fiction:** Will consider feminist, social issues, Pacific rim-related (Asian) material for picture books, young readers and middle readers. Recently published *Berchick*, by Blanc (5-11 year olds, illustrated).
**Nonfiction:** Will consider feminist, social issues, Pacific-rim related (Asian) material for picture books, young readers and middle readers. Published *Period*, by Gardner-Loulan et al (10-15 year olds, illustrated health book); *Periodo* (Spanish edition of *Period*, by Gardner-Loulan et al).

**How to Contact/Writers:** Fiction: Query. Nonfiction: Submit outline/synopsis and sample chapters. SASE (IRC) for answer to query and/or return of ms; include Social Security number with submission. Reports on queries in approximately one month. Publishes a book 12 months after acceptance. Will consider photocopied and computer printout submissions.

**Terms/Writers and Illustrators:** Sends galleys to authors; dummies to illustrators. Book catalog for #10 SAE.

**WALKER AND CO.,** div. of Walker Publishing Co. Inc., 720 Fifth Ave., New York NY 10019. (212)265-3632. Book publisher. Editor-in-Chief: Amy C. Shields. Publishes 5 picture books/year; 10 young reader titles/year; 10 middle reader titles/year; 15 young adult titles/year. 15% of books by first-time authors; 65% of books from agented writers.
**Fiction:** Picture books: animal, contemporary, easy-to-read, fantasy, history. Young readers: animal, contemporary. Middle readers: animal, contemporary, fantasy, science fiction, sports, spy/mystery/adventure. Young adults: animal, contemporary, fantasy, history, problem novels, romance, science fiction, sports, spy/mystery/adventure. Recently published *Whale Brother*, by B. Steiner (picture book, science and nature); *The Revenge of HoTai*, by Hoobler (young adults, novel); *A Place of Silver Silence*, by Mayhar (young adults, science fiction).
**Nonfiction:** Picture books, young readers, middle readers, young adults: animal, biography, education, history, hobbies, music/dance, nature/environment, religion, sports. Recently published *A First Look At Horned Animals*, by Selsam/Hunt (young readers, science and nature); *From Abenaki to Zuni*, by Wolfson (young adults, American history); *Chuck Yeager, A Bio*, by Levinson (young adults, biography).
**How to Contact/Writers:** Fiction/nonfiction: Submit outline/synopsis and sample chapters. SASE (IRC) for return of ms. Report on queries/mss in 8-10 weeks. Publishes a book 12 months after acceptance. Will consider simultaneous, photocopied, and computer printout submissions.
**Illustration:** Number of illustrations used for fiction: picture books—32-48; young readers—30; middle readers—30. Number of illustrations used for nonfiction: picture books—32-48; young readers—20-30; middle readers—20-30; young adults—20-30. Editorial will review ms/illustration packages submitted by authors/artists; ms/illustration packages submitted by authors with illustrations done by separate artists; and illustrator's work for possible use in author's texts.
**How to Contact/Illustrators:** Ms/illustration packages: 5 chapters of ms with 1 piece of final art, remainder roughs. Illustrations only: "Tear sheets." Reports on art samples only if interested. Original artwork returned at job's completion.
**Terms/Writers & Illustrators:** Pays authors in royalties of 5-10% based on wholesale price "depends on contract." Offers average advance payment of $2,000-$4,000. Factors used to determine final payment include "quality, name recognition." Pay for separate authors and illustrators: "If a picture book, royalty is split 50/50. Beyond that we try to make equitable arrangements." Pay for illustrators: By the project, $500-$2,000; royalties from 10%. Sends galleys to authors; blues to illustrators. Book catalog available for 8½×11 SASE; manuscript guidelines for SASE.
**Tips:** Writers: "Keep writing, keep trying. Don't take rejections personally and try to consider them objectively. If 10 publishers reject a work, put it aside and look at it again after a month. Can it be improved?" Illustrators: "Have a well-rounded portfolio with different styles." Looks for: "Science and nature series for young and middle readers. Good contemporary young adult fiction."

**\*WARNER JUVENILE BOOKS,** Warner Publishing Inc., 666 Fifth Ave., New York NY 10103. (212)484-2900. Associate Editor: Alison Weir. Book publisher.
**Fiction:** Picture books, young readers: animal, easy-to-read, history, sports, seasonal books.
**How to Contact/Writers:** Fiction: submit complete ms. SASE for answer to query. Will consider simultaneous, computer printout submissions.
**Illustration:** Will review ms/illustrations packages submitted by authors/artists; ms/ illustration packages submitted by authors with illustrations done by separate artist; illustrator's work for possible use in authors' texts.
**How to Contact/Illustrators:** Ms/illustration packages: query first, no original art. Illustrations only: send slides or photocopies.
**Terms/Writers & Illustrators:** Pays authors in royalties based on retail price. Additional payment for ms/illustrations packages varies.

**WATERFRONT BOOKS,** 98 Brookes Ave., Burlington VT 05401. (802)658-7477. Book publisher. Publisher: Sherrill N. Musty. 100% of books by first-time authors.
**Fiction:** Picture books, young readers, middle readers, young adults: mental health, family/parenting, health, special issues involving barriers to learning in children. Recently published *JOSH: A Boy With Dyslexia*, by Caroline Janover (ages 8-12, paperback).
**Nonfiction:** Picture books, young readers, middle readers, young adults: education, guidance, health, mental health, social issues. "We publish books for both children and adults on any subject that helps to lower barriers to learning in children: mental health, family/parenting, education, and social issues." Recently published *Changing Families*, by David Fassler, M.D., Michele Lash, A.T.R., Sally B. Ives, Ph.D. (ages 4-12, paper and plastic comb binding).
**How to Contact/Writers:** Fiction/nonfiction: Query. SASE (IRC) for answer to query. Reports on queries in 2 weeks; on mss in 6 weeks. Publishes a book 6 months after acceptance. Will consider photocopied and computer printout submissions.
**Illustration:** Editorial will review ms/illustration packages submitted by authors/artists and ms/illustration packages submitted by authors with illustrations done by separate artists.
**How to Contact/Illustrators:** Ms/illustration packages: Query first. Illustrations only: Resume, tear sheets. Reports on art samples only if interested.
**Terms/Writers & Illustrators:** Pays authors in royalties of 10-15% based on wholesale price. Pays illustrators by the job. Additional payment for ms/illustration packages: Negotiable. Factors used to determine final payment: Number of illustrations used. Pay for separate authors and illustrators: "amount is negotiable but it would be within industry standards." Sends galleys to authors; dummies to illustrators. Book catalog available for #10 SAE and 1 first-class stamp.
**Tips:** "Have your manuscript thoroughly reviewed and even copy edited, if necessary. If you are writing about a special subject, have a well-qualified professional in the field review it for accuracy and appropriateness. It always helps to get some testimonials before submitting it to a publisher. The publisher then knows she/he is dealing with something worthwhile."

**\*WEEKLY READER BOOKS,** imprint of Field Publications, 245 Longhill Rd., Middletown CT 06457. (203)638-2472. Book publisher. Senior Editor: Stephen Kraser. Publishes 3 "original" picture books/year; 2 "original" middle reader titles/year. 50% of books by first-time authors.
**Fiction:** Picture Books: animal, fantasy. Middle readers: contemporary, fantasy, sports. Young adult titles: problem novels, romance, science fiction, sports, spy/mystery/adventure. Average word length: picture books—900; middle readers—10,000; young adult titles—20,000.

# Close-up

## Amy Shields
*Editor-in-Chief, Walker & Co.*
*New York City*

When researching new children's book ideas, writers can feel "there is nothing new under the sun." Editor-in-Chief Amy Shields of Walker & Co. acknowledges this situation. Naturally she has an interest in a new or different story plot, but, she qualifies, "What I really look for is a uniqueness in the spirit of the work, if the writer has approached something differently. Books are a lot like cooking," Shields explains. "Every recipe, supposedly, has been created and cooked before. Every book really has been done before, but if you can come up with a different way to do it or if you have a special way to say it, then I think that makes a valuable book." An example she uses to illustrate this point are the numerous books that have been written about the life of Abraham Lincoln, two of which have won major literary awards. The method of presentation the authors (and illustrators) incorporated into their works created unique books.

Shields, who worked for two publishing companies before joining Walker two years ago, has edited a range of juvenile material — children's picture books through young adult novels. A majority of Walker's titles are aimed at young adults. Some of this interest in young adult — and middle reader — titles among publishers, she adds, is based on their awareness that the older group of "baby boomlets" is now ready for this type of material.

One regret she has about the state of middle and young adult titles, Shields shares, is the lack of any real, honest and moral heroes to inspire readers. "The tendency is to be so realistic that everybody has faults, and everybody is so human that you can really see where they are falling down as characters," she says. "It used to be with Nancy Drew and some of the classic children's characters that their lives were perfect and . . . they never did anything wrong and never had any bad thoughts. That's kind of nice." Shields is quick to point out that we can never return to that sort of "cartoon" character in books today because children and teens are exposed to so much more realism through the media that such plots wouldn't have credibility, but her desire is to have writers provide text that bridges this gap. "I think a lot of writers are coming in the middle of these two very different characters (i.e., Nancy Drew and 'realistic characters with human failings'). It's a very hard kind of writing to do, to make the character believable, and current and on the level of not really being a hero but being somebody that a kid could aspire to."

Shields estimates that she and Walker's other editors receive about 3,000 unsolicited and agented manuscripts per year, and that the company publishes about 30-40 titles per year, partly drawn from these submissions. "Everything does get read," she reassures. "I think we probably have a higher percentage than most houses of buying things from the slush pile." She warns beginning writers to make sure they are submitting a solid story with a beginning, middle and end. Though this sounds like basic advice, she admits to amazement at the number of manuscripts that recount a little boy's afternoon adventures instead of incorporating a developed plot. "Whether the book is a picture book or a novel, whether it's fiction or nonfiction," she emphasizes, "you need to finish reading it with a sense of having gotten somewhere, and these pastiches which come in . . . just are not satisfying for the very reason that they don't have a beginning, middle and end. They don't take you anywhere, and I think this is the biggest failing."

Writers also want to be careful about submitting rhyming text, because so many times it just doesn't work, she warns. "There used to be a feeling among publishers not to do rhymed manuscripts. There is a very valid reason behind it," she explains, "either for scanning problems or plot problems. It's just like writing a picture book—an incredibly difficult format, a deceptive form."

When submitting a manuscript or query and outline, be sure to check for grammar, punctuation and spelling, Shields advises. "I think that's key to both business and marketing skills; if you don't know those basics, how can you expect someone to take you seriously as a writer?" In addition, she advises writers to not only keep working constantly to improve their craft but to also stay on top of the market by knowing what types of books are currently being published. "Look at the books being done to find out if you can do it better or if you can do it differently. You've got to write from the heart, and you've got to illustrate from the heart."

Though Shields acknowledges that writers and illustrators should know their audience, she and fellow editors are also busy researching the market to determine a special subject need for books. "We look at sales histories," she begins. "We listen to what people are saying at conferences; we read reviews from journals," plus talk to teachers and librarians regularly. "Occasionally," Shields adds, "a teacher will say, 'Gee, it's nice to have a biography of a discoverer. I wish there were more of them because it's coming up next year in our curriculum.' We'll respond to that," she says.

Writers and illustrators also need to be aware of what is involved in an average negotiation process, Shields advises. "It's my belief that writers and illustrators shouldn't be one-sided in getting advice from only one side of the desk or one corner of the ring. They really should listen to their editor, and if they've got a good editor, the editor should be trying to strike a fair deal for both parties—for both publisher and author. Too often," she adds, "a writer will either leave a deal or feel like he has been mishandled because he's getting advice that may be beyond what his skills are or may be beyond his own personal marketability. Expectations should be at the proper level, I think."

She is happy to note the increased growth—and popularity—of children's books which is largely based on parental and teachers' interests. "There are some interesting things happening in children's books at this point in time," she says. "With so many books being published for children, you've got to increase the number of books that are really special, and I think that is being seen."

*— Connie Eidenier*

**How to Contact/Writers:** Fiction: Query, submit outline/synopsis and sample chapters, submit complete ms. Reports on queries in 3 weeks; mss in 6 weeks. Publishes a book 12 months after acceptance. Will consider simultaneous, photocopied and computer printout submissions.

**Illustration:** Number of illustrations used for fiction: picture books—30; middle readers—4; young adult titles—1. Will review ms/illustration packages submitted by authors/artists; ms/illustrations submitted by authors with illustrations done by separate artists; illustrator's work for possible use in authors' texts.

**How to Contact/Illustrators:** Ms/illustration packages: Send slides or photos of final art; a few representative samples. Reports on ms/art samples in 6 weeks. Original artwork returned at job's completion.

**Terms/Writers and Illustrators:** Pays authors on royalty. Offers "competitive" advance. Manuscript guidelines free on request.

**Tips:** Writers: "Keep at it. It's a good manuscript that catches our attention, not a famous name. There's always room for a good writer." Looks for "a book that doesn't try to teach, but entertains." Trends in children's publishing: "More and better books, more competition and higher standards."

**\*WEIGL EDUCATIONAL PUBLISHERS,** 2114 College Ave., Regina Saskatchewan S4P 1C5 Canada. (306)569-0766. Book publisher. Project Coordinator: Catherine Pritchard.

**Nonfiction:** Young reader/middle reader/young adult: education, history, social studies. Average word length: young reader/middle reader/young adult—64 pages. Recently published *Links Between Canadian Communities*, by Wilma Birchill (grades 2-4, social studies); *Canadian Neighbours*, by Carlotta Hacker (grades 1-3, social studies); and *Early Canada*, by Emily Odynak (grades 4-6, history).

**How to Contact/Writers:** Nonfiction: Submit query and résumé. Reports on queries in 4 weeks. Publishes a book 24 months after acceptance. Will consider simultaneous and photocopied submissions.

**Illustration:** Number of illustrations used in nonfiction: young reader/middle reader/young adult—20. Editorial will review ms/illustration packages submitted by authors/artists; ms/illustration packages submitted by authors with illustrations done by separate artists; illustrator's work for possible use in authors' texts.

**How to Contact/Illustrators:** Ms/illustration packages: "Query first." Illustrations only: Send "résumé and photocopies of completed works." Reports back only if interested or when appropriate project comes in.

**Terms/Writers and Illustrators:** Pays "either royalty or fee." Separate authors and illustrators: "royalty or fee." Illustrators paid by the project. Sends galleys to author; sends dummies to illustrator. Book catalog free on request.

**Tips:** Looks for "educational material suited to a specific curriculum topic."

**WESTERN PRODUCER PRAIRIE BOOKS,** Box 2500, Saskatoon SK S7K 2C4 Canada. (306)665-3548. FAX: (306)653-1255. Book publisher. Editorial Director: Jane McHughen. Publishes 1 middle reader title/year; 2 young adult titles/year. 80% of books by first-time authors.

**Fiction:** Middle readers, young adults: contemporary, fantasy, history, problem novels, sports. Average word length: middle readers—40,000; young adults—50,000. Recently published *Dog Runner*, by Don Meredith (young adult, contemporary); *The Doll*, by Cora Taylor (middle reader, fantasy/history); *Last Chance Summer*, by Diana Wieler (young adult, problem).

**How to Contact/Writers:** Fiction: Submit outline/synopsis and sample chapters. SASE (IRC) for return of ms. Reports on queries in 4 weeks; on mss in 8-12 weeks. Publishes a book 12 months after acceptance. Will consider simultaneous (if we are advised they are simultaneous), photocopied and computer printout submissions (provided they are clear).

**Terms/Writers & Illustrators:** Pays authors in royalties of 10% based on retail price. Offers average advance payment of $1,000. Sends galleys to authors. Book catalog, manuscript guidelines free on request.

**Tips:** "Submit to publishers who have a strong list in the genre of your manuscripts." Looks for ms "with a Canadian connection, strong descriptions of settings, realistic dialogue, and development of the main character during the course of the story." Does not publish mysteries, adventures, who-dunnits, science fiction or new age.

**\*WINSTON-DEREK PUBLISHERS, INC.**, Box 90883, Nashville TN 37209. (615)321-0535. Book publisher. Editorial contact (picture books): Matalyn Rose Peebles. Editorial contact (young reader titles): Maggie Ella Sims. Editorial contact (middle reader/young adult titles): Candi Williams. Publishes 35-40 picture books/year; 25-30 young reader titles/year; 10-15 middle reader titles/year; 10-15 young adult titles/year. 70% of books by first-time authors; 5% through agents. Subsidy publishes 15-20% of books/year.

**Fiction:** Picture books: animal, easy-to-read, fantasy. Young reader: contemporary. Middle reader: problem novels, science fiction, African-American. Young adult: history, romance, spy/mystery/adventure, African-American. Average word length: picture book—600-1200; young reader—3,000-5,000; middle reader—2,000; young adult—10,000-40,000. Recently published *Nia and the Golden Stool*, by C.W. Sheerman (ages 5-8); *The Russians In the Attic*, by R. Forman (ages 8-12, adventure); and *Maude the Mare*, by Jo Washburn (ages 10-12).

**Nonfiction:** Picture books: animal. Young reader: history, religion, African American biographies. Middle reader: African-American biographies. Young adult: biography, education, history, nature/environment, religion, African-American biographies. Average word length: picture book—600-800; young readers—2,500-4,000; middle reader—1,000-2,500; young adult—10,000-30,000. Recently published *My Rainbow Friends*, by Betty Hammond (ages 9-12); *The Computer Zone*, by Marlan Orseth (ages 4-5, educational); and *The Secret Friendship*, by V. Brosseit (ages 8-13).

**How to Contact/Writers:** Fiction: Query or submit outline/synopsis and sample chapters. Nonfiction: Submit complete ms. SASE (IRC) for answer to query and/or return of ms. Reports on queries in 6 weeks; on mss in 8 weeks. Publishes a book 10 months after acceptance. Will consider simultaneous, photocopied and computer printout submissions.

**Illustration:** Number of illustrations used in fiction/nonfiction: picture book—20; young reader—10; middle reader—5. Editorial will review ms/illustration packages submitted by authors/artists; ms/illustration packages submitted by authors with illustrations done by separate artists. Editor, Robert Earl, will review an illustrator's work for possible use in authors' texts.

**How to Contact/Illustrators:** Ms/illustration packages: 3 chapters of ms with 1 piece of final art. Illustrations only: Send résumé and tear sheets. Reports in 3 weeks. Original art work returned at job's completion.

**Terms/Writers and Illustrators:** Pays authors in royalties of 10-15% based on wholesale price. Also pays in copies. Factors to determine final payment: "color art vs. black-and-white, and number of illustrations used." Separate authors and illustrators: 12½% royalty to writer and 2½% royalty to illustrator. Illustrators paid $30-150 or 2½-8½% royalty. Sends galleys to author; dummies to illustrator. Book catalog for SAE; ms/artist's guidelines free on request.

**Tips:** Writers: "Use current themes. Keep and maintain good taste; originality." Illustrators: Use "action illustrations plus send good work and variety of subjects such as male/female; b&w." Looks for: "educational, morally sound subjects, multi-ethnic; historical facts."

# Other Book Publishers

The following book publishers are not included in this edition of *Children's Writer's & Illustrators Market* for the reasons indicated in parenthesis. The phrase "did not respond" means the publisher was in 1989 *Children's Writer's & Illustrator's Market* but did not respond to our written and phone requests for updated information for a 1990 listing.

Abingdon Press (out of juvenile market)

Augsburg (declined to be listed)

Calico Books (deleted per request)

Crossway Books (too many submissions)

Crown Publishers (declined to be listed)

Dell Publishing Co. (declined to be listed)

Dodd, Mead & Co. (declined to be listed)

Fawcett Juniper (did not respond)

Fleet Press Corporation (did not respond)

Greenwillow Books (too many submissions)

Harper & Row (declined to be listed)

Harper Trophy (declined to be listed)

Hunter House Publishers (did not respond)

Little Simon/Wanderer Books (declined to be listed)

New Readers Press (out of juvenile market)

Oxford University Press (declined to be listed)

Parent's Magazine Press (declined to be listed)

Picture Book Studio (declined to be listed)

Pleasant Company (declined to be listed)

Puffin Books (declined to be listed)

G.P. Putnam (declined to be listed)

Simon & Pierre Publishing Co. Ltd. (out of juvenile market)

Twenty-First Century Books (deleted per request)

Viking Kestrel (declined to be listed)

Frederick Warne (declined to be listed)

# Magazine Publishers

Books aren't the only reading tools being promoted to today's youth by parents, teachers and publishers. Magazines are also providing a valuable educational tool in the fight against poor reading skills. In an April 24, 1989 edition of *Time*, Don Stoll, executive director of the Educational Press Association of America, reported the number of children's and teen's magazines as doubling from 85 to 160 titles during the past two years.

The subject matter contained in all these periodicals ranges from student-read *Weekly Reader*, *Junior Scholastic* and *Science Weekly* pieces to church-oriented material in *Group* and *HiCall* to general interest pieces for *Highlights for Children* and *'TEEN* magazine to a host of special-interest needs for publications such as *Insights* (the National Rifle Assoc.), *Exploring* (Boy Scouts of America) and *Listen* (Narcotics Education Inc.).

Interestingly, advertisers have come to realize that many of the more commercial publications such as *Sports Illustrated For Kids, Sesame Street* and *Alf* are excellent vehicles for a generation with a large discretionary income and input into their parents' spending habits. According to the July 1989 issue of *The SRDS Report*, less than 30 percent of children in the U.S. live in what is called a "traditional" home (i.e., working father, home-based mother). Because these children either live in single-parent homes or homes in which both parents work, they are bound to exercise a greater degree of consumer decision-making than children did even a generation ago. Add to this consumer awareness, spending money earned from allowances, odd jobs and gifts, and you have a scenario that advertisers recognize as a healthy market to target. The effect such ads will have on the editorial slant in each publication will have to be determined by you, the writer or illustrator, as you research the type of audience to whom each magazine is geared.

The larger-circulation, ad-carrying publications will generally pay a better pay rate than denominational or nonprofit magazines. But, for beginning writers and artists, remember these smaller magazines may be more open to reviewing the work of newcomers. They can provide an excellent vehicle for you to compile clipping files as you work your way toward the more lucrative markets.

Be sure when studying each listing in this section to look for those that provide writer's or artist's guidelines as well as sample copies. Many larger circulation periodicals can also be found on the newsstand and in the local library. Becoming familiar with the "slant" of each publication will save valuable time in submitting appropriate articles or artwork to magazines.

Once you have determined which magazines you are interested in contacting, take another look at the listing to review their preferred method of receiving submissions. Some may wish to see an entire manuscript, others may wish to see a query letter and outline, especially for nonfiction articles. In all situations, you can count on the editor appreciating any graphics you can provide with the piece. Remember, nine times out of ten, you are dealing with a readership comprised of TV-viewers accustomed to pictures with their text.

You may want to refer to the Business of Children's Writing & Illustrating at the beginning of this book to learn the proper form for submitting a manuscript, the mechanics of writing a query letter, the methods of tracking expenses and income, as well as updates in the copyright law.

Since magazines are in a growth pattern, you will want to periodically check your bookstore for any new titles that may have missed the *Children's Writer's & Illustrator's* deadline and are not included in this section.

**AIM MAGAZINE,** America's Intercultural Magazine, Box 20554, Chicago IL 60620. (312)874-6184. Articles Editor: Ruth Apilado. Fiction Editor: Mark Boone. Art Director: Bill Jackson. Quarterly magazine. Circ. 8,000. Readers are high school and college students, teachers, adults interested in helping, through the written word, to create a more equitable world. 15% of material aimed at juvenile audience.

**Fiction:** Young adults: history, "stories with social significance." Wants stories that teach children that people are more alike than they are different. Does not want to see religious fiction. Buys 20 mss/year. Average word length: 1,000-4,000. Byline given.

**Nonfiction:** Young adults: interview/profile, "stuff with social significance." Does not want to see religious nonfiction. Buys 20 mss/year. Average word length: 500-2,000. Byline given.

**How to Contact/Writers:** Fiction: Send complete ms. Nonfiction: Query with published clips. SASE (IRC) for return of ms. Reports on queries/mss in 1 month. Will consider simultaneous and photocopied submissions.

**Illustration:** Buys 20 illustrations/issue. Preferred theme or style: Overcoming social injustices through nonviolent means. Will review ms/illustration packages submitted by authors/artists; ms/illustration packages submitted by authors with illustrations done by separate artists; illustrator's work for possible use with fiction/nonfiction articles.

**How to Contact/Illustrators:** Ms/illustration packages: Query first. Illustrations only: "Send examples of art, ask for a job." Reports on art samples in 2 months. Original art work returned at job's completion "if desired."

**Terms/Writers & Illustrators:** Pays on publication. Buys first North American serial rights. Publication not copyrighted. Pays $5-25 for assigned/unsolicited articles. Pays in contributor copies if copies are requested. Pays $5-25/b&w cover illustration. Sample copy $3.50.

**Tips:** "Always typed, proofed. We need material of social significance, stuff that will help promote racial harmony and peace."

**\*ANIMAL TALES,** 6015 N. 35th Ave., Phoenix AZ 85017. (602)246-7144. Articles/Fiction Editor and Art Director: Berta I. Cellers. Bimonthly magazine. Estab. 1989. Circ. 1,000. Publishes "stories about animals and the people who love them." 50% of material aimed at juvenile audience."

**Fiction:** Young adult: animal, contemporary, humorous. Does not want to see dedications to a deceased pet. Buys 75 mss/year. Average word length: 2,000-6,000. Byline given.

**Nonfiction:** Young adult: animal, humorous. Buys 6 mss/year. Average word length: 2,000-6,000. Byline given.

**Poetry:** Reviews "light verse and traditional poems about animals." Will accept 5 submissions/author.

**How to Contact/Writers:** Fiction/nonfiction: Send complete ms. SASE (IRC) for answer to query and return of ms; include Social Security number with submission. Reports on queries in 6 weeks. Will consider simultaneous and computer printout submissions.

**Illustrations:** Buys 10-15 illustrations/issue; buys 70 illustrations/year. Prefers "sketches used to illustrate a story and decorate front cover." Will review ms/illustration packages submitted by authors/artists; ms/illustration packages submitted by authors with illustrations done by separate artists; illustrator's work for possible use with fiction/nonfiction articles.

**How to Contact/Illustrators:** Ms/illustrations packages: Complete ms with final artwork. Illustrations only: Samples of artwork. Reports on art samples in 6 weeks. Original art work returned at job's completion.

**Terms/Writers and Illustrators:** Pays on publication. Buys first rights. Pays $5-25 for unsolicited articles. Additional payment for ms/illustration packages is $10-75. Pays $5-25/b&w cover illustration or inside illustration. Sample copy $5. Writer's/illustrator's guidelines free with SAE and 1 first class stamp.

**Tips:** "We are looking for unique material that communicates the animal/human relationship. Should be easy to read but not childish. Especially seeking illustrations that accompany a manuscript."

*Cindy Connor, Phoenix, Arizona, rendered this pen & ink piece for cover use on* Animal Tales. *She is a staff member for the magazine which, according to Editor Berta I. Cellers, looks "for unique material that communicates the animal/human relationship." In addition, Cellers says that she is looking for manuscript/illustration packages for* Animal Tales.

©Animal Tales 1989

*ATALANTIK, 7630 Deer Creek Dr., Worthington OH 43085. (614)885-0550. Articles/Fiction Editor: Prabhat K. Dutta. Art Director: Tanushree Bhattacharya. Quarterly magazine. Estab. 1980. Circ. 400. "*Atalantik* is the first Bengali (Indian language) literary magazine published from the USA. It contains poems, essays, short stories, translations, interviews, opinions, sketches, book reviews, cultural information, scientific arti-

 **The asterisk before a listing indicates that the listing is new in this edition.**

cles, letters to the editor, serialized novels and a children's section. The special slant may be India and/or education." 10% of material aimed at juvenile audience.

**Fiction:** Young reader: animal. Middle readers: history, humorous, problem-solving, math puzzles, travel. Young adult/teens: history, humorous, problem-solving, romance, science fiction, sports, spy/mystery/adventure, math puzzles, travel. Does not want to see: "religious, political, controversial or material without any educational value." Buys 20-40 mss/year. Average word length: 300-1,000. Byline given, "sometimes."

**Nonfiction:** Middle readers: history, how-to, humorous, problem solving, travel. Young adults/teens: history, how-to, humorous, interview/profile, problem solving, travel. Puzzles. Does not want to see: "religious, political, controversial or material without any educational value." Buys 20-40 mss/year. Average word length: 300-1,000. Byline given, "sometimes."

**Poetry:** Reviews 20 line humorous poems that rhyme; maximum of 5 submissions.

**How to Contact/Writers:** Fiction/nonfiction: Send complete ms. SASE (IRC) for answer to query/return of ms. Reports on queries in 2 weeks; mss in 4 weeks. Will consider simultaneous, photocopied and computer printout submissions.

**Illustration:** Buys 4-20 illustrations/year. Prefers to review juvenile education, activities, sports, culture and recreations. Will review ms/illustration packages submitted by authors/artists; ms/illustration packages submitted by authors with illustrations done by separate artists; illustrator's work for possible use with fiction/nonfiction articles and columns by other authors.

**How to Contact/Illustrators:** Ms/illustration packages: Send "complete manuscript with final art." Illustrations only: Send "résumé with copies of previous published work." Reports only if interested.

**Terms/Writer & Illustrators:** Pays on publication. Buys all rights. Usually pays in copies for all circumstances. Sample copy $6. Writer's/illustrator's guidelines free with 1 SAE and 1 first class stamp.

**Tips:** Writers: "Be imaginative, thorough, flexible and educational. Most importantly, be a child." Illustrators: "Be picturesque, eye-catching and true to the occasion or writing."

**\*BOYS' LIFE**, Boy Scouts of America, 1325 W. Walnut Hill La., Box 152079, Irving TX 75015-2079. (214)580-2000. Articles Editor: Jeffrey Csatari. Fiction Editor: William Butterworth. Art Director: Elizabeth Hardaway Morgan. Director of Design: Joseph P. Connolly. Monthly magazine. Estab. 1911. Circ. 1,300,000. *Boys' Life* is "primarily boys 8 to 18 who are members of the Cub Scouts, Boy Scouts or Explorers. A general interest magazine for all boys." 100% of material aimed at juvenile audience.

**Fiction:** Middle readers: animal, contemporary, fantasy, history, humorous, problem-solving, science fiction, sports, spy/mystery/adventure. Does not want to see "talking animals and adult reminiscence." Buys 12 mss/year. Average word length: 500-1,500. Byline given.

**Nonfiction:** Average word length: 300-500. Byline given.

**How to Contact/Writers:** Fiction/nonfiction: Send complete ms/query. SASE (IRC) for answer to query/return of ms. Reports on queries/mss in 2-3 weeks. Will consider photocopied and computer printout submissions.

**Illustration:** Buys 5-7 illustrations/issue; buys 23-50 illustrations/year. Will review ms/illustration packages submitted by authors with illustrations done by separate artists; illustrator's work for possible use with fiction/nonfiction articles and columns by other authors. Works on assignment only.

**How to Contact/Illustrators:** Ms/illustration packages: "Query first." Illustrations only: Send tearsheets. Reports on art samples only if interested. Original artwork returned at job's completion. Buys first rights.

**Tips:** "Study at least a year's issues to better understand type of material published."

**BRILLIANT STAR,** National Spiritual Assembly of the Baha'is of the U.S., 2512 Allegheny Dr., Chattanooga TN 37421. Articles/Fiction Editor: Deborah L. Bley. Art Director: Ms. Pepper Oldziey. Bimonthly magazine. Circ. 2,200. We look for "sensitivity to multi-racial, multi-cultural audience and a commitment to assisting children in understanding the oneness of the human family." 95% of material aimed at juvenile audience.
**Fiction:** Picture material: animal. Young readers, middle readers: animal, fantasy, history, humorous, problem solving, spy/mystery/adventure. Does not want to see material related to traditional Christian holidays or to secular holidays. Nothing that pontificates! Acquires 20 mss/year. Average word length: 750-1,500. Byline given.
**Nonfiction:** Picture material: animal, history, travel. Young readers, middle readers: animal, history, how-to, humorous, interview/profile, problem solving, travel. Does not want to see crafts or activities specific to holidays. Buys 12-15 mss/year. Average word length: 500-1,000. Byline given.
**How to Contact/Writers:** Fiction/nonfiction: Send complete ms. SASE (IRC) for return of ms. Report on mss in 6-10 weeks. Will consider simultaneous, photocopied and computer printout submissions.
**Illustration:** "Illustration assignments made after layout and typesetting done." Will review ms/illustration packages by authors/artists "but must understand that we finalize after layout"; ms/illustration packages submitted by authors with illustrations done by separate artists; illustrators work for possible use with fiction/nonfiction articles. Works on assignment only.
**How to Contact/Illustrators:** Ms/illustration packages: Prefer samples of illustration sent to art director separate from mss. Illustrations only: Résumé, tear sheets, slides, photos. Reports on art samples in 1-2 months. Original artwork returned at job's completion "only if specifically requested by artist."
**Terms/Writers & Illustrators:** Provides 1 complimentary copy of issue in which work appears. Sample copy with 9x12 SAE and 5 oz. worth of postage; writer's/illustrator's guidelines free with business SAE and 2 oz. worth of postage.
**Tips:** Writers: "Have a story to tell! Make sure you have a conflict or problem to be resolved by the characters that gives energy and life to the story. General Editorial office is open to fiction, articles, activities." Illustrators: "Don't be too cute. Get past the one thing you like to draw best and be ready to expand your range. Really look at other illustrators' work for variety and use of space. Art director is open to reviewing general submissions. Need artists who can illustrate diversity of peoples without stereotyping, and in a sensitive way that affirms the beauty of different racial characteristics."

**CALLI'S TALES,** Box 1224, Palmetto FL 34220. (813)722-2202. Articles/Fiction Editor, Art Director: Annice E. Hunt. Quarterly magazine. Circ. 100. Magazine for animal lovers of all ages. 25% of material aimed at juvenile audience.
**Fiction:** Young readers: animal. Does not want to see religious material. Buys 20 mss/year. Average word length: 250-800. Byline given.
**Nonfiction:** Young readers: animal, interview/profile. Does not want to see religious material. Buys 25 mss/year. Average word length: 250-800. Byline given.
**How to Contact/Writers:** Fiction/nonfiction: Send complete ms. SASE (IRC) for answer to query and return of ms. Reports on queries/mss in 9 months. Will consider simultaneous, photocopied and computer printout submissions.
**Illustration:** Buys 4-6 illustrations/issue; buys 30 illustrations/year. Will review an illustrator's work for possible use with fiction/nonfiction articles and columns by other authors.
**How to Contact/Illustrators:** Ms/illustration packages: Send complete ms. Illustrations only: Send tear sheets. Reports on art samples in 9 months.
**Terms/Writers & Illustrators:** Pays on publication. Buys one-time rights. Pays in one free copy of issue. Sample copy $2; writer's/illustrator's guidelines free with SAE and first-class stamps.

**Tips:** "We do not need any more manuscripts until June, 1991. We are overstocked."

**CAREERS,** E.M. Guild, 1001 Avenue of the Americas, New York NY 10018. (212)354-8877. Editor-in-Chief: Mary Dalheim. Senior Editor: Don Rauf. Art Director: Michele Weisman. Magazine published 4 times during school year (Sept., Nov., Jan., March). Circ. 600,000. This is a magazine for high school juniors and seniors, designed to prepare students for their futures. 100% of material aimed at juvenile audience.

**Fiction:** Young adults: contemporary, fantasy, humorous, science fiction, sports, spy/mystery/adventure. Buys 2 mss/year. Average word length: 1,000-1,250. Byline given.

**Nonfiction:** Young adults: how-to, humorous, interview/profile, problem solving. Buys 30-40 mss/year. Average word length: 1,000-1,250. Byline given.

**How to Contact/Writers:** Fiction/nonfiction: Query. SASE (IRC) for answer to query. Reports on queries/mss in 6 weeks. Will consider photocopied, computer printout and electronic submissions via disk or modem.

**Illustration:** Buys 10 illustrations/issue; buys 40 illustrations/year. Will review ms/illustration packages by authors/artists; ms/illustration packages submitted by authors with illustrations done by separate artists; illustrator's work for possible use with fiction/nonfiction articles. Works on assignment "mostly."

**How to Contact/Illustrators:** Ms/illustration packages: Query first. Illustrations only: Send tear sheets, cards. Reports on art samples only if interested. Original artwork returned at job's completion.

**Terms/Writers & Illustrators:** Pays 90 days after publication. Buys first North American serial rights. Pays $250-300 assigned/unsolicited articles. Additional payment for ms/illustration packages "must be negotiated." Pays $500-1,000/color illustration; $300-700 b&w/color (inside) illustration. Sample copy $1 with SAE and $1 postage; writer's guidelines free with SAE and 1 first-class stamp.

**Tips:** "Know the audience of the magazine you would like to contribute to. There is as wide a scope in children's magazines as there is in adult's."

**CHICKADEE,** for Young Children from OWL, Young Naturalist Foundation, 56 The Esplanade, Ste. 306, Toronto Ontario M5E 1A7 Canada. (416)868-6001. Editor-in-Chief: Sylvia Tunston. Art Director: Tim Davin. Publishes 10 times/year, magazine. Circ: 160,000. *Chickadee* is a "hands-on" publication designed to interest 4-9 year olds in the world and environment around them.

**Fiction:** Picture material, young readers: animal, contemporary, history, humorous, sports, spy/mystery/adventure. Does not want to see religious, anthropomorphic animal, romance material. Buys 8 mss/year. Average word length: 200-800. Byline given.

**Nonfiction:** Picture material, young readers: animal, how-to, interview/profile, travel. Does not want to see religious material. Buys 2-5 mss/year. Average word length: 20-200. Byline given.

**How to Contact/Writers:** Fiction/nonfiction: Send complete ms. SAE and $1 money order for answer to query and return of ms. Report on queries/mss in 8 weeks. Will consider simultaneous, photocopied and computer printout submissions.

**Illustration:** Buys 3-5 illustrations/issue; buys 40 illustrations/year. Preferred theme or style: Gentle realism/humor (but not cartoons). Will review ms/illustration packages by authors/artists; ms/illustration packages submitted by authors with illustrations done by separate artists; illustrators work for possible use with fiction/nonfiction articles. Works on assignment only.

**How to Contact/Illustrators:** Ms/illustration packages: Story with sample of art. Illustrations only: Tear sheets. Reports on art samples only if interested.

**Terms/Writers & Illustrators:** Pays on publication. Buys all rights. Pays $25-200 for assigned/unsolicited articles. Additional payment for ms/illustration packages is $25-600. Pays $500 color (cover) illustration, $50-500 b&w (inside), $50-650 color (inside). Sample copy $3.25. Writer's guidelines free.

**Tips:** "Study the magazine carefully before submitting material. 'Read-to-me selection' most open to freelancers. Uses fiction stories. Kids should be main characters and should be treated with respect." (See listing for *Owl*.)

**\*CHILD LIFE**, Children's Better Health Institute, 1100 Waterway Blvd., Indianapolis IN 46206. (317)636-8881. Articles Fiction Editor: Steve Charles. Art Director: Janet Moir. Magazine published 8 times/year. Estab. 1923. Circ. 80,000. "Adventure, humor, fantasy and health-related stories with an imaginative twist are among those stories we seek. We try to open our readers' minds to their own creative potential, and we want our stories and articles to reflect this." 100% of material aimed at juvenile audience.

**Fiction:** Young readers: animal, contemporary, fantasy, history, humorous, problem-solving, science fiction, sports, spy/mystery/adventure. Middle readers: fantasy, history, humorous, science fiction. Buys 30-35 mss/year. Average word length: 1,500. Byline given.

**Nonfiction:** Middle readers: animal, history, how-to, humorous, interview/profile, problem solving, travel. Average word length: 1,200. Byline given.

**Poetry:** Reviews poetry.

**How to Contact/Writers:** Fiction/nonfiction: Send complete ms. Reports on queries/mss in 8-10 weeks. Will consider simultaneous, photocopied and computer printout submissions.

**Illustration:** Buys 8-10 illustrations/issue; buys 65-80 illustrations/year. Preferred theme: "Need realistic styles especially." Will review an illustrator's work for possible use with fiction/nonfiction articles and columns by other authors. Works on assignment only.

**How to Contact/Illustrators:** Illustrations only: Send "résumé, tearsheets, photocopics and/or slides. Samples must be accompanied by SASE for response and/or return of samples." Reports on art samples in 4-6 weeks.

**Terms/Writers & Illustrators:** Editorial: Pays on publication; minimum 8¢/word; buys all rights. Pays 3 weeks prior to publication. Pays $225/color cover; $15-65/b&w inside; $60-125 color inside. Writer's/illustrator's guidelines free with SAE and 1 first class stamp.

**Tips:** Illustrators: "Make sure you can draw children well and draw them accurately as far as age. Be able to illustrate a story situation. I assign poems, fiction stories and factual articles about health subjects and animals. I look for samples that portray a story, that involve children interacting with others in a variety of situations. Most of my assignments are for realistic styles, but I also use humorous, cartoony styles and unusual techniques like cut-paper, collage and woodcut."

**CHILDREN'S DIGEST**, Children's Better Health Institute, Box 567, Indianapolis IN 46206. (317)636-8881. Articles/Fiction Editor: Elizabeth Rinck. Art Director: Lisa Nelson. Magazine published eight times/year. Circ. 125,000. For preteens; approximately 33% of content is health-related.

**Fiction:** Middle readers: animal, contemporary, fantasy, history, humorous, problem solving, science fiction, sports, spy/mystery/adventure. Buys 25 mss/year. Average word length: 500-1,500. Byline given.

*"Picture books" are geared toward the preschool — 8 year old group; "Young readers" to 5-8 year olds; "Middle readers" to 9-11 year olds; and "Young adults" to those 12 and up.*

**Nonfiction:** Middle readers: animal, history, how-to, humorous, problem solving. Buys 16-20 mss/year. Average word length: 500-1,200. Byline given.

**How to Contact/Writers:** Fiction/nonfiction: Send complete ms. SASE (IRC) for return of ms; include Social Security number with submission. Reports on mss in 10 weeks. Will consider photocopied and computer printout submissions.

**Illustration:** Will review an illustrator's work for possible use with fiction/nonfiction articles and columns by other authors. Works on assignment only.

**How to Contact/Illustrators:** Ms/illustration packages: Query first. Illustrations only: Send resume and/or slides or tear sheets to illustrate work. Reports on art samples in 8-10 weeks.

**Terms/Writers & Illustrators:** Pays on acceptance for illustrators, publication for writers. Buys all rights. Pays 8¢/word for accepted articles. Pays $225/color (cover) illustration; $24-100/b&w (inside); $60-125/color (inside). Sample copy 75¢. Writer's/illustrator's guidelines for SAE and 1 first-class stamp. (See listings for *Children's Playmate, Humpty Dumpty's Magazine, Turtle Magazine*.)

**CHILDREN'S PLAYMATE,** Children's Better Health Institute, Box 567, Indianapolis IN 46206. (317)636-8881. Articles/Fiction Editor: Elizabeth Rinck. Art Director: Steve Miller. Magazine published 8 times/year. Circ. 135,000. For children between 6 and 8 years; approximately 33% of content is health-related.

**Fiction:** Young readers: animal, contemporary, fantasy, history, humorous, problem solving, science fiction, sports, spy/mystery/adventure. Buys 25 mss/year. Average word length: 200-700. Byline given.

**Nonfiction:** Young readers: animal, history, how-to, humorous, problem solving. Buys 16-20 mss/year. Average word length: 200-700. Byline given.

**How to Contact/Writers:** Fiction/nonfiction: Send complete ms. SASE (IRC) for return of ms; include Social Security number with submission. Reports on mss in 8-10 weeks. Will consider photocopied and computer printout submissions.

**Illustration:** Will review an illustrator's work for possible use with fiction/nonfiction articles and columns by other authors. Works on assignment only.

**How to Contact/Illustrators:** Ms/illustration packages: Query first. Illustrations only: "Resume and/or slides or tear sheets to illustrate work." Reports on art samples in 8-10 weeks.

**Terms/Writers & Illustrators:** Pays on acceptance for illustrators, publication for writers. Buys all rights. Pays 8¢/word for assigned articles. Pays $225/color (cover) illustration; $25-100/b&w (inside); $60-125/color (inside). Sample copy 75¢. Writer's/illustrator's guidelines for SAE and 1 first-class stamp. (See listings for *Children's Digest, Humpty Dumpty's Magazine, Turtle Magazine*.)

**\*CLASS ACT,** Harvard Publishing Co., 315 Queenston St., Winnipeg, Manitoba R3N OW9 Canada. (204)488-6419. Articles Editor: Guy Rochon. Monthly tabloid. Estab. 1985. Circ. 18,000. "Articles are aimed at a teen market (relationships, how-to's, entertainment, fashion)."

**Fiction:** Young adults/teens: contemporary, fantasy, history, humorous, problem-solving, romance. Buys 10 mss/year. Average word length 800-2,000. Byline given.

**Nonfiction:** Young adults/teens: history, how-to, humorous, interview/profile, problem solving, travel, fashion, new products. Buys 20 mss/year. Average word length: 400-1,000. Byline given.

**How to Contact/Writers:** Fiction/nonfiction: SASE (IRC) for answer to query/return of ms. Reports on queries/mss in 4 weeks. Will consider simultaneous and photocopied submissions.

**Illustration:** Buys 5 illustrations/issue. Prefers "school settings." Will review ms/illustration packages submitted by authors with illustrations done by separate artists.
**How to Contact/Illustrators:** Ms/illustration packages: "Query first." Illustrations only: Send tearsheets. Reports in 4 weeks only if interested. Original art work returned at job's completion.
**Terms/Writers & Illustrators:** Pays on publication. Buys first rights, second serial (reprint rights) and simultaneous rights. Pays 5¢/word assigned/unsolicited articles. Other payment: "Local writers receive merchandise (coupons, film, albums, etc.)." Pays $5-10/b&w cover illustration; $5-10 color cover illustrations. Sample copy $1.50 with SAE. Writer's guidelines free with SAE and 1 first class stamp.

**CLUBHOUSE**, Your Story Hour, Box 15, Berrien Springs MI 49103. (616)471-3701. Articles/Fiction Editor, Art Director: Elaine Trumbo. Bimonthly magazine. Circ. 15,000. 100% of material aimed at juvenile audience.
**Fiction:** Middle readers, young adults: animal, contemporary, history, humorous, problem solving, religious. Does not want to see science fiction/fantasy/Halloween or Santa-oriented fiction. Buys 50 mss/year. Average word length: 800-1,300. Byline given.
**Nonfiction:** Middle readers, young adults: how-to. "We do not use articles except 200-500 word items about good health: anti—drug, tobacco, alcohol; pro—nutrition." Buys 10-12 mss/year. Average word length: 200-400. Byline given.
**How to Contact/Writers:** Fiction/nonfiction: Send complete ms. SASE (IRC) for return of ms. Reports on queries/mss in 6 weeks. Will consider simultaneous, photocopied and computer printout submissions.
**Illustration:** Buys 20-25 illustrations/issue; buys 120+ illustrations/year. Preferred theme or style: "variety." Will review an illustrator's work for possible use with fiction/nonfiction articles and columns by other authors. Works on assignment only.
**How to Contact/Illustrators:** Illustrations only: Send photocopies or prints of work which we can keep on file. Reports on art samples in 6 weeks. Originals usually not returned at job's completion, but they can be returned if desired.
**Terms/Writers & Illustrators:** Pays on acceptance. Buys first North American serial rights. Pays $25-35 for articles. "Writers and artists receive 2 copies free in addition to payment." Pays $30/b&w (cover) illustration; $7.50-25/b&w (inside). Sample copy for business SAE and 3 first-class stamps; writers/illustrator's guidelines free for business SAE and 1 first class stamp.
**Tips:** Writers: "Take children seriously—they're smarter than you think! Respect their sense of dignity, don't talk down to them and don't write stories about 'bad kids.'" Illustrators: "Keep it clean, vigorous, fresh-whatever your style. Send samples we can keep on file. B&w line art is best."

**COBBLESTONE**, The History Magazine for Young People, Cobblestone Publishing, Inc., 30 Grove St., Peterborough NH 03458. (603)924-7209. Articles/Fiction Editor: Carolyn P. Yoder. Art Directors: Jim Fletcher and Marilyn Moran. Monthly magazine. Circ. 45,000. "*Cobblestone* is theme-related. Writers should request editorial guidelines which explain procedure and list upcoming themes. Queries must relate to an upcoming theme. Fiction is not used often, although a good fiction piece offers welcome diversity. It is recommended that writers become familiar with the magazine (sample copies available)." 100% of material aimed at juvenile audience.
**Fiction:** Middle readers, young adults: history. Does not want to see pieces that do not relate to an upcoming theme. Buys 6-10 mss/year. Average word length: 750. Byline given.
**Nonfiction:** Middle readers, young adults: history, interview/profile, travel. Does not want to see material that does not relate to an upcoming theme. Buys 120 mss/year. Average word length: 300-1,000. Byline given.

**How to Contact/Writers:** Fiction/nonfiction: Query with published clips. SASE (IRC) for answer to query and return of ms. Reports on queries in 5-6 months before publication; mss in 2 months before publication. Will consider photocopied, computer printout and electronic submissions via disk or modem.

**Illustration:** Buys 3 illustrations/issue; buys 36 illustrations/year. Preferred theme or style: Material that is simple, clear and accurate but not too juvenile. Sophisticated sources are a must. Will review ms/illustration packages by authors/artists; ms/illustration packages submitted by authors with illustrations done by separate artists; illustrators work for possible use with fiction/nonfiction articles. Works on assignment only.

**How to Contact/Illustrators:** Ms/illustration packages: Illustrations are done by assignment. Roughs required. Illustrations only: Send samples of black and white work. Illustrators should consult issues of *Cobblestone* to familiarize themselves with our needs. Reports on art samples in 1-2 months. Original artwork returned at job's completion.

**Terms/Writers & Illustrators:** Pays on publication. Buys all rights. Pays 10-15¢ word for assigned articles. Pays $10-125/b&w (inside) illustration. Sample copy $3.95 with 7½×10½ SAE and 5 first-class stamps; writer's/illustrator's guidelines free with SAE and 1 first-class stamp.

**Tips:** Writers: "Submit detailed queries which show attention to historical accuracy and which offer interesting and entertaining information. Be true to your own style. Study past issues to know what we look for. All feature articles, recipes, activities, fiction and supplemental nonfiction are freelance contributions." Illustrators: "Submit black and white samples, not too juvenile. Study past issues to know what we look for. The illustration we use is generally for stories, recipes and activities." (See listing for *Faces, The Magazine About People*.)

**\*COCHRAN'S CORNER,** Cochran's Publishing Co., Box 2036, Waldorf MD 20604. (301)843-0485. Articles Editor: Ada Cochran. Fiction Editor/Art Director: Debby Thompkins. Quarterly magazine. Estab. 1985. Circ. 1,000. "Our magazine is open to most kinds of writing that is wholesome and suitable for young children to read. It is a 52 page, 8½×11 devoted to short stories, articles and poems. Our children's corner is reserved for children up to the age of 14." 30% of material aimed at juvenile audience.

**Fiction:** Picture-oriented material: religious. Young readers: animal, fantasy, humorous, problem-solving, religious. Middle readers: religious. Young adults/teens: contemporary, history, religious, romance, science fiction. Does not want to see "anything that contains bad language or violence." Buys 150 mss/year. Average word length: 1,000 words maximum.

**Nonfiction:** Picture-oriented material: religious, travel. Young readers: animal, how-to, problem solving, religious, travel. Middle readers: religious, travel. Young adults/teens: history, humorous, interview/profile, religious, travel. Does not want to see "editorials or politics." Buys 100 mss/year. Average word length: 150. Byline given.

**Poetry:** Reviews 20-line poetry on any subject.

**How to Contact/Writers:** Fiction/nonfiction: Send complete ms. SASE (IRC) for answer to query. Reports on mss in 3 months. Will consider simultaneous or photocopied submissions.

**Terms/Writers:** Sample copy $3 with 6×9 SASE. Writer's guidelines free for SASE.

**Tips:** "Read as much children's writing as possible. Try to have as much contact with children as you can. Stay young/think young."

*Refer to the Business of Children's Writing & Illustrating for up-to-date marketing, tax and legal information.*

**\*CRICKET MAGAZINE**, Carus Corporation, 315 Fifth St., Peru IL 61354. (815)224-6656. Articles/Fiction Editor: Marianne Carus. Art Director: Ron McCutchan. Monthly magazine. Estab. 1973. Circ. 130,000. Children's literary magazine for ages 6-12.
**Fiction:** Picture-oriented material: animal, contemporary, fantasy, history, humorous, problem-solving, science fiction, sports, spy/mystery/adventure. Middle readers: animal, contemporary, fantasy, history, humorous, problem-solving, science fiction, sports, spy/mystery/adventure. Buys 180 mss/year. Average word length: 1,500. Byline given.
**Nonfiction:** Picture-oriented material: animal, history, how-to, humorous, interview/profile, problem solving, travel. Middle readers: animal, history, how-to, humorous, interview/profile, problem solving, travel. Buys 180 mss/year. Average word length: 1,000. Byline given.
**Poetry:** Reviews 1 page maximum length poems.
**How to Contact/Writers:** Send complete ms. SASE (IRC) necessary for return of ms; include Social Security number with submission. Reports on mss in 3 months. Will consider simultaneous, photocopied and computer printout submissions.
**Illustration:** Buys 50 (18 separate commissions)/issue; 600 illustrations/year. Preferred theme or style: "strong realism; strong people, esp. kids; good action illustration; no cartoons." Will review ms/illustration packages submitted by authors/artists "but reserve option to re-illustrate." Will review an illustrator's work for possible use with fiction/nonfiction articles and columns by other authors.
**How to Contact/Illustrators:** Ms/illustrations packages: complete manuscript with sample and query. Illustrations only: tearsheets or good quality photocopies. Reports on art samples in 8 weeks. Original art work returned at job's completion.
**Terms/Writers & Illustrators:** Pays on publication. Buys first North American serial rights. Pays up to 25¢/word for unsolicited articles; up to $3/line for poetry. Pays $500/color cover; $75-150/b&w inside. Writer's/illustrator's guidelines free with SAE and 1 first class stamp.
**Tips:** "Nonfiction, historical articles and how-to's" most open to freelancers.

**CRUSADER**, Calvinist Cadet Corps, Box 7259, Grand Rapids MI 49510. (616)241-5616. Editor: G. Richard Broene. Art Director: Robert DeJonge. Magazine published 7 times/year. Circ. 12,000. Our magazine is for members of the Calvinist Cadet Corps—boys aged 9-14. Our purpose is to show how God is at work in their lives and in the world around them. 100% of material aimed at juvenile audience.
**Fiction:** Middle readers: contemporary, humorous, problem solving, religious, sports. Does not want to see fantasy, science fiction. Buys 12 mss/year. Average word length: 800-1,500.
**Nonfiction:** Middle readers: animal, how-to, humorous, interview/profile, problem solving, religious. Buys 6 mss/year. Average word length: 400-900.
**How to Contact/Writers:** Fiction/nonfiction: Send complete ms. SASE (IRC) for answer to query/return of ms. Reports on queries in 1-3 weeks; mss in 1-5 weeks. Will consider simultaneous, photocopied and computer printout submissions.
**Illustration:** Buys 1 illustration/issue; buys 6 illustrations/year. Works on assignment only.
**Terms/Writers & Illustrators:** Pays on acceptance. Buys first rights; one-time rights; second serial (reprint rights). Pays 4-5¢/word for assigned articles; 2-5¢/word for unsolicited articles. Sample copy free with 9 × 12 SAE and 3 first-class stamps.
**Tips:** Publication is most open to fiction: write for a list of themes (available yearly in January).

**DAY CARE AND EARLY EDUCATION**, Human Sciences Press, 233 Spring St., New York NY 10013. (212)620-8000. Articles/Fiction Editor: Randa Nachbar. Art Director: Bill Jobson. Quarterly magazine. Circ. 2,500. Magazine uses material "involving children from birth to age 7." 5% of material aimed at juvenile audience.

**Fiction:** Picture material, young readers: contemporary, fantasy, humorous, problem solving. Average word length: 1,000-3,000. Byline given.

**Nonfiction:** Picture material, young readers: animal, how-to, humorous, problem solving. Average word length: 1,000-3,000. Byline given.

**How to Contact/Writers:** Fiction/nonfiction: Send complete ms. SASE (IRC) for answer to query and return of ms. Reports on queries in 1 month; mss in 2-3 months. Will consider photocopied submissions.

**Illustration:** Will review ms/illustration packages by authors/artists; ms/illustration packages submitted by authors with illustrations done by separate artists; illustrator's work for possible use with fiction/nonfiction articles.

**How to Contact/Illustrators:** Ms/illustration packages: Send complete ms with final art. Reports on art samples only if interested. Original artwork returned at job's completion.

**Terms/Writers & Illustrators:** Pays in 2 copies. Free sample copy; free writer's guidelines.

**DISCOVERIES,** Children's Ministries, 6401 The Paseo, Kansas City MO 64131. (816)333-7000. Editor: Molly Mitchell. Executive Editor: Robert D. Troutman. Weekly tabloid. *Discoveries* is a leisure reading piece for third through sixth graders. It is published weekly by the Department of Children's Ministries of the Church of the Nazarene. "The major purposes of *Discoveries* are to: provide a leisure reading piece which will build Christian behavior and values; provide reinforcement for Biblical concepts taught in the Sunday School curriculum. The focus of the reinforcement will be life-related, with some historical appreciation. *Discoveries'* target audience is children ages 8-12 in grades three through six. The readability goal is fourth to fifth grade." 100% of material aimed at juvenile audience.

**Fiction:** "Fiction—stories should vividly portray definite Christian emphasis or character-building values, without being preachy. The setting, plot and action should be realistic." Average word length: 400-800. Byline given.

**How to Contact/Writers:** Fiction: Send complete ms. SASE (IRC) for return of ms. Report on mss in 4-6 weeks.

**Illustration:** Preferred theme or style: Cartoon—humor should be directed to children and involve children. It should not simply be child-related from an adult viewpoint. Some full color story illustrations are assigned. Samples of art may be sent for review.

**Terms/Writers & Illustrators:** Pays on acceptance. Buys first rights; second serial (reprint rights). Pays 3.5¢/word (first rights). Contributor receives complimentary copy of publication. Writer's guidelines free with #10 SAE.

**Tips:** "*Discoveries* is committed to reinforcement of the Biblical concepts taught in the Sunday School curriculum. Because of this, the themes needed are mainly as follows: faith in God, obedience to God, putting God first, choosing to please God, accepting Jesus as Savior, finding God's will, choosing to do right, trusting God in hard times, prayer; trusting God to answer, Importance of Bible memorization, appreciation of Bible as God's Word to man, Christians working together, showing kindness to others, witnessing." (See listing for *Together Time*.)

**DOLPHIN LOG,** The Cousteau Society, 8440 Santa Monica Blvd., Los Angeles CA 90069. (213)656-4422. Articles Editor: Pamela Stacey. Bimonthly magazine. Circ. 90,000. Subject matter encompasses all areas of science, history and the arts which can be related to our global water system. The philosophy of the magazine is to delight, instruct and instill an environmental ethic and understanding of the interconnectedness of living organisms, including people. Of special interest are articles on ocean- or water-related themes which develop reading and comprehension skills. 100% of material aimed at juvenile audience.

**Nonfiction:** Picture material, middle readers: animal, environmental, ocean. Does not want to see talking animals. Buys 15 mss/year. Average word length: 500-1,200. Byline given.

**How to Contact/Writers:** Nonfiction: Query. SASE (IRC) for answer to query; include Social Security number with submission. Reports on queries in 4 weeks; mss in 8 weeks. Will consider photocopied, computer printout and electronic IBM-PC Wordstar compatible submissions via disk or modem with manuscript.

**Illustration:** Buys 1 illustration/issue; buys 6 illustrations/year. Preferred theme or style: Biological illustration. Will review ms/illustration packages by authors/artists; ms/illustration packages submitted by authors with illustrations done by separate artists; illustrator's work for possible use with nonfiction articles.

**How to Contact/Illustrators:** Ms/illustration packages: No original artwork, copies only. Illustrations only: Send tear sheets, slides. Reports on art samples in 8 weeks only if interested. Original artwork returned at job's completion.

**Terms/Writers & Illustrators:** Pays on publication. Buys first North American serial rights; "translation rights." Pays $25-150 for assigned/unsolicited articles. Additional payment for ms/illustration packages is in the $25-150 range. Pays $25-150/b&w illustration; $25-200/color (cover); $25-200/color (inside). Sample copy $2 with SAE and 2 first-class stamps. Writer's/illustrator's guidelines free with SAE and 1 first-class stamp.

**Tips:** Writers: "Write simply and clearly and don't anthropomorphize." Illustrators: "Be scientifically accurate and don't anthropomorphize. Some background in biology is helpful, as our needs range from simple line drawings to scientific illustrations which must be researched for biological and technical accuracy."

**EQUILIBRIUM[10]**, Everyone's Entertainment, Eagle Publishing Productions, Box 162, Golden CO 80401. President: Gary Eagle. Quarterly magazine. Circ. 10,000. Material on or relating to balance is best. Material on antonyms (opposites) is even better but not required. 10% of material aimed at juvenile audience.

**Fiction:** Young readers, young adults: animal, contemporary, fantasy, history, humorous, problem solving, religious, romance, science fiction, sports, spy/mystery/adventure. Buys 40 mss/year. Average word length: 500-2,000. Byline given sometimes.

**Nonfiction:** Middle readers, young adults: animal, history, how-to, humorous, interview/profile, problem solving, religious, travel. Buys 60 mss/year. Average word length: 500-2,000. Byline given sometimes.

**How to Contact/Writers:** Fiction/nonfiction: Query first. SASE (IRC) for answer to query. Reports on queries in 8 weeks; mss in 16 weeks. Will consider simultaneous, photocopied, computer printout and electronic submissions via disk (3.5 inch) or modem.

**Illustration:** Buys 10 illustrations/issue; buys 150 illustrations/year. Will review ms/illustration packages by authors/artists; ms/illustration packages submitted by authors with illustrations done by separate artists for a fee; illustrator's work for possible use with fiction/nonfiction articles. Works on assignment only.

**How to Contact/Illustrators:** Ms/illustration packages: Query first, (quick summary of ms) and final art included, captions too. Illustrations only: Send tear sheets, photographed, copied pieces. Reports on art samples in 3 months. Original artwork returned at job's completion.

**Terms/Writers & Illustrators:** Pays on publication. Buys second serial (reprint rights). Pays $50-100 for assigned/unsolicited articles (shorts). "Contributor copies are free with signed contract." Additional payment for ms/illustration packages within the $50-100 range; "photos help pay range." Pays $50-200/b&w (cover) illustration; $100-200/color (cover); $25/b&w (inside); $50/color (inside). Sample copy free with 9×14 SAE and 5 first-class stamps. Writer's/illustrator's guidelines free with #10 SAE and 2 first-class stamps. "For serious inquiries, we offer a special package as an investment on your behalf. Besides author's guidelines, you'll receive: *Equilibrium* [10] Magazine; Generic

Word Search; the Pyramid Edition (mini-newspaper); variety of pamphlets; business opportunities at our company; and any other future publications for $15. We will critique your work and query for $5."
**Tips:** Writers: "Be specific in your query as to why readers would enjoy your material. If on balance, state so. If on antonyms, state them. Shorter the better. Enter the Cheapstakes Sweepstakes Contest. Query with SASE."

**EXPLORING,** Boy Scouts of America, Box 152079, 1325 Walnut Hill Ln., Irving TX 75015-2079. (214)580-2365. Executive Editor: Scott Daniels. Art Director: Joe Connally. Magazine published "4 times a year—not quarterly." *Exploring* is a 12 page, 4-color magazine published for members of the Boy Scouts of America's Exploring program who are young men and women between the ages of 14-21. Interests include careers, computers, camping, hiking, canoeing. 100% of material aimed at juvenile audience.
**Nonfiction:** Young adults: interview/profile, problem solving, travel. Buys 12 mss/year. Average word length: 600-1,200. Byline given.
**How to Contact/Writers:** Nonfiction: Query with published clips. SASE (IRC) for answer to query/return of ms. Reports on queries/mss in 1 week. Will consider computer printout submissions.
**Illustration:** Buys 3 illustrations/issue; buys 12 illustrations/year. Will review an illustrator's work for possible use with fiction/nonfiction articles and columns by other authors. Works on assignment only.
**How to Contact/Illustrators:** Reports on art samples in 2 weeks. Original art work returned at job's completion.
**Terms/Writers & Illustrators:** Pays on acceptance. Buys first North American serial rights. Pays $300-500 for assigned/unsolicited articles. Pays $500-800/b&w (cover) illustration; $800-1,000/color (cover); $250-500/b&w (inside); $500-800/color (inside). Sample copy with 8½ × 11 SAE and 5 first-class stamps. Free writer's/illustrator's guidelines.
**Tips:** "Read previous issues of the magazine." Looks for "short, crisp career profiles of 1,000 words with plenty of information to break out into graphics." (See listing for *Boy's Life*.)

**FACES,** The Magazine About People, Cobblestone Publishing, Inc., 30 Grove St., Peterborough NH 03458. (603)924-7209. Articles/Fiction Editor: Carolyn P. Yoder. Art Director: Coni Porter. Magazine published 10 times/year (Sept.-June). Circ. 13,500. "Although *Faces* operates on a by-assignment basis, we welcome ideas/suggestions in outline form. All manuscripts are reviewed by the American Museum of Natural History in New York before being accepted. *Faces* is a theme-related magazine; writers should send for theme list before submitting ideas/queries." 100% of material aimed at juvenile audience.
**Fiction:** Middle readers, young adults: contemporary, history, religious, anthropology. Does not want to see material that does not relate to a specific upcoming theme. Buys 10 mss/year. Average word length: 750. Byline given.
**Nonfiction:** Middle readers, young adults: history, interview/profile, religious, travel, anthropology. Does not want to see material not related to a specific upcoming theme. Buys 70 mss/year. Average word length: 300-1,000. Byline given.
**How to Contact/Writers:** Fiction/nonfiction: Query with published clips. SASE (IRC) for answer to query and return of ms. Reports on queries in 5-6 months before publication; mss 2 months before publication. Will consider photocopied, computer printout and electronic submissions via disk or modem.
**Illustration:** Buys 3 illustrations/issue; buys 30 illustrations/year. Preferred theme or style: Material that is meticulously researched (most articles are written by professional anthropologists); simple, direct style preferred, but not too juvenile. Will review ms/illustration packages by authors/artists; ms/illustration packages submitted by authors

with illustrations done by separate **artists;** illustrator's work for possible use with fiction/ nonfiction articles. Works on assignment only.

**How to Contact/Illustrators:** Ms/illustration packages: Illustration is done by assignment. Roughs required. Illustrations only: Send samples of black and white work. Illustrators should consult issues of *Faces* to familiarize themselves with our needs. Reports on art samples in 1-2 months. Original artwork returned at job's completion.

**Terms/Writers & Illustrators:** Pays on publication. Buys all rights. Pays 10-15¢/word for assigned articles. Pays $10-125/b&w (inside) illustration. Sample copy $3.95 with 7½ × 10½ SAE and 5 first-class stamps. Writer's/illustrator's guidelines free with SAE and 1 first-class stamp.

**Tips:** "Writers are encouraged to study past issues of the magazine to become familiar with our style and content. Writers with anthropological and/or travel experience are particularly encouraged; *Faces* is about world cultures. All feature articles, recipes and activities are freelance contributions." Illustrators: "Submit black and white samples, not too juvenile. Study past issues to know what we look for. The illustration we use is generally for retold legends, recipes and activities." (See listing for *Cobblestone, The History Magazine for Young People.*)

**FRIEND** (formerly *Primary Friend*), Wesleyan Publishing House, 6060 Castleway W. Dr., Box 50434, Indianapolis IN 46250. (317)842-0444, ext. 196. Articles/Fiction Editor/Art Director: Kathy Nelson. Quarterly magazine. Circ. 31,000. "*Friend* is a Sunday School take-home paper for children ages 6-8 years old. All contributors need to keep in mind the ages of the children this publication is for." 100% of material aimed at juvenile audience.

**Fiction:** Young readers: animal, contemporary, history, humorous, problem solving, sports, spy/mystery/adventure. Does not want to see animals praying, romance, science fiction, fantasy. Buys 4 mss/year. Average word length: 450-600. Byline given.

**Nonfiction:** Young readers: animal, history, humorous, problem solving, religious, travel. Does not want to see animals praying, science fiction, fantasy. Buys 4 mss/year. Average word length: 450-600. Byline given.

**How to Contact/Writers:** Fiction/nonfiction: Send complete ms. SASE (IRC) for answer to query and return of ms; include Social Security number with submission. Report on mss in 1-2 months. Will consider computer printout submissions.

**Illustration:** Will review ms/illustration packages by authors/artists; ms/illustration packages submitted by authors with illustrations done by separate artists; illustrators work for possible use with fiction/nonfiction articles.

**How to Contact/Illustrators:** Ms/illustration packages: Send complete ms and final art. Illustrations only: Send color slides. Reports on art samples in 1-2 months.

**Terms/Writers & Illustrators:** Pays on publication. Buys first rights. Publication not copyrighted. Sample copy free with #10 SAE and 1 first-class stamp. Writer's/illustrator's guidelines free with #10 SAE and 1 first-class stamp.

**Tips:** "The following are turn-offs: a letter of recommendation from a teacher, a letter of recommendation from a pastor, tear sheets. The ability of the writer will be apparent. A résumé might be a way for the editor to become acquainted with the writer without the use of a letter of recommendation." Advice to new writers: "Be yourself. Don't copy someone else's writing technique. Use a technique that is you—not your teacher's or your friend's. Remember your childhood and how it was for you to be a child. Have the children in your stories act in a developmentally appropriate manner." Advice to new artists: "Use bright, clear colors which captivate the action and attract reader interest. Draw children (not little adults)."

**THE FRIEND MAGAZINE,** The Church of Jesus Christ of Latter-day Saints, 50 E. North Temple, Salt Lake City UT 84150. (801)240-2210. Managing Editor: Vivian Paulsen. Art Director: Dick Brown. Monthly magazine. Circ. 225,000. Magazine for 3-11 year olds. 100% of material aimed at juvenile audience.

**Fiction:** Uses history, humorous, religious, ethnic, mainstream, nature, adventure pieces. Does not want to see controversial issues, political, horror, fantasy. Buys 200 mss/year. Average word length: 400-1,000. Byline given.

**Nonfiction:** Uses animal, how-to, religious. Does not want to see controversial issues, political, horror, fantasy. Buys 200 mss/year. Average word length: 400-1,000. Byline given.

**How to Contact/Writers:** Fiction/nonfiction: Send complete ms. Reports on mss in 2 months. Will consider computer printout submissions.

**Terms/Writers & Illustrators:** Pays on acceptance. Buys all rights. Pays 8-11¢/word for unsolicited articles. Free sample copy with 9×11 envelope and 85¢ postage. Free writer's guidelines.

**Tips:** "The *Friend* is published by the Church of Jesus Christ of Latter-day Saints for boys and girls up to twelve years of age. All submissions are carefully read by the *Friend* staff, and those not accepted are returned within two months when a self-addressed stamped envelope is enclosed. Submit seasonal material at least eight months in advance. Query letters are not encouraged. Authors may request rights to have their work reprinted after their manuscript is published."

**\*GROUP,** Thom Schultz Publications, Box 481, Loveland CO 80537. (303)669-3836. Articles Editor: Joani Schultz. "We are a religious publication for youth ministries and their teachers. Our readers are from the junior high age and up." 50% of publication aimed at juveniles.

**Fiction/Nonfiction:** Young adults: religious.

**How to Contact/Writers:** Fiction/nonfiction: query, query with published clips. SASE for answer to query/return of ms. Will consider simultaneous, photocopied, computer printout and electronic submissions.

**Illustration:** Will review ms/illustration packages by authors/artists.

**How to Contact/Illustrators:** Ms/illustration packages: query first with SASE.

**Terms/Writers & Illustrators:** Pays on acceptance. Buys first North American serial rights or one-time rights. Pays $20-200/assigned or unsolicited article.

**\*GUIDE MAGAZINE,** Review and Herald Publishing Association, 55 West Oak Ridge Dr., Hagerstown MD 21740. (301)791-7000. Articles Editor: Jeannette Johnson. Art Director: Stephen Hall. Weekly magazine. Estab. 1953. Circ. 42,000. "Ours is a weekly Christian journal written for 10- to 14-year-olds, presenting true stories relevant to the needs of today's young person, emphasizing positive aspects of Christian living. 100% of material aimed at juvenile audience."

**Fiction:** Young adults: Animal, contemporary, history, humorous, problem-solving, religious, character-building. "We like 'true-to-life,' that is, based on true happenings."

**Nonfiction:** Young adults: animal, history, how-to, humorous, interview/profile, problem solving, religious, character-building. Does not want to see violence, hunting nonfiction. Buys 300+ mss/year. Average word length: 500-600 minimum, 1,600-1,800 maximum. Byline given.

**How to Contact/Writers:** Nonfiction: Send complete ms. SASE (IRC) for answer to query or return of ms; include Social Security number with submission. Reports in 1-2 weeks. Will consider simultaneous, photocopied, computer printout and electronic submissions via disk or modem.

**Illustration:** Buys 4-6 illustrations/issue: buys 350+ illustrations/year. Works on assignment only.

**How to Contact/Illustrators:** Ms/illustration packages: "art is by assignment only. Glad to look at portfolios." Artists interested in illustrations only: "Send tear sheets and slides." Original artwork returned at job's completion.

**Terms/Writers and Illustrators:** Pays on acceptance. Buys first North American serial rights; first rights; one-time rights; second serial (reprint rights) simultaneous rights. Pays 4¢/word/assigned articles; 3-4¢/word/unsolicited articles. "Writer receives several complimentary copies of issue in which work appears." Pays $150-250/b&w (cover) illustration; $175-300/color (cover); $125-175/b&w (inside); 150-175/color (inside). Sample copy free with 5×9 SAE and 2 first-class stamps; writer's/illustrator's guidelines for SASE.

**Tips:** "Study our magazine carefully—get a feel for style and content."

*HiCall **staff artist Jeffrey Jansen, Springfield, Missouri, was assigned to do this acrylic cover piece which Director of Publications William Eastlake says "conveys a wholesomeness that appeals to a Christian high school-age audience."***

© Gospel Publishing House 1989

**\*HICALL,** Gospel Publishing House, 1445 Boonville Ave., Springfield MO 65802-1894. (417)862-2781, ext. 4349. Articles/Fiction Editor, Art Director: Deanna Harris. Quarterly newsletter (Sunday school take-home paper). Estab. 1920. Circ. 80,000. "Slant articles and art style toward the 15-to 17-year old teen. We are a Christian publication, so all articles should focus on the Christian's responses to life. Fiction should be realistic, not syrupy nor too graphic. Fiction should have a Christian slant also." 100% of material aimed at juvenile audience.

**Fiction:** Young adults/teens: contemporary, fantasy, history, humorous, problem-solving, religious, romance. Buys 100 mss/year. Average word length 1,000-1,500. Byline given.

**Nonfiction:** Young adults/teens: animal, history, humorous, problem solving, religious. Buys 25 mss/year. Average word length: 1,000. Byline given.

**Poetry:** Reviews 40-line poetry.

**How to Contact/Writers:** Fiction/nonfiction: Send complete ms. Do *not* send query letters. SASE (IRC) for return of ms; include Social Security number with submission. Reports on mss in 4-6 weeks. Will consider simultaneous, photocopied and computer printout submissions.

**Illustration:** Buys 10-30 illustrations/year. "Freelance art used only when in-house art department has a work overload." Prefers to review "realistic, cartoon, youth-oriented styles." Will review an illustrator's work for possible use with fiction/nonfiction articles and columns by other authors. Works on assignment only. "Any art sent will be referred to the art department. Art department will assign freelance art."

**How to Contact/Illustrators:** Illustrations only: Send "tearsheets, slides, photos. Résumé helpful." Reports in 4-6 weeks.

**Terms/Writers & Illustrators:** Pays on acceptance. Buys first North American serial rights, first rights, one-time rights, second serial (reprint rights), simultaneous rights. Pays 4¢/word/assigned articles; 3-4¢/word unsolicited articles. Pays $25-35/b&w cover illustration; $30-35 color cover illustration; $25/b&w inside illustration; $30 color inside illustration. Sample copy free with 6×9 SASE. Writer's guidelines free with SASE.

**HIGH ADVENTURE,** Assemblies of God, 1445 Boonville Ave., Springfield MO 65802. (417)862-2781, Ext. 4181. Articles Editor: Ken Hunt. Quarterly magazine. Circ. 86,000. Magazine is designed to provide boys with worthwhile, enjoyable, leisure reading; to challenge them in narrative form to higher ideals and greater spiritual dedication; and to perpetuate the spirit of Royal Rangers through stories, ideas and illustrations. 75% of material aimed at juvenile audience.

**Fiction:** Buys 100 mss/year. Average word length: 1,200. Byline given.

**Nonfiction:** Articles: Christian living, devotional, Holy Spirit, salvation, self-help; biography; missionary stories; news items; testimonies.

**How to Contact/Writers:** Fiction/nonfiction: Send complete ms. SASE (IRC) for return of ms; include Social Security number with submission. Reports on queries in 6-8 weeks. Will consider simultaneous and photocopied submissions. Will review ms/illustration packages by authors/artists; ms/illustration packages submitted by authors with illustrations done by separate artists; illustrator's work for possible use with fiction/nonfiction articles.

**How to Contact/Illustrators:** Ms/illustration packages: Send complete ms with final art. Illustrations only: Most of our artwork is done inside building.

**Terms/Writers & Illustrators:** Pays on acceptance. Buys first rights. Pays 2-3¢/word for unsolicited articles. Sample copy free with 8½×11 SASE. Free writer's/illustrator's guidelines.

**HIGHLIGHTS FOR CHILDREN,** 803 Church St., Honesdale PA 18431. (717)253-1080. Articles/Fiction Editor: Leah White. Art Director: Rosanne Guararra. Monthly (July-August issue combined) magazine. Circ. 2.5 million. "Our motto is 'Fun With a Purpose.' We are looking for quality fiction and nonfiction that appeals to children, will encourage them to read, and reinforces positive values." All art is done on assignment. 100% of material aimed at juvenile audience.

**Fiction:** Picture-oriented material: animal, contemporary, fantasy, history, humorous, problem solving. Young readers, middle readers: animal, contemporary, fantasy, history, humorous, problem solving, science fiction, sports, mystery/adventure. Does not want to see: war, crime, violence. Buys 150+ mss/year. Average word length: 600-900. Byline given.

**Nonfiction:** Picture-oriented material: animal, history, how-to, humorous, problem solving. Young readers, middle readers: animal, history, how-to, humorous, interview/profile, problem solving, foreign, science, nature, arts, sports. Does not want to see: trendy topics, fads, personalities who would not be good role models for children, guns, war, crime, violence. Buys 75+ mss/year. Average word length: 900. Byline given.

**How to Contact/Writers:** Fiction: Send complete ms. Nonfiction: Query. SASE (IRC) for return of ms; include Social Security number with submission. Reports on queries in 1-3 weeks; mss in 4-8 weeks. Will consider photocopied and computer printout submissions (good quality—would rather not see dot matrix).

**Illustration:** Preferred theme or style: Realistic, some stylization, cartoon style acceptable. Works on assignment only.

**How to Contact/Illustrators:** Ms/illustration packages: Art is done on assignment only. Illustrations only: Photocopies, tear sheets, or slides. Résumé optional. Reports on art samples in 4-6 weeks.

**Terms/Writers & Illustrators:** Pays on acceptance. Buys all rights. Pays 14¢/word for unsolicited articles. Pays $400-$550 color (cover) illustration; $200-$350 color (inside) illustration. Writer's/illustrator's guidelines for 9x12 SAE and $1.05 postage.

**Tips:** Writers: "Study the market. Analyze several issues of the magazines you want to write for. Send for writer's guidelines. Send in professional-looking work." Illustrators: "Fresh, imaginative work presented in a professional portfolio encouraged. Flexibility in working relationships a plus. Illustrators in presenting their work need not confine themselves to just children's illustrations as long as work can translate to our needs. We also use animal illustrations, real and imaginary. We need party plans, crafts and puzzles—any activity that will stimulate children mentally and creatively. Some cover subjects from past and upcoming issues: picnic scene, kite flying, building a snowman, trick or treating, children blowing bubbles, clowns at a circus, carnival scene, sledding downhill, cookie baking, playing in leaves, tree house, St. Bernard puppies, beach sandcastle, elephants at zoo, magic show, horseback riding, winter feeding birds, library scenes, playing in attic, dinosaurs, ocean fishing, vegetable garden, bathing dog, mice in pumpkin house, ice skating, art class, city scene, bears camping, baseball game, at the beach. Additional seasonal themes such as Thanksgiving plays, Valentine parties, 4th of July outings, fall foliage, skiing holidays. These can be either realistic or imaginary using animals, elves, etc."

**HOB-NOB**, 994 Nissley Rd., Lancaster PA 17601. (717)898-7807. Articles/Fiction/Poetry Editor, Art Director: M. K. Henderson. Semiannual magazine. Circ. 350. *Hob-Nob* began as a "family" publication and prefers to avoid any material that could or should not be read by younger readers. Occasional stories by or for children/teenagers are used, depending on submissions. 20% of prose in current issue aimed at juvenile audience.

**Fiction:** Young readers: animal, humorous. Middle readers: animal, contemporary, fantasy, humorous. Young adults: contemporary, fantasy, humorous, problem solving, religious, romance, science fiction, sports, spy/mystery/adventure. Does not want to see religious proselytizing material geared to specific denominations or categories of denominations (i.e., "fundamentalist"); "clean" only, no bathroom language. Buys 60 mss/year, (all age levels—7 juveniles in current issue). Average word length: 2,000. Byline given.

**Nonfiction:** Young readers: animal, humorous. Middle readers: humorous, interview/profile. Young adults: humorous, interview/profile, problem solving. Buys 10 mss/year, (all ages); juvenile—none in current issue. Average word length: 1,000. Byline given.

**How to Contact/Writers:** Fiction/nonfiction: Send complete ms. SASE (IRC) for answer to query/return of ms. Reports on queries/mss in 2 months or less. Will consider photocopied and computer printout submissions.

**Illustration:** "I don't have space for large illustrations so I use cuts, suitable drawings from miscellaneous small ones sent by certain readers." Preferred theme or style: black and white only, no intermediate values. Will review ms/illustration packages submitted by authors/artists. Small picture(s) appropriate to a submitted ms.

**How to Contact/Illustrators:** Ms/illustration packages: Send complete ms and final b&w drawing, small size (or I'll reduce it). Reports on art samples in 2 months or less. Original artwork returned at job's completion if requested and SASE supplied.

**Terms/Writers & Illustrators:** Acquires first North American serial rights. Pays in contributor copies. Sample copy for $3. Writer's guidelines free or sent with sample if requested.

**Tips:** Will consider short poetry (up to 16 lines) by and for juveniles. "Write what children will enjoy—test out on your own children if possible." Looks for: "shorter fiction, especially humor or whimsy. First time contributors may submit only in January and February. (Established contributors may submit September through February only)." Publication most open to "cartoons." Current minimum of two years before new contributors' work can appear.

**\*HOBO STEW REVIEW,** 2 Eliot St. #1, Somerville MA 02143. (617)628-4032. Editor: Hobo Stew. Quarterly magazine. Estab. 1984. Circ. 40. "*HSR* supports that once you are comfortable with your emotional self, you just might be an honest person. Writing is a honest craft: invoke and emote." 25% of material aimed at juvenile audience.

**Fiction:** Picture-oriented material: contemporary, fantasy, history, humorous, science fiction, spy/mystery/adventure. Young readers: contemporary, fantasy, history, humorous, science fiction, spy/mystery/adventure. Middle readers: contemporary, fantasy, history, humorous, science fiction, spy/mystery/adventure. Young adult/teens: contemporary, fantasy, history, humorous, science fiction, spy/mystery/adventure. Does not want to see: "surprise ending, dirges, hateful material." Buys 8-12 mss/year. Average word length: 2,000. Byline given.

**Nonfiction:** Picture-oriented material: animal, history, how-to, humorous, interview/profile. Young readers: animal, history, how-to, humorous, interview/profile. Middle readers: animal, history, how-to, humorous, interview/profile. Young adult/teens: animal, history, how-to, humorous, interview/profile. Does not want to see: self-aggrandizing sermons. Buys 5-10 mss/year. Average word length: 2,000. Byline given.

**Poetry:** Reviews all kinds of poetry; maximum of 5 submissions.

**How to Contact/Writers:** Fiction/nonfiction: Send complete ms. SASE (IRC) for answer to query/return of ms. Reports on queries in 2 weeks; mss in 2-4 weeks. Will consider photocopied and computer printout submissions (no dot matrix; prefer near or at letter quality).

**Illustration:** Buys 2-4 illustrations/issue; buys 8-16 illustrations/year. Prefers to review "black ink on 8½×11 paper, leaving a good border, with humor and compassion in mind." Will review ms/illustration packages submitted by authors/artists; ms/illustration packages submitted by authors with illustrations done by separate artists; illustrator's work for possible use with fiction/nonfiction articles and columns by other authors.

**How to Contact/Illustrators:** Ms/illustration packages: "Send complete ms, SASE *and* complete illustrations." Illustrations only: "Send a variety of drawings ready for reproduction. Inquire about other needs if desired; or suggest your approach, ideas of what you'd like to draw." Reports back in 2-4 weeks.

**Terms/Writers & Illustrators:** Buys one-time rights. "Pay is always, and only, one copy. There is no cash payment." Writer's/illustrator's guidelines free with SASE.

**Tips:** Writers: "Don't mistake simplicity for shallowness. Don't patronize your reader. Be willing to rewrite, to act on an editor's suggestions and engage others in your craft. Keep a regard for communicating, speaking *and* listening—soundly written, your piece will find a home. But it takes a lot of work to make that home comfortable." Illustrators: "Don't muddy your illustration with filler; depict your theme and portray it honestly."

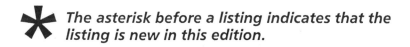

**\*** *The asterisk before a listing indicates that the listing is new in this edition.*

**HUMPTY DUMPTY'S MAGAZINE**, Children's Better Health Institute (div. Benjamin Franklin Literary & Medical Soc.), 1100 Waterway Blvd., Box 567, Indianapolis IN 46206. (317)636-8881. Articles/Fiction Editor: Christine French Clark. Art Director: Larry Simmons. Magazine published 8 times/year — Jan/Feb; Mar/April; May/June; July/Aug;Sept., Oct., Nov., Dec. *HDM* is edited for kindergarten children, approximately ages 4-6. It includes fiction (easy-to-reads; read alouds; rhyming stories; rebus stories), nonfiction articles (some with photo illustrations), poems, crafts, recipes and puzzles. Much of the content encourages development of better health habits. "All but 2 pages aimed at the juvenile market. The remainder may be seasonal and/or more general."

**Fiction:** Picture material: animal, contemporary, fantasy, humorous, sports, health-related. Young readers: animal, contemporary, fantasy, humorous, science fiction, sports, spy/mystery/adventure, health-related. Does not want to see bunny-rabbits-with-carrot-pies stories! Also, talking inanimate objects are very difficult to do well. Beginners (and maybe everyone) should avoid these. Buys 35-50 mss/year. Maximum word length: 700. Byline given.

**Nonfiction:** Picture material, young readers: animal, how-to, humorous, interview/profile, health-related. Does not want to see long, boring, encyclopedia rehashes. "We're open to almost any subject (although most of our nonfiction has a health angle), but it must be presented creatively. Don't just string together some facts." Buys 6-10 mss/year. Average word length: 700. Byline given.

**How to Contact/Writers:** Send complete ms. Nonfiction: Send complete ms with bibliography if applicable. SASE (IRC) for return of ms; include Social Security number with submission. "No queries, please!" Reports on mss in 8-10 weeks. Will consider photocopied and computer printout (letter quality) submissions.

**Illustration:** Buys 13-16 illustrations/issue; buys 90-120 illustrations/year. Preferred theme or style: Realistic or cartoon. Will review ms/illustration packages by authors/artists; ms/illustration packages submitted by authors with illustrations done by separate artists; illustrator's work for possible use with fiction/nonfiction articles. Works on assignment only.

**How to Contact/Illustrators:** Ms/illustration packages: Send slides, printed pieces, or photocopies. Illustrations only: Send slides, printed pieces or photocopies. Reports on art samples only if interested.

**Terms/Writers & Illustrators:** Writers: Pays on publication. Artists: Pays within 6-8 weeks. Buys all rights. "One-time book rights may be returned if author can provide name of interested book publisher and tentative date of publication." Pays about 8¢/word for unsolicited stories/articles; payment varies for poems and activities. Up to 10 complimentary issues are provided to author with check. Pays $225/color cover illustration; $35-65 per page b&w (inside); $40-125/color (inside). Sample copy for 75¢. Writer's/illustrator's guidelines free with SASE.

**Tips:** Writers: "Study current issues and guidelines. Observe, especially, word lengths and adhere to requirements. It's sometimes easier to break in with recipe or craft ideas, but submit what you do best. Don't send your first, second, or even third drafts. Polish your piece until it's as perfect as you can make it." Illustrators: "Please study the magazine before contacting us. Your art must have appeal to three- to seven-year-olds." (See listings for *Children's Digest, Children's Playmate, Jack and Jill, Turtle Magazine*.)

**IN-BETWEEN**, Art and Entertainment Between the Lakes, Six Lakes Arts Communications Inc., 43 Chapel St., Seneca Falls NY 13148. (315)568-4265. Articles/Fiction Editor: Stephen Beals. Art Director: Wayne Lohr. Bimonthly magazine. Estab. 1987. Circ. 1,500. Magazine includes "arts and entertainment, music, theatre, exhibitions, history, short stories and poetry." Annual Young Artist and Writers Contest Edition aimed at juvenile audience.

# Close-up

### Christine Clark
*Editor, Humpty Dumpty*
*Indianapolis, Indiana*

"What few writers fail to understand is: Writing for children requires both talent and skill," says Christine Clark, editor of *Humpty Dumpty*. "Writers with discipline to learn the craft are often able to overcome any lack of gift. They have a passion for what they're doing and don't view the children's market as a training ground or patronizingly speak of writing 'little stories for kiddies' as an amusing diversion."

*Humpty Dumpty* was acquired from Parents' Magazine Press in 1980. Its format was revised to fit into Children's Better Health Institute's (CBHI) group of general interest children's magazines with a health emphasis. The magazine is edited especially for children ages 4-6. The CBHI editors share information and writers; manuscripts are considered for all of CBHI's titles, so a writer need not send the same manuscript to more than one of the editors. "We tend to be rather general in the health information we relay to readers of *Humpty Dumpty*. We stick to the basics, laying a foundation for more detailed lessons to come later in the other magazines. We cover the same ground again and again, and we're always looking for a different, more interesting way to cover it. This is probably the easiest place to break in, but, beginners, beware! Health material is very difficult to write. The most common reason for rejection of manuscripts is that they're too preachy, too heavy-handed.

"It's difficult to make generalizations about juvenile magazines—there are so many today, and they're all so different. But there does seem to be a general trend toward shorter pieces—less copy, more art," says Clark. She says that although graphics are important, some teachers and librarians are concerned that children aren't reading when photos or art dominate the pages. "At CBHI we concentrate on 'good reads.' We ask writers to 'think short' and 'write tight,' especially when creating nonfiction. This trend toward less copy, more graphics is one result of TV's impact on children. But the booming children's book industry has had an influence as well. Most of the books produced today look beautiful. It's only natural for kids who read these brightly colored, delightfully illustrated books to expect the same kind of quality in the magazines they read.

"I feel good about what I do, because I believe it makes a difference in people's lives. I am continually excited by the challenge of exploring the ways children's magazines nurture relationships of grown-ups and children."

*—Deborah Cinnamon*

**Fiction:** Young readers, middle readers, young adults: history, spy/mystery/adventure. Does not want to see religious, romance, sports, science fiction material. Publishes 1-2 mss/year. Byline given.
**Nonfiction:** Young readers, middle readers, young adults: history, how-to, interview/profile. Does not want to see religious material. Publishes 1-2 mss/year. Average word length: 500-2,500. Byline given.
**How to Contact/Writers:** Fiction/nonfiction: Send complete ms. SASE (IRC) for answer to query and return of ms. Reports on queries in 2 months; mss in 3 months. Will consider simultaneous, photocopied, computer printout and electronic submissions via disk or modem (Apple MacIntosh).
**Illustration:** Publishes 1 illustration/issue; Publishes 3-4 illustrations/year. Preferred theme or style: Pen and ink. Will review ms/illustration packages by authors/artists; ms/illustration packages submitted by authors with illustrations done by separate artists; illustrator's work for possible use with fiction/nonfiction articles.
**How to Contact/Illustrators:** Ms/illustration packages: Send complete ms with final art or samples. Illustrations only: Send samples—copies OK. Reports on art samples in 2 months. Original art work returned at job's completion.
**Terms/Writers & Illustrators:** Pays in copies. "We hope to begin paying writers and illustrators in the future." Sample copy and writer's guidelines for $1.
**Tips:** "We have a young writers and artists annual contest."

**INSIGHTS**, NRA News for Young Shooters, National Rifle Assoc. of America, 1600 Rhode Island Ave. NW, Washington DC 20036. (202)828-6290. Articles Editor: Brenda Dalessandro. Monthly magazine. Circ. 40,000. "*Insights* promotes the shooting sports. We teach the safe and responsible use of firearms for competition shooting, hunting or recreational shooting. Our articles are instructional yet entertaining. We teach but don't preach. We emphasize safety." 100% of material aimed at juvenile audience.
**Fiction:** Young adults: animal, history, humorous, sports. "Fiction that does not relate to the shooting sports or positively promote the safe and ethical use of firearms will not be considered." Buys 12 mss/year. Average word length: 600-1,500. Byline given.
**Nonfiction:** Young adults: animal, history, how-to, humorous, interview/profile, "all these categories must involve the shooting sports." Buys 40 mss/year. Average word length: 600-1,500. Byline given.
**How to Contact/Writers:** Fiction/nonfiction: Query, send complete ms. SASE (IRC) for answer to query; include Social Security number with submission. Reports on queries/mss in 2 months. Will consider photocopied and computer printout submissions.
**Illustration:** Buys 1 illustration/issue; buys 7 illustrations/year. Will review ms/illustration packages submitted by authors with illustrations done by separate artists. Works on assignment only.
**How to Contact/Illustrators:** Ms/illustration packages: Query first. Illustrations only: Tear sheets or slides would be great! Illustrator should have technical knowledge of firearms and shooting.
**Terms/Writers & Illustrators:** Pays on acceptance. Buys first North American serial rights, second serial (reprint rights). Pays $200 for assigned/unsolicited articles. Additional payment for ms/illustration packages: $300. Pays $150-200 b&w (inside) illustration. Sample copy free with 10x12 SAE and 3 first class stamps; writer's/illustrator's guidelines free with business SAE and 1 first-class stamp.
**Tips:** Writers: "You have to know your subject. Kids are smart and quickly pick up on inaccuracies. As an authority, your credibility is then zilch. Material should instruct without sounding preachy. We do not buy material that shows shooting in a bad light. We show our readers the correct, safe and ethical way to use a firearm." Illustrators: "When illustrating a story, stick to the description in the plot. We find young readers don't like illustrations when they differ from the story. Forego creative license this time. Wildlife art must be anatomically and environmentally correct. Shooting scenes must

be safe and instructionally correct. We will be sponsoring a wildlife art contest for our readers. Entrants must be in 12th grade or below."

**\*INTERNATIONAL GYMNAST,** Sundbysports, Inc., 225 Brooks, Box G, Oceanside CA 92054. (619)722-0030. Monthly publication. "We are a magazine about gymnasts for ages up to 17." 100% of publication aimed at the juvenile market.
**Nonfiction:** Gymnastics material only.
**How to Contact/Writers:** Nonfiction: query, query with published clips. SASE for answer to query/return of ms. Will consider simultaneous submissions (please advise).
**Illustration:** Will review ms/illustration packages by authors/artists; ms/illustration packages by authors with illustrations by separate artists; illustrator's work for possible use with nonfiction articles.
**How to Contact/Illustrators:** Ms/illustration packages: query first. Illustrations only: send slides or prints.
**Terms/Writers & Illustrators:** Pays on publication by arrangement. Buys one-time rights. Pay "varies; negotiated." Additional payment for ms/illustration packages or illustrations only also "varies; negotiated."

**\*JACK AND JILL,** Children's Better Health Institute, 1100 Waterway Blvd., Indianapolis IN 46206. (317)636-8881. Articles Fiction Editor: Steve Charles. Art Director: Ed Cortese. Magazine published 8 times/year. Estab. 1938. Circ. 360,000. "Write entertaining and imaginative stories *for* kids, not just *about* them. Writers should understand what is funny to kids, what's important, what excites them. Don't write from an adult 'kids are so cute' perspective. We're also looking for health and healthy lifestyle stories and articles, but don't be preachy." 100% of material aimed at juvenile audience.
**Fiction:** Young readers: animal, contemporary, fantasy, history, humorous, problem-solving. Middle readers: contemporary, humorous. Buys 30-35 mss/year. Average word length: 1,200. Byline given.
**Nonfiction:** Young readers: animal, history, how-to, humorous, interview/profile, problem solving, travel. Buys 8-10 mss/year. Average word length: 1,000. Byline given.
**Poetry:** Reviews poetry.
**How to Contact/Writers:** Fiction/nonfiction: Send complete ms. SASE (IRC) for return of ms. Reports on queries in 2 weeks; mss in 8-10 weeks. Will consider simultaneous, photocopied and computer printout submissions.
**Terms/Writers:** Pays on publication; minimum 8¢/word. Buys all rights. (See listing for *Children's Digest, Children's Playmate, Humpty Dumpty's Magazine, Turtle Magazine.*)

**JACKIE,** D.C. Thomson and Co. Ltd., Albert Square, Dundee DD1 9QJ Scotland. (0382)23131 Ext. 4146. Fiction Editor: Tracy Thow. Weekly magazine. 100% of material aimed at teenage audience.
**Fiction:** Young adults: contemporary, humorous, problem solving, romance. Buys 100 mss/year. Average word length: 1,200-1,500. Byline given.
**Nonfiction:** Young adults: interview/profile, problem solving. Buys "very few" mss/ year. Average word length: 1,200-1,500.
**How to Contact/Writers:** Fiction/nonfiction: Send complete ms. SASE (IRC) for answer to query and return of ms. Reports on queries in 1 week; mss in 2 weeks. Will consider simultaneous submissions.
**Illustration:** Will review an illustrator's work for possible use with fiction/nonfiction articles and columns by other authors. Works on assignment only.
**How to Contact/Illustrators:** Ms/illustration packages: Query first, but packages not usually accepted. Illustrations only: Send tear sheets. Reports on art samples in 1 week. Original artwork returned at job's completion (depending on contract).

**Terms/Writers & Illustrators:** Pays on acceptance. Buys all rights. Pays 50-70 pounds (English currency) for assigned/unsolicited articles. Pays 60-80 pounds (English currency)/color (inside) illustration.

**Tips:** "Study the magazine and market before contributing." Looks for "fiction which is aimed at teenage girls with some emphasis on romance."

**JUNIOR TRAILS,** Gospel Publishing House, 1445 Boonville Ave., Springfield MO 65802. (417)862-2781. Articles/Fiction Editor: Sinda Zinn. Quarterly magazine. Circ. 70,000. Junior Trails is a 4-page take-home paper for fifth and sixth graders. Its articles consist of fiction stories of a contemporary or historical nature. The stories have a moral slant to them to show how modern-day people can work out problems in acceptable ways, or give examples in history from which we can learn.

**Fiction:** Middle readers: contemporary, history, humorous, problem solving, religious, sports, spy/mystery/adventure. Does not want to see science fiction, mythology, ghosts and witchcraft. Buys 80 mss/year. Average word length: 800-1,800. Byline given.

**Nonfiction:** Middle readers: animal, history, how-to, humorous, problem solving, religious, travel. Buys 30 mss/year. Average word length: 300-1,000. Byline given.

**How to Contact/Writers:** Fiction/nonfiction: Send complete ms. SASE (IRC) for answer to query; return of ms; include Social Security number with submission. Reports on queries in 2 weeks; mss in 6-8 weeks. Will consider simultaneous, photocopied and computer printout submissions.

**Terms/Writers & Illustrators:** Pays on acceptance. Buys first rights; one-time rights; second serial (reprint rights); simultaneous rights. Pays 2-3¢/word for unsolicited articles. Sample copy free with 9 × 12 SASE.

**Tips:** "Submit stories with which children can identify. Avoid trite, overused plots and themes. Make children be children — not babies or super, adult-like people. Let your characters weave the story. Don't fill up space with unnecessary details. We are always in need of good fiction stories. We tend to get a lot of very long stories that will not fit in our available space. Short fiction stories seem hard to find at times." Looks for: "fiction that presents believable characters working out their problems according to Bible principles, in other words, present Christianity in action, without being preachy; articles with reader appeal, emphasizing some phase of Christian living, presented in a down-to-earth manner; biography or missionary material using fiction technique; historical, scientific or nature material with a spiritual lesson; fillers that are brief, purposeful, usually containing an anecdote, and always with a strong evangelical emphasis."

**KEYNOTER,** Key Club International, 3636 Woodview Trace, Indianapolis IN 46268. (317)875-8755. Articles Editor: Tamara P. Burley. Art Director: James Patterson. Monthly magazine. Circ. 128,000. As the official magazine of the world's largest high school service organization, we publish nonfiction articles that interest teenagers and will help our readers become better students, better citizens, better leaders.

**Nonfiction:** Young adults: how-to, humorous, problem solving. Does not want to see first-person accounts; short stories. Buys 15 mss/year. Average word length: 1,800-2,500. Byline given.

**How to Contact/Writers:** Nonfiction: Query. SASE (IRC) for answer to query and return of ms; include Social Security number with submission. Reports on queries/mss in 1 month. Will consider simultaneous, photocopied and computer printout submissions.

*"Picture books" are geared toward the preschool — 8 year old group; "Young readers" to 5-8 year olds; "Middle readers" to 9-11 year olds; and "Young adults" to those 12 and up.*

**Illustration:** Buys 2-3 illustrations/issue; buys 15 illustrations/year. Will review ms/illustration packages by authors/artists; ms/illustration packages submitted by authors with illustrations done by separate artists; illustrator's work for possible use with nonfiction articles. Works on assignment only.

**How to Contact/Illustrators:** Ms/illustration packages: Because of our publishing schedule, we prefer to work with illustrators/photographers within Indianapolis market. Illustrators only: Send résumé, tearsheets, slides, samples or photos. Reports on art samples only if interested. Original artwork returned at job's completion if requested.

**Terms/Writers & Illustrators:** Pays on acceptance. Buys first North American serial rights. Pays $75-300 for assigned/unsolicited articles. Sample copy free with 8½×11 SAE and 65¢ postage. Writer's guidelines free with SAE and 1 first-class stamp.

**Tips:** "We are looking for light or humorous nonfiction, self help articles."

**KID CITY,** Children's Television Workshop, 1 Lincoln Plaza, New York NY 10023. (212)595-3456. Editor: Maureen Hunter-Bone. Magazine published 10 times a year. Circ. 260,000.

**Fiction:** Young readers: animal, contemporary, history, humorous, science fiction, sports, spy/mystery/adventure. Buys 3 mss/year. Average word length: 500-750. Byline given.

**Nonfiction:** Young readers: animal, history, how-to, interview/profile. Does not want to see religious material. Buys 10 mss/year. Average word lenth: 200-300. Byline given.

**How to Contact/Writers:** Fiction: Send complete ms. Nonfiction: Query. SASE (IRC) for answer to query and return of ms. Reports on queries/mss in 4 weeks. Will consider photocopied and computer printout submissions.

**Illustration:** Buys 5 illustrations/issue. Works on assignment only.

**Terms/Writers & Illustrators:** Pays on acceptance. Buys all rights. Pays $25-250 for assigned articles. Writer's guidelines free with SASE. Sample copy with SASE and $1.50.

**Tips:** Writers: "Be deft, original, not cutesy or moralistic. Avoid clichés but be real, too—don't go off the deep end into fantasy, either." Illustrators: "Send lots of sample cards to art directors. Write or call to bring in portfolios." Looks for: "fiction, photoessays." (See listing for *3-2-1 Contact*.)

**LIGHTHOUSE,** Lighthouse Publications, Box 1377, Auburn WA 98071-1377. Fiction Editor: Lynne Trindl. Bimonthly magazine. Circ. 500. Magazine contains timeless stories and poetry for family reading. 15-20% of material aimed at juvenile audience.

**Fiction:** Young readers, middle readers: animal, contemporary, humorous, sports, spy/mystery/adventure. Young adults: animal, contemporary, humorous, problem solving, romance, sports, spy/mystery/adventure. Does not want to see anything not "G-rated," any story with a message that is not subtly handled. Buys 15 mss/year. Average word length: 2,000. Byline given.

**How to Contact/Writers:** Fiction: Send complete ms. SASE (IRC) for return of ms and/or response; include Social Security number with submission. Reports on mss in 2 months. Will consider photocopied and computer printout submissions.

**Terms/Writers:** Pays on publication. Buys first North American serial rights; first rights. Sample copy for $2 (includes guidelines). Writer's guidelines free with regular SAE and 1 first-class stamp.

**Tips:** "All sections are open to freelance writers—just follow the guidelines and stay in the categories listed above."

**LISTEN,** Celebrating Positive Choices, Narcotics Education, Inc., 12501 Old Columbia Pike, Silver Spring MD 20904. (301)680-6726. Articles/Fiction Editor: Gary B. Swanson. Art Director: Paul Hey. Monthly magazine. Circ. 100,000. *Listen* offers positive alternatives to drug use for its teenage readers. 100% of material aimed at juvenile audience.

**Fiction:** Young adults: contemporary, humorous, problem solving. Buys 12 mss/year. Average word length: 1,000-1,500. Byline given.

**Nonfiction:** Young adults: how-to, interview/profile, problem solving. Buys 50 mss/year. Average word length: 1,000-1,200. Byline given.

**How to Contact/Writers:** Fiction/nonfiction: Send complete ms. SASE (IRC) for answer to query and return of ms. Reports on queries/mss in 2 months. Will consider photocopied and computer printout submissions.

**Illustration:** Buys 2 illustrations/issue. Will review ms/illustration packages submitted by authors/artists. Works on assignment only.

**How to Contact/Illustrators:** Illustrations only: Résumé and tear sheets should be sent to art director, Pacific Press Publishing Assoc., Box 7000, Boise ID 83707.

**Terms/Writers & Illustrators:** Pays on acceptance. Buys first North American serial rights. Pays $150 for assigned articles; $100 for unsolicited articles. Sample copy for $1.50 and SASE. Writer's guidelines free with SASE.

**Tips:** *Listen* is a magazine for teenagers. It encourages development of good habits and high ideals of physical, social and mental health. It bases its editorial philosophy of primary drug prevention on total abstinence from alcohol and other drugs. Because it is used extensively in public high-school classes, it does not accept articles and stories with overt religious emphasis. Four specific purposes guide the editors in selecting materials for *Listen*: 1) To portray a positive lifestyle and to foster skills and values that will help teenagers deal with contemporary problems, including smoking, drinking and using drugs. This is *Listen*'s primary purpose. 2) To offer positive alternatives to a lifestyle of drug use of any kind. 3) To present scientifically accurate information about the nature and effects of tobacco, alcohol and other drugs. 4) To report medical research, community programs and educational efforts which are solving problems connected with smoking, alcohol and other drugs. *Positive Alternatives.* These articles should offer their readers activities that increase one's sense of self-worth through achievement and/or involvement in helping others. They are often categorized by three kinds of focus: 1) Hobbies—Recent subjects have been model railroading, autograph collecting, remote-control aircraft, amateur radio, photography, genealogy. 2) Recreation—*Listen* has recently featured articles on canoeing, orienteering, amateur golf, horseback riding, ice-boating. 3) Community Service—Recent subjects have been caring for injured raptor birds, working at summer camps for children with cancer, serving as teenage police cadets, volunteering for rescue work. Cartoons: May be slanted against using tobacco, alcohol and other drugs; or may be of general interest to teenagers. Pays $15 each.

**\*MAD MAGAZINE,** E.C. Publications, Inc., 485 Madison Ave., New York NY 10022. (212)752-7685. Articles Editor: John Ficarra. Art Director: Lenny Brenner. Magazine published every 6 weeks. Estab. 1952. Circ. 1.2 million. *MAD* deals with humor and satire.

**Fiction:** Picture-oriented material/middle readers/young adult/teens. Buys all work from freelancers. "We're looking for *visual* articles with captioned illustrations." Byline given.

**Nonfiction:** Satire. Picture-oriented material/middle readers/young adult/teens. "Buy all our work from freelancers." Byline given.

**How to Contact/Writers:** Fiction/nonfiction: Query with 3 or 4 examples of premise. SASE (IRC) for answer to query. Reports on queries in 4 weeks. Will consider photocopied and computer printout submissions.

**Illustration:** Buys all illustrations/issue from freelancers. "The whole magazine is freelanced. Every submission is welcomed and considered! Look at a current issue for idea of styles we prefer." Will review ms/illustration packages submitted by authors/artists; ms/illustration packages submitted by authors with illustrations done by separate artists; illustrator's work for possible use with fiction/nonfiction articles and columns by other authors.

**How to Contact/Illustrators:** Ms/illustration packages: "Query with 3 or 4 examples of artwork." Illustrators only: Send tearsheets. Reports back in 4 weeks.

**Terms/Writers & Illustrators:** Pays on acceptance. Buys all rights. Pay: "Starts $350/ page of art or writing." Additional payment for ms/illustration packages, "starts $350 art and $350 script/per page." Sample copy $1.75 with SAE and 90¢ postage. Writer's/ illustrator's guidelines free with SAE and 1 first class stamp.

**Tips:** "Read several *MAD*s to get our style down. Remember, 95% (of art) is b&w work."

**MY FRIEND,** A Magazine for Children, Daughters of St. Paul/St. Paul Books and Media, 50 St. Paul's Ave., Jamaica Plain, Boston MA 02130. (617)522-8911. Articles/Fiction Editor: Sister Anne Joan, fsp. Art Director: Sister Helen Rita, fsp. Magazine published 10 times/year. Magazine. Circ. 10,000. *My Friend* is a magazine of inspiration and entertainment for a predominantly Catholic readership. We reach ages 6-12. "100% of material aimed at juvenile audience."

**Fiction:** Picture-oriented material: animal, contemporary, religious. Young readers: contemporary, fantasy, history, humorous, problem solving, religious, sports, adventure. Middle readers: contemporary, history, humorous, problem solving, religious, science fiction, sports, adventure. Young adults: religious. Does not want to see poetry, animals as main characters in religious story, stories whose basic thrust would be incompatible with Catholic values. Buys 50 mss/year. Average word length: 450-750. Byline given.

**Nonfiction:** Picture-oriented material: animal, religious. Young readers: history, how-to, humorous, interview/profile, religious. Middle readers: history, interview/profile, problem solving, religious. Does not want to see material that is not compatible with Catholic values; "new age" material. Buys 10 mss/year. Average word length: 450-750. Byline given.

**How to Contact/Writers:** Fiction/nonfiction: Send complete ms. SASE (IRC) for answer to query and return of ms. Reports on queries in 3 weeks; mss in 3-4 weeks. Will consider photocopied and computer printout submissions.

**Illustration:** Buys 8 illustrations/issue; buys 60-80 illustrations/year. Preferred theme or style: Realistic depictions of children, but open to variety! Looking for a "Bible stories" artist, too. Will review ms/illustration packages by authors/artists; ms/illustration packages submitted by authors with illustrations done by separate artists; illustrator's work for possible use with fiction/nonfiction articles.

**How to Contact/Illustrators:** Ms/illustration packages: Send complete ms with copy of final art. Reports on art samples in 3-4 weeks. Original artwork not returned at job's completion "unless previously requested and arranged."

**Terms/Writers & Illustrators:** Pays on publication. Buys one-time rights. Pays 3-7¢ per word. Additional payment for ms/illustration packages: "I suppose this would be negotiable. Rarely happens." Sample copy free with 9 × 12 SAE and 4 first-class stamps. Writer's/illustrator's guidelines free with SAE and 1 first-class stamp.

**Tips:** Writers: "Right now, we're especially looking for stories that would appeal to boys. We are not interested in poetry unless it is humorous." Illustrators: "Please contact us! For the most part, we need illustrations for fiction stories; usually one 'main' illustration and a second supporting picture."

**NATIONAL GEOGRAPHIC WORLD,** National Geographic Society, 17th and M Streets NW, Washington DC 20036. (202)857-7000. Editor: Pat Robbins. Submissions Editor: Eleanor Shannahan. Photo Editor: Larry Nighswander. Art Director: Ursula Vosseler. Monthly magazine. Circ. 1.3 million. "National Geographic *World* features factual stories on outdoor adventure, natural history, sports, science and history for children ages 8 and older. Full-color photographs are used to attract young readers and the text easily guides them through the story." 100% of material aimed at juvenile audience. Does not publish fiction.

**Nonfiction:** "*World* does not publish manuscripts from outside writers. Story ideas that lend themselves to photo stories will be considered, and, if accepted, a finder's fee will be paid for an original idea. All writing is done by staff." Picture material: animal, history, how-to, travel. Middle readers: animal, history, how-to, travel. Average word length: 90-600.

**How to Contact/Writers:** Nonfiction: Query only—no ms please. SASE (IRC) for answer to query. Reports on queries in 6-8 weeks.

**Illustration:** Assignment only.

**How to Contact/Illustrators:** Ms/illustration packages: Query story idea first. Illustrations only: Submit samples in slide form or tear sheets. Reports on art samples only if interested. Original artwork returned at job's completion; NGS retains copyright.

**Terms/Writers & Illustrators:** Pays on publication. Buys one-time rights. Pays $75-350 for assigned articles. Free sample copy; contributor's guidelines available free.

**Tips:** "All *World* stories are written by staff. For *World*, the story proposal is the way to break in. Think through the focus of the story and outline what action photos are available. Keep in mind that *World* is a visual magazine. A story will work best if it has a very tight focus and if the photos show children interacting with their surroundings as well as with each other."

**\*NATURE FRIEND MAGAZINE,** Pilgrim Publishers, 22777 State Road 119, Goshen IN 46526. (219)534-2245. Articles Editor: Stanley Brubaker. Monthly magazine. Estab. 1983. Circ. 11,000. "See our writers guide *before* submitting articles."

**Nonfiction:** Picture-oriented material: animal, nature. Young readers: animal, nature. Middle readers: animal, nature. Young adult/teens: animal, nature. Does not want to see evolutionary material. Buys 50-80 mss/year. Average word length: 350-1,500. Byline given.

**How to Contact/Writers:** Nonfiction: Send complete ms. SASE (IRC) for return of ms; reports on mss in 4-16 weeks. Will consider simultaneous, photocopied and computer printout submissions.

**Illustration:** Buys 10 illustrations/year. See samples of magazine for styles of art used. Will review ms/illustration packages submitted by authors/artists; ms/illustration packages submitted by authors with illustrations done by separate artists.

**Terms/Writers & Illustrators:** Pays on publication. Buys one-time rights. Pays $15-45. Payment for ms/illustration packages: $15-40. Payment for illustrations: $15-40/b&w inside. Two sample copies for $2 with 7 × 10 SAE and 85¢ postage. Writer's/illustrator's guidelines for $1.

**Tips:** "Study the magazine to get their mood." Looks for "main articles, puzzles and simple nature and science projects."

**\*THE NEW YABA WORLD,** Young American Bowling Alliance, 5301 South 76th St., Greendale WI 53129. (414)421-4700. Media Relations Manager: Mark Schaefer. Editor: Marie Cox. Tabloid published 3 times/bowling season. Estab. 1987. Circ. 600,000. "Our audience is youth bowlers between the ages of 3-21. Our paper is predominantly nonfiction news regarding our membership, leagues and tournaments. On occasion we use puzzles, fiction and cartoons." 85% of material directed to children.

**Nonfiction:** Does not want to see "anything not pertaining to YABA sanctioned leagues or tournaments." Average word length: 500-1,500. Byline sometimes given.

**How to Contact/Writers:** Nonfiction: Query. SASE (IRC) for answer to query. Reports on queries in 2 weeks. Will consider simultaneous, photocopied and computer printout submissions.

*Refer to the Business of Children's Writing & Illustrating for up-to-date marketing, tax and legal information.*

**Illustration:** Buys 1 illustration/issue; 3 illustrations/year. Preferred theme or style: "Relating to youth bowling." Works on assignment only.

**How to Contact Illustrators:** Ms/illustration packages: "Query first." Illustrations only: Send tearsheets. Reports on art samples only if interested. Original artwork returned at job's completion "if requested."

**Terms/Writers and Illustrators:** Pays on publication. Buys first North American serial rights. Publication not copyrighted. Pays $40-50/assigned articles. Sample copy for 9 × 12 SAE; writer's/illustrator's guidelines free with SAE.

**NOAH'S ARK,** A Newspaper for Jewish Children, 8323 Southwest Freeway, #250, Houston TX 77074. (713)771-7143. Articles/Fiction Editor: Debbie Israel Dubin. Art Director: Nachman. Monthly tabloid. Circ. 450,000. All submissions must have Jewish content and positive Jewish values. The newspaper is sent to more than 400 religious schools and submissions must be appropriate for educational use as well. 100% of material aimed at juvenile.

**Fiction:** Young readers, middle readers: contemporary, history, religious, sports. Does not want to see Christian and secular material. Buys 3 mss/year. Average word length: 650. Byline given.

**Nonfiction:** Young readers, middle readers: history, how-to, humorous, interview/profile, problem solving, religious, travel. Does not want to see secular, Christian nonfiction. Buys 1 ms/year, "only because more not submitted." Average word length: 500. Byline given.

**How to Contact/Writers:** Fiction/nonfiction: Send complete ms. SASE (IRC) for answer to query and return of ms. Report on mss 6-8 weeks. Will consider photocopied and computer printout submissions.

**Terms/Writers & Illustrators:** Pays on acceptance. Buys first North American serial rights. Pays 5¢/word for unsolicited articles. Sample copy free with #10 SAE and 1 first-class stamp. Writer's guidelines free with SAE and 1 first-class stamp.

**Tips:** "Send appropriate material. We receive mostly inappropriate submissions; very few submissions have Jewish values as required."

**ODYSSEY,** Kalmbach Publishing Co., 21027 Crossroads Cr., Box 1612,Waukesha WI 53187. (414)796-8776. FAX (414)796-0126. Articles Editor: Nancy Mack. Art Director: Jane Borth-Lucius. Monthly magazine. Circ. 104,148. Magazine covers astronomy and space exploration for children ages 8-14. 100% of material aimed at juvenile audience.

**Nonfiction:** Middle readers, young adults: how-to, humorous, astronomy, space science. Does not want to see very general or overview articles. Buys 20-30 mss/year. Average word length: 600-2,000. Byline given.

**How to Contact/Writers:** Nonfiction: Query. SASE (IRC) for answer to query and return of ms. Reports in 10 weeks. Will consider simultaneous, photocopied and computer printout submissions.

**Illustration:** Buys 10-12 illustrations/year. Will review ms/illustration packages by authors/artists; ms/illustration packages submitted by authors with illustrations done by separate artists; illustrator's work for possible use with fiction/nonfiction articles. Works on assignment only.

**How to Contact/Illustrators:** Ms/illustration packages: Query first. Illustrations only: Send tear sheets and/or slides. Reports on art samples in 10 weeks. Original artwork returned at job's completion.

**Terms/Writers & Illustrators:** Pays on publication. Buys one-time rights. Pays $100-350 for assigned/unsolicited articles. Additional payment for ms/illustration packages is $350-1,000. Pays $100-350/color (cover/inside) illustration; $100-300/b&w (cover/inside). Sample copy free with 9 × 11 SAE and 4 first-class stamps. Writer's guidelines free with SAE and 1 first-class stamp.

**Tips:** "At *Odyssey*, short, offbeat articles have the best chance of acceptance. Major articles are usually handled by staff or contributing editors." Looks for "short, humorous articles and experiments. Keep the writing very simple (usually the topic will be technical)."

**ON THE LINE,** Mennonite Publishing House, 616 Walnut Ave., Scottdale PA 15683. (412)887-8500. Editor: Mary Meyer. "Monthly in weekly parts" magazine. Circ. 10,000. 100% of material aimed at juvenile audience.
**Fiction:** Buys 52 mss/year. Average word length: 900-1,200. Byline given.
**Nonfiction:** Middle readers: animal, history, how-to, humorous, interview/profile, problem solving, religious. Does not want to see articles written from an adult perspective. Average word length: 200-900. Byline given.
**How to Contact/Writers:** Fiction/nonfiction: Send complete ms. SASE for return of ms. Reports on queries/mss in 1 month. Will consider simultaneous, photocopied and computer printout submissions "if print is good quality."
**Illustration:** Buys 1-2 illustrations/issue; buys 52 illustrations/year. "Illustrations are done on assignment only, to accompany our stories and articles—our need for new artists is very limited." Will review ms/illustration packages submitted by authors/artists. Works on assignment only.
**How to Contact/Illustrators:** Illustrations only: Prefer samples they do not want returned; these stay in our files. Reports on art samples only if interested. Original art work returned at job's completion.
**Terms/Writers & Illustrators:** Pays on acceptance. Buys one-time rights; second serial (reprint rights). Pays 2-4¢/word for assigned/unsolicited articles. Pays $12-50/color (inside) illustration. Sample copy free with 7×10 SAE. Free writer's guidelines.

**OWL MAGAZINE,** The Discovery Magazine for Children, Young Naturalist Foundation, Ste. 306, 56 The Esplanade, Toronto Ontario M5E 1A7 Canada. (416)868-6001. Editor-in-Chief: Sylvia Funston. Managing Editor: Debora Pearson. Art Director: Tim Davin. Magazine published 10 times/year. Circ. 160,000. *Owl* helps children over eight discover and enjoy the world of science and nature. We look for articles that are fun to read, that inform from a child's perspective and that motivate hands-on interaction. *Owl* explores the reader's many interests in the natural world in a scientific, but always entertaining, way.
**Fiction:** Middle readers, young adults: animal, contemporary, fantasy, humorous, science fiction, sports, spy/mystery/adventure. Does not want to see romance, religion, anthropomorphizing. Average word length: 500-1,000. Byline given. "We publish only 3-4 pieces of fiction per year, and they are usually only excerpts from books."
**Nonfiction:** Middle readers, young adults: animal, biology, high-tech, how-to, humor, interview/profile, travel. Does not want to see religious topics, anthropomorphizing. Buys 20 mss/year. Average word length: 200-1,500. Byline given.
**How to Contact/Writers:** Fiction/nonfiction: Query with published clips. SASE (IRC) for return of ms. Report on queries in 4-6 weeks; mss in 6-8 weeks. Will consider photocopied and computer printout submissions.
**Illustration:** Buys 3-5 illustrations/issue; buys 40-50 illustrations/year. Preferred theme or style: lively, involving, fun, with emotional impact and appeal. Works on assignment only.
**How to Contact/Illustrators:** Illustrations only: Send tear sheets and slides. Reports on art samples only if interested. Original artwork returned at job's completion.
**Terms/Writers & Illustrators:** Pays on acceptance. Buys all rights. Pays $35-600 for assigned/unsolicited articles. Pays $600-700/color (inside) illustration. Sample copy $3.25. Free writer's guidelines.

**Tips:** Writers: "Talk to kids and find out what they're interested in; read kid's magazines; make sure your research is thorough and find good consultants who are doing up-to-the-minute research. Be sure to read the magazine carefully to become familiar with *Owl*'s style." Illustrators: "Talk to kids and find out what work appeals to them; look at kid's magazines and books. Look through *Owl* to see what styles we prefer." (See listing for *Chickadee*.)

**PENNYWHISTLE PRESS,** Gannett, Box 500-P, Washington DC 20044. (703)276-3796. Articles/Fiction Editor: Anita Sama. Art Director: Eileen Kelly. Weekly tabloid. Circ. 2.5 million. "We are an educational supplement for kids from 7 to 14 years old. We generally buy fiction from freelancers about kids in real life situations." 100% of material aimed at juvenile audience.
**Fiction:** Picture material, middle readers, young adults: animal, contemporary, history, humorous, problem solving, science fiction, sports, spy/mystery/adventure. Does not want to see stories that include talking animals. Buys 30 mss/year. Average word length: 200-600. Byline given.
**How to Contact/Writers:** Fiction: Send complete ms. Large SASE for return of ms. Reports on mss in 2-3 months. Will consider photocopied and computer printout submissions.
**Illustration:** Buys 2 illustrations/issue; buys 4 illustrations/year. Will review ms/illustration packages by authors/artists; ms/illustration packages submitted by authors with illustrations done by separate artists; illustrator's work for possible use with fiction/nonfiction articles.
**How to Contact/Illustrators:** Illustrations only: Send tear sheets. Reports on art samples only if interested. Original artwork returned at job's completion.
**Terms/Writers & Illustrators:** Pays on acceptance. Buys all rights. Pays $125 for unsolicited articles. Additional payment for ms/illustration package is $250-300. Sample copy 75¢.

**PIONEER,** Brotherhood Commission, SBC, 1548 Poplar Ave., Memphis TN 38134. (901)272-2461. Articles Editor: Tim Bearden. Monthly magazine. Circ. 30,000. Magazine contains boy interests, sports, crafts, sports personalities, religious.
**Nonfiction:** Young adults: animal, how-to, humorous, interview/profile, problem solving, religious, travel. Buys 15 mss/year. Average word length: 600-800. Byline given.
**How to Contact/Writers:** Nonfiction: Send complete ms. SASE (IRC) for return of ms; include Social Security number with submission. Reports on queries in 1 month; mss in 2 months. Will consider simultaneous, photocopied, and computer printout submissions.
**Illustration:** Buys 1-2 illustrations/issue; buys 12 illustrations/year. Will review ms/illustration packages by authors/artists; ms/illustration packages submitted by authors with illustrations done by separate artists; illustrator's work for possible use with fiction/nonfiction articles.
**How to Contact/Illustrators:** Ms/illustration packages: Send ms with final art.
**Terms/Writers & Illustrators:** Pays on acceptance. Buys one-time rights, simultaneous rights. Pays $25-35 for unsolicited articles. Sample copy free with #10 SAE and 2 first-class stamps. Writer's/illustrator's guidelines free with SAE and 1 first-class stamp.

**POCKETS,** Devotional Magazine for Children, The Upper Room, 1908 Grand, Box 189, Nashville TN 37202. (615)340-7333. Articles/Fiction Editor: Janet M. Bugg. Art Director: Chris Schechner, Ste. 206, 3100 Carlisle Plaza, Dallas TX 75204. Magazine published 11 times/year. Circ. 60,000. Stories should help children 6 to 12 experience a Christian lifestyle that is not always a neatly wrapped moral package, but is open to the continuing revelation of God's will.

**Fiction:** Young readers, middle readers: contemporary, fantasy, history, religious, "Retold Bible stories." Does not want to see violence. Buys 26-30 mss/year. Average word length: 800-2,000. Byline given.

**Nonfiction:** Young readers, middle readers: history, interview/profile, religious, "communication activities." Does not want to see how-to articles. Our nonfiction reads like a story. History is in form of role-model stories as is profile. Buys 10 mss/year. Average word length: 800-2,000. Byline given.

**How to Contact/Writers:** Fiction/nonfiction: Send complete ms. SASE (IRC) for return of ms. Report on mss in 4 weeks. Will consider simultaneous, photocopied and computer printout submissions.

**Illustration:** Buys 30 illustrations/issue. Preferred theme or style: varied; both 4-color and 2-color. Will review ms/illustration packages by authors/artists; ms/illustration packages submitted by authors with illustrations done by separate artists; illustrator's work for possible use with fiction/nonfiction articles. Works on assignment only.

**How to Contact/Illustrators:** Ms/illustration packages: No final art. Illustrations only: Send résumé, tear sheets, slides to Chris Schechner, Ste. 206, 3100 Carlisle Plaza, Dallas TX 75204. Reports on art samples only if interested. Original artwork returned at job's completion.

**Terms/Writers & Illustrators:** Pays on acceptance. Buys first North American rights. Pays $250 for assigned articles; 10¢/word for unsolicited articles. Pays $500/color (cover) illustration; $50-500/color (inside). Sample copy free with 7×9 SAE and 4 first-class stamps. Writer's/illustrator's guidelines free with SAE and 1 first-class stamp.

**Tips:** "Ask for our themes first. They are set yearly in the fall."

**R-A-D-A-R**, Standard Publishing, 8121 Hamilton Ave., Cincinnati OH 45231. (513)931-4050. Articles/Fiction Editor: Margaret Williams. Art Director: Frank Sutton. Weekly magazine. Circ. 110,000. *R-A-D-A-R* is a weekly take-home paper for boys and girls who are in grades 3-6. Our goal is to reach these children with the truth of God'sWord, and to help them make it the guide of their lives. Many of our features, including our stories, now correlate with the Sunday-school lesson themes. Send for a quarterly theme list and sample copies of *R-A-D-A-R*. Keep in mind that others will be submitting stories for the same themes—this is not an assignment.

**Fiction:** Middle readers: animal, contemporary, history, humorous, problem solving, religious, sports, spy/mystery/adventure. Does not want to see fantasy or science fiction. Buys 150 mss/year. Average word length: 400-1,000. Byline given.

**Nonfiction:** Middle readers: animal, history, how-to, humorous, interview/profile, problem solving, religious, travel. Buys 50 mss/year. Average word length: 400-1,000. Byline given.

**How to Contact/Writers:** Fiction/nonfiction: Send complete ms. SASE (IRC) for answer to query and return of ms; include Social Security number with submission. Reports on queries/mss 6-8 weeks. Will consider simultaneous (but prefer not to), photocopied (must be clean copies) and computer printout submissions. Reprint submissions must be retyped.

**Illustration:** Will review ms/illustration packages by authors/artists; ms/illustration packages submitted by authors with illustrations done by separate artists; illustrator's work for possible use with fiction/nonfiction articles. Works on assignment only; there have been a few exceptions to this.

**How to Contact/Illustrators:** Illustrations only: Send résumé, tear sheets; samples of art can be photocopied. Reports on art samples only if interested.

**Terms/Writers & Illustrators:** Pays on acceptance. Buys first rights, one-time rights, second serial; all rights to art. Pays 3¢/word for unsolicited articles, few are assigned. Contributor copies given "not as payment, but all contributors receive copies of their art/articles." Pays $70-150 for color illustrations; $40-60 for line art only. Sample copy and writer's/illustrator's guidelines free with 9⅜ × 4¼ SAE and 1 first-class stamp. (See listing for *Straight*.)

**RANGER RICK**, National Wildlife Federation, 8925 Leesburg Pike, Vienna VA 22184. (703)790-4000. Editor: Gerald Bishop. Art Director: Donna Miller. Monthly magazine. Circ. 950,000. "Our audience ranges from ages six to twelve, though we aim the reading level of most material at nine-year-olds or fourth graders." 100% of material aimed at juvenile audience.

**Fiction:** Animal, fantasy, humorous, science fiction. Buys 4 mss/year. Average word length: 900. Byline given.

**Nonfiction:** Animal, humorous. Buys 20-30 mss/year. Average word length: 900. Byline given.

**How to Contact/Writers:** Fiction: Query with published clips; send complete ms. Nonfiction: Query with published clips. SASE (IRC) for answer to query and return of ms; include Social Security number with submission. Reports on queries/mss in 6 weeks. Will consider computer printout submissions.

**Illustration:** Buys 6-8 illustrations/issue; buys 75-100 illustrations/year. Preferred theme or style: Nature, wildlife. Will review an illustrator's work for possible use with fiction/nonfiction articles and columns by other authors. Works on assignment only.

**How to Contact/Illustrators:** Illustrations only: Send resume, tear sheets. Reports on art samples in 6 weeks. Original artwork returned at job's completion.

**Terms/Writers & Illustrators:** Pays on acceptance. Forms, buys all rights (first N.A. serial rights negotiable). Pays up to $550 for full-length of best quality. For illustrations, buys one-time rights. Pays $250-1,000 for color (inside, per page) illustration. Sample copy $2. Writer's guidelines free with SAE.

**Tips:** "Fiction and nonfiction articles may be written on any aspect of wildlife, nature, outdoor adventure and discovery, domestic animals with a 'wild' connection (such as domestic pigs and wild boars), science, conservation, or related subjects. To find out what subjects have been covered recently, consult our annual indexes and the *Children's Magazine Guide*. These are available in many libraries. The National Wildlife Federation (NWF) discourages the keeping of wildlife as pets, so the keeping of such pets should not be featured in your copy. Avoid stereotyping of any group. For instance, girls can enjoy nature and the outdoors as much as boys can, and mothers can be just as knowledgeable as fathers. The only way you can write successfully for *Ranger Rick* is to know the kinds of subjects and approaches we like. And the only way you can do that is to read the magazine. Recent issues can be found in most libraries or are available from our office for $2 a copy." Illustrators: "Start small, with less demanding magazines." (See listing for *Your Big Backyard*.)

**\*SCHOLASTIC MATH MAGAZINE**, Scholastic, Inc., 730 Broadway, New York NY 10003. (212)505-3135. Editor: Tracey Randinelli. Artist: Leah Bossio. Art Director: Joan Michael. Magazine published 14 times/year; September-May. Estab. 1980. Circ. 307,000. "We are a math magazine for 7, 8, 9 grade classrooms. We present math in current, relevant, high-interest topics. Math skills we focus on include whole number, fraction, and decimal computation, percentages, ratios, proportions, geometry." 100% of material aimed at juvenile audience.

**Fiction:** Buys 14 mss/year "in the form of word problems." Average line length 80-100.

**Nonfiction:** Young adult/teens: animal, history, how-to, humorous, interview/profile, problem solving, travel. Does not want to see "anything dealing with *very* controversial issues — ie, teenage pregnancy, AIDS, etc." Buys 20 mss/year. Average line length 80-100. Byline given.

**How to Contact/Writers:** Fiction/nonfiction: Query. SASE (IRC) for answer to query. Reports on queries/mss in 1 month. Will consider photocopied submissions.
**Illustration:** Buys 4 illustrations/issue; 56 illustrations/year. Prefers to review "humorous, young adult sophistication" types of art. Will review ms/illustration packages submitted by authors/artists; ms/illustration packages submitted by authors with illustrations done by separate artists; illustrator's work for possible use with fiction/nonfiction articles and columns by other authors. Works on assignment only.
**How to Contact/Illustrators:** Ms/illustration packages: "Query first." Illustrations only: Send tearsheets. Reports back only if interested. Original art work returned at job's completion.
**Terms/Writers & Illustrators:** Pays on acceptance. Pays $100-350/assigned article.
**Tips:** "For our magazine, stories dealing with math concepts and applications in the real world are sought." (See listing for *Scope*.)

**SCHOOL MAGAZINE, BLAST OFF!, COUNTDOWN, ORBIT, TOUCHDOWN,** New South Wales Dept. of Education, Box A242, Sydney NSW 2000 Australia. (02)261-7231. Editor: Anna Fienberg. 4 monthly magazines. Circ. 305,000. *School Magazine* is a literary magazine that is issued free to all N.S.W. public schools. Private schools and individuals subscribe for a small fee. We include stories, articles, plays, poems, crosswords. The 4 magazines issued each month are graded according to age level, 8-12 years. 100% of material aimed at juvenile audience.
**Fiction:** Young readers: animal, contemporary, fantasy, humorous. Middle readers: animal, contemporary, fantasy, history, humorous, problem solving, romance, science fiction, spy/mystery/adventure. Buys 30 mss/year. Average word length: 500-2,500. Byline given.
**Nonfiction:** Young readers: animal, humorous, interview/profile. Middle readers: animal, history, humorous, interview/profile, problem solving, travel. Does not want to see political topics. Buys 30 mss/year. Average word length: 500-2,000. Byline given.
**How to Contact/Writers:** Fiction/nonfiction: Send complete ms. SASE (IRC) for return of ms. Reports on queries in 2 months. Will consider photocopies and computer printout submissions "as long as it is clear and legible."
**Terms/Writers & Illustrators:** "Payment when accounts done, usually 2 weeks after acceptance." Buys one-time rights. "Pays $112 per thousand words." Free sample copy.
**Tips:** "Subscribe to *School Magazine*—read as much children's literature as possible." Looks for: "Both fiction and articles. Fantasy, real-life both acceptable for fiction. Good quality is the main criteria."

**\*SCIENCELAND,** To Nurture Scientific Thinking, Scienceland Inc., 501 Fifth Ave. #2108, New York NY 10017-6102. (212)490-2180. FAX: 986-2077. Editor/Art Director: Al Matano. Magazine published 8 times/year. Estab. 1977. Circ. 16,000. This is "a content reading picture-book for K-3rd grade to encourage beginning readers; for teachers and parents." 100% of material aimed at juvenile audience.
**Nonfiction:** Picture-oriented material: animal, how-to, humorous, problem solving. Young readers: animal, how-to, humorous, problem solving. Does not want to see "unillustrated material."
**How to Contact/Writers:** Nonfiction: Query with published clips. SASE (IRC) for answer to query. Reports on queries in 3-4 weeks. Will consider photocopied submissions.
**Illustration:** Prefers to review "detailed, realistic, full color art. No abstracts." Will review ms/illustration packages submitted by authors/artists; ms/illustration packages submitted by authors with illustrations done by separate artists; illustrator's work for possible use with fiction/nonfiction articles and columns by other authors.

**How to Contact/Illustrators:** Ms/illustration packages: "Query first." Illustrations only: Send résumé and tearsheets. Reports back in 3-4 weeks. Original art work returned at job's completion, "depending on material."

**Terms/Writers & Illustrators:** Pays on publication. Buys first North American serial rights or all rights. Payment for ms/illustration packages: $50-500. Payment for illustrations: $25-300 color cover; $25-300 color inside. Sample copy free with 9×12 SASE.

**Tips:** "Must be top-notch illustrator or photographer. No amateurs."

**\*SCOPE**, Scholastic Inc., 730 Broadway, New York NY 10003. (212)505-3000. Senior Editor: Deborah Sussman. Art Director: Joy Makon. Biweekly magazine. Estab. 1964. Circ. 700,000. "*Scope* is directed at middle-school and high school students who often wish they weren't at school. Many are poor readers. *Scope* aims to motivate them to read and to think about their world." 100% of material is directed to children.

**Fiction:** Middle readers, young adults: animal, contemporary, fantasy, humorous, problem-solving, science fiction, sports and spy/mystery/adventure. Young adults: romance. Buys 20 mss/year. Average word length: 200-2,500. Byline given.

**Nonfiction:** Middle readers, young adults: animal, how-to, humorous, interview/profile and problem solving. Buys 35 mss/year. Average word length: 200-2,000. Byline "sometimes given."

**How to Contact/Writers:** Fiction: Send complete ms. Nonfiction: Query with published clips. SASE (IRC) for return of ms; include Social Security number with submission. Reports on queries in 1 month; mss in 2 months. Will consider photocopied and computer printout submissions.

**Illustration:** Buys 6-10 illustrations/issue; buys 100-150 illustrations/year. Preferred theme or style: "varies. Prefer sophisticated, non-childish styles." Works on assignment only.

**How to Contact/Illustrators:** Ms/illustration packages: "Submit portfolio; leave samples/tearsheets." Illustrations only: "Submit portfolio; leave samples/tearsheets. Do not send any non-returnable materials." Original artwork returned at job's completion.

**Terms/Writers & Illustrators:** Pays on acceptance. Pays $75-400 for assigned articles; $50-250 for unsolicited articles. Additional payment for ms/illustration packages. Sample copy for $1.25 with 9×12 SAE. Writer's guidelines free with SASE.

**Tips:** Illustrators: "Do not telephone art department. Submit portfolio of sample styles; leave samples/tearsheets to keep on file." (See listing for *Scholastic Math*.)

**\*SEVENTEEN MAGAZINE**, Triangle Communication, 850 Third Ave., New York NY 10022. (212)759-8100. Articles Editor: Roberta Myers. Fiction Editor: Adrian Nicole LeBlanc. Art Director: Kay Spear. Monthly magazine. Estab. 1944. Circ. 1,750,000. "General-interest magazine for teenage girls." 100% of material aimed at juvenile audience.

**Fiction:** Young adults: animal, contemporary, fantasy, history, humorous, problem-solving, religious, romance, science fiction, sports, spy/mystery/adventure, adult. "We consider all good literary short fiction." Buys 12-20 mss/year. Average word length 900-3,500. Byline given.

**Nonfiction:** Young adults: animal, history, how-to, humorous, interview/profile, problem solving, religious, travel. Buys 150 mss/year. Word length: "all different lengths." Byline given.

**Poetry:** Reviews poetry "only by teenagers younger than 21."

**How to Contact/Writers;** Fiction: Send complete ms. Nonfiction: Query with published clips or send complete ms. SASE (IRC) for answer to query. Reports on queries/mss in 3 weeks. Will consider simultaneous, photocopied and computer submissions.

**Illustration:** 1 illustration per short story. Will review ms packages submitted by authors/artists; ms/illustration packages submitted by authors with illustrations done by separate artists. Illustrators paid by the project. Writer's guidelines for business-size envelope and 1 first-class stamp.

**SHOFAR**, Sr. Publications Ltd., 43 Northcote Dr., Melville NY 11747. (516)643-4598. Articles Editor: Gerald H. Grayson. Magazine published monthly Oct. through May—double issues Dec./Jan. and April/May. Circ. 10,000. For Jewish children 8-13. 100% of material aimed at juvenile audience.
**Fiction:** Middle readers: contemporary, humorous, religious, sports. Buys 10-20 mss/year. Average word length: 500-1,000. Byline given.
**Nonfiction:** Middle readers: history, humorous, interview/profile, religious. Buys 10-20 mss/year. Average word length: 500-1,000. Byline given.
**How to Contact/Writers:** Fiction/nonfiction: Send complete ms. Will consider simultaneous, photocopied, computer printout and electronic submissions via disk or modem (only Macintosh).
**Illustration:** Buys 3-4 illustrations/issue; buys 15-20 illustrations/year. Works on assignment only.
**How to Contact/Illustrators:** Ms/illustration packages: Query first. Illustrations only: Send tear sheets. Reports on art samples only if interested. Original artwork returned at job's completion.
**Terms/Writers & Illustrators:** Buys one-time rights. Pays $25-125 for assigned articles. Additional payment for ms/illustration packages $50-250. Pays $25-100/b&w cover illustration; $50-150/color (cover). Sample copy free with 9 × 12 SAE and 3 first-class stamps. Free writer's/illustrator's guidelines.

**\*SING OUT!**, The Folk Song Magazine, Sing Out! Corp., Box 5253, 125 E. 3rd St., Bethlehem PA 18015-5253. (215)865-5366. Editor: Mark D. Moss. Contributing Editor: Jeff Eilenberg. Managing Director: Diane C. Petro. Quarterly magazine. Estab. 1950. Circ. 5,000 member; 1,500 newstand. Readers are "a diverse group of music lovers, who believe in preserving the folk music of America as well as the native music of all countries. Additionally, *Sing Out!* explores the new musical fusions being created daily by rising new troubadors." 20% (Kidsbeat column) of material aimed at juvenile audience.
**Fiction:** Middle readers, Young adult/teens: storytelling. "We have a storytelling column, Endless Tale."
**Nonfiction:** Picture-oriented material: music. Young readers: music. Middle readers: history, interivew/profile, music. Young adult/teens: history, how-to, humorous, interview/profile, religious, music. Does not want to see "non-music material."
**How to Contact/Writers:** Fiction/nonfiction: "Query first." SASE (IRC) for return of ms. Will consider simultaneous, photocopied, computer printout and electronic submissions via disk or modem.
**Illustration:** Prefers to review "music-oriented themes—folk preferred." Will review ms/illustration packages submitted by authors/artists "after query"; ms/illustration packages submitted by authors with illustrations done by separate artists; illustrator's work for possible use with fiction/nonfiction articles and columns by other authors.
**How to Contact/Illustrators:** Ms/illustration packages: "Query first and foremost!" Illustrations only: Send tearsheets. Reports only if interested.
**Terms/Writers & Illustrators:** Pays on publication. Buys first North American serial rights or first rights. Pay is "negotiable." Writers/illustrator's guidelines free with SASE.
**Tips:** "Be as pertinent as possible to folk music needs and interests. We accept many freelance reviews of artists and their work."

**THE SINGLE PARENT**, Journal of Parents Without Partners, Inc., Parents Without Partners, Inc., 8807 Colesville Rd., Silver Spring MD 20910. (301)588-9354. Articles/Fiction Editor/Art Director: Allan Glennon. Bimonthly magazine. Circ. 125,000. Members of PWP are single parents who are divorced, widowed or never married. All our material is related to this basic fact. We look at the positive side of our situation and are interested in all aspects of parenting, and in the particular situation of single parenting. 10% of material aimed at juvenile audience.

**Fiction:** Young readers, middle readers, young adults: contemporary, fantasy, humorous, problem solving, science fiction, spy/mystery/adventure. No anthropomorphic material. Buys 12 mss/year. Average word length: 800-1,500. Byline given.

**Nonfiction:** Young readers, middle readers, young adults: humorous, problem solving. "We do not ordinarily use nonfiction aimed at children, but could be persuaded by a particularly good piece." Does not want to see material unrelated to single-parent children and families. Average word length: 800-1,800. Byline given.

**How to Contact/Writers:** Fiction/nonfiction: Send complete ms. SASE (IRC) for answer to query and return of ms. Reports on queries/mss in 3 weeks. Will consider simultaneous, photocopied and computer printout submissions.

**Illustration:** Buys 4-6 illustrations/issue. Preferred theme or style: Line art, sometimes with mechanicals. No special preference for style, but lean toward realistic. Will review ms/illustration packages by authors/artists; ms/illustration packages submitted by authors with illustrations done by separate artists; illustrator's work for possible use with fiction/nonfiction articles. Works on assignment only.

**How to Contact/Illustrators:** Ms/illustration packages: Send complete ms with final art with prepaid return envelope. Illustrations only: Send nonreturnable samples in whatever form the artist prefers. Reports on art samples only if interested. Original artwork returned at job's completion.

**Terms/Writers & Illustrators:** Pays on publication. Buys one-time rights. Pays $50-175 for assigned articles; $35-175 for unsolicited articles. Additional payment for ms/illustration packages: $50-75. Pay $100-150/color (cover) illustration; $50-75/b&w (inside); $50-75/color (inside). Sample copy $1. Writer's/illustrator's guidelines free with SASE.

**Tips:** Writers: "Study your target; do not submit material if you've never seen the magazine. In stories where the protagonist undergoes a behavior change, build up a credible reason for it. 'Comes to realize' is not a credible reason. We are overstocked at the moment with children's stories, but still buy one occasionally that we're unable to resist. Our greatest need is for articles for adults, in particular, articles on parenting from the single father's perspective." Illustrators: "Get examples of your work to as many editors as possible, but remember, there are hundreds of others doing the same thing. I review all samples that are submitted, and put those that appeal to me in a separate file as potential illustrators for the magazine. To get into the 'may call on' file, provide me with nonreturnable samples that illustrate the broadest range of your work—I may not appreciate your cartoon style, but think your realistic style is super or vice versa."

**SKYLARK**, 2233 171st St., Hammond IN 46323. (219)989-2262. Editor: Marcia Jaron. Art Director: Cathy Kadow. Children's Editor: Beverly Thevenin. Annual magazine. Circ. 500-750. 15% of material aimed at juvenile audience.

**Fiction:** Picture material, young readers, middle readers, young adults: animal, contemporary, fantasy, history, humorous, problem solving, religious, romance, science fiction, sports, spy/mystery/adventure. Does not want to see material about Satan worship, graphic sex. Byline given.

**Nonfiction:** Picture-oriented material, young readers, middle readers, young adults: animal, history, how-to, humorous, interview/profile, problem solving, religious, travel. Does not want to see material about Satan worship, graphic sex. Byline given.

**How to Contact/Writers:** Fiction/nonfiction: Send complete ms. SASE (IRC) for return of ms. Reports on queries/mss in 3 months. Will consider simultaneous, photocopied and computer printout submissions.

**Illustration:** Will review ms/illustration packages by authors/artists; ms/illustration packages submitted by authors with illustrations done by separate artists; illustrators work for possible use with fiction/nonfiction articles.

**How to Contact/Illustrators:** Illustrations only: Artwork. Reports on art samples in 3 months. Original artwork returned at job's completion "if SASE is included with artwork."

**Terms/Writers & Illustrators:** Pays in contributor's copies. Sample copy $3 with SAE. Writer's/illustrator's guidelines free with SASE.

**Tips:** Writers: "Do not send handwritten material, typed double-spaced only." Illustrators: "Use ink; pencil does not reproduce well. Also, send black and white only."

**\*STARWIND,** Starwind Press, Box 98, Ripley OH 45167. (513)392-4549. Editor: David F. Powell. Quarterly magazine. Estab. 1974. Circ. 2,000. "*Starwind* is a science fiction magazine which also publishes science and technology-related nonfiction along with the stories. Although the magazine is not specifically aimed at children, we do number teenagers among our readers. Such readers are the type who might enjoy reading science fiction (both young adult and adult), attending science fiction conventions, using computers, be interested in such things as astronomy, the space program, etc."

**Fiction:** Young adult/teens: fantasy, science fiction. Buys 8-10 mss/year. Average word length 2,000-10,000.

**Nonfiction:** Young adult/teens: how-to (science), interview/profile, travel, informational science book review. Does not want to see crafts. Buys 8-10 mss/year. Average word length: 1,500-5,000. Byline given.

**How to Contact/Writers:** Fiction/nonfiction: Send complete ms. SASE (IRC) for answer to query/return of ms, "proper postage please!" Reports on queries/mss in 2-3 months. Will consider photocopied, computer printout and submissions via disk or Macintoshin MacWrite, WriteNow, IBM PC or compatible in Multimate or ASCII format.

**Illustration:** Buys 12-15 illustrations/issue; buys 20-30 illustrations/year. Prefers to review "science fiction, fantasy or technical illustration." Will review ms/illustration packages submitted by authors/artists; ms/illustration packages submitted by authors with illustrations done by separate artists, (must be very impressed with art, though); illustrator's work for possible use with fiction/nonfiction articles and columns by other authors.

**How to Contact/Illustrators:** Ms/illustration packages: "Would like to see clips to keep on file (black and white only, preferably photocopies)." Illustrations only: "If we have an assignment for an artist, we will contact him/her with the ms we want illustrated. We like to see roughs before giving the go-ahead for final artwork." Reports in 2-3 months. Original art work returned at job's completion, "sometimes, if requested. We prefer to retain originals, but a high-quality PMT or Velox is fine if artist wants to keep artwork."

**Terms/Writers & Illustrators:** Pays 50% on acceptance (for art), 50% on publication. Pays 25% on acceptance (for writing), 75% on publication. Buys first North American serial rights; first rights; second serial (reprint rights). Pays $5-100/article. Additional payment for ms/illustration packages: $5-10. Payment for illustrations: Pays $30-50/b&w cover; $25/b&w inside. Sample copy $3.50 with 9 × 12 SAE and 5 first class stamps; Writer's/illustrator's guidelines free with business-size SAE and 1 first class stamp. "Specify fiction or nonfiction guidelines, or both."

**Tips:** Writers: "Read the magazines you're thinking of submitting to and familiarize yourself with children's magazines in general. Also, read lots of children's writing in general, especially specific genre if you're writing a genre story. (SF, romance, mystery, etc.). We list upcoming needs in our guidelines; writers can study these to get an idea of what we're looking for." Illustrators: "Show an editor your best work; study illustrations in back issues of magazines you're interested in illustrating for, and be able to work in a genre style if that's the type of magazine you want to publish your work. Everything is open to freelancers, as almost all our artwork is done out-of-house. (We occasionally use public domain illustrations, copyright-free illustrations and photographs.)"

**STRAIGHT**, Standard Publishing, 8121 Hamilton Ave., Cincinnati OH 45231. (513)931-4050. Articles/Fiction Editor: Carla J. Crane. Art Director: Frank Sutton. "Quarterly in weekly parts" magazine. Circ. 60,000. *Straight* is a magazine designed for today's Christian teenagers.
**Fiction:** Young adults: contemporary, humorous, problem solving, religious, sports. Does not want to see science fiction, fantasy, historical. Buys 100-115 mss/year. Average word length: 1,100-1,500. Byline given.
**Nonfiction:** Young adults: how-to, humorous, interview/profile, problem solving, religious. Does not want to see devotionals. Buys 24-30 mss/year. Average word length: 500-1,000. Byline given.
**How to Contact/Writers:** Fiction/nonfiction: Query or send complete ms. SASE (IRC) for answer to query and return of ms; include Social Security number with submission. Report on queries in 1-2 weeks; mss in 4-6 weeks. Will consider simultaneous, photocopied and computer printout submissions.
**Illustration:** Buys 40-45 illustrations/year. Preferred theme or style: Realistic, cartoon. Will review ms/illustration packages submitted by authors/artists "on occasion." Works on assignment only.
**How to Contact/Illustrators:** Ms/illustration packages: Query first. Illustrations only: Art done on assignment only. Artists must work through the art director.
**Terms/Writers & Illustrators:** Pays on acceptance. Buys first rights; one-time rights; second serial (reprint rights). Sample copy free with business SAE. Writer's/illustrator's guidelines free with business SAE.
**Tips:** "Study the copies and guidelines and get to know teenagers: how they talk, act and feel. Write fiction from the teenager's point of view. Fiction must appeal to teenagers and have an interesting, well-constructed plot. The main characters should be contemporary teens who cope with modern-day problems using Christian principles. Stories should be uplifting, positive and character-building, but not preachy. Conflicts must be resolved realistically, with thought-provoking and honest endings. Accepted length is 1,100 to 1,500 words. Nonfiction is accepted. We use devotional pieces, articles on current issues from a Christian point of view, and humor. Nonfiction pieces should concern topics of interest to teens, including school, family life, recreation, friends, part-time jobs, dating and music." (See listing for *R-A-D-A-R*.)

**\*'TEEN MAGAZINE**, Petersen Publishing Co., 8490 Sunset Blvd., Los Angeles CA 90069. (213)854-2950. Articles Editor: Whitney Woodward. Fiction Editor: Karle Dickerson. Art Director: Laurel Finnerty. Monthly magazine. Estab. 1957. Circ. 1,100,000. "We are a pure junior high and senior high female audience. *'TEEN* teens are upbeat and want to be informed." 100% of material is directed to children.
**Fiction:** Young adults: humorous, problem-solving, romance and spy/mystery/adventure. Does not want to see "that which does not apply to our market—i.e., science fiction, history, religious, adult-oriented." Buys 12 mss/year. Length for fiction: 10-15 pages typewritten, double-spaced.
**Nonfiction:** Young adults: animal, how-to, humorous, interview/profile, problem solving and young girl topics. Does not want to see adult oriented, adult point of view." Buys 25 mss/year. Length for articles: 10-20 pages typewritten, double-spaced. Byline given.

**Poetry:** "Only teen reader poetry accepted."
**How to Contact/Writers:** Fiction/nonfiction: Query. SASE (IRC) for answer query and return of ms. Reports on queries/mss in 10 weeks. Will consider photocopied, computer printout and electronic submissions via disk or modem.
**Illustration:** Buys 0-4 illustrations/issue. Preferred theme or style: "Various styles for variation. Use a lot of b&w illustration. Light, upbeat." Will review ms/illustration packages submitted by authors/artists; ms/illustration packages packages submitted by authors with illustrations done by separate artists; illustrator's work for possible use with fiction/nonfiction articles and columns by other authors.
**How to Contact/Illustrators:** Ms/illustration packages: "Query first." Illustrations only: "Want to see samples whether it be tearsheets, slides, finished pieces showing the style."
**Terms/Writers & Illustrators:** Pays on acceptance. Buys all rights. Pays $25-400 for assigned articles. Pays $25-250/b&w inside; $100-$400/color inside. Writer's/illustrator's guidelines free with SASE.
**Tips:** Illustrators: "Present professional finished work. Get familiar with magazine and send samples that would be compatible with the style of publication." There is a need for artwork with "fiction/specialty articles. Send samples or promotional materials on a regular basis."

**\*TEENAGE,** for Christian young people. Box 481, Loveland CO 80539. (303)669-3836. Articles Editor: Jolene L. Roehlkepartain. Art Director: Lisa Kretsch. Monthly (September-May, June/August issue) magazine. Estab. 1983. Circ. 32,000. *Teenage* is "an interdenominational religious magazine for Christian teenagers. We're interested in articles that will help teenagers grow spiritually."
**Nonfiction:** Young adults: how-to, humorous, interview/profile, problem solving and religious. "Do not want to see general nonfiction. We want nonfiction that will encourage teenagers to grow spiritually."
**How to Contact/Writers:** Nonfiction: Query with published clips. SASE (IRC) for answer to query and return of ms. Reports in 1 month. Will consider photocopied and computer printout submissions.
**Illustrations:** Buys 0-1 illustration/issue; buys 5-10 illustrations/year. Preferred theme or style: "Youthful, contemporary, cartoonish." Will review ms/illustration packages submitted by authors with illustrations done by separate artists; illustrator's work for possible use with fiction/nonfiction articles and columns by other authors. Works on assignment only.
**How to Contact/Illustrators:** "Query first." Reports on art samples only if interested. Original artwork returned at job's completion.
**Terms/Writers & Illustrators:** Pays on acceptance. Buys all rights. Pays $75-100 for assigned articles and unsolicited articles. Pays $200-$300 color cover illustration; $50-100 b&w inside illustration; $100-300 color inside illustration. Sample copy for $1 with 9×12 SAE and 3 first class stamps; writer's guidelines free for SASE.
**Tips:** Writers: "Include teenage anecdotes, current statistics and write about contemporary issues." Illustrators: "Be youthful and contemporary in your illustrations."

**3-2-1 CONTACT,** Children's Television Workshop, One Lincoln Plaza, New York NY 10023. (212)595-3456. Articles Editor: Jonathan Rosenbloom. Fiction Editor: Eric Weiner. Art Director: Al Nagy. Magazine published 10 times/year. Circ. 440,000. This is a science and technology magazine for 8-14 year olds. Features cover all areas of science and nature. 100% of material aimed at juvenile audience.
**Fiction:** Middle readers: science fiction, spy/mystery/adventure. Young adults: science fiction, spy/mystery/adventure. "All of our stories must have a science slant. No fantasy, history, religion, romance." Buys 10 mss/year. Average word length: 750-1,000. Byline given.

# Close-up

**Karle Dickerson**
*Managing Editor, 'TEEN*
*Los Angeles, California*

Thirty-three year old *'TEEN* magazine "has a long
history of being at the forefront of teen trends and
happenings, successfully addressing the most
pressing concerns of today's teens," says Karle
Dickerson, managing editor. There have been
magazine format changes over the years,
Dickerson says, "but the fundamentals of the teen
experience remain unchanged. Teens today want to feel good about
themselves," she points out. "They want information on how to make the most
of their looks, and want to know how to deal with parents, siblings, friends and
boys—as well as serious global issues."

Dickerson, a 7½ year veteran of the magazine, is no stranger to teens. Her
background as a junior and senior high school teacher, helps her to understand
teen concerns.

Because *'TEEN* is aimed at the teen market, adults need to be aware of
some of the heavy-hitting social problems that teens need to discuss, such as
drugs, pregnancy, runaways, adoption and incest. Dickerson admits to a
problem with some adult writers who handle such controversial problems in a
less than empathetic way. Approaching them from an adult point of view
frequently results in the message becoming too preachy. The solution to this
problem, in part, is to research *'TEEN*'s distinctive style.

She warns aspiring writers that teens are more sophisticated than they may
think. "Don't leave out details (in nonfiction) thinking teens won't be able to
understand," she warns. "You may need to tailor your writing for the teen
market, but don't skimp on research."

Much of *'TEEN* magazine's editorial material is decided upon at yearly
projection meetings to determine, based on reader mail, the topics that will be
addressed. A stable of freelancers is frequently used to write these pieces. "We
are receptive to new writers, " she adds, "because we want fresh perspectives."
Illustrators, also, should send samples and queries. Dickerson does warn
against artists getting "too complicated" with their art. "Artists sometimes get
lost in their artwork and lose track of what they're illustrating." Most of the
freelance artwork used is commissioned and is used to illustrate a specific
article. She suggests writers and illustrators study back issues of *'TEEN* to get
a feel for the style and topics used before submitting work.

*—Connie Eidenier*

**Nonfiction:** Middle readers: animal, how-to, interview/profile. Young adults: animal, how-to, interview/profile. Does not want to see religion, travel or history. Buys 20 mss/year. Average word length: 750-1,000. Byline given.

**How to Contact/Writers:** Fiction/nonfiction: Query with published clips. SASE (IRC) for answer to query. Reports on queries in 3 weeks. Will consider photocopied submissions.

**Illustration:** Buys 15 illustrations/issue; buys 150 illustrations/year. Works on assignment only.

**How to Contact/Illustrators:** Illustrations only: Send tearsheets. Reports on art samples only if interested. Original artwork returned at job's completion.

**Terms/Writers & Illustrators:** Pays on acceptance. Pays $100-400 for assigned/unsolicited articles. Pays $500-1,000/color (cover) illustration; $150-300/b&w (inside); $175-350/color (inside). Sample copy for $1.50 and 8 × 14 SASE; writer's/illustrator's guidelines free with 8½ × 11 SASE.

**Tips:** Looks for "features. We do not want articles based on library research. We want on-the-spot interviews about what's happening in science now." (See listing for *Kid City*.)

**\*TIGER BEAT**, DS Magazines, 1086 Teaneck Rd., Teanecck NJ 07666. (201)833-1800. Editor: Louise A. Barile. Art Director: Tracy Bucek. Monthly magazine. Estab. 1965. Circ. 150,000. "Tiger Beat is essentially a teen entertainment magazine. We are primarily interested in articles, fiction and illustrations of young celebrities in music, movies and TV. Readership ages 11-17." 100% of material directed to children.

**Fiction:** Young adult: fantasy, humorous, problem-solving, romance, spy/mystery/adventure and celebrity-oriented. Does not want to see "science fiction, talking animals. No religious or political material." Buys 5-10 mss/year. Average word length: 0-1,000. Byline given.

**Nonfiction:** Young adults: animal, how-to, humorous, interview/profile, problem solving and travel. Buys 12-24 mss/year. Average word length. 0-1,000. Byline given.

**How to Contact/Writers:** Fiction/nonfiction: Query, send complete ms. SASE (IRC) for answer to query and return of ms; include Social Security number with submission. Reports in 2 months. Will consider photocopied and computer printout submissions.

**Illustrations:** Buys 12-24 illustrations/year. Preferred theme or style: "Celebrity oriented." Will review ms/illustration packages submitted by authors/artists; ms/illustration packages submitted by authors with illustrations done by separate artists; illustrator's work for possible use with fiction/nonfiction articles and columns by other authors.

**How to Contact/Illustrators:** Ms/illustration packages: "Query." Illustrations only: send "resume, tearsheets." Reports in 2 months. Original artwork returned at job's completion.

**Terms/Writers & Illustrators:** Pays on publication. Buys first North American serial rights. Additional payment for ms/illustration packages is $50. Pays $50-150 for assigned articles. Pays $10-75/b&w cover illustration; $35-200 color cover illustration; $10-50 b&w inside illustration; $35-100 color inside illustration. Sample copy for 9 × 12 SAE and 3 first class stamps; writer's guidelines for SAE.

**\*TIGER BEAT STAR**, DS Magazines, 1086 Teaneck Rd., Teaneck NJ 07666. (201)833-1800. Articles Editor: Louise A. Barile. Art Director: Paul Castori. Bimonthly magazine. Estab. 1968. Circ. 150,000. *Tiger Beat Star* is an "entertainment magazine for teens (ages 11-17) featuring the latest stars in music, movies and TV." 100% of material aimed at juvenile audience.

**Fiction:** Young adults: contemporary, fantasy, humorous, problem-solving, romance and celebrity. Buys 1-5 mss/year. Average word length: 0-1,000. Byline given.
**Nonfiction:** Young adults: how-to, humorous, interview/profile, problem solving and travel. Buys 12-24 mss/year. Average word length: 0-1,000. Byline given.
**How to Contact/Writers:** Fiction: Send complete ms. Nonfiction: Query. SASE (IRC) for answer to query and return of ms; include Social Security number with submission. Reports in 2 months. Will consider photocopied and computer printout submissions.
**Illustration:** Buys 1-10 illustrations/year. Preferred theme or style: "Celebrity oriented." Will review ms/illustration packages submitted by authors/artists; submitted by authors with illustrations done by separate artists; illustrator's work for possible use with fiction/nonfiction articles and columns by other authors.
**How to Contact/Illustrators:** Ms/illustration packages: "Query first." Illustrations only: Send "query, résumé and tearsheets." Reports on art samples in 2 months. Original artwork returned at job's completion.
**Terms/Writers & Illustrators:** Pays on publication. Buys first North American serial rights. Pays $50-200 for assigned articles and unsolicited articles. Additional payment for ms/illustration packages. Pays $35-200/b&w cover illustration; $75-250 color cover illustration; $10-55 b&w inside illustration and $25-75 color inside illustration. Sample copy for 9 × 12 SAE and 3 first-class stamps. Writer's guidelines free with SASE.

**TOGETHER TIME,** Children's Ministries, 6401 The Paseo, Kansas City MO 64131. Editor: Lynda T. Boardman. Executive Editor: Robert D. Troutman. Weekly tabloid. "*Together Time* is a take-home reading piece for 2 and 3 year-olds and their parents. It correlates with Adldersgate Graded Curriculum for twos and threes. The major purposes of *Together Time* are to: provide a home-reading piece to help parents build Christian behavior and values in their children, provide life-related home reinforcement for Biblical concepts taught in the Sunday School curriculum." 100% of material aimed at juvenile audience.
**Fiction:** Picture material: religious. "Fiction stories should have definite Christian emphasis or character-building values, without being preachy. The setting, plot and action should be realistic." Average word length: 150-200. Byline given.
**How to Contact/Writers:** Fiction: Send complete ms. SASE (IRC) for return of ms. Reports on mss in 10-12 weeks.
**Terms/Writers:** Pays on acceptance. Buys all rights. Pays 3.5¢/word for unsolicited articles. Complimentary copy mailed to contributor. Writer's guidelines free with #10 SAE.
**Tips:** "*Together Time* is planned to reinforce the Biblical concepts taught in the S.S. curriculum. Because of this, the basic themes needed are as follows: security in knowing there is a God, God is creator and giver of good gifts, Jesus is God's son, Jesus is a friend and helper, the Bible is God's special book, introduction to God's love and forgiveness, asking forgiveness (from parents, teacher, friends and God), expressing simple prayers, church is a special place where we learn about God, each person is special and loved by God, accept failure without losing self-confidence, desire to be like Jesus, desire to be helpful, appreciate God's world, appreciate community helpers." (See listing for *Discoveries*.)

**TOUCH,** Calvinettes, Box 7259, Grand Rapids MI 49510. (616)241-5616. Editor: Joanne Ilbrink. Managing Editor: Carol Smith. Art Director: Chris Cook. Monthly (with combined issues May/June, July/Aug.) magazine. Circ. 14,300. "*Touch* is designed to help girls ages 9-14 see how God is at work in their lives and in the world around them." 100% of material aimed at juvenile audience.
**Fiction:** Middle readers: animal, contemporary, history, humorous, problem solving, religious, romance. Does not want to see unrealistic stories and those with trite, easy endings. Buys 40 mss/year. Average word length: 400-1,000. Byline given.

**Nonfiction:** Middle readers: how-to, humorous, interview/profile, problem solving, religious. Buys 5 mss/year. Average word length: 200-800. Byline given.

**How to Contact/Writers:** Fiction/nonfiction: Send complete ms. SASE (IRC) for return of ms. Report on mss in 2 months. Will consider simultaneous, photocopied and computer printout submissions.

**Illustration:** Buys 1-2 illustrations/issue; buys 10-15 illustrations/year. Prefers illustrations to go with stories. Will review ms/illustration packages by authors/artists; ms/illustration packages submitted by authors with illustrations done by separate artists. Works on assignment only.

**How to Contact/Illustrators:** Ms/illustration packages: "We would prefer to consider finished art with a ms." Illustrations only: "A sample of work could be submitted in tear sheets or rough drafts." Reports on art samples only if interested.

**Terms/Writers & Illustrators:** Pays on publication. Buys first North American serial rights; first rights; second serial (reprint rights); simultaneous rights. Pays $20-50 for assigned articles; $5-30 for unsolicited articles. "We send complimentary copies in addition to pay." Additional payment for ms/illustration packages: $5-20. Pays $25-50/b&w (cover) illustration; $15-25/b&w (inside) illustration. Writer's guidelines free with SAE and first class stamps.

**Tips:** Writers: "The stories should be current, deal with children's problems and joys, and help girls see God at work in their lives through humor as well as problem solving." Illustrators: "Keep trying! Write for guidelines and our biannual update. It is difficult working with artists who are not local."

**TQ,** Teen Quest, Good News Broadcasting Assoc., Box 82808, Lincoln NE 68501. (402)474-4567. Articles/Fiction Editor: Karen Christianson. Art Director: Victoria Valentine. Monthly (combined July/August issue) magazine. Circ. 70,000. Ours is a magazine for Christian teenagers. Articles and fiction purchased from freelancers must have a Christian basis, be relevant to contemporary teen culture, and be written in a style understandable and attractive to teenagers. Artwork must be likewise appropriate. 100% of material aimed at teen audience.

**Fiction:** Young adults: contemporary, fantasy, humorous, problem solving, religious, romance, science fiction, sports, spy/mystery/adventure. Does not want to see historical material. Buys 40 mss/year. Average word length: 1,500-3,000. Byline given.

**Nonfiction:** Young adults: how-to, humorous, interview/profile, problem solving, religious, travel. Buys 30 mss/year. Average word length: 500-2,000. Byline given.

**How to Contact/Writers:** Fiction/nonfiction: Query. SASE (IRC) for answer to query and return of ms. Reports on queries in 6 weeks; mss in 6-8 weeks. Will consider simultaneous, photocopied and computer printout submissions.

**Illustration:** Buys 5 illustrations/issue; buys 50 illustrations/year. Preferred theme or style: Realistic, somewhat contemporary, but not too far out of the mainstream. Works on assignment only.

**How to Contact/Illustrators:** Ms/illustration packages: Query only. Illustrations only: Send tearsheets. Reports on art samples only if interested. Original art work returned at job's completion.

**Terms/Writers & Illustrators:** Pays on completion of assignment. Buys one-time rights. Pays 8-10¢/word for assigned articles; 4-7¢/word for unsolicited articles. Sample copy for 10×12 SAE and 5 first-class stamps; writer's/illustrator's guidelines for business-size envelope and 1 first-class stamp.

**Tips:** Writers: "Just familiarize yourself with the magazine to which you're submitting. Get to know what we like, our style. Fiction: be current; Christian message without being 'preachy.' Most stories we buy will center on the lives and problems of 14 to 17 year-old characters. The problems involved should be common to teens (dating, family, alcohol and drugs, peer pressure, school, sex, talking about one's faith to nonbelievers, standing up for convictions, etc.) in which the resolution (or lack of it) is true to our reader's experiences. In other words, no happily-ever-after endings, last-page spiritual conversions or pat answers to complex problems. We're interested in the everyday (though still profound) experiences of teen life—stay away from sensationalism." Illustrators: "Fiction: assignment only; send samples of work."

**TURTLE MAGAZINE,** For Preschool Kids, Ben Franklin Literary & Medical Society, Children's Better Health Institute, Box 567, Indianapolis IN 46206. (317)636-8881. Articles/Fiction Editor: Beth Wood Thomas. Art Director: Bart Rivers. Monthly/bimonthly magazine, Jan/Feb., Mar/April, May/June and July/August. Circ. approx. 650,000. *Turtle* uses bedtime or naptime stories that can be read to the child. Also used are health-related articles. 100% of material aimed at juvenile audience.
**Fiction:** Picture material: animal, health. Does not want to see stories about monsters or scary things. Stories in which the characters indulge in unhealthy activity like eating junk food—unless a moral is taught. Buys 50 mss/year. Average word length: 200-600. Byline given.
**Nonfiction:** Picture material: animal, contemporary, health. Buys 20 mss/year. Average word length: 200-600. Byline given.
**How to Contact/Writers:** Fiction/nonfiction: Send complete ms. SASE (IRC) for return of ms; include Social Security number with submission. Reports on mss in 8-10 weeks. Will consider computer printout submissions.
**Illustration:** Buys 20-25 illustrations/issue from freelancers; 160-200 illustrations/year from freelancers. Prefers "realistic and humorous illustration."
**Terms/Writers & Illustrators:** Pays $225 color (cover) illustration, $25-65/b&w (inside); $60-125/color (inside). Sample copy 75¢. Writer's/illustrator's guidelines free with SAE and 1 first-class stamp.
**Tips:** "We need more stories that reflect these changing times but at the same time communicate good, wholesome values. We are especially in need of holiday material—stories, articles and activities. Characters in realistic stories should be up-to-date. Many of our readers have working mothers and/or come from single-parent homes." (See listings for *Children's Digest, Children's Playmate, Humpty Dumpty's Magazine, Jack and Jill.*)

**TYRO MAGAZINE,** Tyro Publishing, 194 Carlbert St., Sault Ste. Marie ON P6A 5E1 Canada. (705)253-6402. Articles Editor: George Hemingway. Fiction Editor: Stan Gordon. Art Director: Lorelee. Bimonthly magazine. Circ. 1,000. "*Tyro* is a practice medium for developing writers and accepts almost anything worthy." 15% of material aimed at juvenile audience.
**Fiction:** "We have published material and will consider submissions in any area and level." Buys 80 mss/year. Average word length: 5,000. Byline given.
**Nonfiction:** "We will consider any of these: animal, history, how-to, humorous, interview/profile, problem solving, religious, travel." Buys 6 mss/year. Average word length: 5,000. Byline given.
**How to Contact/Writers:** Fiction: Send complete ms. Nonfiction: Query. SASE (IRC) for answer to query and return of ms. Reports on queries/mss in 1 month. Will consider photocopied and computer printout submissions.
**Illustration:** "We use only camera-ready, b&w art." Buys "up to 5" illustrations/issue; buys "up to 30" illustrations/year. Will review ms/illustration packages by authors/artists; ms/illustration packages submitted by authors with illustrations done by separate artists; illustrator's work for possible use with fiction/nonfiction articles.

**How to Contact/Illustrators:** Ms/illustration packages: Send complete ms with final art. Reports on art samples in 1 month. Original artwork returned at job's completion.
**Terms/Writers & Illustrators:** "Since we are a practice vehicle, no fees paid." Pays in contributor copies. Sample copy $5. Writer's guidelines free with SAE.
**Tips:** "Many believe that because children's literature is often simple it is easy to write. That's not so. It's a discipline that requires as much, if not more, skill as any writing."

**\*U\*S\*KIDS®**, A Weekly Reader Magazine, Field Publications, 245 Long Hill Rd., Middletown CT 06457. (203)638-2400. Articles Editor: Emily Schell. Fiction Editor: Gabriel Davis. Art Director: Nancy Fisher. Bimonthly magazine. Estab. 1987. Circ. 250,000. "*U\*S\*Kids* is a 44-page magazine with a 'real world' focus. Its objective is to teach 5 to 9-year-olds about their world in a fun and entertaining way. Publication includes news, true-life stories, science and nature stories, activities and puzzles." 100% of material aimed at juvenile audience.
**Fiction:** Young readers: animal, contemporary, humorous, spy/mystery/adventure. Middle readers: animal, contemporary, humorous, spy/mystery/adventure. Does not want to see fantasy. Buys 15-20 mss/year. Average word length: 300-400. Byline given.
**Nonfiction:** Young readers: animal, interview/profile, true-life, lifestyles. Middle readers: animal, interview/profile. Buys 15-20 mss/year. Average word length: 200-300. Byline given "sometimes."
**How to Contact/Writers:** Fiction: Send complete ms. Nonfiction: Query with published clips. SASE (IRC) for return of ms. Reports on queries/mss in 4-6 weeks. Will consider computer printout submissions.
**Terms/Writers and Illustrators:** Pays on acceptance. Buys first North American serial rights for fiction, all rights for nonfiction. Pays $150-300 for assigned or unsolicited articles. Writer's guidelines free with SASE.
**Tips:** "Include intriguing title; quick beginning; fast-moving prose; clear treatment of subject matter; humor; emphasis on active response of reader; expressions that make the child want to repeat certain phrases. Write on child's reading level; in the case of *U\*S\*Kids*, grade 2 reading level."

**VENTURE**, Christian Service Brigade, Box 150, Wheaton IL 60189. (312)665-0630. Articles/Fiction Editor: Steven Neideck. Art Director: Robert Fine. Bimonthly magazine. Circ. 23,000. The magazine is designed "to speak to the concerns of boys from a biblical perspective. To provide wholesome, entertaining reading for boys." 100% of material aimed at juvenile audience.
**Fiction:** Middle readers, young adults: animal, contemporary, history, humorous, problem solving, religious, sports, spy/mystery/adventure. Does not want to see fantasy, romance, science fiction. Buys 12 mss/year. Average word length: 1,000-1,500. Byline given.
**Nonfiction:** Middle readers, young adults: animal, history, how-to, humorous, interview/profile, problem solving, religious, travel. Buys 3 mss/year. Average word length: 1,000-1,500. Byline given.
**How to Contact/Writers:** Fiction/nonfiction: Query; send complete ms. SASE (IRC) for answer to query and return of ms. Reports on queries in 1 week; mss in 2 weeks. Will consider simultaneous, photocopied and computer printout submissions.
**Illustration:** Buys 1 illustration/issue; buys 6 illustrations/year. Will review ms/illustration packages by authors/artists; ms/illustration packages submitted by authors with illustrations done by separate artists; illustrator's work for possible use with fiction/nonfiction articles.
**How to Contact/Illustrators:** Ms/illustration packages: query first. Illustrations only: Send tearsheets, slides. Reports on art samples in 2 weeks. Original art work returned at job's completion.

**Terms/Writers & Illustrators:** Pays on publication. Buys first North American serial rights; first rights; one-time rights; second serial (reprint rights). Pays $75-150 for assigned articles; $30-100 for unsolicited articles. Additional payment for ms/illustration packages: $100-200. Pays $35-125/b&w (cover) illustration; $35-50/b&w (inside) illustration. Sample copy $1.50 with 9 × 12 SAE and 85¢ postage. Writer's/illustrator's guidelines free with SAE and 1 first-class stamp.
**Tips:** "Write about children's interests, not your own interests."

*\*VOICE*, Scholastic, Inc., 730 Broadway, New York NY 10003. (212)505-3000. Fiction Editor: Forrest Stone. Art Director: Joy Makon. Bimonthly "during school year (18 issues/year)" magazine. Estab. 1946. Circ. 250,000. *Voice* is "a language-arts magazine for junior high and high school students." 100% of material directed to children.
**Fiction:** Young adults: contemporary, fantasy, history, humorous, problem-solving, romance, science fiction, sports, spy/mystery/adventure, poetry and drama. Does not want to see "anything over 3,000 words unless writer is quite established." Buys 10 mss/year. Average word length: 0-3,000. Byline given.
**Nonfiction:** Young adults: humorous, problem solving and travel. Buys 5 mss/year. Average word length: 0-1,000. Byline given.
**Poetry:** Reviews "good" poetry; send no more than 10 submissions.
**How to Contact/Writers:** Fiction: Send complete ms. Nonfiction: Query with published clips. SASE (IRC) for answer to query; return of ms; include Social Security number with submission. Reports on queries in 2-4 weeks; mss in 1-3 months. Will consider simultaneous, photocopied and computer printout submissions.
**Terms/Writers & Illustrators:** Pays on publication. Pays $100-$500 for assigned and unsolicited articles.
**Tips:** "Parents and teachers have a big advantage in understanding kids." (See listings for *Scholastic Math* and *Scope*.)

**WEE WISDOM MAGAZINE**, A Children's Magazine, Unity School of Christianity, Unity Village MO 64025. (816)524-3550, ext. 329. FAX: (816)251-3550. Editor: Judy Gehrlein. Published 10 times/year, magazine. 100% of material aimed at juvenile audience.
**Fiction:** Picture material, young readers, middle readers: animal, contemporary, fantasy, history, humorous, problem solving, religious, science fiction, sports, spy/mystery/adventure. Does not want to see anything on war, crime; avoid negative perspective. Buys 60 mss/year. Average word length: 800. Byline given. Rarely assign stories.
**How to Contact/Writers:** Fiction: Send complete ms. SASE (IRC) for return of ms. Report on mss in 8 weeks. Will consider computer printout submissions.
**Illustration:** Buys 25 illustrations/issue; buys 250 illustrations/year. Preferred theme or style: "We assign according to literature." Will review ms/illustration packages by authors/artists; ms/illustration packages submitted by authors with illustrations done by separate artists; illustrators work for possible use with fiction articles. Works on assignment only.
**How to Contact/Illustrators:** Ms/illustration packages: No queries, full manuscript, sample illustration package. Illustrations only: Samples. "We are interested in freelancers in children's art. We are most interested in seeing their work—perhaps their range in work." Reports on art samples in 6 weeks. "Originals returned one year after publication."
**Terms/Writers & Illustrators:** Pays on acceptance. Buys first North American serial rights. Pays 5-9¢/word for stories. "We pay the same rate for assigned work and unsolicited. We rarely assign stories. Contributor copies are sent at no charge." Pays $80 full page (2-color) illustration, $30-60 fraction (2-color) illustration; $100 full page (4-color) illustration, $30-60 fraction (4-color) illustration; $200 double cover illustration; $200

calendar (always 4-color, always a package). Free sample copy. Writer's/illustrator's guidelines free with SASE.

**Tips:** Writers: "Use dialogue in stories taken from real life rather than imagination. Develop characters that express real feelings and explore human relationships through behavior and dialogue. Do not over-describe with adjectives. We need to read your fresh, individual approach to children's fiction of no more than 800 words. We're looking for up-to-date kids with basic values. We must have positive yet plausible solutions to real situations. We select very few poems within a year. We are open to puzzles and riddles for 4-12 year olds." Illustrators: "We are always looking for illustrators who project humor, beauty and fun for children."

*Judy Gehrlein, editor of Wee Wisdom magazine, purchased first rights to this piece by Mary Morgan, Kansas City, Missouri. According to Gehrlein, this watercolor cover illustration "communicates warmth and feeling unique to Wee Wisdom."*

**WITH,** Faith & Life Press, Mennonite Publishing House, Box 347, 722 Main, Newton KS 67114. (316)283-5100. Articles/Fiction Editor, Art Director: Susan Janzen. Monthly magazine. Circ. 6,500. Magazine published for teenagers in Mennonite congregations. We deal with issues affecting teens and try to help them make choices reflecting an Anabaptist-Mennonite faith. 100% of material aimed at juvenile audience.

**Fiction:** Teenagers: contemporary, humorous, problem solving, religious, sports. Buys 10 mss/year. Average word length: 1,200-1,500. Byline given.

**Nonfiction:** Young adults: how-to, humorous, interview/profile, problem solving, religious. Buys 5-6 mss/year. Average word length: 1,000-1,750. Byline given.

**How to Contact/Writers:** Fiction: Send complete ms. Nonfiction: Query. SASE (IRC) for answer to query and return of ms. Reports on queries in 1 month; mss in 3 months. Will consider simultaneous, photocopied, and computer printout submissions.

**Illustration:** Buys 6-8 illustrations/issue; buys 70-75 illustrations/year. Preferred theme or style: Candids/interracial. Will review ms/illustration packages by authors/artists; ms/illustration packages submitted by authors with illustrations done by separate artists; illustrator's work for possible use with fiction/nonfiction articles.

**How to Contact/Illustrators:** Ms/illustration packages: Query first. Illustrations only: Send slides 8×10 b&w prints preferred. Reports on art samples in 1 month. Original art work returned at job's completion.

**Terms/Writers & Illustrators:** Pays on acceptance. Buys one-time rights; second serial (reprint rights). Pays $40-80 for assigned articles; $20-80 for unsolicited articles. Additional payment for ms/illustration packages: $30-100. Pays $25-50/b&w (cover) illustration; $25-35/b&w (inside) illustration. Sample copy $1.25 with 9×12 SAE and 85¢ postage. Writer's/illustrator's guidelines free.

**Tips:** Writers: "Fiction and poetry are most open to freelancers." Illustrators: "We use almost exclusively illustrations from freelancers. Since we can't use color photos, I appreciate submissions that are b&w. Art can be 2-color."

**\*WONDER TIME,** Beacon Hill Press, 6401 The Paseo, Kansas City MO 64131. (816)333-7000. Editor: Evelyn Beals. Weekly magazine. Circ. 45,000. "*Wonder Time* is a full-color story paper for first and second graders. It is designed to connect Sunday School learning with the daily living experiences and growth of the primary child. Since *Wonder Time's* target audience is children ages six to eight, the readability goal is to encourage beginning readers to read for themselves. The major purposes of *Wonder Time* are to: Provide a life-related paper which will build Christian values and encourage ethical behavior. Provide reinforcement for the biblical concepts taught in the 'Exploring God's Word' Sunday School curriculum." 100% of material aimed at juvenile audience.

**Fiction:** Young readers: problem-solving, religious. Buys 52 mss/year. Average word length: 400-550. Byline given.

**Poetry:** Reviews religious poetry of 4-8 lines.

**How to Contact/Writers:** Fiction/nonfiction: Send complete ms. SASE (IRC) for return of ms. Reports on queries/mss in 6-8 weeks. Will consider simultaneous, photocopied and computer printout submissions.

**Illustration:** Buys 10-15 illustrations/year. Will review ms/illustration packages submitted by authors/artists; ms/illustration packages submitted by authors with illustrations done by separate artists; illustrator's work for possible use with your fiction/nonfiction articles and columns by other authors. Works on assignment only.

**How to Contact/Illustrators:** Ms/illustration packages: Ms with sketch. Illustrations only: Samples of work. Reports on art samples only if interested.

**Terms/Writers and Illustrators:** Pays 1 month after acceptance. Buys first rights and second serial (reprint rights). Pays 3.5¢/word for stories and a complimentary contributor's copy of publication. Additional payment for ms/illustration package. Sample copy, writer's/illustrator's guidelines with 9½×12 SAE and 2 first class stamps.

**Tips:** "These basic themes reappear regularly: faith in God; putting God first; choosing to please God; understanding that Jesus is God's Son and our Savior; choosing to do right; asking forgiveness; trusting God in hard times; prayer: trusting God to answer; appreciation of the Bible as God's word to man; importance of Bible memorization; understanding both meanings of church: a place where we worship God, a fellowship of God's people working together; understanding each person's value to God and to others; showing love and kindness to others; enriching family life, including non-traditional family units; addressing current problems which children may face."

**\*THE WORLD OF BUSINES$ KIDS,** America's Future, Lemonade Kids, Inc., Suite 330, 301 Almeria Ave., Coral Gables FL 33134. (305)445-8869. Articles Editor: Jacky Robinson. Art Director: Donn Matus. Quarterly newsletter. Estab. 1988. Circ. 75,000. "We cover stories about young entrepreneurs, how teens and preteens can become entrepreneurs, and useful information for effective business operation and management. Our goal is to help prepare America's youth for the complex and competitive world of business by sharing with them every possible business experience, the problems *and* the solutions. And while we're *serious* about business, we want them to know that business can be *fun*. 99% of material aimed at juvenile audience with one article aimed at parents in each issue."

**Nonfiction:** Middle readers: how-to, interview/profile, problem solving. Young adult/teens: how-to, interview/profile, problem solving. "All must relate to business." Does not want to see "any articles which do not deal with business." Buys 15 mss/year. "Our goal is 50% freelance." Average word length: 200-600. Byline: Listed as a contributing writer.

**Poetry:** Reviews free verse, light verse, traditional poetry; 25-50 lines.

**How to Contact/Writers:** Nonfiction: Send complete ms. SASE (IRC) for return of ms; include Social Security number with submission. Reports on mss in 2 months. Prefers letter-quality submissions.

**Terms/Writers:** Pays on publication. Buys all rights. Pays 15¢ word/unsolicited articles; $35-50 for puzzles/games; $15-20 for cartoons; $5-10 for b&w/8 × 10 photos. Sample copies available. Writer's guidelines and sample copy available.

**Tips:** Looking for "any nonfiction pertaining to teens in the business world. How to choose, build, improve, market or advertise a business. When, and how, to hire (or fire) employees. Lots of profiles about successful young entrepreneurs. The latest in *any* field—entertainment, sports, medicine, etc.—where teens are making megabucks (or just movie money!). New products; book reviews on children and money; motivational articles; how-to invest/save money; news releases; tax information; stock market tips; bonds; banking; precious metals; cartoons; puzzles; poetry; games" also sought.

**YOUNG AMERICAN,** America's Newspaper for Kids, Young American Publishing Co., Inc., Box 12409, Portland OR 97212. (503)230-1895. Articles/Fiction Editor: Kristina Linden. Art Director: Tim Stevens. Biweekly (national) tabloid. Circ. 5,000,000+.

**Fiction:** Young readers, middle readers, young adults: animal, contemporary, fantasy, history, humorous, problem solving, science fiction, sports, spy/mystery/adventure. Does not want to see religious themes. Buys 12-15 mss/year. Average word length: 500-1,000. Byline given.

**Nonfiction:** Young readers, middle readers, young adults: animal, history, how-to, humorous, interview/profile, problem solving. Does not want to see preachy, moralistic themes. Buys 75 mss/year. Average word length: 350. Byline given sometimes.

**How to Contact/Writers:** Fiction/nonfiction: Send complete ms. SASE (IRC) for return of ms; include Social Security number with submission. Reports on mss in 4 months. Will consider photocopied and computer printout submissions.

**Illustration:** "Future plans are to increase freelance illustrations." Will review ms/illustration packages by authors/artists; ms/illustration packages submitted by authors with illustrations done by separate artists; illustrator's work for possible use with fiction/nonfiction articles.

**How to Contact/Illustrators:** Ms/illustration packages: Submit complete ms. Illustrations only: Send examples of style. Reports on art samples in 4 months. Original art work returned at job's completion.

**Terms/Writers & Illustrators:** Pays on publication. Buys first North American serial rights; may buy reprint rights. Pay is "negotiable" for assigned articles. Pay for illustrations is "negotiable." Sample copy for $1.50. Writer's guidelines free with SASE.

**Tips:** "Know today's kids—quote them when possible. Fiction—don't be condescending. Increased frequency means we will be buying more mss."

**THE YOUNG CRUSADER**, National WCTU, 1730 Chicago Ave., Evanston IL 60201. (312)864-1396. Managing Editor: Michael C. Vitucci. Monthly magazine. Circ. 3,500. The magazine is geared to the 8-12 year old child. It stresses high morals and good character. Nature and informational stories are also used. Above all, the stories should not be preachy or religious as the magazine is used in public schools. 100% of material aimed at juvenile audience.

**Fiction:** Middle readers: contemporary, problem solving, positive character building. Does not want to see preachy, religious-type stories. Buys 4 mss/year. Average word length: 550-650. Byline given.

**Nonfiction:** Middle readers: animal, history, interview/profile, problem solving, travel. Buys 10 mss/year. Average word length: 550-650. Byline given.

**How to Contact/Writers:** Fiction/nonfiction: Send complete ms. Will consider simultaneous, photocopied and computer printout submissions. "I require submissions to be copies. If used, I will publish; if not used, the manuscript will be destroyed."

**Terms/Writers & Illustrators:** Pays on publication. Buys second serial (reprint rights); simultaneous rights. Pays ½¢/word for assigned/unsolicited articles. Free sample copy.

**Tips:** "Don't write down to the child. Writers often underestimate their audience." Looks for: "nonfiction stories stressing good character and high morals."

**\*YOUNG JUDAEAN**, Hadassah Zionist Youth Commission, 50 W. 58th St., New York NY 10019. (212)303-8271. Quarterly magazine. Estab. 1910. Circ. 4,000. "Magazine is intended for members—age 9-12—of Young Judaea, which is the Zionist-oriented youth movement sponsored by the Hadassah Women's Organization." 100% of material is directed to children.

**Fiction:** Middle readers: contemporary, fantasy, history, humorous, science fiction, sports and spy/mystery/adventure. Does not want to see "any material that does *not* relate to Jewish themes. Also, no material whose Jewishness is theological rather than cultural." Buys 10-15 mss/year. Average word length: 500-1,500. Byline given.

**Nonfiction:** Middle readers, young adults: history, how-to, humorous, interview/profile, problem solving and travel. Does not want to see "anything that preaches a particular theological outlook. Anything that is *not* related to Jewish life." Buys 30 mss/year. Average word length: 500-1,500. Byline given.

**How to Contact/Writers:** Fiction: Send complete ms. Nonfiction: Send complete ms or query. SASE (IRC) for answer to query and return of ms. Will consider photocopied and computer printout submissions.

**Illustration:** Buys 6 illustrations/issue. Preferred theme or style: "Lively and anecdotal." Will review ms/illustration packages submitted by authors/artists; ms/illustration packages submitted by authors with illustrations done by separate artists; illustrator's work for possible use with fiction/nonfiction articles and columns by other authors.

**How to Contact/Illustrators:** Ms/illustration packages: Send complete ms with final art. Illustrations only: Send tearsheets. Original artwork returned at job's completion "if requested."

**Terms/Writers & Illustrators:** Pays on publication. Buys first North American serial rights. Pays $20-50 for assigned articles; $20-50 for unsolicited articles. Additional payment for ms/illustration packages is "manuscript plus $20 per illustration." Pays $20-40/b&w cover illustration, $20-30 b&w inside illustration. Sample copy 75¢ with SASE; free writer's/illustrator's guidelines.

**\*YOUNG SALVATIONIST**, The Salvation Army, 799 Bloomfield Ave., Verona NJ 07003. (201)239-0606. Articles Editor: Captain Robert R. Hostetler. Monthly magazine. Estab. 1984. Circ. 50,000. "We accept material with clear Christian content written for high school age teenagers. *Young Salvationist* is published for teenage members of The Salvation Army, a fundamental, activist denomination of the Christian Church." 100% of material directed to youth.

**Fiction:** Picture-oriented material, young adults: religious. Buys 12-20 mss/year. Average word length: 750-1,200. Byline given.
**Nonfiction:** Young adults: religious. Buys 40-50 mss/year. Average word length: 750-1,200. Byline given.
**Poetry:** Reviews 16-20 line poetry dealing with a Christian theme. Send no more than 6 submissions.
**How to Contact/Writers:** Query; query with published clips or send complete ms. SASE (IRC) for answer to query/return of ms. Reports on queries in 2-3 weeks; mss in 1 month. Will consider simultaneous, photocopied and computer printout submissions.
**Illustrations:** Buys 2-3 illustrations/issue; 20-30 illustrations/year. Will review ms/illustration packages submitted by authors/artists; ms/illustrations packages submitted by authors with illustrations done by separate artists; illustrator's work for possible use with fiction/nonfiction articles and columns by other authors.
**How to Contact/Illustrators:** Ms/illustration packages: "Query or send manuscript with art." Reports on artwork in 2-3 weeks (with SASE). Original artwork returned at job's completion "if requested."
**Terms/Writers & Illustrators:** Pays on acceptance. Buys first North American serial rights, first rights, one-time rights, second serial (reprint rights) simultaneous rights. Pays $40/assigned articles (depends on length); $25 for unsolicited articles (depends on length). Additional payment for ms/illustration packages "depends on use." Pays $100-150 color (cover) illustration; $50-100 b&w (inside) illustration; $100-150 color (inside) illustration. Sample copy for 9 × 12 SAE and 3 first class stamps. Writer's/illustrator's guidelines free for #10 SASE.
**Tips:** Writers: "Write for our themes." Looking for "nonfiction articles to fit themes."

**\*YOUR BIG BACKYARD,** National Wildlife Federation, 8925 Leesburg Pike, Vienna VA 22184-0001. (703)790-4274. Articles Editor: Sallie A. Luther. Art Director: Kimberly Kerin. Monthly magazine. Estab. 1980. Circ. 512,000. This magazine is "aimed at readers 3-5 years old; full-color; lots of photos of animals, especially young ones; all nature and conservation oriented. We require ability to describe and write to preschoolers, painting word pictures, often with a humorous touch." 100% of material aimed at juvenile audience.
**Fiction:** Picture-oriented material: animal, nature; conservation. Young readers: animal, nature; conservation. Buys 3-4 mss/year. Average word length: 600. Byline given.
**Nonfiction:** Picture-oriented material: animal, crafts; simple games. Young readers: animal, crafts; simple games. Buys 1-2 mss/year. Average word length: 600. Byline given.
**How to Contact/Writers:** Fiction/nonfiction: query. SASE (IRC) for answer to query/return of ms; include Social Security number with submission. Reports on queries/mss in 4-6 weeks. Will consider computer printout submissions.
**Illustration:** Buys 1-2 illustrations/issue; buys 12-15 illustrations/year. Prefers to review "fanciful, realistic, warm and appealing art; lots of bright colors; originality appreciated." Will review ms/illustration packages submitted by authors/artists; ms/illustration packages submitted by authors with illustrations done by separate artists; illustrator's work for possible use with fiction/nonfiction articles and columns by other authors.
**How to Contact/Illustrators:** Ms/illustration packages: "Query first, then send complete ms with sketches." Illustrations only: Send résumé, tearsheets, slides; "samples of work in whatever form available." Reports in 4-6 weeks. Original art work returned at job's completion, "depending on rights sold."
**Terms/Writers & Illustrators:** Pays writers on acceptance; illustrators upon receipt of invoice. Buys first North American serial rights; first rights, one-time rights; second serial (reprint rights); all rights. Pays $250-500/assigned or unsolicited article. Payment for ms/illustration packages: $100-600. Sample copy free with 9 × 12 SASE; writer's guidelines free with SASE.

**Tips:** "This is a very tough market. The edge goes to the writer who can avoid trite situations, or can present an 'old' situation with a new twist. Humor is always a plus, and scientific accuracy for us is mandatory." Illustrators: "Send your best samples to as many people as you can. But take time to look up back copies of the magazines to see what is needed. Color and warmth win out." Looking for: "Fiction stories with an animal, nature, a conservation base. Do your homework: know your subjects, do good research and present stories that avoid trite situations and stereotyping." (See listing for *Ranger Rick*.)

**YOUTH UPDATE**, St. Anthony Messenger Press, 1615 Republic St., Cincinnati OH 45210. (513)241-5615. Articles Editor: Carol Ann Morrow. Art Director: Julie Lonneman. Monthly newsletter. Circ. 36,000. Each issue focuses on one topic only. *Youth Update* addresses the faith and Christian life questions of young people and is designed to attract, instruct, guide and challenge its audience by applying the gospel to modern problems and situations. The students who read *Youth Update* vary in their religious education and reading ability. Write for the average high school student. This student is 15-years-old with a C+ average. Assume that they have paid attention to religious instruction and remember a little of what "sister" said. When writing avoid glib phrases and clichés. Aim more toward "table talk than teacher talk."
**Nonfiction:** Young adults: religious. Does not want to see travel material. Buys 12 mss/year. Average word length: 2,300-2,400. Byline given.
**How to Contact/Writers:** Nonfiction: Query. SASE (IRC) for answer to query; include Social Security number with submission. Reports on queries/mss in 6 weeks. Will consider computer printout and electronic submissions via disk.
**Terms/Writers:** Pays on acceptance. Buys first North American serial rights. Pays $325-400 for assigned/unsolicited articles. Sample copy free with #10 SAE and 1 first-class stamp.

# Other Magazine Publishers

The following magazine publishers are not included in this edition of *Children's Writer's & Illustrator's Market* for the reasons indicated in parenthesis. The phrase "did not respond" means the publisher was in 1989 *Children's Writer's & Illustrator's Market* but did not respond to our written and phone requests for updated information for a 1990 listing.

Action! (declined to be listed)
Animal Kingdom (declined to be listed)
Animal World (did not respond)
Art & Man (declined to be listed)
The Apple Blossom Connection (did not respond)
Barbie Magazine (declined to be listed)
Bible-in-Life Stories (declined to be listed)
Bonjour (declined to be listed)
California Weekly Explorer (declined to be listed)
Ca Va (declined to be listed)

Chez Nous (declined to be listed)
Cinemagic (no longer published)
Classical Calliope (declined to be listed)
Current Events (declined to be listed)
Current Health 1 & 2 (declined to be listed)
Current Science (declined to be listed)
Earth Science (declined to be listed)
El Sol (declined to be listed)
Forecast (declined to be listed)

GI Joe Magazine (declined to be listed)
He Man & the Masters of the Universe Magazine (declined to be listed)
Hoy Dia (declined to be listed)
Junior Scholastic (declined to be listed)
Muppet Magazine (declined to be listed)
Que Tal (declined to be listed)
Read (declined to be listed)
Sesame Street Magazine (declined to be listed)
Thundercats Magazine (declined to be listed)

It should come as no surprise that children's videotapes are selling well. When you consider the popularity of the adult video market and today's crop of TV-oriented children the prognosis looks good for this market to grow steadily.

Usually when we think of children's videos large-scale production houses such as Disney come to mind, but other companies are tapping into this lucrative market as well. Many such production companies are included in this section and have a range of writing and animation needs that include educational as well as entertainment subjects.

Educational films may not pay quite as much as those destined for entertainment distribution, but once you're established as a professional who can create quality work on time, you will find steady work. Many teachers realize that audiovisual aids can facilitate learning much more effectively than simply relying on book reading and teachers' lectures.

Read through each listing carefully to determine the company's needs and methods of contact. You will also notice that video isn't the only format produced by many production houses. A writer or illustrator may find himself working on a film project, film strip or multi-media production.

Be aware that audiovisual media rely more on the "visual" to tell the story. The script plays a "secondary" role and explains only what the visual message doesn't make clear to viewers. This will be a greater challenge to writers than to illustrators as the latter are already trained to think primarily in visual terms.

**\*AERIAL IMAGE VIDEO SERVICES,** #203, 101 W. 31 St., New York NY 10001. (212)279-6026, (800)237-4259. FAX: (212)279-6229. President: John Stapsy. Estab. 1979. Type of company: Video production and post production, and audio production and post production. Uses videotapes and audio. (For list of recent productions consult the Random House catalog of children's videos.)

**Children's Writing:** Submissions returned with proper SASE. Reports in "days."

**Children's Illustration/Animation:** Hires illustrators for: computer and hand animation, storyboarding, live action and comprehensives. Types of animation produced: cel animation, clay animation, stop motion, special effects, 3-D, computer animation, video graphics, motion control and live action. Submission method: send cover letter, resume and demo tape. Art samples returned with proper SASE. Reports in "weeks." Pays "per project."

**Tips:** When reviewing a portfolio/samples, looks for "application to a project, general talent and interests based on examples."

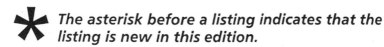 **The asterisk before a listing indicates that the listing is new in this edition.**

**\*KEN ANDERSON FILMS**, P.O. Box 618, Winona Lake IN 46590. (219)267-5774. Contact: Margaret Mauzy. Estab. 1959. Type of company: film production facility. Audience: the evangelical market. Uses film strips, slide sets, films, videotapes.
**Children's Writing:** Needs: Children's adventure; teen (junior high). Submission method: query with synopsis. Submission returned with proper SASE. Reports in 1 month. Guidelines/catalog free.
**Children's Illustration/Animation:** Guidelines/catalog free.
**Tips:** "Don't get discouraged. Keep on trying. We are open to material of children's adventure stories; our slant is to the evangelical market, cannot at the moment consider full scripts. We need to see one-page gist of the story, and from this we will decide to have the material developed. Payment is by prior negotiation with the author."

**\*EDWARD BAKST**, 160 West 96th St., New York NY 10025. (212)666-2579 or 6395. Designer/Director: Edward Bakst. Estab. 1978. Type of company: independent designer/director/producer. Audience: commercial agencies, cable TV, corporate clients, children's TV. Uses: film, videotapes. Recent children's productions: *Nickelodeon ID*, written and illustrated by Edward Bakst. This is a computer animation station ID for Nickelodeon Cable TV. *Illustrated Songs*, written and illustrated by Edward Bakst. Format comprised of clay animation; these are films for children aimed at developing countries. *Snacky*, written and illustrated by Edward Bakst. This is a 3D computer animation TV commercial aimed at children and parents.
**Children's Illustration/Animation:** Hires illustrators for: animation inbetweening, pencil testing. Type of animation produced: cel animation, clay animation, stop motion, 3-D, computer animation. Submission method: send demo tape on VHS. Art samples not returned. Reports only if interested. Pays: $500/week.
**Tips:** Illustrators/animators: Looks for "design ability, originality, experience."

**\*CLEARVUE**, 6465 N. Avondale, Chicago IL 60631. (312)775-9433. President: W.O. McDermed (for scripts); V.P. Editorial: Matthew Newman (for illustration/animation). Estab. 1969. Type of company: production house. Audience: educational pre-school through high school. Uses film strips, slide sets, videotapes. 30% of writing is by freelancers; 70% of illustrating/animating is by freelancers.
**Children's Writing:** Needs: educational material; preschool, 5-8, 9-11, 12 and older. Submission method: query with synopsis. Submissions are returned. Reports in 2 weeks. Guidelines/catalog free. Buys material outright.
**Children's Illustration/Animation:** Hires illustrators for: animation, storyboarding. Types of animation produced: cel animation. Art samples returned. Reports in 2 weeks. Guidelines/catalog free. Pay: "open."
**Tips:** "Programs must be designed for educational market—not home or retail."

**\*DIMENSION FILMS**, 15007 Gault St., Van Nuys CA 91405. (818)997-8065. President: Gary Goldsmith. Estab. 1962. Type of company: Production house. Audience: schools and libraries. Uses film strips, films, videotapes. Recent children's productions: *Literature to Write About*, written by Gary Goldsmith; illustrated by various artists. These subjects are comprised of filmstrips and videos dealing with books as a basis of writing for 10-12 year olds. *Legend of the Bluebonnet*, written by Gary Goldsmith, adapted from Tomie dePaola's work. This is a live-action 16mm film for 6-10 year olds. 20% of writing is by freelancers; 20% of illustrating/animating is by freelancers.
**Children's Writing:** Needs: educational material and documentaries for Kindergarten-12th-grade audience. Submission method: query. Submissions filed. Reports in a matter of weeks. "Prefer phone calls" for guidelines. Pays in accordance with Writer's Guild standards.

**Children's Illustration/Animation:** Hires illustrators for: storyboarding, comprehensives. Types of animation produced: cel animation, video graphics, live action. Submission method: send cover letter and résumé. Reports in a matter of weeks. "Call for guidelines." Pays $30-60/frame.
**Tips:** Illustrators/animators: looking for "imagination, clarity and purpose." Portfolio should show "strong composition; action in stillness."

**\*J. DYER, INC.**, Suite 900, 3340 Peachtree Rd., Atlanta GA 30326. (404)266-8022. Studio Manager: Ilene Dyer. Estab. 1984. Type of company: animation studio. Audience: Material intended for TV advertising. Uses film, videotapes and "35 mm film/with motion control computer, then finished on 1″ tape." Recent children's productions: *Gummy Bears*, written by Bockell, Castello & Swagger Advertising, and illustrated by J. Dyer. This is a cel animation 30-second TV commercial, aimed at all youth ages. 20% of writing is by freelancers; 50% of illustrating/animating is by freelancers.
**Children's Writing:** Needs: "Up to this point all of our work is done for advertising and most of that is not aimed at children. However, we are very interested in finding writers who have developed stories and characters who would be interested in having their work animated and produced for television." Submission method: query with synopsis or "call Ilene first and then send story outline." Submissions filed. Reports in 2 weeks. Buys material outright. "If it is a commercial, then it's a flat fee. If it's an original story for entertainment production, then it would be a fee plus percentage of sales."
**Children's Illustration/Animation:** Hires illustrators for: animation, storyboarding, character development, live action, pencil testing/photography. Types of animation produced: cel animation, stop motion, special effects, 3-D, motion control, live action/rotoscoping. Submission method: send demo tape on ¾″. "Call Ilene first before sending anything." Art samples returned with proper SASE. Reports in 2 weeks. Pays: $18-25 for key animator; $12-15 for inbetween artist; $10-20 for background illustrator; $12 for stat camera operator; $10-15 for inker; $6.50-15 for painter; $10-20 for animation camera operator and assistant; $6.50-15 for matte prep; $10-15 for rotoscope; $10-15 for model construction and rigging. "Hourly rates subject to change at any time."
**Tips:** Writers/scriptwriters: "The ad agency selects and hires writers; we very seldom hire. However, since we are experienced animators, children's stories offer a new dimension to our potential market. If the stories and characters are good enough, we will work with the writer to produce his story." Looks for "strong character development and a writer who is capable of creating action as well as being able to compress complex ideas into limited seconds of screen time." Illustrators/animators: "Let us see your work; we'll go from there. Most all freelancers who want to work with us live in and around Atlanta. After the initial phone call to Ilene, we set up a meeting to see the portfolio." Looks for "good taste and draftsmanship first, then diversity and the ability to be flexible." Illustrators in animation should "develop some original characters and include them in your general portfolio. Interview with some animation companies for freelance, entry-level work by the job. Then you'll start seeing what it's all about and whether you even like the animation business. It's a lot harder than straight illustration and *much* more tedious. Remember, there are about 300 renderings in a 30 second TV commercial. You've got to be a team player." Trends: "Commercials are here to stay, but we want to pursue the area of animated children's stories for cable TV and the home video rental markets. Animation can be a universal language. There is a growing market for not only children's books, but children's TV programs."

**\*EDUCATIONAL AUDIO VISUAL, INC.**, 17 Marble Ave., Pleasantville NY 10570. (914)769-6332. FAX: (914)769-6350. Producer: Stephen C. Galleher. Estab. 1953. Type of company: production house and distribution company. Audience: primarily junior and senior high school; some programs for elementary schools. Uses film strips, videotapes. Recent children's productions: *The Crusades*, written by Judith Conway, illustrated by David Prebenna. This is a video dealing with history, aimed at high school students. *The Surprise Symphony*, illustrated by Isaac Abrams. This is a video about Hadyn's composition and music appreciation aimed at elementary through high school students. *Voice: The Universal Instrument*, written by Pete Barton. This is a video on voice/singing instruction aimed at junior and senior high students. 80-90% of writing is by freelancers; 100% of illustrating/animating is by freelancers.

**Children's Writing:** Needs: first, scripts; second, animation/graphics; third, educational material; primarily for junior and senior high students. Subjects include: "basic junior and senior high school curriculum: English literature, art, music, social studies/history, media, language arts, modern language, life skills." Submission method: synopsis/outline. Submissions filed (if relevant); returned (if requested) with proper SASE. Reports only if interested. Guidelines/catalog free. Buys material outright.

**Children's Illustration/Animation:** Hires illustrators for: animation. Types of animation produced: special effects, video graphics, live action. Submission method: send cover letter and résumé with VHS demo tape. Art samples not filed (unless interested); returned with proper SASE. Reports in 4 weeks. Guidelines/catalog free.

**Tips:** "Use illustrations only minimally, as graphics, in particular maps/overlays." Writers/scriptwriters: Looks for "flair and accuracy and succinctness." Illustrators/animators: Looks for "creativity."

**\*EDUCATIONAL VIDEO NETWORK**, 1401 19th St., Huntsville TX 77340. (409)295-5767. Editor: Gary Edmondson. Estab. 1954. Type of company: production house. Audience: educational (school). Uses film strips, videotapes. Recent children's production: *Improvising Your Self-Esteem*, written by Bill Carroll. This is a video for 12-17 year olds. 20% of writing by freelancers; 20% of illustrating/animating is by freelancers.

**Children's Writing:** Needs: "Educational material" for ages 9-11 and 12-18. Submission method: script with video or animation. Submissions returned with proper SASE. Reports in 1 month. Guidelines/catalog free. Pays writers in royalties or buys material outright.

**Children's Illustration/Animation:** Hires illustrators for: acetate cels, animation. Types of animation produced: cel animation stills, video graphics, live action. Submission method: send cover letter and VHS demo tape. Art samples returned with proper SASE. Reports in 1 month. Guidelines/catalog free.

**Tips:** "Materials should fill a curriculum need in grades 6-12." Writers/scriptwriters: "Work must be of professional quality adaptable to video format." Illustrators/animators: Looks for "creativity." "More live-action is being demanded. Go to school library and ask to review most popular A-V titles."

**\*JOHN GATI FILM EFFECTS, INC.**, Suite 832, 154 West 57th St., New York NY 10019. (212)582-9060. Director/Producer: John Gati. Estab. 1982. Type of company: animation studio and production house. Audience: Children from 9-12, and all ages. Uses film, videotapes. Recent children's productions: *An Art Lover's Fantasy*, written by John Gati, illustrated by Danish painters. This is a 16mm or videocassette that includes music from the same period as the paintings; for all age groups. *Happy Times*, comprised of original paintings. 100% of writing is by freelancers; 100% of illustrating/animating is by freelancers.

**Children's Writing:** Needs: "Animation and educational materials for ages 9-11 and 12 and older." Submission method: submit synopsis/outline and/or completed script. Submissions returned with proper SASE. Reports in a matter of weeks.

**Children's Illustration/Animation:** Types of animation produced: stop motion, special effects, motion control, puppets. Art samples returned with proper SASE. Guidelines/catalog free. Pays "according to projects."

**Tips:** Wants illustrators/animators interested in "puppet design, development and building for stop motion cinematography." Illustrator/Animators: Looks for "educational video, cable and educational broadcast quality."

**\*MARSHMEDIA,** 5903 Main St., Kansas City MO 64113. (816)523-1059. FAX: (816)333-7421. Production Director: Janie Fopeano. Estab. 1969. Type of company: production house. Audience: grades K-12. 100% of writing is by freelancers; 100% of illustrating/animating is by freelancers.
**Children's Writing:** Needs: educational materials—filmstrip and video scripts for grades K-12. Subjects include: "health, drug education, guidance, safety, nutrition." Submission method: query with synopsis and submit completed scripts, résumé. Submissions returned with proper SASE. Reports in 1 month. Buys material outright.
**Children's Illustration/Animation:** Submission method: send résumé and VHS demo tape. Art samples returned with proper SASE. Reports in 1 month.

**\*NATIONAL TEXTBOOK COMPANY,** 4255 W. Touhy Ave., Lincolnwood IL 60646. (708)679-5500. FAX: (708)679-2494. Editorial Director: Michael Ross. Art Director: Karen Christoffersen. Estab. 1960. Type of company: publisher. Audience: all ages. Uses film strips, multimedia productions, videotapes, books and audiocassettes. Recent children's productions: *Ready for English,* written by Linda Ventriglia, illustrated by Terry Meider. These are books, tapes, videos and story cards dealing with pre-reading aimed at ages 5-7. *Hello, English,* written by Barbara Zaffran, illustrated by Alan Tansen. These are books, tapes, videos and story cards on reading and writing. *Viva el Espanol,* written by Linda Tibenser, illustrated by Don Wilson. These are texts, filmstrips, cassettes and posters dealing with Spanish aimed at ages 6-14. 40% of writing is by freelancers; 50% of illustrating/animating is by freelancers.
**Children's Writing:** Needs educational material for ages 5-14. Subjects include: "mostly foreign language and English." Submission method: submit synopsis/outline, completed script, résumé and samples. Submission returned with proper SASE only. Reports in 2 months. Guidelines/catalog free. Pays writers in royalties or buys material outright—"depends on project."
**Children's Illustration/Animation:** Hires illustrators for: character development, comprehensives, pencil testing. Types of animation produced: stop motion, video graphics. Submission method: send cover letter, résumé, color print samples, tearsheets, business card. Art samples returned with proper SASE. Reports in 8 weeks. Guidelines/catalog free.
**Tips:** Looking for "experienced professionals only with proven track record in the *educational* field."

**\*PACIFIC RIM PRODUCTIONS, INC.,** Suite 212, 8500 Melrose Ave., Los Angeles CA 90069. (213)273-1730. FAX: (213)659-2208. President: Alan W. Livingston (for scripts); Vice President, Production: Milton D. Vallas (for illustrators/animators). Estab. 1987. Type of company: animation studio. Audience: children's television and animated feature pictures. Uses films, videotapes. Recent children's productions: half-hour series for French company and half-hour series for Spanish company, plus work on 2 features for major American studio." (Identities are confidential per request.)
**Children's Writing:** Needs animation scripts—ages 5 to 11. Submission method: submit synopsis/outline and résumé plus any rights to known characters or properties. Submissions not returned. Reports in 2 weeks. Guidelines/catalog for SAE. Buys material outright.
**Children's Illustration/Animation** Hires illustrators for: storyboarding, character development. Type of animation produced: cel animation. Submission method: send cover letter, résumé, VHS demo tape. Art samples not returned. Reports in 2 weeks. Guidelines/catalog for SAE.

Tips: "Greatest chance of hiring would be if writer has rights to a known property."

*SINNOT & ASSOCIATES, INC., 676 N. LaSalle, Chicago IL 60610. (312)440-1875. Director: Steven A. Jones. Estab. 1975. Type of company: animation studio, special effects. Audience: television. Uses films, videotapes. Recent children's productions: *Ronald McDonald and the Adventure Machine* — a videotape for children, aimed at ages 2-10. *Return to Mocha* — educational film aimed at ages 10-16. *Cap'n Crunch* — cereal commercials aimed at ages 5-25. 75% of work done by freelance illustrators; 25% by freelance animators.

Children's Illustration/Animation: Hires illustrators for: animation, storyboarding, character development, live action, pencil testing. Types of animation produced: cel animation, stop motion, special effects, 3-D, motion control, live action. Submission method: send cover letter, résumé, VHS demo tape. Art samples filed; returned with proper SASE. Reports only if interested.

*STUDIO ANIMATICS, Suite 265, 1950 Sawtelle Blvd., Los Angeles CA 90025. (213)478-7230. FAX: (213)478-5142. Producer: Jim Keeshen. Estab. 1978. Type of company: video storyboard presentation producer. Audience: ad agencies, consumers, children. Uses slide sets, films, videotapes, storyboards and illustrations. Recent productions: *Mattel*, written by Ogilvy & Mather Advertising, illustrated by Helen MacCarthy. This is a video dealing with dolls/Barbie fashion aimed at ages 6-12. *Inca Legends*, written by Jim Keeshen, illustrated by Rusty Mills. This film/video deals with the creation of man, for all ages. 90% of writing by freelancers; 80% of illustrating/animating by freelancers.

Children's Writing: Needs: "stories with value judgement, morals; educational." Submission method: query. Write for release form prior to submitting material. Submissions returned with proper SASE. Reports in 10 days. Pays writers in royalties.

Children's Illustration/Animation: Hires illustrators for: animation, storyboarding, character development. Types of animation produced: cel animation, video graphics, motion control. Art samples returned with proper SASE or not returned. Reports in 10 days. Guidelines/catalog free.

Tips: Writers/scriptwriters: "Must have excellent story sense. Can develop characters with strong personalities." Illustrators/animators: "Must have strong staging ability; good at caricature. Take courses at UCLA extension, talk with screenwriters. Work for animation studio, apprentice as an inbetweener." Trends: "toward simple stories with strong visuals."

*TREEHAUS COMMUNICATIONS, INC., 906 W. Loveland Ave., Loveland OH 45140. (513)683-5716. President: Gerard A. Pottebaum. Estab. 1968. Type of company: production house. Audience: preschool through adults. Uses film strips, multimedia productions, videotapes. Recent children's productions: *The Treehouse Stories*, written by G. Pottebaum. This is a filmstrip dealing with self-esteem, for kindergarten-grade 4 children. *The Christmas Story*, written by G. Pottebaum. This is a video dealing with religion for kindergarten-grade 3 children. *The Sunday Series*, written by Christine Brusselmans and Paule Freeburg. Print/leaflets for kindergarten-age 12. 30% of writing by freelancers; 30% of illustrating/animating by freelancers.

Children's Writing: Needs: educational material/documentories, for all ages. Subjects include: "social studies/religious education/documentaries on all subjects, but primarily about people who live ordinary lives in extraordinary ways." Submission method: query with synopsis. Submissions returned with proper SASE. Reports in 1 month. Guidelines/catalog for SAE. Pays writers in accordance with Writer's Guild standards.

Tips: Illustrators/animators: "Be informed about movements and needs in education, multi-cultural sensitivity." Looks for "social values, originality, competency in subject, global awareness."

**\*WEST INDIGO, INC.**, 9715 Washington Blvd., Culver City CA 90230. (213)202-0263. FAX: (213)202-7596. Producer: Catherine Perow (scriptwriters). Director: Gary Katona (illustrators/animators). Estab. 1984. Type of company: production house — animation, visual effects and combo techniques. Audience: commercials, theatrical. Uses films, videotapes. 75% of illustrating/animating is by freelancers.

**Children's Writing:** "Open to animation or educational scripts at all age levels." Submission method: query with synopsis/outline, send résumé. Submissions returned with proper SASE. Reports only if interested. No guidelines/catalog. Payment "to be determined."

**Children's Illustration/Animation:** Hires illustrators for: traditional/experimental animation, storyboarding, character development, live action, comprehensives, pencil testing. Types of animation produced: cel animation, stop motion, special effects, 3-D, computer animation, video graphics, motion control, live action. Submission method: cover letter, résumé, VHS or ¾" demo tape, color print samples, tearsheets. Reports only if interested. Pays "on project-to-project basis."

**Tips:** Scriptwriters: "Try to appeal to broad audience — think visually." Illustrators/Animators: "Try to define your own style and/or be adaptable to others." Looks for "drawing ability and range of techniques or uniqueness of vision." Trends: "Moving away from commercial TV market toward home video market on a level of high quality." Sees "a *growing* need for original material."

Book and music publishers as well as record companies recognize the growing children's market for book/cassette packages and music tapes. Due to today's baby boomlet and the high percentage of two-career-parent families or single-parent households, there is great demand for music tapes for entertainment as well as for book/cassette packages to develop children's reading habits and skills, since parents aren't free to read to them.

A recent survey of booksellers, conducted by *Publishers Weekly*, showed that 93.5 percent of children's bookstores in the U.S. already stock story or music tapes. Following closely behind were 81.8 percent of the chain bookstores also claiming to sell audiotapes as well as 69.1 percent of the nation's independent bookstores. On the average, these bookstores carried an inventory of 76 tapes.

With these statistics to back up the need for new material, writers and songwriters can look toward the children's audiotape market as a valid marketing outlet. Represented in this section are publishers and record companies looking for good story material or unique children's music to record. Many specify an interest in reviewing both. Be sure to study each listing to determine what subject matter they prefer to review and to what age level such submissions should be geared.

Pay rates to a large degree will be based on royalties for writers and songwriters or, for recording musicians, on record contract. Also, be sure to follow closely the instructions for making contact. This is definitely an expanding industry, but remember that you are competing against established artists who already have a track record. Presenting yourself as a professional by submitting only the material requested, and in the correct format noted, is a good first step toward getting "your foot in the door."

**\*BARRON'S EDUCATIONAL SERIES**, 250 Wireless Blvd., Hauppauge NY 11788. (516)434-3311. FAX: (516)434-3723. Executive Vice President: Ms. Ellen Sibley. Book publisher.
**Stories:** Publishes 7 book/cassette packages/year. 100% of stories are fiction. Tapes aimed at preschool audience. Authors are paid in royalties of 6-10% based on wholesale price. Buys ms outright for $1,500-5,000. Average advance: $2,000. Making contact: query, submit outline/synopsis and sample chapters, submit complete ms. Reports on queries/mss in 4-12 weeks. Book catalog for 9½" × 11" SAE.

**\*THE CHILDREN'S GROUP**, 17 Cadman Plaza West, Brooklyn NY 11201. (718)838-2544. FAX: (718)858-8976. President: Bob Hinkle. Personal management firm. Estab. 1988.
**Music:** Works with composers, lyricists, team collaborators. Making contact: Submit cassette, VHS or ¾" videocassette and lyric sheet. Requirements: "Call to talk with us about who's recording and how the caller's material may fit those recording." Does not return unsolicited material. Reports in a matter of weeks.
**Tips:** Songwriters: "As an artist manager, a submission should be appropriate to the artist(s) in mind." Trends in children's music: "Becoming more sophisticated. Selling more. Careers developing just as in rock, pop, jazz, etc."

**\*FRONTLINE MUSIC GROUP/FRONTLINE BOOKS**, Box 28450, Santa Ana CA 92799. (714)751-2242. FAX: (714)755-6236. Executive Vice President: Brian Tong. Music publisher, record company, book publisher. Record labels include Broken Songs, Carlotta Music, Frontline Kids. Estab. 1985.
**Music:** Releases 80-100 singles/year; 40-50 LPs/year; 40-50 CDs/year. Member of AS-CAP and BMI. Publishes and records 50-60 children's songs/year. Hires staff writers for children's music. Works with composers, lyricists, team collaborators. For music published pays standard royalty of 50%; for songs recorded pays musicians/artists on record contract, musicians on salary for inhouse studio work, and songwriters on royalty contract. Making contact: Submit cassette demo tape and lyric sheet by mail—unsolicited submissions OK. Requirements: only Christian material, no fantasy stuff. SASE for return of submissions. Reports in 3-4 weeks. Recently recorded songs: "Fruits of the Spirit," by Terry Taylor, recorded by Sunny Lovetree on the Frontline Kids label (children's music); and "Megamouth 1 & 2," by Terry Taylor, recorded by Megamouth on the Frontline Kids label (children's music).
**Tips:** Songwriters: "Submit fresh material that is relevant to today's issues. Trends in children's music: "Age groupings are becoming more specialized. There is a distinct difference in likes and dislikes between 6-10 and 10-13 year olds and 14-16 year olds."
**Stories:** Publishes 2-4 book/cassette packages/year. 100% of stories are fiction. Will consider fictional animal, fantasy, history, sports and spy/mystery/adventure stories aimed at all juvenile audiences "if Christian." Will consider nonfictional Bible stories aimed at all juvenile audiences. Authors are paid in royalties based on retail price. Making contact: Submit complete ms. SASE for return of ms. Reports on queries in 4-6 weeks; mss in 6-8 weeks. Book catalog, ms guidelines not available. Recently recorded story tapes: "Mouse Family Christmas," by Terry Taylor (ages 3-7), and "Harry Who-dunit," by Terry Taylor (ages 5-11, mystery).
**Tips:** Writers: "Be unusual." Trends in children's reading material: "More sophistication."

**\*LARRCO IND. OF TX, INC.**, K-Larrco Satellite Radio and T.V. Div., Box 3842, Houston TX 77253-3842. President: Dr. L. Herbst. Music publisher, book publisher. Record labels include Beverly Hills Music Publishing, Total Sound Records, Lawrence Herbst Records, Beverly Hills Records, Larrco Records, Bestway Records, D.T.I Records.
**Music:** Member of BMI. Hires staff writers for children's music. Works with composers, lyricists, team collaborators. For music publishers pays standard royalty of 50%; for songs recorded pays musicians/artists on record contract, musicians on salary for inhouse studio work, songwriters on 50% royalty contract. Making contact: Submit a 7½ IPS reel-to-reel tape or VHS videocassette with 3 minutes worth of song and a lyric or lead sheet by mail—unsolicited submissions are OK. SASE for return of submissions. Reports in 6 weeks.
**Tips:** "Submit professionally recorded works." Looks for "easy to understand lyrics on all labels."
**Stories:** Publishes 12 book/cassette packages/year. 3% of stories are fiction; 97% nonfiction. Will consider fictional animal, fantasy, history, adventure stories aimed at all ages. Will consider all genres of nonfiction aimed at "open" audience. Authors are paid in royalties of 50%. Making contact: submit complete ms or submit cassette tape of story.

*"Picture books" are geared toward the preschool—8 year old group; "Young readers" to 5-8 year olds; "Middle readers" to 9-11 year olds; and "Young adults" to those 12 and up.*

SASE for return of ms; include Social Security number with submission. Reports on queries in 2 weeks; mss in 4-12 weeks.
**Tips:** "Keep trying." Trends in children's reading material: "More of God's stories coming out."

**\*NEW DAY PRESS**, 2355 E. 89th St., Cleveland OH 44106. (216)795-7070. Chair, Editorial Committee: Carolyn Gordon. Book publisher. Estab. 1972.
**Stories:** Publishes "1 or less" book/cassette packages/year. 50% of stories are fiction; 50% are nonfiction. Will consider historical African-American fiction and nonfiction only aimed at 6-12 year olds. Buys mss outright for $100. Making contact: Query. Book catalog free on request. Recently recorded story tape: *Henry Box Brown*, written by Pamela Pruitt and narrated by Carolyn Gordon (African-American History for 6-12 year olds).

**\*OAK STREET MUSIC INC.**, 301-140 Bannatyne Ave., Winnipeg Manitoba R3B 3C5 Canada. (204)957-0085. FAX: (204)943-3588. Director of Marketing: Stephen Berofe. Music publisher, record company, book publisher. Record labels include Oak Street. Estab. 1987.
**Music:** Releases 10-15 LPs/year; 1-5 CDs/year. Member of CAPAC, PROCAN, CM-RRA, Harry Fox Agency. Publishes and records 100 children's songs/year. Hires staff writers for children's music. Works with composers, lyricists. Pays standard royalty of 50% for musicians/artists on record contract, musicians on salary for inhouse studio work, songwriters on royalty contract. Making contact: Submit a cassette demo tape or VHS videocassette with 3-5 songs and a lyric sheet by mail—unsolicited submissions are OK. Requirements: "A press kit is always helpful." Reports in 2 weeks. Recently recorded songs: "Sandwiches," "Sandwich Polka," "The People on My Street," all written and recorded by Bob King on the Oak Street label (children's music).
**Tips:** Songwriters: "Ensure the material is accessible by children and entertaining to *all* family members." Trends: "Recordings for children are becoming more sophisticated in terms of production and attitude towards children."
**Stories:** Publishes 1-2 book/cassette packages/year; 1-2 audio tapes/year. 100% of stories are fiction. Will consider fictional fantasy and adventure stories aimed at 2-10 year olds. Will consider nonfictional history, animal, biography stories aimed at 2-10 year olds. Authors are paid in negotiable royalties based on wholesale price. Making contact: Submit complete ms, cassette tape of story. SASE (IRC) for return of ms. Reports on queries in 2 weeks; mss in 2-3 weeks.
**Tips:** "Research various award-winning stories. Try to analyze the common factors, or the most interesting features of these titles." "A plethora of low material (re-workings of traditional stories) is now available. Try to select stories that are unique, unusual yet entertaining."

**\*PETER PAN INDUSTRIES**, 88 St. Francis St., Newark NJ 07105. (201)344-4214. FAX: (201)344-0465. Vice President of Sales: Shelly Rudin. Music publisher, record company. Record labels include Parade Music, Compose Music, Peter Pan. Estab. 1927.
**Music:** Releases 20 singles/year; 10 12-inch singles; 45 LPs/year; 45 CDs/year. Member of ASCAP and BMI. Publishes 50 children's songs/year; records 80-90 songs/year. Works with composers, lyricists, team collaborators. For music published pays standard royalty of 50%; for songs recorded pays musicians/artists on record contract, songwriters on royalty contract. Making contact: Submit a 15 IPS reel-to-reel demo tape or VHS videocassette by mail—unsolicited submissions OK. SASE (or SAE and IRCs) for return of submissions. Reports in 4-6 weeks.

**Tips:** "Lullabies are popular now."
**Stories:** Publishes 12 book/cassette packages/year. 90% of stories are fiction; 10% non-fiction. Will consider "all" genres of fiction and nonfiction aimed at 6 month olds to 9 year olds. Authors are paid in royalties based on wholesale price. Making contact: Query. Reports on queries in 4-6 weeks. Book catalog, manuscript guidelines free on request.
**Tips:** "Tough business but rewarding. Lullabies are very popular."

**\*PLAYBACK RECORDS**, Box 630755, Miami FL 33163. (305)935-4880. FAX: (305)933-4007. President: Jack Gale. Music publisher, record company. Record labels include Playback, Gallery II, Ridgewood, Caramba. Estab. 1983.
**Music:** Releases 48 singles/year; 12 LPs/year; 10 CDs/year. Member of BMI and AS-CAP. Publishes 10 children's songs/year; records 20 children's songs/year. Works with composers, lyricists, team collaborators. For music published pays standard royalty of 50%. For songs recorded pays musicians on salary for inhouse studio work, songwriters on 50% royalty contract. Making contact: Submit a cassette demo tape or VHS videocassette with 2 songs and a lyric sheet by mail—unsolicited submissions are OK. Does not return unsolicited material. Reports in 10 days. Recently published/recorded songs: "Contando, We Learn," by Neraida Smith, recorded by The Amigos on the Caramba label (Spanish educational); and "My Mother's House," by Robin Zachary, recorded by Benji Wilhaite (country) on the Playback label.
**Stories:** Publishes 2 book/cassette packages/year. 100% of stories are fiction. Authors are paid in royalties. Making contact: submit complete ms. Reports on queries/mss in 10 days.

**\*PRESCRIPTION CO.**, 70 Murray Ave., Port Washington NY 11050. (516)767-1929. VP, Artists & Repertoire: Kirk Nordstrom. Music publisher, record company. Record label Prescription. Estab. 1976.
**Music:** Member of BMI. Works with composers, lyricists, team collaborators. For music published pays standard royalty of 50%. For songs recorded pays musicians/artists on record contract, musicians on salary for inhouse studio work. Write first and obtain permission to submit a cassette tape with up to 5 songs and a lyric sheet. Making contact: Submit cassette, up to 5 songs, lyric sheet. Requirements: "Include SASE or no returns." Reports in 1-2 months. Has not published children's songs yet," but would consider them."
**Tips:** Songwriters: "Check in with us—see what we're looking for. At the moment we need children's songs and Christmas songs for a singer whose style is like Elvis."

**\*PRODUCTIONS DIADEM INC.**, C.P. 33 Pointe-Gatineau, Québec J8T 4Y8 Canada. (819)561-4114. President: Denyse Marleau. Record company. Record label Jouvence. Estab. 1982.
**Music:** Releases 1-2 LPs/year; 1-2 CDs/year. Member of CAPAC. Records 16-20 songs/year. Works with composers, lyricists. For songs recorded pays musicians/artists on record contract, musicians on salary for inhouse studio work, songwriters on 10% royalty contract. Making contact: Write first and obtain permission to submit a cassette tape with 3 songs and a lyric sheet. SASE (or SAE and IRC's). Reports in 1 month. Recently recorded songs: "Vive l'hiver," by Marie Marleau, (children's contemporary music); "Chers grands-parents," by Denyse Marleau, (children's contemporary music); "Mon ami l'ordinateur," (children's popular music), all recorded by DIADEM on the Jouvence label.

**\*REVIEW AND HERALD PUBLISHING ASSOCIATION**, 55 W. Oak Ridge Dr., Hagerstown MD 21740. (301)791-7000. Acquisitions Editor: Penny Estes Wheeler. Book publisher. Estab. 1849.

**Music:** Publishes song books only.
**Stories:** Publishes 1 book/year. 100% of stories are nonfiction. Need stories dealing with contemporary problems of kids age 8-15. Buys material outright. Making contact: query, submit outline/synopsis and sample chapters, submit complete ms. SASE for answer to query and for return of ms; include Social Security number with submission. Reports on queries in 6-8 weeks; mss in 3-4 months. Book catalog free on request. Recently recorded story tapes: "Best of Guide Vols. 1 and 2," aimed at 6-9 year olds, for character building.

**\*RHYTHMS PRODUCTIONS/TOM THUMB MUSIC,** Box 34485, Los Angeles CA 90034. (213)836-4678. President: R.S. White. Record company, cassette and book packagers. Record label, Tom Thumb—Rhythms Productions. Estab. 1955.
**Music:** Releases 4-6 LPs/year. Member of ASCAP. Records 4 albums/year. Works with composers and lyricists. For songs recorded pays musicians/artists on record contract, songwriters on royalty contract. Making contact: Submit a cassette demo tape or VHS videotape by mail—unsolicited submissions are OK. Requirements: "We accept musical stories. Must be produced in demo form, and must have educational content or be educationally oriented." Reports in 2 months. Recently recorded: *Prof. Whatzit & Carmine Cat Series*, written and produced by Dan Brown and Bruce Crook on the Tom Thumb label (musical stories). Other titles include: "The Deep Sea Adventure," "The Dinosaur Adventure," "The Space Adventure," and "The Rainmakers," all on Tom Thumb label (4 cassette and book packages.)

**\*SILVER BURDETT & GINN,** 250 James St., Morristown NJ 07960-1918. (201)285-8003. Music Editor: Donald Scafuri. Music textbook publisher, grades K-8 (each grade package contains a set of recordings). Estab. 1867.
**Music:** Member of ASCAP. Publishes and records 200 songs/year. Hires staff writers for children's music. Works with composers, lyricists, team collaborators. For music published pays standard mechanical royalty rate; $400 set fee per song (melody and lyrics). Write first and obtain permission to submit a cassette tape and lead sheet. SASE. Reports in 3 months. Recently recorded songs: "Whistle While You Work," by Morey/Churchill, recorded by the Houston Vocal Edition on the Silver Burdett & Ginn label (juvenile pop); "The Rainbow Connection," by Williams/Ascher, recorded by Brad Diamond on the Silver Burdett & Ginn label (pop, grade 5); "Those Magic Changes," by Casey/Jacobs, recorded by the Darrell Bledsoe Singers on the Silver Burdett & Ginn label (Broadway, grade 7).
**Tips:** "Songs should reflect the appropriate vocal range, rhythmic sophistication and style for a particular age level. Lyrics should also be age appropriate. The songwriter should become familiar with those types of songs that are most successful in a classroom setting. (Styles could include pop, folk, 2-or 3-part choral.)"

**\*SIMON & SCHUSTER CHILDREN'S BOOKS,** 1230 Ave. of the Americas, New York NY 10020. (212)698-7257. FAX: (212)698-7007. Marketing Director: Ken Geist. Book publisher. Estab. 1927.
**Stories:** Publishes 4 book/cassette packages/year. 100% of stories are fiction. "Storytapes are developed using Simon & Schuster best selling and award winning children's books." Books aimed at 3-8 year olds. Pays authors in royalties of 2%.
**Making Contact:** Submit through agent only. Book catalog free on request. Recently recorded story tapes: *Strega Nona*, by Tomie DePaola and narrated by Dom DeLuise ("Grandmother Witch" is the source of all kinds of magic in her little town; a Caldecott Honor Book aimed at 4-9 year olds); *The Velveteen Rabbit*, by Margery Williams and narrated by Kim Hunter (a children's classic aimed at 6-10 year olds); *Pumpkinville Mystery*, by Bruce Cole and narrated by Fred Gwynne (a thrilling Halloween tale of mystery, magic and suspense aimed at 6-9 year olds).

*SOLID IVORY MUSIC, 3665 Arista Way #1910, Mississauga, Ontario L5A 4A3 Canada. (416)277-3908. A & R Director: Jack P. Moorehouse. Music publisher, record company. Record labels include Bovine International Record Co. Estab. 1978.
**Music:** Releases 2 singles/year; 2 LPs/year. Member of PROCAN. Publishes and records 5 children's songs/year. Works with team collaborators. For music published pays standard royalty of 50%; for songs recorded pays musicians on salary for inhouse studio work; 40% royalty. Making contact: Submit a cassette demo tape and lyric and lead sheet by mail—unsolicited submissions are OK. Requirements: "Please type lyric sheets. Use Canadian stamps for return postage." SASE or SAE and IRC's. Reports in 2 months. Recently recorded songs: "A Child at Christmas," by J. Moorhouse, recorded by J. Moorhouse on the Bovine label (Christmas); "Down the Chimney," by the Solid Ivory Brothers' Band, recorded by Solid Ivory Brothers Band on the Bovine label (Christmas); "It's Time to Go," by J. Moorhouse, recorded by J. Moorhouse on the Bovine label (children's music).
**Tips:** Songwriters: "Get input from the music community or fellow songwriters before submitting tapes. Keep the arrangement simple. Do not overproduce a demo." Trends in children's music: "Kids are interested in environmental topics and safety topics. Christmas music is good."

*WATCHESGRO MUSIC PUBLISHING CO., BMI. Watch Us Climb, ASCAP. Box 1794, Big Bear City CA 92314. (714)585-4645. President: Eddie Lee Carr. Music publisher, record company. Record labels include Interstate 20 Records, Tracker Records. Estab. 1970.
**Music:** Releases 10 singles/year; 5 12-inch singles/year; 1 LP/year; 1 CD/year. Publishes 15 children's songs/year; records 4 children's songs/year. Works with composers, lyricists. For music published pays standard royalty of 50%; for songs recorded pays musicians/artists on record contract, musicians on salary for inhouse studio work. Making contact: Write or call first and obtain permission to submit a cassette tape. Does not return unsolicited material. Reports in 1 week. Recently published songs: "Little Girls," by D.C. McKinnon, recorded by Donna Cox on the Interstate 20 Records label (children's music); "Little Boys," by Donna Cox, recorded by Donna Cox on the Tracker Records label (children's music); "My House," by Donna Cox/D.C. McKinnon, recorded by Donna Cox on the Tracker label (children's music).
**Tips:** Looks for "good demo."

Shakespeare's adage "All the world's a stage" has never been more true for today's children. There isn't a school, church, community group or even scouting organization that hasn't provided a theatrical outlet for its youth.

Despite the attraction contemporary kids have for TV and videos, many fledgling actors have found that nothing can parallel the thrill of performing for a live audience. And audiences still are attracted to the vitality exhibited by "live" actors.

Many of the markets in this section are soliciting material primarily aimed at children and teenagers, as well as subject matter suitable for the whole family.

Writers interested in playwriting should be aware that, more than ever before, the U.S. population is comprised of a wider multitude of ethnic subcultures from which material for plays can be culled. As you read through many of these listings, you will notice requests for material, now in short supply, aimed at minority groups.

Study the listings carefully to determine publishers' and theaters' needs regarding the type of material they want to purchase. Also, since many theater groups produce plays on limited budgets, keep the set and costume changes to a minimum. Some publishers will have catalogs available so you can become more familiar with the type of work typically used.

Payment for playwrights will usually come in the form of royalties, outright sums or a combination of both. Remember that the pay scale isn't going to be quite as lucrative as screen play rates, but writers within this profession have the added enjoyment of seeing their work performed live by a variety of groups employing a multitude of interpretations.

**\*BAKER'S PLAYS**, 100 Chauncy St., Boston MA 02111. (617)482-1280. Editor: John B. Welch. Estab. 1845. Publishes 5-8 children's plays/year; 2-4 children's musicals/year. 80% of plays/musicals written for adult roles; 20% for juvenile roles. Subject matter: "Touring shows for 5-8 year olds, full lengths for family audience and full lengths for teens." Recently published plays: *Goldilocks and the Three Bears*, by Tom McCabe—adaptation of the classic as a touring vehicle; *Tom McKeanna*—play about Louis Bravre for a family audience; *Inner Circle*, by Patrcia Loughrey—play about teens and AIDS for teens. Submission method: Submit complete ms, score and tape of songs. Reports in 4 months. Rights obtained on mss: worldwide rights. Pays writers in royalties (amount varies) or $10-100/performance. SASE for return of submission.
**Tips:** "Looking for writers for the theater, not frustrated poets or novelists." Wants "honest, committed material dealing with today's issues."

**\*CIRCA '21 DINNER THEATRE**, P.O. Box 3784, Rock Island IL 61204-3784. (309)786-2667. Producer: Dennis Hitchcock. Estab. 1977. Produces 2-3 children's plays/year; 1-2 children's musicals/year. "Prefer a cast no larger than 12." Produces children's plays for professional productions. 95% of plays/musicals written for adult roles; 5% written for juvenile roles. Recently produced plays: *Cinderella, Emperor's New Clothes* and *Jack and the Beanstalk*, all by Prince St. Players. Submission method: query with synopsis, character breakdown, tape and set description. Reports in 2 months. Payment negotiable. SASE for return of submission.

**\*CONTEMPORARY DRAMA SERVICE**, a Div. of Meriwether Publishing Ltd., 885 Elkton Dr., Colorado Springs CO 80907. (719)594-4422. FAX: (719)594-9916. Editor: Arthur Zapel. Estab. 1970. Publishes 35-40 children's plays/year; 3 children's musicals/year. 15% of plays/musicals written for adult roles; 85% for juvenile roles. Recently published plays: *Phantom of the Op'ry*, by Tim Kelly—comedy three-act spoof for teens; *The Substitute*, by David Powell—comedy about education for teens and adults; *Twinkle, the Christmas Star*, by Mary Brendon Conlon—a fantasy tableau for children aimed at children and adults. "We do not publish plays for elementary level except for church plays for Christmas and Easter. All of our secular plays are for teens or college level." Submission method: query with synopsis, character breakdown and set description; "query first if a musical." Rights obtained on mss: all first rights. Payment varies according to type: royalty or purchase.
**Tips:** "Manuscripts should be professionally prepared and presented—typewritten, organized, etc."

**\*THE COTERIE**, 2450 Grand, Kansas City MO 64108. (816)474-6785. Artistic Director: Pamela Sterling. Estab. 1978. Produces 7 children's plays/year; 2 children's musicals/year. "Prefer casts of between 5-7, no larger than 15. Props and staging should be relatively simple." Produces children's plays for professional productions. 80% of plays/musicals written for adult roles; 20% for juvenile roles. "We do *not* produce puppet shows, although we may use puppets in our plays. We produce original plays, musicals and literary adaptations for ages 5 through adult." Recently produced plays: *Great Expectations*, by Barbara Field (from Charles Dickens)—a classic novel for 10 year old through adult; *Takunda*, by Charles Smith—deals with race relations and apartheid and aimed at 12 year old through adult; *Dirty Beasts*, by Judy Yeckel/Cheryl Benge (from Roald Dahl)—about friendship and intended for a 5 year old through adult audience. "We do *not* want to see 'camp' adaptations of fairytales." Submission method: query with synopsis, character breakdown and set description. Reports in 3 weeks. Rights obtained on mss: "negotiable." Pays writers in royalties; buys material outright for $500-1,500; pays $20-35/performance. SASE for return of submission.
**Tips:** There are "smaller casts, simpler staging requirements, strong thematic, character and plot development, 'risky' issues; (i.e. teen pregnancy, substance abuse, race relations, etc.). There is a need for non-condescending material for younger age groups (5-8) and for middle school (ages 9-13). Fairytales are fine, but they should be straightforward and non-condescending."

**\*DRAMATIC PUBLISHING, INC.**, 311 Washington St., Woodstock IL 60098. (815)338-7170. Contact: Editor. Publishes plays and musicals for children and young adults. Submission method: send script, (with a cassette if a musical) and include an SASE if you wish to have manuscript returned. Reports in 3-4 months. Pays writers in royalties.
**Tips:** Scripts should be from ½ to 1½ hours long, and not didactic or condescending. Original plays dealing with hopes, joys and fears of today's children are preferred to adaptations of old classics.

**\*ELDRIDGE PUBLISHING CO. INC.**, P.O. Box 216, Franklin OH 45005. (513)746-6531. Editor: Nancy Vorhis. Estab. 1906. Publishes approximately 20 children's plays/year (5-8 for elementary; 10-12 for junior and senior high); 2-3 children's musicals/year. Prefers simple staging; flexible cast size. We "publish for elementary, middle, junior and high school, all genres." Recently published plays: *Frumpled Fairy Tales*, by Bill Springer—humorous retelling of 3 fairy tales, for elementary audience; *Louder Than Words*, by

*Refer to the Business of Children's Writing & Illustrating for up-to-date marketing, tax and legal information.*

Linda Dumas—a collection of mimes for junior high students; *It's A Howl*, by Tim Kelley—a humorous 3-act play for high audiences. Does not want to see "anything suggestive; anything with a subject matter that is too mature." Submission method: submit complete ms, score and tape of songs (if a musical). Reports in 2 months. Rights obtained on mss: all dramatic rights. Pays writers 10% of copy sales or 35% of royalties; buys material outright for $150-300. SASE for return of submissions.

**Tips:** "We always need material which offers flexible casting; parts which can be played by boys or girls or 'group' parts which may include one or several students. We like upbeat themes with humor and physical action."

**\*SAMUEL FRENCH, INC.**, 45 W. 25th St., New York NY 10010. (212)206-8990. FAX: (212)206-1429. Editor: Lawrence Harbison. Estab. 1830. Publishes 2 or 3 children's plays/year; "variable number of musicals." Subject matter: "All genres, all ages. No puppet plays." Recently published plays/musicals: *No More Secrets*, by Paul Lenzi and Geraldine Snyder—musical about child abuse; *The Gemshield Sleeper*, by Richard Slocum—sci-fi; *The Love Song of A. Nellie Goodrock*, by Richard Slocum—"mellerdrammer." "No adaptations of any of those old 'fairy tales.' No 'Once Upon a time, long ago and far away.' No kings, princesses, fairies, trolls, etc." Submission method: submit complete ms and demo tape (if a musical). Reports in 2-8 months. Rights obtained on mss: "Publication rights, amateur and professional production rights, option to publish next 3 plays." Pay for writers: "book royalty 10%; professional production royalty: 90%; amateur production royalty: 80%." SASE for return of submissions.

**Tips:** "Children's theater is a very tiny market, as most groups perform plays they have created themselves or have commissioned."

**\*HONOLULU THEATRE FOR YOUTH**, 2846 Ualena St., Honolulu HI 96819. (808)839-9885. Artistic Director: John Kauffman. Produces 6 children's plays/year. Subject matter: Looks for plays "celebrating cultures of the Pacific Rim, especially. Also, plays that deal with issues of concern to today's young audiences (varying in age from 6-18)." Submission method: query first. Reports in a matter of weeks. SASE for return of submission.

**Tips:** "Writers are encouraged to talk first to John Kauffman before beginning any work. Adaptations of published fiction for children to play form are the most frequently accepted types; queries could produce commissions to proceed with an adaptation, or possibly even an original work if it meets our needs and agrees with our philosophy."

**\*PIONEER DRAMA SERVICE**, P.O. Box 22555, Denver CO 80222. (303)759-4297. FAX: (303)759-0475. Editor: Steven Fendrich. Estab. 1960. Publishes 7 children's plays/year; 2 children's musicals/year. Subject matter: Publishes plays for ages 9-high school. Recently published plays/musicals: *Lucky Dollar—Private Eye*, by Tim Kelly, Arne Christiansen and Ole Kittleson—musical satire for ages 10 and up; *School for Nerds*, by R. Eugene Jackson—full-length satire, for ages 10 and up; *Little Luncheonette of Terror*, by Tim Kelly, Bill Francoeur and Steve Fendrich—musical for ages 10 and up. Does not want to see "script, scores, tapes, pics and reviews." Submission method: query with synopsis, character breakdown and set description. Reports in 2 months. Rights obtained on mss: all rights. Pays writers in royalties (10% on sales, 50% royalties on productions); or buys material outright for $200-1,000. SASE for return of submission.

**\*PLAYERS PRESS, INC.**, P.O. Box 1132, Studio City CA 91614-0132. (818)789-4980. Vice President: R. W. Gordon. Estab. 1965. Publishes 5-25 children's plays/year; 2-15 children's musicals/year. Subject matter: "We publish for all age groups." Recently published plays/musicals: *A Frog King's Daughter*, by Cheryl Miller Thurston—comic musical about a plain princess, for grades K-6; *Nessie*, by William Hezlep—comic story about the Loch Ness monster, for ages 9-15; *Rhyme Tyme*, by William-Alan Landes—a musical dealing with nursery rhymes and fractured stories, for preschool through adult audiences. Submission method: query with synopsis, character breakdown and set description; include #10 envelope SASE with query. Reports in 3 months. Rights obtained on mss: stage, screen, TV rights. Payment varies; outright purchases are available upon written request.

**Tips:** "Entertainment quality is on the upswing and needs to be directed at the world, no longer just the USA."

**\*PLAYS FOR YOUNG AUDIENCES**, P.O. Box 22555, Denver CO 80222. (303)759-4297. FAX: (303)759-0475. Editor: Steven Fendrich. Estab. 1989. Publishes 3 children's plays/ year; 1 children's musical/year. Subject matter: Publishes plays for preschool-8th grade audience. Recently produced plays: *Follow That Rabbit*, by Tim Kelly, Pam Hughes and Karen Selby—play based on *Alice in Wonderland*, for preschool-age 8 audience; *Emma Lou and the Big Ragout*, by Karen Boettcher-Tate—for preschool-age 10 audience; *Life and Adventures of Santa Claus*, by R. Eugene Jackson and Carl Alette—Christmas theme, for preschool-age 10 audience. Does not want to see script, score, tape, pictures and reviews. Submission method: query first; query with synopsis, character breakdown and set description. Reports in 2 months. Rights obtained on mss: all rights. Pays writers in royalties of 10% in sales, 50% on productions; or buys material outright for $200-1,000. SASE for return of submission.

**\*PLAYS, THE DRAMA MAGAZINE FOR YOUNG PEOPLE**, 120 Boylston St., Boston MA 02116. (617)423-3157. Managing Editor: Elizabeth Preston. Estab. 1941. Publishes 70-75 children's plays/year. "Props and staging should not be overly elaborate or costly. Our plays are performed by children in school." 100% of plays written for juvenile roles. Subject matter: Audience is lower grades through junior/senior high. Recently published plays: *A Laundromat Romance*, by John Murray—comedy about a young man and woman who meet and fall in love at the laundromat, aimed at junior and senior high audiences; *Author! Author!*, by Christine Hamlett—spoof of a talk show featuring fairy tale characters who have written books, aimed at the middle grade level students; *Prince and the Pauper*, by Joellen Bland—dramatization of the Mark Twain classic, for junior and senior high audiences. Send "nothing downbeat—no plays about drugs, sex or other 'heavy' topics." Submission methods: query first on adaptations of folk tales and classics; otherwise submit complete ms. Reports in 2-3 weeks. Rights obtained on mss: all rights. Pay rates vary, on acceptance. SASE for return of submission.

**Tips:** "Above all, plays must be entertaining for young people with plenty of action and a satisfying conclusion."

**\*PATRICIA B. SNYDER**, Esipa, Empire State Plaza, Albany NY 12223. (518)443-5222. FAX: (518)442-5318. Artistic Director: Patricia B. Snyder. Estab. 1976. Produces 1-2 children's plays and 1-2 children's musicals/year. Produces family plays for professional theater. 90% of plays/musicals are written for adult roles; 10% for juvenile roles. Recently produced children's plays: *The Snow Queen*, by Adrian Mitchell and Richard Peaslee—deals with rite of passage, for a family audience; *Knockabout Boy*, by William A. Frankonis—deals with rite of passage, for a family audience; *Pied Piper*, by Adrian Mitchell and Dominick Muldowney—social commentary, for a family audience. Does not want to see plays for children only. Submission method: submit complete ms and tape of songs (if a musical). Reports in 2-3 months. Rights obtained on mss: "varies." Pay for writers: "fees vary in nature and in degree." SASE for return of submission.

**Tips:** Writers should be mindful of "audience *sophistication*!"

**\*STAGE ONE: THE LOUISVILLE CHILDREN'S THEATRE**, 425 W. Market, Louisville KY 40202. (502)589-5946. FAX: (502)589-5779. Producing Director: Moses Goldberg. Estab. 1946. Produces 10 children's plays/year 1-3 children's musicals/year. Stage One is an equity company producing children't plays for professional productions. 100% of plays/musicals written for adult roles. "Sometimes do use students in selected productions." Recently produced plays: *Vasilsa*, by Moses Goldberg—fairy tale for 4-8 year old audiences; *Glass Menagerie*, by Tennessee Williams—deals with family tension, for a 12 year old through adult audience; *Odyssey*, by Greg Falls and Kent Beattie—a classic poem for 8-12 year old audiences. Submission method: submit complete ms, score and tape of songs (if a musical); include the author's résumé if desired. Reports in 3-4 months. Pays writers in royalties or per performance.
**Tips:** Looking for "stageworthy and respectful dramatizations of the classic tales of childhood, both ancient and modern; plays relevant to the lives of young people and their families; and plays directly related to the school curriculum."

**\*TADA!**, 120 West 28th St., New York NY 10001. (212)627-1732. Co-Artistic Directors: Janine Trevens and James Learned. Estab. 1984. Produces 3-4 children's plays/year; 3-4 children's musicals/year. "All actors are children, ages 6-17." Produces children's plays for professional, year-round theater. 100% of plays/musicals written for juvenile roles. Recently produced plays: *Once a Year on Christmas*, by Jeremy Beck—adventure in mythic town of children, for ages 2 through adult; *Wide Awake Jake*, by Alice Elliott, Robby Mecken and Faye Greenberg—boy learning to fall asleep, for ages 2 through adult; *Apt. 3*, by Davidson Lloyd—boys seek source of music in their apartment building, for ages 2 through adult. Submission method: query with synopsis, character breakdown and set description; submit complete ms, score and tape of songs (if a musical). Reports in 2 months. Rights obtained on mss: "Depends on the piece." Pays writers in royalties.
**Tips:** "Too many authors are writing productions, not plays. Our company is multi-racial and city-oriented. We are not interested in fairy tales."

**\*THEATRE FOR YOUNG AMERICA**, 7204 W. 80th St., Overland Park KS 66204. (913)648-4600. Artistic Director: Gene Mackey. Estab. 1974. Produces 10 children's plays/year; 3-5 children's musicals/year. We use a "small cast (4-7), open thrust stage." Theatre for Young America is a professional equity company. 80% of plays/musicals written for adult roles; 20% for juvenile roles. Recently produced plays: *The Wizard of Oz*, by Jim Eiler and Jeanne Bargy—for ages 6 and up; *A Partridge in Pear Tree*, by Lowell Swortzell—deals with the 12 days of Christmas, for ages 6 and up; *Three Billy Goats Gruff*, by Gene Mackey and Molly Jessup—Norwegian folk tales, for ages 6 and up. Submission method: query with synopsis, character breakdown and set description. Reports in 2 months. Rights obtained on mss: "production, tour rights in local area." Pays writers in royalties or $10-50/per performance. SASE for return of submission.
**Tips:** Looking for "cross-cultural material that respects the intelligence, sensitivity and taste of the child audience."

**\*THEATREWORKS/USA**, 890 Broadway, New York NY 10003. (212)672-5959. Artistic Director: Jay Harnick. Estab. 1964. "We only produce musicals." Uses musicals with "five actors; highly tourable, no lights. We are an equity company which produces and tours shows to schools and theaters across the country." 100% of plays/musicals written for adult roles. Recently produced plays: *Jekyll & Hyde*, by David Crane, Marten Kauffman and Michael Skloff—deals with drugs, aimed at grades 4 through junior high; *The Secret Garden*, by Linda Kline, Robert Jeff Roth, Kim Oler and Alison Hubbard—literary adaptation for grades 3 through junior high; *Footprints on the Moon*, by Art Perlman and Jeff Lunden—deals with early days of space exploration, for grades 4 through junior high. No "stuff that reads like Saturday Afternoon Specials; traditional fairy tales—especially sexist ones; musicals with nothing to say; fractured fairy tales."

Submission method: query with synopsis, character breakdown and set description. Reports in 6 months. Rights obtained on mss: all performance rights. Pays writers in royalties of 6% (divided by collaborators); also pays a $1,500 commission (to be divided by collaborators). SASE for return of submission.

**Tips:** "It's always a good idea to see any organization's work before submitting material to get an idea of our 'style.' We look for *good theater* — theater that kids and families can enjoy together."

**\*THE YOUNG COMPANY**, P.O. Box 225, Milford NH 03055. (603)673-4005. Associate Director/Literary Manager: Austin Tichenor. Estab. 1984. Produces 10-12 children's plays/year; 1-2 children's musicals/year. "Scripts should not be longer than an hour, small cast preferred; very small production budgets, so use imagination." The Young Company is a professional training program associated with American Stage Festival, a professional theater. Recently produced plays/musicals: *Dancing on the Ceiling*, by Austin Tichenor — adaptation of Kafka's *Metamorphosis*, for ages 7 and up; *High Pressure Zone*, music by Andrew Howard, book and lyrics by Austin Tichenor — musical about addictive behavior, for middle school and older audience; *The First Olympics*, by Eve Muson and Austin Tichenor — deals with mythology/Olympic origins, for 6 year old through adult audience. Does not want to see condescending material. Submission method: Query with synopsis, character breakdown and sample score. Rights obtained on mss: first production credit on all future materials. Pays small fee and housing for rehearsals; SASE for return of submission.

**Tips:** Looks for "concise and legible presentation, songs that further dramatic action. Develop material with strong marketing possibilities. See your work in front of an audience and be prepared to change it if your audience doesn't 'get it.' Don't condescend to your audience. Tell them a *story*."

The "special markets" in this section include greeting cards for children, coloring books, comics, and word games and puzzles. You will find that many publishers included in the Book Publishers section of *Children's Writer's & Illustrator's Market* express a need for coloring books and games as well.

Though this year's section is small, don't be fooled into thinking this may not be a profitable market over the long term. A recent survey of national booksellers showed that 78 percent of children's bookstores carry greeting cards and related paper products, and that 58 percent of these same children's bookstores—as well as 50 percent of chain bookstores—stock educational games. Such items wouldn't be stocked without a customer demand for them, and more companies will soon realize this.

As with any section of this book, read through the listings carefully to determine subject needs and methods of submission. Since there is a variety of product needs represented by each company the materials requested for review will vary greatly.

**\*COLORMORE, INC.,** P.O. Box 111249, Carrollton TX 75011-1249. (214)245-1059. President: Susan C. Koch. Estab. 1987. 50% of material written and illustrated by freelancers. Buys 2 freelance projects/year; receives 10 submissions/year. Greeting card line(s): "color-your own postcards and seasonal cards." Coloring books: "travel-related/geography/social studies." Illustrators: looks for "color-your own postcards with Texas themes."
**Making Contact & Terms:** Submit greeting cards 12 months in advance, special coloring books 12 months in advance. SASE. Reports in 2-4 weeks. Material copyrighted. Buys all rights, Pays on publication. Pay for greeting cards "varies"; pay for coloring books is within a 5-8% royalty range. Writer's/illustrator's guideline sheets for legal-size SAE and 1 first class stamp. Market list is regularly revised.
**Tips:** Target age-groups: 5-10 years old.

**\*ECLIPSE COMICS,** P.O. Box 1099, Forestville CA 95436. (707)887-1521. FAX: (707)887-7128. Editor-in-Chief: Catherine Yronwode. Art Director: Stan Woch. Estab. 1978. 100% of material written and illustrated by freelancers. Buys "approximately 100" freelance projects/year; receives 500 submissions/year. Comic books: looks for "realistic art and stories that appeal to a broad spectrum and a variety of ages." Writers: "All material submitted should be in (brief) outline form with 5-6 sample pages of script." Illustrators: "We will only look at samples of continuity art and cover illustrations; display pieces are not needed."
**Making Contact & Terms:** SASE. Pays on acceptance. Pay for comic books "varies; writer and artist split 8% royalty." Guideline sheets for #10 SAE and 1 first class stamp; guidelines and a sample comic for $1.75 and 9×12 SAE.

**HIGHLIGHTS FOR CHILDREN,** Hidden Pictures, Puzzlemania, Activity Books, 803 Church St., Honesdale PA 18431. (717)253-1080. FAX: (717)253-0179. Editor: Kent L. Brown Jr. Art Director: Rosanne Guararra. Estab. 1946. 90% of materials freelance written and illustrated. Freelance projects purchased last year: "several thousand to start inventory; following years may be significantly lower." Receives 7,000-8,000 submissions annually. Needs "independent activities targeting children 5-12 years in age. We favor visually stimulating puzzles free of violent themes."

**Making Contact & Terms:** Special puzzle submissions accepted year round. SASE for return of submission. Reports in 1-2 months. Purchases all rights. Pays on acceptance. Writer's guidelines for SASE.

**Tips:** Looking for "codes, matching, crosswords, dot-to-dots, math and logic puzzles, hidden pictures, mazes, quizzes, riddles." Illustrators: "In illustration almost any range of art is accepted these days. Children are more sophisticated now in terms of graphics and design — the illustrator should be aware of this."

**\*PRICE STERN SLOAN**, 360 N. La Cienega Blvd., Los Angeles CA 90048. Editor: Lisa Ann Marsoli. Estab. 1964. 90% of material written and illustrated by freelancers. Buys 50 freelance projects/year; receives hundreds of submissions/year. Publishes "word searches, word games, hidden picture coloring books."

**Making Contact & Terms:** SASE. Reports in 4-6 weeks. Rights purchased: "depends on project." Payment depends on project. Writer's/illustrator's guidelines for business-size SAE and 1 first-class stamp. "Seasonal (fall or spring issue) catalog available with SASE and $2.50 postage."

**Tips:** Target age group: preschool-YA. Trend toward "children's nonfiction."

**\*STANDARD PUBLISHING**, 8121 Hamilton Ave., Cincinnati OH 45231. (513)931-4050. FAX: (513)931-0904. Editor: Henrietta Gambill. Art Director: Frank Sutton. Estab. 1866. 100% of material illustrated by freelancers. Buys 75 freelance projects/year; receives 1,200 submissions/year. Publishes religious/value-oriented material.

**Making Contact & Terms:** Submit seasonal coloring books, games and puzzles 12-18 months in advance. SASE. Reports in 3 months. Material copyrighted. Buys all rights. Pays on acceptance. Writer's guidelines for SAE and 1 first class stamp.

**Tips:** Looks for "Bible-oriented" material, for a preschool-6th grade audience.

**\*WARNER PRESS**, P.O. Box 2499, Anderson IN 46018. Editor: Cindy Maddox. Art Director: Dianne Deckert. Estab. 1880. 60% of material written by freelancers; 75% illustrated by freelancers. Publishes children's birthday cards, coloring and activity books, all religious-oriented. "We are expanding our line, so specific needs are still undetermined."

**Making Contact & Terms:** Submit seasonal greeting cards and coloring books 18 months in advance. Reports in 6 weeks. Material copyrighted. Buys all rights. Pays on acceptance. Guidelines sheet for SASE.

# Young Writer's/ Illustrator's Markets

Children and teens—the listings in this section are for you. You may notice some of the magazines listed here are the ones you already read. Many adult magazines have special sections set aside to feature the work of younger writers and illustrators, and may provide special writer's and artist's guidelines upon request. Be sure to check each listing to determine if such guidelines are available. Some of the smaller, literary magazines here may not be easily found in the bookstore or library. In such a case, you may need to contact the magazine to see if a sample copy is available, and what the cost might be. It is important for all writers and artists to be familiar with the type of editorial material contained in those magazines they are interested in submitting work to.

Don't be discouraged if your work is rejected at first as unsuitable for a magazine. Many of our best known writers and artists were turned down more times than they can count at the beginning of their careers, yet went on to be successful at their craft. The key to becoming published lies in persistence as well as talent. Just keep sending out your stories and artwork—there will come a time when an editor wants to use it because it is right for his needs.

As the adult writers and artists have been advised in other parts of this book, refer to the Business of Children's Writing & Illustrating at the beginning of this book if you're not sure how a proper query letter or manuscript looks. We have included a step by step explanation of what to include in each. Good luck in your writing or art career—I hope to hear of your successes!

**\*THE ACORN**, 1530 7th St., Rock Island IL 61201. (309)788-3980. Newsletter. Audience consists of "kindergarten-12th grade, teachers and other adult writers." Purpose in publishing works by children: to expose children's manuscripts to others and provide a format for those who might not have one. Children must be K-12 (put grade on manuscripts).
**Magazines:** 99% of magazine written by children. Word length: 500 fiction, 500 nonfiction, 32 lines poetry. Pays 1 copy of the issue the work is in. Sample copy $1. Subscription $5 for 6 issues. Submit mss to Betty Mowery, editor. Send complete ms. Will accept typewritten, legibly handwritten and/or computer printout. SASE. Reports in 1 week.
**Artwork:** Publishes artwork by children. Looks for "all types, size—3 × 4½ (the size of a business card). Use black ink in artwork." Pays in 1 copy of issue the work is in. Submit artwork either with manuscript or separately to Betty Mowery, editor.
**Tips:** "I will use occasional articles by adults, but it must relate to something that will help children with their writing—submitting or publishing. Manuscripts without SASE will not be returned."

**\*ATALANTIK**, 7630 Deer Creek Dr., Worthington OH 43085. (614)885-0550. Magazine published quarterly. "This bilingual (English and Bengali) magazine endeavors to keep the Bengali language alive to the Bengalis in USA." Purpose in publishing works by children: to encourage them to write more and develop their hidden talents. Requirements to be met before work is published: age or location is no restriction; about originality, parent/teacher's assurance is enough.

**Magazines:** Approximately 5% at most of magazine written by children. Uses 1-2 short fiction stories (500-1,000 words); 1-2 short, educational nonfiction pieces (500-1,000 words); 1-2 poems (20 lines or less). Pays in one or two magazines. Submit mss to Prabhat K. Dutta, editor. Submit complete ms. Will accept typewritten and computer printout mss. SASE. Reports in 6-8 weeks.

**Artwork:** Publishes artwork by children. Pays in one or two magazines. Submit b&w; pen or pencil work, size not exceeding 6 × 9 to Prabal Rana Dutta, art director. SASE. Reports in 6-8 weeks.

**Tips:** "Ours is an international magazine. As such, the audience is all over the globe. International themes as well as Asian Indian themes are most welcome. Educational, scientific and (math) puzzle writings are also very welcome."

**BITTERROOT,** Box 489, Spring Glen NY 12483. Magazine. Published 3 times/year. Purpose in publishing works by children: we encourage all poets who seek their own identity through original poetry, realistic or fantastic. We discourage stereotyped forms in poetry that imitate fixed patterns and leave no individual mark. Requirements to be met before work is published: contributors are "usually high school level."

**Poetry:** 1% of magazine written by children. Uses poetry, poetry book reviews. "Short poems preferred." Pays in copies. Submit mss to Menke Katz, editor-in-chief. Send 3 or 4 poems with SASE. Will accept typewritten mss. Include SASE. Reports in 6 weeks.

**Artwork:** Looks for only black and white line drawings. Pays in copies. Submit artwork to Rivke Katz, art editor. SASE. Reports in 6 weeks.

**\*BOY'S LIFE,** 1325 Walnut Hill Ln., Box 152079, Irving TX 75015-2079. (214)580-2000. Magazine published monthly. Audience consists of boys 8-18. Requirements to be met before work is published: must be 18 or under.

**Magazines:** One page, which does not run every month, is written by children. Uses 3-10 fiction stories (500 words or less); nonfiction pieces (500 words or less); poetry. "We do not pay for mss." Submit mss to Jeff Csatari, special features editor. Will accept typewritten, legibly handwritten, computer printout mss. "We do not acknowledge receipt or use of ms."

**\*CHILDREN'S CONNECTIONS,** Bat Publishing, 316 S. Therese, Box 132, Holgate OH 43527. Magazine "pamphlet softcover." Publishes "stories all by Children's Connections contributors." Readers are 18 and under. Purpose in publishing works by children: to encourage young writers in the craft of writing and provide audiences; to encourage handwork projects, quality of the writing craft in a too-fast-paced world. Requirements to be met before work is published: Need name, school, age, town identifications; must meet length requirements. Writer's guidelines available on request.

**Magazines:** 100% of magazine written by children. "At present, there is no mss limit, as we are still getting our feet wet." Uses fiction (typed, double-spaced, 4 pages); nonfiction (only personal experience stories or articles; typed, double spaced, 4 pages); poetry and communicative letters (writer to writers about writing experience/problems, 2 pages). Pays in 2 copies of edition to writer. Submit complete ms. Will accept typewritten and very legibly handwritten form mss. SASE. Reports in 1 month.

 *The asterisk before a listing indicates that the listing is new in this edition.*

**Tips:** "We publish three 'Connections' editions: Children's—18 and under; 'Connections'—19 and over; 'Calendar Connections'—by BAT writers; as well as separate pamphlets and works."

**CHILDREN'S DIGEST,** Box 567, Indianapolis IN 46206. (317)636-8881. Magazine. Published 8 times/year. Audience consists of preteens. Purpose in publishing works by children: to encourage children to express themselves through writing. Requirements to be met before work is published: require proof of originality before publishing stories. Writer's guidelines available on request.
**Magazines:** 10% of magazine written by children. Uses 1 fiction story (about 200 words), 6-7 poems, 15-20 riddles, 7-10 letters/issue. "There is no payment for manuscripts submitted by readers." Submit mss to *Children's Digest* (Elizabeth A. Rinck, editor). Submit complete ms. Will accept typewritten, legibly handwritten, computer printout mss. Reports in 8-10 weeks.

**CHILDREN'S PLAYMATE,** Box 567, Indianapolis IN 46206. (317)636-8881. Magazine. Audience consists of children between 6 and 8 years of age. Purpose in publishing works by children: to encourage children to write. Writer's guidelines available on request.
**Magazines:** 10% of magazine written by children. Uses 6-7 poems, 8-10 jokes, 8-10 riddles/issue. "There is no payment for manuscripts submitted by children." Submit mss to *Children's Playmate* (Elizabeth A. Rinck, editor). Submit complete ms. Will accept typewritten, legibly handwritten, computer printout mss. Reports in 8-10 weeks. "No material may be returned."
**Artwork:** Publishes artwork by children. "Prefers dark-colored line drawings on white paper. No payment for children's artwork published." Submit artwork to *Children's Playmate.*

**CLUBHOUSE,** Box 15, Berrien Springs MI 49103. (616)471-9009. Magazine. Publishes 1 section by kids in each issue, bimonthly. "Audience consists of kids 9-14; philosophy is God loves kids, kids are neat people." Purpose in publishing works by children: encouragement; demonstration of talent. Requirements to be met before work is published: age 9-14; parent's note verifying originality.
**Magazines:** 1/16th of magazine written by children. Uses adventure, historical, everyday life experience (fiction/nonfiction-1,200 words); health-related short articles; poetry (4-24 lines of "mostly mood pieces and humor"). Payment for ms: prizes for children, money for adult authors. Query. Will accept typewritten, legibly handwritten, computer printout mss. SASE—"will not be returned without SASE." Reports in 6 weeks.
**Artwork:** Publishes artwork by children. Looks for all types of artwork-white paper, black pen. Pays in prizes for kids. Send black pen on white paper to Elaine Trumbo, editor. SASE—"won't be returned without SASE."
**Tips:** "All items submitted by kids are held in a file and used when possible. We normally suggest they do not ask for return of the item. We will not be accepting manuscripts or unassigned artwork until April of 1990."

**CREATIVE KIDS,** Box 6448, Mobile AL 36660. (205)478-4700. Magazine. Published 8 times/year (Oct.-May). "All of our material is by children, for children." Purpose in publishing works by children: to create a product that is good enough for publication and to offer an opportunity to see their work in print. Requirements to be met before work is published: age 5-18—must have statement by teacher or parent verifying originality. Writer's guidelines available on request.

*Refer to the Business of Children's Writing & Illustrating*
*for up-to-date marketing, tax and legal information.*

**Magazines:** Uses "about 6" fiction stories (200-750 words); "about 6" nonfiction stories (200-750 words); poetry, plays, ideas to share (200-750 words)/issue. Pays in "free magazine"/ms. Submit mss to Fay L. Gold, editor. Will accept typewritten, legibly handwritten mss. SASE. Reports in 4 weeks.

**Artwork:** Publishes artwork by children. Looks for "any kind of drawing, cartoon, or painting." Pays in "free magazine." Send original or a photo of the work to Fay L. Gold, editor. No photocopies. SASE. Reports in 4 weeks.

**Tips:** "*Creative Kids* is a magazine by kids, for kids. The work represents children's ideas, questions, fears, concerns and pleasures. The material never contains racist, sexist or violent expression. The purpose is to encourage youngsters to create a product that is good enough for publication. A person may submit one or more pieces of work. Each piece must be labeled with the student's name, birth date, grade, school, home address, and school address. Include a photograph, if possible. Recent school pictures are best. Material submitted to *Creative Kids* must not be under consideration by any other publisher. Items should be carefully prepared, proofread and double checked. All activities requiring solutions must be accompanied by the correct answers. We're looking for current topics of interest: nutrition, ecology, cleaner environment, etc."

**CREATIVE WITH WORDS PUBLICATIONS,** Box 223226, Carmel CA 93940. (408)649-1862. Books. Estab. 1975. Published 1 time/year. Audience consists of children, schools, libraries, adults, reading programs. Purpose in publishing works by children: to offer them an opportunity to get started in publishing. "Work must be of quality, original, unedited, and not published before; age must be given (up to 19 years old)." Writer's guidelines available on request.

**Books:** Uses fairy tales, folklore items (1,000 words); poetry "language art work" (not to exceed 30 lines). Recently published *We Are Writers, Too!* (anthology, children of all ages); *A Scary Halloween!* (children and adults of all ages); *A CWW Easter!* (anthology, children and adults of all ages). Pay: 20% off each copy of publication in which fiction or poetry by children appears. Submit mss to Brigitta Geltrich, editor. Send query or submit complete ms; teacher must submit; teacher and/or parents must verify originality of writing. Will accept typewritten and/or legibly handwritten mss. SASE. Reports in 2-8 weeks.

**Artwork:** Publishes artwork by children (language art work). Pay: 20% off every copy of publication in which work by children appears. Submit artwork to Brigitta Geltrich, editor. "There is more use of illustrations to accompany text."

**THE FLYING PENCIL PRESS,** Box 7667, Elgin IL 60121. Books. Publishes 1 book by children/year. "Audience is general (family, schools, libraries). Philosophy is freedom of expression and creativity." Purpose in publishing works by children: to encourage and support young writers. Requirements to be met before work is published: age 8-14, following current guidelines. Writer's guidelines available on request.

**Books:** Uses fiction stories (200-2,000 words); nonfiction (200-2,000 words); poems (4-32 lines). Pays in author's copy, awards/ms. Submit ms to Charlotte Towner Graeber, editor. "We prefer fiction, nonfiction and poems to be typewritten, but will accept handwritten material if it is clear and readable. Material must be the original work of the submitting author. Enclose a self addressed stamped envelope (SASE) if you wish material we do not accept for publication to be returned. Remember to keep a copy of your writing in case the original is lost in handling or mailing. You will be notified by mail in 4-6 weeks if your work is accepted for Flying Pencil publication."

**Artwork:** Publishes artwork by children. Artwork—black and white line art, size limit 8×10; cartoons—1 to 8 frames, black and white, size limit 8×10. Pays in copies. Artwork, illustrations and cartoons should be on unlined white paper. SASE. "Keep a copy of artwork in case original is lost in the mail." Submit to Charlotte Towner Graeber, editor. Reports in 4-6 weeks.

**FUTURIFIC, INC.**, the Foundation for Optimism, Futurific, 280 Madison Ave., New York NY 10016. (212)684-4913. Magazine. Published monthly. Audience consists of people interested in an accurate report of what is ahead. "We do not discriminate by age. We look for the visionary in all people. They must say what will be. No advice or 'may-be.' " Writer's guidelines available on request.
**Magazines:** Submit mss to B. Szent-Miklosy, publisher. Will accept typewritten, legibly handwritten, computer printout mss. SASE.
**Artwork:** Publishes artwork by children. Looks for "what the future will look like." Pay is negotiable. Send b&w drawings or photos. Submit artwork to B. Szent-Miklosy, publisher. SASE.

**\*GHOST TOWN QUARTERLY**, Box 714, Philipsburg MT 59858. (406)859-3365. Magazine published quarterly. "We work to preserve the history surrounding ghost towns and abandoned sites throughout the U.S., Canada and Mexico and to present this history in a manner both interesting and informative. We also feature museums and historical sites." Purpose in publishing works by children: "to add to the scope of our magazine and to give children a chance to gain recognition for their abilities." Requirements to be met before work is published: K through 12th grade; include contributor's name and address, age and name and address of school attended. Writer's guidelines available upon request.
**Magazines:** 4% of magazine written by children. Uses very little fiction. Uses 1-4 nonfiction articles about ghost towns and abandoned sites, museums, historical sites, interviews with people who have lived in an area now abandoned (1,000 words maximum length). Uses 1-4 poems (500 word maximum length). Pays 5¢/word on publication. Submit mss to Donna B. McLean, editor, Student's Corner. Submit complete ms. Will accept typewritten, legibly handwritten, computer printout mss. SASE. Reports in 2-4 months.
**Artwork:** Publishes artwork by children "up to 8×10 vertical or 5×7 horizontal; cartoons and sketches related to our themes, depicting something based on facts." Pays $10 per cartoon; $15 per sketch, on publication. Submit "on plain paper kept free of smudges" to Donna B. McLean, editor Student's Corner. SASE. Reports in 2-4 months.
**Tips:** "We also accept photographs and pay $5 if they are published as b&w, $10 if we publish in color. Eligible for cover consideration (covers pay $50—need to include information about photo). Best to include at least a short article with photo submission."

**GIFTED CHILDREN MONTHLY**, Box 115, Sewell NJ 08080. (609)582-0277. Newsletter. Audience is parents of gifted children. There is a 4-page insert for kids; complements adult section. Requirements to be met before work is published: 4-14 years old. Writer's guidelines available on request.
**Magazines:** 18% of magazine written by children. Uses 5 fiction stories (50 words average); 10 nonfiction articles. "Respond to regular departments that run throughout the year." Pays $3 or a product from our catalog. Submit ms to Robert Baum, managing editor. Will accept typewritten, legibly handwritten, computer printout mss. "Only responds if material used—sometimes many months. Contributor copies sent."
**Artwork:** Publishes artwork by children. Interested in poster contest, editorial cartoons. Pays $3 or a product from our catalog. Submit artwork to Robert Baum, managing editor.

**HIGHLIGHTS FOR CHILDREN**, 803 Church St., Honesdale PA 18431. (717)253-1080. Magazine. Published monthly (July-August issue combined). "We strive to provide wholesome, stimulating, entertaining material that will encourage children to read. Our audience is children 2-12." Purpose in publishing works by children: to encourage children's creative expression. Requirements to be met before work is published: age limit is 15.

**Magazines:** 15-20% of magazine written by children. Uses 9-15 pieces of prose and poetry: "Our Own Pages"; 15-20 jokes and riddles; 3-5 letters to the editor. Submit mss to the Editor. Submit complete ms. Will accept typewritten, legibly handwritten, computer printout mss. Responds in 3-6 weeks.

**Artwork:** Publishes artwork by children. No cartoon or comic book characters. No commercial products. Submit black-and-white artwork for "Our Own Pages." Color for others. Responds in 3-6 weeks.

**MERLYN'S PEN: The National Magazine of Student Writing**, Box 1058, East Greenwich RI 02818. (401)885-5175. Magazine. Published every 2 months during the school year, September to May. "We publish 150 manuscripts annually by students in grades 7-10. The entire magazine is dedicated to young adults' writing. Our audience is classrooms, libraries and students from grades 7-10." Requirements to be met before work is published: writers must be in grades 7-10 and must follow submission guidelines for preparing their manuscripts. When a student is accepted, he/she, a parent and a teacher must sign a statement of originality.

**Magazines:** 100% of magazine written by adolescents. Uses 6-8 short stories, plays (fiction); 2-3 nonfiction essays; poetry; letters to the editor; editorials; reviews of previously published works; reviews of books, music, movies. No word limit on any material. Pays for ms in three copies of the issue and a paperback copy of *The Elements of Style* (a writer's handbook). Also, a discount is offered for additional copies of the issue. Submit mss to R. Jim Stahl, editor. Submit complete ms. Will only accept typewritten mss. SASE. "All rejected manuscripts have an editor's constructive critical comment in the margin." Reports in 11 weeks.

**Artwork:** Publishes artwork by children. Looks for black and white line drawings, cartoons, color art for cover. Pays in 3 copies of the issue to the artist, and a discount is offered for additional copies. Send unmatted original artwork. Submit artwork to R. Jim Stahl, editor. SASE. Reports in 11 weeks.

**Tips:** "All manuscripts and artwork must be submitted with a cover sheet listing: name, age and grade, home address, home phone number, school name, school phone number, school address, teacher's name and principal's name. SASE must be large enough and carry enough postage for return."

**MY FRIEND**, 50 St. Paul's Ave., Jamaica Plain, Boston MA 02130. (617)522-8911. Magazine. Published 10 times/year. Audience consists of children ages 6-12, primarily Roman Catholics. Purpose in publishing works by children: to stimulate reader participation and to encourage young Catholic writers. Requirements to be met before work is published: we accept work from children ages 6-16. Requirements regarding originality included in guidelines. Writer's guidelines available for SASE.

**Tips:** "Our 'Junior Reporter' feature gives young writers the chance to do active research on a variety of topics. Children may ask for an 'assignment' or suggest topics they'd be willing to research and write on. This would be mainly where our interest in children's writing would lie."

**THE MYTHIC CIRCLE**, Mythopoeic Society, Box 6707, Altadena CA 91001. Editor: Lynn Maudlin and Christine Lowentrout. Art Director: Lynn Maudlin. Quarterly magazine. Circ. 150. We are a fantasy writer's workshop in print featuring reader comments in each issue. 5% of publication aimed at juvenile market.

**Nonfiction:** How-to, interview/profile. "We are just starting with nonfiction — dedicated to how to write and publish." Buys "maximum of 4" mss/year. Average word length: 250-2,000. Byline given.

**How to Contact/Writers:** Fiction: send complete ms. Nonfiction: query. SASE (IRC) for answer to query and return of ms. Reports on queries/mss in 1 month. Will consider photocopied, computer printout (dark dot matrix) and electronic submissions via disk (query for details).

**Illustration:** Buys 10 illustrations/issue; buys 40 illustrations/year. Preferred theme or style: fantasy, soft science fiction. Will review ms/illustration packages submitted by authors/artists; ms/illustration packages submitted by authors with illustrations done by separate artists; illustrator's work for possible use with fiction/nonfiction articles and columns by other authors.

**How to Contact/Illustrators:** Ms/illustration packages: complete with art. Illustrations only: Send tear sheets. Reports on art samples in 3-6 weeks. Original artwork returned at job's completion (only if postage paid).

**Terms/Writers and Illustrators:** Pays on publication. Buys one-time rights. Pays in contributor copies. Sample copy $3.50. Writer's guidelines free with SAE and 1 first-class stamp.

**Tips:** "We are a good outlet for a story that hasn't sold but 'should' have — good feedback and tips on improvement. We do have a 'Mythopoeic Youth' section with stories and art by those under 18 years."

**PRISM MAGAZINE**, Lauderdale Publishing, Box 7375, Ft. Lauderdale FL 33338. (305)563-8805. Newspaper. Bimonthly. "While many people realize the need to develop young talent, there has been little opportunity for gifted young people to see their creations published and to create a network of communication with other gifted young people. We see *Prism* as a vehicle not only for the publication of work, but also as the beginning of that vital network. For the first issue, we have gathered contributions from as many geographic areas and age groups as possible. We found that some young people were shy about creating materials, because they were unsure of the format, but we are sure once you have seen *Prism* you will understand the wide latitude we have built into the concept." Writer's guidelines available on request.

**Magazines:** "Math, science, philosophy, history, literature, the future, your personal experiences, humor, current events — all are topics we would like to see discussed in *Prism*." Pays in copies. Submit ms to Sherry Friedlander, publisher, or T. Constance Coyne, editor.

**Artwork:** Publishes artwork by children. Artwork, photos and cartoons are the expressions and feelings of young people all over the United States and in many foreign countries. Pays in copies. Submit artwork to Sherry Friedlander, publisher, or T. Constance Coyne, editor.

**REFLECTIONS**, Box 368, Duncan Falls OH 43734. (614)674-5209. Magazine. Published January and June. Purpose in publishing works by children: to encourage writing. Requirements to be met before work is published: statement of originality and signed by teacher or parent. Writer's guidelines available on request (with SASE).

**Magazines:** 100% of magazine written by children. Uses 1-3 fiction stories (1,000-2,000 words); 1-3 nonfiction articles (1,000-2,000 words); poetry. Pays in contributor's copy. Editor: Dean Harper. Submit complete ms. Will accept typewritten, legibly handwritten, computer printout mss. "Please include your name, age, school, address, and your teacher's name. Be certain to include a self-addressed stamped envelope with your manuscripts. Make the statement that this is your own original work, then date it and sign your name. Your teacher or parent should also sign it." Reports in 2 weeks.

**Artwork:** Publishes artwork by children. Pays in contributor's copy. Editor: Dean Harper. SASE. Reports in 2 weeks.

**Tips:** "We hope we are encouraging young people to read and write."

**\*SCHOLASTIC SCOPE**, 730 Broadway, New York NY 10003. (212)505-3000. Magazine published weekly. "*Scope* is a language arts magazine for junior high and high school students reading below level (approximately 5th grade level)." Purpose in publishing works by children: to encourage readers to write, to entertain readers. Requirements to be met before work is published: proof of original work, signed by parent or teacher. Writer's guidelines available on request.
**Magazines:** 20% of magazine written by children. Uses fiction, nonfiction and poetry. Submit ms to Adrienne Su, assistant editor. Submit complete ms. Will accept typewritten, legibly handwritten, computer printout mss. SASE.

**SHOE TREE**, National Association for Young Writers, 215 Valle del Sol Dr., Santa Fe NM 87501. (505)982-8596. Magazine. Published 3 times/year. "We encourage young writers to use writing as a serious form of communication to raise their performance standards and improve skills. We accept only the finest work. The goal of the NAYW is the encouragement of children's writing." We publish work by young writers, ages 6-14. Writer's guidelines available on request.
**Magazines:** 95% of magazine written by children; one adult author-to-author column. Uses 5-10 fictional stories; 2-6 nonfiction articles; and personal narratives, humor, book reviews, 6-10 poems. Pays with 2 complimentary copies. Sheila Cowing, editor-in-chief. Submit complete ms. Will accept typewritten, legibly handwritten, computer printout mss. Reports in 2 months.
**Artwork:** Publishes artwork by children. "We use art mostly for illustration so we solicit. Send, or have teacher send, samples of artwork and then we solicit. Also use pictures for full-color or b&w cover." Pays with 2 complimentary copies. Submit artwork by student or teacher, either photocopy or original. Sheila Cowing, editor-in-chief. Reports in 2 months.

**STONE SOUP**, The Magazine by Children, Children's Art Foundation, Box 83, Santa Cruz CA 95063. (408)426-5557. Articles/Fiction Editor, Art Director: Ms. Gerry Mandel. Magazine. Bimonthly. Circ. 10,000. "We publish fiction, poetry and artwork by children through age 13. Our preference is for work based on personal experiences and close observation of the world."
**Magazines:** 100% of magazine written by children. Uses animal, contemporary, fantasy, problem-solving, science fiction, spy/mystery/adventure fiction stories. Does not want to see classroom assignments and formula writing. Buys 50 mss/year. Byline given. Uses animal, interviews/profile, problem solving, travel nonfiction articles. "We don't publish straight nonfiction, but we do publish stories based on real events and experiences." Buys 10 mss/year. Byline given. Send complete ms. SASE. Reports in 6 weeks. Will accept computer printout submissions.
**Artwork:** Buys 6 illustrations/issue; 30/year. Send samples of artwork. Reports in 6 weeks. Original artwork returned at job's completion.
**Terms/Writers and Illustrators:** Pays on acceptance. Buys all rights. Pays $5-15/solicited article. Pays $5-15/b&w inside illustration. All other contributors paid in copies. Sample copy $2. Free writer's/illustrator's guidelines.
**Tips:** "Look closely at the magazine to get an idea of the kind of work we publish."

**STRAIGHT MAGAZINE**, Standard Publishing, 8121 Hamilton Ave., Cincinnati OH 45231. (513)931-4050. Magazine. Weekly magazine includes fiction pieces and articles for Christian teens 13-19 years old to inform, encourage and uplift them. Purpose in publishing works by children: give them an opportunity to express themselves. Requirements to be met before work is published: must submit their birth date and Social Security number (if they have one). Writer's guidelines available on request, "included in regular guidelines."

# Close-up

**Gerry Mandel**
*Co-Editor, Stone Soup*
*Santa Cruz, California*

Adult writers and illustrators can research hundreds of magazines before they decide which is the best market for their articles, poems and illustrations. Children and younger teens, however, have fewer options. It was this situation that Gerry Mandel and her *Stone Soup* co-founder William Rubel decided to rectify 18 years ago.

"We started out with a good idea," she begins, "a good business sense and the ability to recognize top writing and art by children." Mandel and Rubel, who started *Stone Soup* while students at the University of California at Santa Cruz, have enjoyed watching circulation grow to 10,000 along with an increased number of writing and art submissions that now average 200 per week.

Since more students are aware of *Stone Soup*, there are more submissions so Mandel offers valuable advice about the type of material that is published. "A good deal of the writing we reject is formula writing of some kind, like 'The Mystery of the Haunted House' or 'My Life as a Pencil.' Our advice is write about the things you really care about. We look for stories," she says, "that reveal something about the deepest concerns of the author. Often, these stories are based on an experience that had a big impact on the author, like the death of a pet or moving to a new town. Sometimes they may be purely fiction, but with observations drawn from experience about people and places."

One story sticks in Mandel's mind as being particularly memorable— "Midnight Crossing," by 12 year old Marci Sanchez. The story, based on tales Sanchez's grandmother has shared with her, recounts the family's struggle to leave Mexico and take up residence in the United States. "Not only is the subject matter both moving and fascinating," Mandell explains, "but Marci successfully conveys her love of her grandmother and how happy she is to be learning about this important part of her family's history."

Her advice to artists, not surprisingly, parallels her suggestions to writers: "Draw the things you know best and draw them the way they look to you."

Mandel tells her contributors to read lots of books, go to museums and galleries, and to generally be observant of what they see around them. "Pay close attention to how people talk, what they wear, how they act toward each other, and how they solve their problems," she suggests. "Look at how light reflects off a puddle of water and how a cat looks curled up by the fire. We advise our writers to do lots of writing and our artists to draw lots of pictures."

*— Connie Eidenier*

**Magazines:** 15% of magazine written by children. Uses fiction (500-1,000 words); personal experience pieces (500-700 words); poetry (approx. 1 poem per issue). Pays flat fee for poetry; per word for stories/articles. Submit mss to Carla J. Crane, editor. Submit complete ms. Will accept typewritten and computer printout mss. SASE. Reports in 4-6 weeks.
**Artwork:** Publishes artwork by children. Looks for "anything that will fit our format." Pays flat rate. Submit artwork to Carla Crane, editor. SASE. Reports in 4-6 weeks.

**\*SUNSHINE MAGAZINE,** Henrichs Publications, Inc., Box 40, Sunshine Park, Litchfield IL 62056. (217)324-3425. Magazine published monthly. "General audience."
**Magazines:** "Two pages/issue written by children." Uses fiction, nonfiction and poetry (up to 200 words). Pays in copies. Submit mss to Editor. Submit complete ms. Will accept typewritten, legibly handwritten, computer printout mss. SASE. Reports in 3 months.

**\*TEXAS HISTORIAN,** Texas State Historical Association, 2/306 Sid Richardson Hall, Univ. Station, Austin TX 78731. (512)471-1525. Articles Editor: David De Boe. Magazine published 5 times a year in January, March, May, September and November. Estab. 1940. Circ. 2,200. "The *Texas Historian* is the official publication of the Junior Historians of Texas. Articles accepted for publication must be written by members of the Junior Historians of Texas." 75% of material directed to children.
**Nonfiction:** Young adult: history. Average word length: 2,500.

**THUMBPRINTS,** 928 Gibbs St., Caro MI 48723. (517)673-6653. Newsletter. Monthly. "Our newsletter is designed to be of interest to writers and allow writers a place to obtain a byline." Purpose in publishing works by children: to encourage them to seek publication of their work. Writer's guidelines available on request, "same guidelines as for adults."
**Newsletter:** Percentage of newsletter written by children "varies from month to month." Pays in copies. Submit ms to Janet Ihle, editor. Submit complete ms or have teacher submit. Will accept typewritten and computer printout mss. SASE. Reports in 6-8 weeks.
**Artwork:** Publishes artwork by children. Looks for art that expresses our monthly theme. Pays in copies. Send pencil or ink drawing no larger than 3 × 4. Submit artwork to Janet Ihle, editor.
**Tips:** "We look forward to well written articles and poems by children. It's encouraging to all writers when children write and are published."

**TURTLE,** Ben Franklin Literary & Medical Society, Children's Better Health Institute, 1100 Waterway Blvd., Box 567, Indianapolis IN 46206. (317)636-8881. Magazine. "*Turtle* is generally a health-related magazine geared toward children from ages 2-5. Purpose in publishing works by children: we enjoy giving children the opportunity to exercise their creativity." Requirements to be met before work is published: for ages 2-5, publishes artwork or pictures that you have drawn or colored all by yourself. Writer's guidelines available on request.
**Artwork:** Publishes artwork by children. There is no payment for children's artwork. All artwork must have the child's name, age and complete address on it. Submit artwork to *Turtle* Magazine Executive Editorial Director: Beth Wood Thomas. "No artwork can be returned."

**WOMBAT: A JOURNAL OF YOUNG PEOPLE'S WRITING AND ART,** 365 Ashton Dr., Athens GA 30606. (404)549-4875. Newspaper, (slick cover/ newsprint interior). Published 4 times a year. "Illiteracy in a free society is an unnecessary danger which can and must be remedied. *Wombat*, by being available to young people and their parents and teachers, is one small incentive for young people to put forth the effort to learn to read and write (and draw) better, to communicate better, to comprehend better and — hopefully — consequently, to someday possess greater discernment, judgment and wisdom as a result." Purpose in publishing works by children: to serve as an incentive, to encourage them to work hard at their reading, writing and — yes — drawing/art skills, to reward their efforts. Requirements to be met before work is published: ages 6-16; all geographic regions; statement that work is original is sufficient.

**Magazines:** 95% of magazine written by children. Have one 2-4 page "Guest Adult Article" in most issues/when available (submitted). Uses any kind of fiction (3,000 words maximum) but avoid extreme violence, religion or sex (approaching pornography); uses any kind of nonfiction of interest to 6-16 year olds (3,000-4,000 words); cartoons, puzzles and solutions, jokes and games and solutions. Pays in copies and frameable certificates. Submit mss to Publisher: Jacquelin Howe. Submit complete ms. Teacher can submit; parents, librarians, students can submit. Will accept typewritten, legibly handwritten, computer printout mss. Responds in 1-2 weeks with SASE; up to 12 months with seasonal or holiday works (past season or holiday). Written work is not returned. SASE permits *Wombat* to notify sender of receipt of work.

**Artwork:** Publishes artwork by children. Looks for: works on paper, not canvas. Photocopies OK if clear and/or reworked for clarity and strong line definition by the artist. Pays in copies and frameable certificates. Submit artwork to Publisher: Jacquelin Howe. "Artwork, only, will be returned if requested and accompanied by appropriate sized envelope, stamped with sufficient postage."

**Tips:** *"Wombat* is, unfortunately, on 'hold' probably throughout this entire school year; therefore, we are asking people to please query as to when/if we will resume publication, before subscribing or submitting works to *Wombat* right now."

**\*WRITER'S GAZETTE**, Trouvere Co., Rt. 2 Box 290, Eclectic AL 36024. Newsletter published monthly. Readers are other writers. Purpose in publishing work by children: to give them the early experience and encouragement to continue to write.

**Magazines:** 1% of magazine written by children. Uses 1-3 fictional stories (800 words average); and 1-4 nonfiction articles (800 words average). Pays $1-50 or copy of publication. Submit ms to Brenda Williamson, editor. Will accept typewritten, legibly handwritten, computer printout form. SASE. Reports in 1-6 weeks.

**Artwork:** Publishes artwork by children. Looks for "simple drawings." Pays in copy of publication.

**WRITERS NEWSLETTER**, 1530 7th St., Rock Island IL 61201. (309)788-3980. Newsletter. Audience consists of adults and children, to present good creative writing to others. Purpose in publishing works by children: giving children a chance to have their work read and published.

**Newsletter:** 25% of newsletter written by children. Uses 1-2 fiction stories (500 words); 1-2 nonfiction articles; poetry (1 page any kind — no more than 25 lines). Pays in 1 copy. Submit mss to Betty Mowery, editor. Submit complete ms. Will accept typewritten, legibly handwritten, computer printout mss. SASE. Reports in 1 week.

**Artwork:** Publishes artwork by children. Looks for "any kind" of artwork. Pays in 1 copy. Send drawing with black ink submitted flat. Submit artwork to Betty Mowery, editor. SASE. Report in 1 week.

**Tips:** "Sample copies can be obtained for $1." Will not return rejected ms unless SASE is sent with ms.

"Nothing ventured, nothing gained" certainly holds true for those ambitious writers and artists who strive to submit a perfected story or piece of artwork to a competition geared for fellow professionals. The sense of satisfaction felt when being awarded a prize by your peers can be a boost to anyone's ego. Even for those who don't place, many competitions offer the chance to obtain valuable feedback from judges and other established writers or artists.

The popularity of contests among writers and illustrators is evident this year in our 40 new listings. Not all of these contests are geared strictly for professionals. Many are designed for "amateurs" who haven't yet been published, still others are open only to students. (For proof of a student writer/artist who "hit the big time" refer to the Close-up interview with Elizabeth Haidle in this section.) Contests really can be viable vehicles to gain recognition in the industry.

Read through the listings that interest you, then send away for more information to gain specifics about the types of written or illustrated material reviewed, word length and any qualifications you should know about such as rights to prize winning material.

You will notice that some contests can't be directly applied to, that is, some require nominations. If you are interested in being recommended for such an award, be sure to bring it to your editor's or art director's attention. Such a nomination is a good publicity tool for the publisher as well as yourself.

**\*AIM Magazine Short Story Contest**, P.O. Box 20554, Chicago IL 60620. (312)874-6184. Contest Directors: Ruth Apilado, Norma Jones, Mark Boone. Annual contest. Estab. 1983. Purpose of the contest: "We solicit stories with social significance. Youngsters can be made aware of social problems through the written word and hopefully they will try solving them." Unpublished submissions only. Deadline for entries: August 15, 1990. SASE for contest rules and entry forms. SASE for return of work. No entry fee. Awards $100. Judging by members of staff. Contest open to everyone. Winning work will be published in the Autumn issue, 1990.

**AMERICA & ME ESSAY CONTEST**, Farm Bureau Insurance, 7373 W. Saginaw, Box 30400, Lansing MI 48909. (517)323-7000. Communications/Advertising Technician: Blythe Redman. Annual contest/award. Estab. 1968. Purpose of the contest/award: to give Michigan 8th graders the opportunity to express their thoughts/feelings on America and their roles in America. Unpublished submissions only. Deadline for entries: mid-November. SASE for contest/award rules and entry forms. "We have a school mailing list. Any school located in Michigan is eligible to participate." Entries not returned. No entry fee. Awards savings bonds and plaques for state top ten ($500-1,000), certificates and plaques for top 3 winners from each school. Judging by home office employee volunteers. Requirements for entrants: "participants must work through their schools or our agents' sponsoring schools. No individual submissions will be accepted. Top ten essays and excerpts from other essays are published in booklet form following the contest. State capital/schools receive copies."

**ANNUAL CONTEST**, Creative With Words Publications, Box 223226, Carmel CA 93922. (408)649-1862. Contest/Award Director: Brigitta Geltrich. Annual contest/award. Unpublished submissions only. Deadline for entries: December 31. SASE for contest/award

rules and entry forms. SASE for return of entries "if not winning poem." Entry fee is $1/poem. Awards: $15; $10; $5, $1; honorable mention. Judging by selected guest editors. Contest open to any writer 18 years old and older.
**Tips:** Writer must request contest rules.

**AVON FLARE YOUNG ADULT NOVEL COMPETITION**, Avon Books, 105 Madison Ave., New York NY 10016. (212)481-5609. Contest held every two years. Estab. 1983. Purpose of the contest/award: to find and encourage teenage writers. Unpublished submissions only. Deadline for entries: August 31 of odd numbered years. SASE for contest/award rules and entry forms. SASE for return of entries. No entry fee. Awards a $2,500 advance. Judging by the editors of Avon Books. Rights to winning material purchased. Requirements for entrants: "you are eligible to submit a manuscript if you will be no younger than 13 and not older than 18 years of age as of December 31. The book will be published one year after selection."
**Tips:** "Each manuscript should be approximately 125 to 200 pages, or about 30,000 to 50,000 words. All manuscripts must be typed, double-spaced, on a single side of the page only. Be sure to keep a copy of your manuscript; we cannot be responsible for the manuscripts. With your manuscript, please enclose a letter that includes your name, address, telephone number, age, and a short description of your novel." For information contact Gwen Montgomery, associate editor.

**MARGARET BARTLE ANNUAL PLAYWRITING AWARD**, Community Children's Theatre of Kansas City, 8021 E. 129th Terrace, Grandview MO 64030. (816)761-5775. Chairman: E. Blanche Sellens. Annual contest/award. Estab. 1950. Unpublished submissions only. Deadline for entries: January. SASE for contest/award rules and entry forms. SASE for return of entries. No entry fee. Awards $500. Judging by a committee of five.

**BOOK OF THE YEAR FOR CHILDREN**, Canadian Library Association, Ste. 602, 200 Elgin St., Ottawa ON K2P 1L5 Canada. (613)232-9625. Chairperson, Canadian Association of Children's Librarians. Annual contest/award. Estab. 1947. "The main purpose of the award is to encourage writing and publishing in Canada of good books for children up to and including age 14. If, in any year, no book is deemed to be of award calibre, the award shall not be made that year. To merit consideration, the book must have been published in Canada and its author must be a Canadian citizen or a permanent resident of Canada." Previously published submissions only; must be published between January 1 and December 1. Deadline for entries: January 1. SASE for contest/award rules and entry forms. Entries not returned. No entry fee. Awards a medal. Judging by committee of members of the Canadian Association of Children's Librarians. Requirements for entrants: contest open only to Canadian authors or residents of Canada. "Winning books are on display at CLA headquarters."

**CALDECOTT AWARD**, Association for Library Service to Children, division of the American Library Association, 50 E. Huron, Chicago IL 60611. (312)944-6780. Executive Director ALSC: Susan Roman. Annual contest/award. Estab. 1938. Purpose of the contest/award: to honor the artist of the most distinguished picture book for children

**✶** *The asterisk before a listing indicates that the listing is new in this edition.*

published in the U.S. Must be published year preceding award. Deadline for entries: December. SASE for contest/award rules and entry forms. Entries not returned. No entry fee. "Medal given at ALA Annual Conference during the Newbery/Caldecott Banquet."

**\*CALIFORNIA WRITERS' CONFERENCE AWARDS**, California Writers' Club, 2214 Derby St., Berkeley CA 94705. (415)841-1217. "Ask for contest rules before submitting entries." Contest/award offered every two years. Next conference, July 14-16, 1991. Purpose of the contest/award: "the encouragement of writers. Categories: adult fiction, adult nonfiction, juvenile fiction or nonfiction, poetry and scripts." Unpublished submissions only. SASE for contest/award rules and entry forms. SASE for return of entries. Entry fee is $5. Awards: "First prize in each category is free tuition to the Conference; second prize is cash and third a certificate." Judging by "published writer-members of California Writers' Club." Requirements for entrants: "Open to any writer who is not a member of California Writers' Club. Winners in previous contests of California Writers' Club not eligible."

**CANADIAN AUTHOR & BOOKMAN CREATIVE WRITING CONTEST**, CA&B/Canadian Authors Association, Ste. 104, 121 Avenue Rd., Toronto ON M5R 2G3 Canada. (416)926-8084. Contest/Award Director: Editor. Publisher: Diane Kerner. Annual contest/award. Estab. 1983. Categories: fiction, nonfiction, poetry. Unpublished submissions only (except in school paper). Deadline for entries: mid-February. "Form must come from magazine. Teacher nominates." Entries not returned. No entry fee. Awards $100 for each fiction, poetry and nonfiction—teachers get matching award; $500 scholarship. Judging by CA&B staff-selected judges. Contest open to high school, private school, college and university students. Works published in summer issue of magazine.

**\*CHILD STUDY CHILDREN'S BOOK AWARD**, Child Study Children's Book Committee at Bank St. College, 610 West 112 St., New York NY 10025. (212)222-6700. Chairperson: Anita Dore. Annual contest/award. Estab. 1943. Purpose of the contest/award: "To honor a book for children or young people which deals realistically and in a positive way with problems in their world." Must be previously published "within the current year." Submissions: "From publisher's review copies that are submitted for our annual recommended booklist, we select a winner." Entries not returned. No entry fee. Awards $500 and plaque. Judging by committee members. Works will be listed and annotated "in our annual booklist and on display for one year in Bank St. College library."

**\*CHILDREN'S BOOK AWARD**, Sponsored by Federation of Children's Book Groups. 30 Senneleys Park Rd., Northfield Birmingham B31 1AL England. (021)427-4860. Coordinator: Jenny Blanch. Annual contest/award. Estab. 1981. Purpose of the contest/award: "The C.B.A. is an annual prize for the best children's book of the year judged by the children themselves." Previously unpublished submissions only. Deadline for entries: December 31. Charges an entry fee. Entries not returned. Awards "a magnificent silver and oak trophy worth over $6,000 and a portfolio of children's work." Judging by children. Requirements for entrants: Work must be fiction and published during the current year (poetry is ineligible). Work will be published in our current "Pick of the Year" publication.

**CHILDREN'S BOOK AWARD**, Sponsored by the Institute for Reading Research-IRA, 800 Barksdale Rd., Newark DE 19714-8139. (302)731-1600. FAX (302)731-1057. Public Information Associate: Patricia C. DuBois. Annual contest/award. To submit a book for consideration, send 10 copies to : Walter Barbe, 823 Church St., Honesdale PA 18431. Categories: young readers—4-10, older readers—10-16. Must be published between January 1990 and December 1990. Deadline for entries: December 1 of each

year. SASE for contest/award rules and entry forms. Awards a $1,000 stipend. Requirements for entrants: Must be a writer's first or second book.
**Tips:** "Award is presented each year at our annual convention."

**\*CHILDREN'S CHOICE AWARD,** Harris County Public Library, Suite 200, 49 San Jacinto, Houston TX 77002. (713)221-5350. Director: Elizabeth J. Ozbun, children's specialist. Annual contest/award. Estab. 1978. Purpose of the contest/award: "The objective of the program is for children to select their favorite author, to read and to use the public library. Children are free to select any published author." Deadline for entries: "Election is held in March. Children are given a blank ballot and are invited to fill in the name of their favorite author. The winning author receives a framed certificate." Judging by "children. The author with the most votes wins. Dr. Seuss 1978, Judy Blume 1979-1989."
**Tips:** "Each child receives a pin with the theme, 'I VOTED.' Starting in 1988 the design used on the pin was from a child's design which was selected from entries in the Design the Button contest. The winning child receives a book of his/her choice."

**THE CHRISTOPHER AWARD,** The Christophers, 12 E. 48 St., New York NY 10017. (212)759-4050. Christopher Awards Coordinator: Peggy Flanagan. Annual contest/award. Estab. 1969 (for young people; books for adults honored since 1949). Previously published submissions only; must be published between January 1 and December 31. Deadline for entries: "books should be submitted all year." Entries not returned. No entry fee. Awards a bronze medallion. Books are judged by both reading specialists and young people. Requirements for entrants: "only published works are eligible and must be submitted during the calendar year in which they are first published."
**Tips:** "The award is given to works, published in the calendar year for which the award is given, that 'have achieved artistic excellence, affirming the highest values of the human spirit.' They must also enjoy a reasonable degree of popular acceptance."

**\*THE MARIE-LOUISE D'ESTERNAUX POETRY SCHOLARSHIP CONTEST,** The Brooklyn Poetry Circle, Apt. 51, 61 Pierrepont St., Brooklyn NY 11201. (718)875-8736. Chairperson: Gabrielle Lederer. Annual contest/award. Estab. 1965. Purpose of the contest/award: "to encourage students between the age of 16 and 21 to write poetry." Previously unpublished submissions only. Deadline for entries: April 15. SASE for contest rules. Entries not returned. No entry fee. Awards first place: $50 and 2nd place: $25. Judging by three members (critics) of the Brooklyn Poetry Circle. Requirements for entrants: Open to *students* between 16 and 21 years of age.

**\*ETHICAL CULTURE SCHOOL BOOK AWARD,** Ethical Culture School, 33 Central Park West, New York, NY 10023. (212)874-5200. Resource Specialist: Nancy Bautz. Annual contest/award. Estab. 1975. Purpose of the contest/award: "The children choose the winning book." Previously published submissions only: must have been originally published in the preceding year. Deadline for entries: December 15. "Letters are sent to publishers, who submit the books." Entries not returned. No entry fee. Awards consist of "a scroll with the winner's name and the name of the book." Judging by the children. "The books are displayed in the library during the contest—January through April."

**FICTION CONTEST,** *Highlights for Children,* 803 Church St., Honesdale PA 18431. (717)253-1080. "Mss should be addressed to Fiction Contest. Editor: Kent L. Brown Jr." Annual contest/award. Estab. 1980. Purpose of the contest/award: to stimulate

*Refer to the Business of Children's Writing & Illustrating for up-to-date marketing, tax and legal information.*

interest in writing for children and reward and recognize excellence. Unpublished submissions only. Deadline for entries: February 28; entries accepted after January 1 only. SASE for contest/award rules and entry forms. SASE for return of entries. No entry fee. Awards 3 prizes of $750 each in cash, (or, at the winner's election, attendance at the Highlights Foundation Writers Workshop at Chautauqua). Judging by *Highlights* editors. Winning pieces are purchased for the cash prize of $750. Requirements for entrants: contest open to any writer. Winners announced in June.

**Tips:** "This year's contest is for humorous stories up to 900 words. Stories should be consistent with *Highlights* editorial requirements."

**\*CAROLYN W. FIELD AWARD**, Pennsylvania Library Association, 3107 N. Front St., Harrisburg PA 17110. (717)233-3113. Executive Director: Margaret S. Bauer, CAE. Annual contest/award. Estab. 1983. Purpose of the contest/award: "To honor outstanding Pennsylvania children's authors/illustrators." Previously published submissions only; must be published January-December of year of award. Deadline for entries: March 1. SASE for contest/award rules and entry forms. SASE for return of entries. No entry fee. Awards a medal, citation and luncheon honoring award winner. Judging by "children's librarians." Requirements for entrants: "Writer/illustrator must be a Pennsylvania resident." Works displayed at "PLA annual conference each fall."

**DOROTHY CANFIELD FISHER CHILDREN'S BOOK AWARD**, Vermont Department of Libraries, Vermont State PTA and Vermont Congress of Parents and Teachers, % Southwest Regional Library, Pierpoint Ave., Rutland VT 05701. Chairman (currently): Betty Lallier. Annual contest/award. Estab. 1957. Purpose of the contest/award: to encourage Vermont children to become enthusiastic and discriminating readers by providing them with books of good quality by living American authors published in the current year. Previously published entries are not eligible. Deadline for entries: "January of the following year." SASE for contest/award rules and entry forms. No entry fee. Awards a scroll presented to the winning author at an award ceremony. Judging is by the children grades 4-8. They vote for their favorite book. Requirements for entrants: "the book must be copyrighted in the current year. It must be written by an American author living in the U.S."

**\*FLORIDA STATE WRITING COMPETITION/Juvenile Division**, Florida Freelance Writers Assoc., P.O. Box 9844, Fort Lauderdale FL 33310. (305)485-0795. Chairman: Ginger Kuh. Annual contest/award. Estab. 1984. Fiction: all age groups judged together/ Ages 6-8—400-900 words; Tween (9-12 yrs.)—500-1,900 words; Teen/Young Adult— 1,500-2,000 words. Nonfiction: All age groups judged together/Ages 9-12: 1,000 words maximum. Nonfiction ages 6-8—500 words maximum, ages teen/Young Adult—2,000 words maximum—Special Categories: Edwin V. Pugh Award—Best historical article; Florida Federation of Wildlife Award—Best Conservation Article. Book Chapter Fiction or Nonfiction: All age groups will be judged together, intended age of book will be major criteria for judging ages 6-8—800 words; ages 9-12—1,000 words; teen/YA—1,500 words. Children's Verse—maximum length: 20 lines.

**\*DON FREEMAN MEMORIAL GRANT-IN-AID and WORK-IN-PROGRESS GRANT**, (Grant for a Contemporary Novel for young people, nonfiction research grant, grant for a work whose author has never had a book published), SCBW, P.O. Box 296, Mar Vista Stn., Los Angeles CA 90066. Estab. 1974. Purpose of contest/award: to assist illustrator members of The SCBW. SASE for contest/award rules and entry forms. SASE for return of entries. No entry fee. Awards $1,000. Judging by panel of people in the field. Requirements for entrants: must be SCBW member.

**Tips:** Write for specific information.

**\*GOLD MEDALLION BOOK AWARDS**, Evangelical Christian Publishers Association, Suite 106B, 950 W. Southern Ave., Tempe AZ 85282. (602)966-3998. Director: Doug Ross. Annual contest/award. Estab. 1975. Deadlines for entries: December 30. SASE for contest/award rules and entry form. "The work must be submitted by the publisher." Entry fee is $150 for non-members. Awards a Gold Medallion plaque.

**\*GOLDEN KITE AWARDS**, Society of Children's Bookwriters, Box 296, Mar Vista Station, Los Angeles CA 90066. (818)347-2849. Coordinator: Sue Alexander. Annual contest/award. Estab. 1973. "The works chosen will be those that the judges feel exhibit excellence in writing, and in the case of the picture-illustrated books—in illustration, and genuinely appeal to the interests and concerns of children. For the fiction and nonfiction awards, original works and single-author collections of stories or poems of which at least half are new and never before published in book form are eligible—anthologies and translations are not. For the picture-illustration awards, the art or photographs must be original works (the texts—which may be fiction or nonfiction—may be original, public domain or previously published). Deadline for entries: December 15. SASE for contest/award rules. SASE for return of entries. No entry fee. Awards statuettes and plaques. The panel of judges will consist of two children's book authors, a children's book artist or photographer (who may or may not be an author), a children's book editor and a librarian." Requirements for entrants: "Must be a member of SCBW." Works will be displayed "at national conference in August."
**Tips:** Books to be entered, as well as further inquiries, should be submitted to: The Society of Children's Book Writers, % Sue Alexander, 6846 McLaren, Canoga Park, CA 91307.

**\*GOLDEN PEN AWARD**, Spokane Public Library Young Adult Advisory Committee, West 906 Main, Spokane WA 99201. (509)838-3361. Attn: Dave Davis. Annual contest/award. Estab. 1980. Purpose of the contest/award: for the "author who has given us the most reading pleasure." Entry fee is a free copy of the *published book*. (No manuscripts or galley proofs). Award is a gold pen and pen holder.

**\*GOVERNOR GENERAL'S LITERARY AWARDS**, Canada Council, 99 Metcalfe St., Ottawa, Ontario K1P 5V8 Canada. (613)598-4376. Officer, Writing and Publishing Section: Gwen Hoover. Annual contest/award. Estab. 1976. Purpose of contest/award: to encourage Canadian authors and illustrators of books for young people as well as to recognize the importance of their contribution to literary activity. Previously published submissions only. Must be published between December 1, 1988 and November 30, 1989. "We collect through booksellers all eligible books published in Canada. For Canadian writers publishing outside of Canada, either writer or publisher writes us. There are no entry terms nor nomination procedures." Entries not returned. No entry fee. Awards $10,000 Canadian plus specially bound copy of winning book. Judging by practicing writers, illustrators plus librarian or critic.

**\*GRAFFITI**, *LISTEN* **Magazine**, 12501 Old Columbia Pike, Silver Spring MD 20904. (301)680-6726. Editor: Gary B. Swanson. Monthly contest/award. Estab. 1984. "*LISTEN* magazine seeks to publish well-written, thought-provoking manuscripts by teenage writers. Poems should be no longer than 20 lines; essays or stories between 300-500 words." Previously unpublished submissions only. No deadline; "since the contest is monthly, submissions are rolled from one issue to the next." SASE for contest award/rules and entry forms. SASE for return of entries. No entry fees. Prize "poems printed receive a $10 prize; stories or essays are awarded $15 to $20." Judging by the editor. First serial rights to winning material purchased. Requirements for entrants: "Graffiti" is open only to teenage writers between the ages of 12 and 19. Writers should specify their age. Winning entries will be pubilshed monthly in a specially designed "Graffiti" spread.

**Tips:** Submissions for "Graffiti" should be concise and well-written. Any subject of interest to teens is acceptable. We especially look for positive rather than negative attitudes within the works.

**AMELIA FRANCES HOWARD-GIBBON MEDAL,** Canadian Library Association, Ste. 602, 200 Elgin St., Ottawa ON K2P 1L5 Canada. (613)232-9625. Chairperson, Canadian Association of Children's Librarians. Annual contest/award. Estab. 1971. Purpose of the contest/award: "the main purpose of the award is to honor excellence in the illustration of children's book(s) in Canada. To merit consideration the book must have been published in Canada and its illustrator must be a Canadian citizen or a permanent resident of Canada." Previously published submissions only; must be published between January 1 and December 31. Deadline for entries: February 1, 1990. SASE for contest/award rules and entry forms. Entries not returned. No entry fee. Awards a medal. Judging by selection committee of members of Canadian Association of Children's Librarians. Requirements for entrants: illustrator must be Canadian or Canadian resident. Winning books on display at CLA Headquarters.

**\*INDIAN PAINTBRUSH BOOK AWARD,** Wyoming Library Assoc., Box 304, Laramie WY 82070. (307)745-8662. Contest/Award Director: Kay Nord. Annual contest/award. Estab. 1986. Purpose of contest/award: to encourage the children of Wyoming to read good books. Previously published submissions only, published between 1985 and 1989 (for 1990 nominations list). Deadline for entries: April 1. Books can only be submitted for the nominations list by the children of Wyoming. No entry fee. Awards a plaque. Judging by the children of Wyoming (grades 4-6) voting from a nominations list of 20. Requirements for entrants: only Wyoming children may nominate: books must be published in last 5 years, be fiction, have good reviews: final list chosen by a committee of librarians.

**\*IOWA CHILDREN'S CHOICE AWARD,** Iowa Educational Media Association, RR1 Box 1B, Calamus IA 52729. (319)246-2342. Director: Pat Bernard. Annual contest/award. Estab. 1979. Purpose of the contest/award: to encourage children to read more and better books; to provide an avenue for positive dialogue between teacher, parent and children about books and authors; to give recognition to those who write books for children. The award is unique in that it gives children an opportunity to choose the book to receive the award and to suggest books for the yearly reading list. Deadline for entries: February 15. "Students in grades 3-6 throughout Iowa nominate." Awards a brass-plated school bell. Judging by "students in grades 3-6 through Iowa."

**\*IOWA TEEN AWARD,** Iowa Educational Media Association, 2211 Northwestern, Ames IA 50010. (515)232-0307. Co-Chairmen: Norma Sisson and Twyla Kerr. Annual contest/award. Estab. 1983. Purpose of contest/award: to allow students to read high quality literature and to have opportunity to select their favorite from this list. Must have been published "in last 3-4 years." Deadline for entries: August 1. "Media specialists, teachers and students nominate possible entries." Awards a brass apple and opportunity to speak at IEMA annual convention. Judging by students in 6-9th grade. Requirements: To be of recent publication, so copies can be ordered for media center collections and to be nominated by media specialists on a scale of 1-5. Works displayed "at participating schools in Iowa."

**\*THE EZRA JACK KEATS NEW WRITER AWARD,** Director: Dr. Bernice Cullinan and Selection Committee. Writing Contact: Hannah Nuba, Director, %The New York Public Library Early Childhood Resource and Information Center, 66 Leroy St., New York, NY 10014. (212)929-0815. Biennial contest/award. Estab. 1986. Purpose of the contest/award: "Award to writers of books done in the tradition of Ezra Jack Keats that appeal to very young children, capture universal qualities of childhood in a multicultural world and portray strong family relationships." Previously published submissions only: Must be published the year of contest or the year before. Deadline for entries: December. SASE for contest/award rules and entry form. Entries not returned. No entry fee. Awards silver Ezra Jack Keats Medal and $500. Judging by Dr. Bernice Cullinan, Dr. Dorothy Strickland, Dr. Jane Hornberger, Bobbye Goldstein, Dr. Claudia Lewis, Dr. Dorothy Carter. Works will be displayed "at the Ezra Jack Keats New Writer Award Reception at the New York Public Library Early Childhood Resource and Information Center."

**\*KERLAN AWARD**, Kerlan Collection, 109 Walter Library, 117 Pleasant St. SE, University of Minnesota, Minneapolis MN 55455. (612)624-4576. Curator: Karen Nelson Hoyle. Annual award. Estab. 1975. "Given in recognition of singular attainments in the creation of children's literature and in appreciation for generous donation of unique resources to the Kerlan Collection." Previously published submissions only. Deadline for entries: November 1. Anyone can send nominations for the award, directed to the Kerlan Collection. No materials are submitted other than the person's name. No entry fee. Award is a laminated plaque. Judging by the Kerlan Award Committee—three representatives from the University of Minnesota faculty (from the College of Education, the College of Home Economics, and the College of Liberal Arts); one representative from the Kerlan Collection; one representative from the Kerlan Friends; one representative from the Minnesota Library Association. Requirements for entrants: open to all who are nominated. Anyone can submit names. "Obviously, for serious consideration, entrant must be a published author and/or illustrator of children's books (including young adult fiction) and have donated original materials to the Kerlan Collection."

**ELIAS LIEBERMAN STUDENT POETRY AWARD**, Poetry Society of America, 15 Gramercy Park, New York NY 10003. (212)254-9628. Contest/Award Director: Elise Paschen. Annual contest/award. Purpose of the contest/award: award is for the best unpublished poem by a high or preparatory school student (grades 9-12) from the U.S. and its territories. Unpublished submissions only. Deadline for entries: December 31. SASE for contest/award rules and entry forms. Entries not returned. No entry fee. Award: $100. Judging by a professional poet. Requirements for entrants: contest open to all high school and preparatory students from the U.S. and its territories. School attended, as well as name and address, should be noted. Line limit: none. "The award-winning poem will be included in a sheaf of poems that will be part of the program at the award ceremony, and sent to all PSA members."

**VICKY METCALF BODY OF WORK AWARDS**, Canadian Authors Association, Ste. 104, 121 Avenue Rd., Toronto ON M5R 2G3 Canada. (416)926-8084. Contest/Award Director: Awards Chairman. Annual contest/award. Estab. 1963. Purpose of the contest/award: to honor writing inspirational to Canadian youth. Previously published submissions only. Deadline for entries: December 31. SASE for contest/award rules and entry forms. Entries not returned. No entry fee. Awards $2,000. Judging by panel of CAA-appointed judges including past winner.
**Tips:** "The prizes are given solely to stimulate writing for children by Canadian writers," said Mrs. Metcalf when she established the award. "We must encourage the writing of material for Canadian children without setting any restricting formulas."

**VICKY METCALF SHORT STORY AWARD**, Canadian Authors Association, Ste. 104, 121 Avenue Rd., Toronto ON M5R 2G3 Canada. (416)926-8084. Contest/Award Director: Awards Chairman. Annual contest/award. Estab. 1982. Purpose of the contest/award: to honor writing by a Canadian inspirational to Canadian youth. Previously published submissions only; must be published between January 1 and December 31. Deadline for entries: December 31. SASE for contest/award rules and entry forms. Entries not returned. No entry fee. Awards $1,000 to Canadian author and $1,000 to Canadian editor of winning story. Judging by CAA-selected panel including past winners.

**\*THE MILNER AWARD,** Atlanta-Fulton Public Library/Friends of the Atlanta Library, One Margaret Mitchell Square, Atlanta GA 30303. (404)730-1710. Exec. Director: Rennie Jones Davant. Annual contest/award. Estab. 1983. Purpose of the contest/award: "The Milner Award is an annual award to a living American author of children's books. Selection is made by the children of Atlanta voting for their favorite author during Children's Book Week." Previously published submissions only. "The winning author is awarded a specially commissioned work of the internationally famous glass sculptor, Hans Frabel, and a $1,000 honorarium." Requirements for entrants: "Winner must be able to appear personally in Atlanta to receive the award at a formal program."

**NATIONAL JEWISH BOOK AWARD FOR CHILDREN'S LITERATURE,** (Shapolsky Award), JWB Jewish Book Council, 15 E. 26th St., New York NY 10010. (212)532-4949. Awards Coordinator: Dr. Marcia W. Posner. Annual contest/award. Estab. 1950. Previously published submissions only; must be published in 1989 for 1990 award. Deadline for entries: November 30. SASE for contest/award rules and entry forms. Entries not returned. No entry fee. Awards $750. Judging by 3 authorities in the field. Requirements for entrants: contest for best Jewish children's books, published only for ages 8-14. Books will be displayed at the awards ceremony in NYC in June.

**\*NEW JERSEY AUTHOR AWARD,** Alumni Association, NJ Institute of Technology, Newark NJ 07076. (201)596-3449. Director: Dr. Herman A. Estrin. Annual contest/award. Estab. 1960. Purpose of the contest/award: "To honor New Jersey authors of published books." Previously published submissions only; must be published September 1988 to September 1989. Deadline for entries: January 30, 1990. SASE for contest/award rules and entry forms. Entries not returned. No entry fee. Awards "an author's citation and a guest invitation to NJ Authors Banquet." Judging by "publishers of books written by NJ authors. March 10, 1990, NJ Authors' works will be displayed in the lounge of student center at NJIT."

**NEW JERSEY POETRY CONTEST,** NJIT Alumni Association, 323 Martin Luther King Blvd., Newark NJ 07102. (201)596-3441. Contest Director: Dr. Herman A. Estrin. Annual contest/award. Estab. 1977. Purpose of the contest/award: to encourage young poets to write poetry and to have it eventually published. Unpublished submissions only. Deadline for entries: February 10. SASE for contest rules and entry forms. Entries not returned. No entry fee. Awards a citation with the poet's name and the name of the poem. Also, the poem will be published in an anthology. Judging by teachers of English. Requirements for entrants: poet must be a NJ resident. "The published anthology can be obtained through NJIT Alumni office."

**NEWBERY MEDAL AWARD,** Association for Library Service to Children—division of the American Library Association, 50 E Huron, Chicago IL 60611. (312)944-6780. Executive Director, ALSC: Susan Roman. Annual contest/award. Estab. 1922. Purpose of the contest/award: for the most distinguished contribution to American children's literature published in the U.S. Previously published submissions only; must be published prior to year award is given. Deadline for entries: December. SASE for contest/award rules and entry forms. Entries not returned. No entry fee. Medal awarded at banquet during annual conference. Judging by Newbery Committee. Works displayed at ALA Midwinter Meeting where announcement of winner is made.

**THE 1990 NATIONAL WRITTEN & ILLUSTRATED BY . . . AWARDS CONTEST FOR STUDENTS**, Landmark Editions, Inc., Box 4469, Kansas City MO 64127. (816)241-4919. Contest/Award Director: Alida Braden. Annual awards contest with 3 published winners. Purpose of the contest/award: to encourage and celebrate the creative efforts of students. There are three age categories (6-9 years of age; 10-13; and 14-19). Unpublished submissions only. Deadline for entries: May 1, 1990. Contest rules available for self-addressed, business-sized envelope, stamped with 50¢ postage."Need to send a self-addressed, sufficiently stamped book mailer with book entry" for its return. No entry fee. Prize: "book is published." Judging by national panel of educators, editors, illustrators and authors. "Each student winner receives a publishing contract allowing Landmark to publish the book. Copyright is in student's name and student receives royalties on sale of book. Author/illustrators may enter who are ages 6-19. Books must be in proper contest format and submitted with entry form signed by a teacher or librarian. Students may develop their illustrations in any medium of their choice, as long as the illustrations remain two-dimensional and flat to the surface of the paper." Works will be published in 1991, Kansas City, MO for distribution nationally and internationally. Winner and runners-up in each age category will receive college scholarships from the R.D. and Joan Dale Hubbard Foundation: winner, $5,000; second place, $2,000; third, fourth, and fifth places, $1,000 each.

**\*THE NOMA AWARD FOR PUBLISHING IN AFRICA**, Kodansha Ltd., % Hans Zell Associates, 11 Richmond Rd., Oxford OX1 3EL England. (0865)511428. Secretary of the Managing Committee: Hans M. Zell. Annual contest/award. Estab. 1979. Purpose of contest/award: To encourage publications of works by African writers and scholars in Africa, instead of abroad, as is still too often the case at present. Categories of books eligible for the Award are scholarly or academic, books for children, literature and creative writing, including fiction, drama and poetry. Previously published submissions only; in the preceding year the Award i.e. in 1989 for the 1990 Award. Deadline for entries: end of February 1990. Submissions must be made through publishers. Conditions of entry and submission forms are available from the secretariat. Entries not returned. No entry fee. Awards US $5,000. Judging by the Managing Committee (jury): African scholars and book experts and representatives of the international book community. Chairman: Professor Eldred Jones. Requirements for entrants: author must be African, and book published in Africa. "Winning titles are displayed at appropriate international book events."

**\*THE SCOTT O'DELL AWARD FOR HISTORICAL FICTION**, 1100 E. 57th St., Chicago IL 60037. Award Director: Mrs. Zena Sutherland. Annual contest/award. Purpose of the contest/award: "To promote the writing of historical fiction of good quality." Previously published submissions only; must be published between January 1 and December 31 of each year. Deadline for entries: December 31. "Publishers send books, although occasionally a writer sends a note or a book." SASE for contest/award rules and entry forms. No entry fee. Awards $5,000. Judging by the advisory committee of *The Bulletin of the Center for Children's Books* at the University of Chicago. Requirements for entrants: "Must be published by a U.S. publisher in the preceding year; must be by an American citizen; must be set in the North or South American continent; must be historical fiction."

**\*OHIOANA BOOK AWARDS**, Ohioana Library Association, 1105 State Departments Bldg., 65 S. Front St., Columbus OH 43215. (614)466-3831. Director: Linda R. Hengst. Annual contest/award. "The Ohioana Book Awards are given to books of outstanding literary quality. Up to 6 Book Awards are given each year. Awards may be given in the categories of: fiction, non-fiction, children's literature, poetry and books about Ohio or an Ohioan. Books must be received by the Ohioana Library during the calendar year

# Close-up

**Elizabeth Haidle**
*Writer/Illustrator*
*Beaverton, Oregon*

Writing and illustrating a children's book is the dream of many — but imagine your first book being published at age 13. Elizabeth Haidle, author and illustrator of *Elmer the Grump* and winner of the 10 to 13 age category in Landmark Edition's 1988 National Written & Illustrated by ... Awards Contest for Students didn't have to dream for long. "I always thought I would like to have a book published when I was older," says the now 15 year old high-school sophomore, "but I never thought it would happen this young."

Elizabeth's picture book began during her 5th grade school year. "I made up these little elf characters," she begins, noting that the concept for them may have come from her mother who, during long family trips, would tell the sometimes "grumpy" Elizabeth and her siblings to "Watch out. Don't frown or the grumps will get you." But, it was in the 6th grade, when her mother home-schooled Elizabeth, that work on the book was completed. She wrote the text for *Elmer the Grump* after detailing the story plot via use of black and white drawings. Though her artistic ability comes naturally, as with most artists, Elizabeth acknowledges that her father, also an artist, gave her a lot of instruction. "He gave me a lot of pointers — and a lot of art supplies," she explains.

When Elizabeth first learned about Landmark's annual contest through a newspaper article, she only had a month and a half left until the May, 1988 deadline. "I rewrote my old book," she points out, then redrew the original black and white sketches in colored pencil. Once her book won the contest even more work was necessary to polish the text and artwork. Since the prize was publication of *Elmer the Grump*, she, on her editor's advice, rewrote the text four times until the story's flow and sentence structure were perfected. This process, which ran from November, 1988 through March 1, 1989, seemed a bit drawn out but paid off in a well written story.

Revising artwork, however, was more enjoyable since this is Elizabeth's forté. She found this to be a much more creative undertaking because she could play with adding material to each illustration, fixing something she didn't like or even re-drawing a picture new and different ways. Once final text was approved, spring had arrived and Elizabeth was nearing her final April deadline. "When the text was finalized, we looked at where the illustrations could go," she says explaining that changes in the story line involved reworking the art. "I highlighted parts of sentences that conveyed the action I wanted to illustrate," Elizabeth says. It was difficult sometimes, she acknowledges, because she could envision multiple scenes based on each page of text, yet knew she had to choose the image that best represented the edited story line.

Since envisioning art can be such a nebulous process, Elizabeth had to send in one set of drawings to Landmark for review, then make a second set of drawings based on suggestions from the previous material submitted. Added to this complexity was the fact that the final art had to be rendered in watercolor which takes a much longer time than colored pencil, Elizabeth explains. It was her father's suggestion to use watercolor she says, a suggestion which was endorsed by Elizabeth and David Melton, creative coordinator at Landmark. "Watercolor does look more professional and realistic," she says. In order to finish her book on time, Elizabeth worked daily from 8 a.m. to 10 p.m. during her spring break from school.

What advice does this veteran have for other aspiring writers and illustrators? "What they need to learn first," she shares, "is that they have to go over the story a lot, go over each sentence, then do the illustrations over a lot. If they're working with a publisher—or even if they're working alone," she adds, "they need to learn to take constructive criticism" to improve their work. "I thought advice from editors would involve fixing sentence structure," she explains, "but they suggested adding more to the part of the story about Rosy and took out some other things." She admits she didn't always see how these suggestions would really improve the story, but acknowledges that they did. "I trusted that they knew what they were doing because they've been in the business so many years."

*— Connie Eidenier*

*This watercolor illustration from* **Elmer the Grump** *is only one of the selections that attracted Editorial Coordinator Nan Thatch and other judges to Haidle's work at Landmark Edition's National Written & Illustrated By . . . Awards for Students. "Her artwork caught the eye first," Thatch explains. "It's unusual talent for that age. Also, her story had a good beginning, middle and end, and certainly showed promise." More than 4,000 submissions are received annually, Thatch adds, noting that the competition is intense.*

The house that Elmer builds.

prior to the year the Award is given and must have a copyright date within the last two calendar years." Deadline for entries: December 31. SASE for contest/award rules and entry forms. No entry fee. "Any book that has been written or edited by a person born in Ohio or who has lived in Ohio for at least five years" is eligible.

**\*HELEN KEATING OTT AWARD FOR OUTSTANDING CONTRIBUTION TO CHILDREN'S LITERATURE**, Church and Synagogue Library Association, Box 19357, Portland OR 97219. (503)244-6919. Chair of Committee: Eleanor S. Courtney. Annual contest/award. "This award is given to a person or organization that has made a significant contribution to promoting high moral and ethical values through children's literature." Deadline for entries: February 1, 1990. "Recipient is honored in July during the conference." Awards certificate of recognition and a conference package consisting of registration, meals and housing. "A nomination for an award may be made by anyone. It should include the name, address and telephone number of the nominee plus the church or synagogue relationship where appropriate. Nominations of an organization should include the name of a contact person. A detailed description of the reasons for the nomination should be given, accompanied by documentary evidence of accomplishment. The person(s) making the nomination should give his/her name, address and telephone number and a brief explanation of his/her knowledge of the nominee's accomplishments." Elements of creativity and innovativion will be given high priority by the judges.

**\*EDGAR ALLAN POE AWARD**, Mystery Writers of America Inc., #600, 236 W. 27th St., New York NY 10001. (212)255-7005. Executive Secretary: Priscilla Ridgway. Annual contest/award. Estab. 1945. "Each year the Mystery Writers of America honors the best of mystery fiction, nonfiction, television and film with awards in the following categories: BEST NOVEL, BEST FIRST NOVEL BY AN AMERICAN AUTHOR, BEST PAPERBACK ORIGINAL, BEST SHORT STORY, BEST CRITICAL/BIOGRAPHICAL WORK, BEST FACT CRIME, BEST JUVENILE, BEST YOUNG ADULT, BEST TELEVISION FEATURE, BEST EPISODE IN A TELEVISION SERIES and BEST MOTION PICTURE. When warranted, an award is given for BEST MYSTERY PLAY." Deadline for entries: December 1. SASE for contest rules. Entries not returned. No entry fee. Awards ceramic bust of Edgar Allan Poe and nomination scroll. Judging by committees chosen every year from the active membership. Requirements for entrants: "All books, short stories, television shows and films in the mystery, crime, suspense and intrigue fields are eligible for this year's Edgar awards in their respective category if they were published or shown for the first time in the United States during this calendar year. Authors nominated for the BEST FIRST NOVEL BY AN AMERICAN AUTHOR may have published previous non-crime novels, and both paperback and hardcover books may be submitted. Nominees for BEST SHORT STORY are eligible if the story first appeared in a book published in the United States during the calendar year, or in a magazine published in the United States bearing the cover date of this calendar year. In all book categories, date of publication takes precedence over copyright date."

**PUBLISH-A-BOOK CONTEST**, Raintree Publishers, 310 W. Wisconsin Ave., Milwaukee WI 53203. (414)273-0873. FAX: (414)273-0887. Vice President for Marketing and Sales: Julia G. Mayo. Send written entries: PAB Contest. Annual contest/award. Estab. 1984. Purpose of the contest/award: to stimulate 4th, 5th and 6th graders to write outstanding stories for children. Unpublished submissions only. Deadline for entries: January 31. SASE for contest/award rules and entry forms. "Entries must be sponsored by a teacher or librarian." Entries not returned. No entry fee. Grand prizes: Raintree will publish four winning entries in the fall of 1990. Each winner will receive a $500 author's fee and ten free copies of the published book. The sponsor named on each of these entries will receive 20 free books from the Raintree catalog. Honorable mentions: each of the twenty honorable mention writers will receive $25. The sponsor named on each of these entries will receive ten free books from the Raintree catalog. Judging by an editorial team. Contract issued for Grand Prize winners. Payment and royalties paid. Requirements for entrants: contest is open only to 4th, 5th and 6th graders enrolled in a school program in the United States or other countries. Books will be displayed and sold in the United States and foreign markets. Displays at educational association meetings, book fairs.

**\*ANNA DAVIDSON ROSENBERG AWARD FOR POEMS ON THE JEWISH EXPERI-ENCE**, Judah L. Magnes Museum, 2911 Russell St., Berkeley CA 94705. (415)849-2710. Poetry Award Coordinator: P. Friedman. Award has been annual; "may become triennial." Estab. 1986-87. Purpose of the contest/award: to encourage poetry in English on the Jewish experience. Previously unpublished submissions only. Deadline for entries: August 31. SASE for contest/award rules and entry forms. SASE for list of winners. Awards $100-1st Prize, $50-2nd Prize, $25-3rd Prize; honorable mention certificates; *$25 Youth Commendation (poets under 19)*. Judging by committee of 3. There will be a reading of winners in December at Museum. Prospective anthology of winning entries. **Tips:** Write for entry form and guidelines *first*; entries must follow guidelines.

**\*SEVENTEEN/SMITH CORONA FICTION CONTEST**, Smith Corona, 9th Fl., 850 Third Ave., New York NY 10022. (212)759-8100. Fiction Editor: Adrian Nicole LeBlanc. Annual contest/award. Unpublished submissions only. Deadline for entries: January 31. SASE for contest/award rules and entry forms. Entries not returned. No entry fee. Awards cash prize and Smith-Corona word processor. Judging by "external readers, in-house panel of editors." If first prize, acquires first North American rights for piece to be published. Requirements for entrants: "Our annual fiction contest is open to anyone between the ages of 13 and 21 on January 31. Submit only original fiction that has never been published in any form other than in school publications. Stories should be between 1,500 and 3,000 words in length (six to twelve pages). All manuscripts must be typed double-spaced on a single side of paper. Submit as many original stories as you like, but each story must include your full name, address, birth date and signature in the top right-hand corner of the first page. Your signature on submission will constitute your acceptance of the contest rules."

**\*SFWA NEBULA AWARDS**, Science Fiction Writers of America, Inc., Box 4236, West Columbia SC 29171. (803)791-5942. Executive Secretary: Peter Dennis Pautz. Annual contest/award. Estab. 1966. Purpose of the contest/award: to recognize meritorious achievement of short stories, novelettes, novellas and novels published the previous calendar year in the science fiction/fantasy genre. Previously published submissions only; must be published between January 1 and December 31 of the previous calendar year. "Works are nominated and selected by our active membership." Entries not returned. Awards a trophy. Judging by the active membership of the SFWA, Inc.

**SHOE TREE CONTESTS**, National Association for Young Writers, Inc., 215 Valle del Sol Dr., Santa Fe NM 87501. (505)982-8596. Editor: Sheila Cowing. Contest/award offered 3 times a year/one each fiction, nonfiction, poetry. Estab. 1984. "The purpose of the awards is to stimulate young writers to do their best work. Fiction, poetry, nonfiction." Unpublished submissions only. Deadline for entries: December 1, fiction; April 1, poetry; June 1, nonfiction. SASE for contest/award rules and entry forms. No entry fee. Awards first prize $25, second prize $10, honorable mention; all receive publication in *Shoe Tree*. "All writers may have work reprinted elsewhere after they write requesting permission, providing credit is given to *Shoe Tree*." Works will be published in the issue of *Shoe Tree* following due date.

**Tips:** "Contests are open to all children between the ages of 6-14, first grade through eighth, at the time of entry. A statement of authenticity signed by the student and by a parent, teacher, or guardian must accompany the entry. Student's name, address, age and the names of his or her school and teacher must accompany the entry."

**\*CHARLIE MAY SIMON BOOK AWARD**, Arkansas Elementary School Council, Arkansas Dept of Education, #4 Capitol-301-B, Little Rock AR 72201. (501)682-4371. Award Director: James A. Hester. Annual contest/award. Estab. 1970. Purpose of contest/ award: to promote reading—to encourage reading of good literature. Previously published submissions only; must be published between January 1 and December 31 of calendar year; all books must have re    ᵐmendations from 3 published sources. No entry fee. Awards a medallion. Contest ᴗ    ᵗ to entry by any writer, provided book is printed in year being considered.

**\*KAY SNOW WRITING CONTEST**, Willamet     Vriters, Suite 120, 811 E. Burnside, Portland OR 97233. (503)233-1877. Director: Pᴀ   ᵗia Wyckoff. Annual contest/award. Estab. 1973. Purpose of the contest/award: "To enᴄ   ᵘrage Northwest writers." Unpublished submissions only. Deadline for entries: early ᴊ   ᵉ. SASE for contest/award rules and entry forms. Entries not returned. Entry fee is $1ᴜ    ᵗ non-member; $7 for member of WW; $5 for student writer 17 and under. Awards ᴄ  ᵗʰ for 1st, 2nd and 3rd place winners. Judging by local published writers. "WW reservᴇ   ʰe right to print any of the winning entries. Publishing rights will then revert to the      ʰor." Requirements for entrants: "Open only to residents of Oregon, Washington oᵢ   daho and current members of Willamette Writers except board members, advisors aᵢ ᵈ conference chairpersons." Works to be published "in chapbook by Willamette Writ  ᵣs (if this is done)."
**Tips:** "Categories: fiction (1,500-word maximum); nonfiction (1,ᵗ00-word maximum); juvenile (1,500-word maximum); script (1-act to 20 page maximum); poetry—structured, unstructured (40-line maximum); student writer (age 17 or under—ms in any of above categories)."

**GEORGE G. STONE CENTER FOR CHILDREN'S BOOKS RECOGNITION OF MERIT AWARD**, George G. Stone Center for Children's Books, The Claremont Graduate School, 131 E. 10th St., Claremont CA 91711-6188. (714)621-8000 ext. 3670. Contest/ Award Director: Doty Hale. Annual contest/award. Estab. 1965. Purpose of the contest/ award: given to an author or illustrator of a children's book or for a body of work for the "power to please and expand the awareness of children and teachers as they have shared the book in their classrooms." Previously published submissions only. SASE for contest/award rules and entry forms. Entries not returned. No entry fee. Awards a scroll by artist Richard Beasley. Judging by a committee of teachers, professors of children's literature and librarians. Requirements for entrants: "nominations are made by students, teachers, professors and librarians. Award made at annual Claremont Reading Conference in spring (March)."

**\*VERY SPECIAL ARTS YOUNG PLAYWRIGHTS PROGRAM**, Very Special Arts Education Office, John F. Kennedy Center for the Performing Arts, Washington D.C. 20566. (202)662-8899. Annual contest/award. Estab. 1984. "All scripts must address or incorporate some aspect of disability." Unpublished submissions only. Deadline for entries: February 19, 1990. Deadline changes each year according to production date. Write to Young Playwrights Coordinator for contest/award rules and entry forms. No entries returned. No entry fee. Judging by Artists Selection Committee. "Very Special Arts retains the rights for videotaping and broadcasting on television and/or radio." Requirements for entrants: Scripts must be written by students between the ages of 12 and 18. "Script will be selected for production at the John F. Kennedy Center for the Performing Arts, Washington D.C."

**VFW VOICE OF DEMOCRACY**, Veterans of Foreign Wars of the U.S., 34th & Broadway, Kansas City MO 64111. (816)756-3390. Director: Gordon Thorson. Annual contest/award. Estab. 1960. Purpose of the contest/award: to give high school students the opportunity to voice their opinions about their responsibility to our country and to convey them via the broadcast media to all of America. Deadline for entries: November 15. SASE for contest/award rules and entry forms. SASE for return of entries. No entry fee. Awards 1st-9th place; $18,000, $10,000, $8,000, $5,500, $4,000, $1,500, $1,000, $1,000, $1,000 respectively. Requirements for entrants: "10th, 11th and 12th grade students in public, parochial and private schools in the United States and overseas are eligible to compete. Former national and/or 1st place state winners are not eligible to compete again. U.S. citizenship is required."

**LAURA INGALLS WILDER AWARD**, Association for Library Service to Children—a division of the American Library Association, 50 E. Huron, Chicago IL 60611. (312)944-6780. Executive Director, ALSC: Susan Roman. Contest/award offered every 3 years. Purpose of the contest/award: to recognize an author or illustrator whose books, published in the U.S., have over a period of years made a substantial and lasting contribution to children's literature. Awards a medal. Judging by committee which chooses several authors—winner is chosen by vote of ALSC membership.

**PAUL A. WITTY OUTSTANDING LITERATURE AWARD**, International Reading Association, Special Interest Group, Reading for Gifted and Creative Learning, School of Education, Box 32925, Fort Worth TX 76129. (817)921-7660. Contest/Award Director: Dr. Cathy Collins. Annual contest/award. Estab. 1979. Categories of entries: poetry/prose at elementary, junior high and senior high levels. Unpublished submissions only. Deadline for entries: February 1, 1989. SASE for contest/award rules and entry forms. SASE for return of entries. No entry fee. Awards $25 and plaque, also certificates of merit. Judging by 2 committees for screening and awarding. Works will be published in Reading Association publications.
**Tips:** "The elementary students' entries must be legible and may not exceed 1,000 words. Secondary students' prose entries should be typed and may exceed 1,000 words if necessary. At both elementary and secondary levels, if poetry is entered, a set of 5 poems must be submitted. All entries and requests for applications must include a self-addressed, stamped envelope."

**\*YOUNG ADULT CANADIAN BOOK AWARD**, % Unionville Library, 15 Liberty Lane, Markham, Ontario L3R 5C4 Canada. (416)477-2641. Contest/Award Director: Nancy E. Black. Annual contest/award. Purpose of contest/award: "To recognize the author of an outstanding English-language Canadian book which appeals to young adults between the ages of 13 and 18 that was published the preceding calendar year." "Information is available for anyone requesting. We approach publishers, also send news releases to various journals, i.e. *Quill & Quire*." Entries are not returned. No entry fee. Awards a leather-bound book, sometimes author tour. Requirement for entrants: a work of fiction (novel or short stories), the title must be a Canadian publication in either hardcover or paperback, and the author must be a Canadian citizen or landed immigrant. Award given at the Canadian Library Association Conference.

**\*YOUNG PLAYWRIGHT FESTIVAL**, Foundation of the Dramatists Guild, 234 W. 44th St., New York NY 10036. (212)575-7796. Director: Nancy Quinn. Annual contest/award. Deadline for entries: October 1. "Write and request information." SASE. Entries are not returned. No entry fee. Award: Production of play. Judging by YPF Selection Committee. Requirements for entrants: writers 18 years old and under.

**\*YOUNG READER'S CHOICE AWARD**, Pacific Northwest Library Association Children's and Young Adult Services Division, Alaska State Library, Box G, Juneau AK 99811. Award Director: Terry Hyer, 812 E. Clark, Pocatello, ID 83201. Annual contest/ award. Estab. 1940. Purpose of the contest/award: to promote reading. To give recognition to books young readers endorse as being an excellent story. Previously published submissions only; must be published 3 years before award year. Deadline for entries: February 1. SASE for contest/award rules and entry forms. Entries not returned. No entry fee. Awards a silver medal plus increased booksales for list of 15 nominated titles. "Librarians and teachers read books and nominate those they would like to see on the list. Children read from a list of 15 books and vote for their favorite."

**YOUNG WRITER'S CONTEST**, Young Writer's Contest Foundation, Box 6092, McLean VA 22106. (703)893-6097. Executive Director: Kathie Janger. Annual contest/award. Estab. 1984. Purpose of the contest/award: "to challenge first through eighth graders and to give them recognition; in so doing, we aim to improve basic communication skills." Unpublished submissions only. Deadline for entries: November 30. SASE for contest/award rules and entry forms. Entries not returned. Entry fee is $15 per school (or, if school does not participate, the individual may pay the fee). "All participating students and schools receive certificates; winners' entries are published in our anthology: *RAINBOW COLLECTION: Stories and Poetry by Young People.*" Judging by writers, editors, journalists, teachers, reading specialists. "All rights surrounding winners' entries are given to YWCF, via consent and release form. Participants must be currently enrolled in grades 1-8; no more than 12 entries per school may be submitted; we accept poems, stories and essays. *RAINBOW COLLECTION: Stories and Poetry by Young People* is published in May of each year, and is distributed (25,000 cc. in 1989) to libraries, school systems and charitable organizations. The YWCF complements classroom writing programs and creates a cycle of encouragement and performance; writing is critical to all fields of endeavor; we reward the students' efforts—not just the winning."

# Resources

## Agents

Many times writers and illustrators have a difficult time deciding when, and if, they need the services of an agent. There are those established professionals who sometimes also find their own negotiation skills are polished enough to work out contract specifics with a publisher. Others find that marketing their work and the negotiation process that ensues rob them of valuable writing or illustrating time. Before you put any thought into whether to contact an agent, read on to become familiar with what an agent can — and can't — do for you.

Generally the agent will evaluate your manuscript or artwork to determine its salability in the marketplace. If it is deemed work that can be sold, the agent can call upon many contacts in different publishing houses to query their interest. Following a positive response he is authorized to negotiate for a favorable contract on your behalf and collect the fees for you. An agent won't, however, maintain your financial records or act as a writing or art coach. Even though many have reading and/or critique services (available at a nominal fee), time spent on such services is reserved for promising work.

Agents typically charge a 10 to 15 percent commission from the sale of your writing or art material. Such fees will be taken from your advance and royalty earnings. If your agent sells foreign rights to your work, he will deduct 20 percent because he will most likely be dealing with an overseas agent with whom he must split the fee.

As mentioned earlier, some agents offer reading services, though this isn't an industry standard. If you are a new writer, you will probably be charged a fee of less than $75. Many times, if an agent agrees to represent you, the fee will be reimbursed (though not always). If you take advantage of an agency's critique service, you will probably pay a range of $25-200 depending on the length of the manuscript. Be aware also that the purpose of this service isn't to edit your manuscript, but rather to offer "pointers" based on the agent's knowledge of what sells in juvenile publishing. Prior to engaging in a reading or critique service, you should find out up front what results you can expect. The listings in this section specify whether such services are available, the fee, and whether the fee is refundable upon an agreement to represent you.

The only other fees you may incur from an agent, once he agrees to represent you, include photocopying costs, phone expenses or postage for mailings or messenger services. Now that you know a bit more about what an agent's role in your career involves, be advised that not every agent is open to representing a writer or artist who doesn't have some sort of track record. This means that your manuscript or artwork, and query or cover letters, must be polished and professional looking. Your first impression must be that of an organized, articulate person.

You should feel free to conduct some research prior to contacting an agent to determine how familiar—and successful—he is with selling to children's publishers. Scanning through these listings will provide you with an important first step because you will be advised of reporting time on queries, manuscripts or art samples, or possible reading or critique fees as well as the "hidden" expenses of postage and phone calls mentioned earlier, what rights are marketed, contract requirements (i.e., how long the agreement runs and what expenses you are responsible for), as well as any special services offered such as lecture/promotional tours or tax/legal consultations. Talking to an agent's other clients could provide you with useful information as well, though a few may balk at providing you with such names.

**\*ARTISTS INTERNATIONAL,** 7 Dublin Hill Road, Greenwich CT 06830. (203)869-8010. Contact person: Michael Brodie. Estab. 1971. Represents 25 artists. 15 artists in picture books, 12 in young readers, 20 in middle readers, 6 in young adults/teens, 20 illustrators who specialize in juvenile art. Prefers to review new material via slide, tearsheets and SAE. Commission: 30% on domestic and foreign sales. 100% of business derived from commission on ms sales.

**\*CAROL BANCROFT & FRIENDS,** 185 Goodhill Rd., Weston CT 06883. (203)226-7674. Owner: Carol Bancroft. Estab. 1972. Member of SCBW. Represents 40 illustrators. Prefers to review new material via a portfolio. Reports in 2 months on illustrations. Handles 30% picture books, 10% young readers, 10% middle readers, 10% young adults. Commission: 25% on domestic sales. Offers a criticism service.

**BARBARA BAUER LITERARY AGENCY, INC.,** 179 Washington Ave., Matawan NJ 07747. (201)739-5210, 16. Contact: Kay Morgan. Estab. 1984. Branch Office: 59 W. Front St., Keyport NJ 07735. (201)583-4988. Represents 12 clients. Specializes in new and unpublished authors. "Our success with *The Mystery of the Singing Mermaid* (Weekly Reader Book Club) is well-known. We have earned plenty of royalties for Ann Young. Barbara Bauer is that rare literary agent who holds a Ph.D. in English. Combined with her marketing expertise and multitude of publishing contacts, she is a powerful resource to have. Charges a low commission. Has been very successful with first time authors. Query with SASE or phone. Also offers training to new agents."

**BOOKSTOP LITERARY AGENCY,** 67 Meadow View Rd., Orinda CA 94563. (415)254-2664. Agent: Kendra Marcus. Estab. 1984. Member of SCBW. Clients specialize in picture books, young readers, middle readers, young adult books, illustration of own books, juvenile art. 50% of clients are new/unpublished writers; 30% new/unpublished illustrators. Qualifications for representation: must have high-quality work that will sell to the trade market. Prefers to review new material via the entire ms. Reports in 6 weeks on a ms or ms/illustration package. Has sold *Silicon Song*, by Buzz King (YA novel—Delacorte); *Korean Cinderella*, by Clinco/Heller (K-3, picture book—Harper); *Eye of the Needle*, by Sloat (K-4, picture book—Dutton). Commission: 15% on domestic sales, 20% on foreign sales. Criticism service fee: $25 an hour. "I charge for postage, copies and telephone." 75% of business derived from commission on ms sales; 25% from criticism services.

**ANDREA BROWN, LITERARY AGENCY,** 301 W. 53 St., 13B, New York NY 10019. (212)581-7068. President: Andrea Brown. Estab. 1981. Member of ILAA. 15-18 clients specialize in picture books, 10 in young readers, 20-25 in middle readers, 10-12 in young adult books, many writers illustrate own books, 10 clients specialize in juvenile art. 25% of clients are new/unpublished writers; 5% new/unpublished illustrators. Qualifications for representation: "Illustrators—who have published children's book material only. Writers—queries only by unpublished writers with a SASE. Other writers should send samples of work published. Taking on few brand new writers." Prefers to review new material via a query with outline/proposal; ms/illustration packages (queries with photos of art—SASE). Reports in approximately 2 weeks on a query, 8 weeks on a ms, 6 weeks on a ms/illustration package, 2 weeks on illustrations. Handles (approximately) 30% nonfiction, 40% fiction, 10% ms/illustration package, 20% illustrations only. Has sold *The Teacher From the Black Lagoon*, by Mike Thaler (grades 2-3, Scholastic); *Snake and Wild Goat*, by Caroline Arnold (grades 2-3, Morrow); *Mole and Shrew*, by Jackie French Koller (grades 2-3, Atheneum). Commission: 15% on domestic sales, 20% on foreign sales. "We call new, unpublished authors collect." All business derived from commission on ms sales.

**Tips:** "We do exclusively children's books. Young adults is slow now, but we can't get enough good middle-group books. Not interested in unpublished picture book people. I want more middle-group and nonfiction, especially science related."

**MARIA CARVAINIS AGENCY, INC.,** 235 W. End Ave., New York NY 10023. (212)580-1559. President: Maria Carvainis. Estab. 1977. Member of Independent Literary Agents Association, Writers Guild of America, Authors Guild of America, and Romance Writers of America. Represents 60 clients. 15% of clients specialize in young adult books. 15% of clients are new/unpublished writers. Accepting new clients. Qualifications for representation: "I look for three criteria to be met: 1) a strong writing talent 2) a special story or book concept and 3) a strong execution of the story or book concept." Prefers to learn of new authors and their projects via a letter query with SASE. Reports in 2-3 weeks, if not earlier, on a query, 4-12 weeks on a ms. Handles 100% fiction (10% middle readers, 90% young adults). "I would like to see more children's and middle-grade books and nonfiction. Has sold *The Tub People*, by Pam Conrad (children's, Harper & Row); *Stonewords*, by Pam Conrad (young adult, Harper & Row); *The Most Embarrassing Mother in the World*, by Peter Filichia (young adult, Avon). Commission: 15% on domestic sales, 20% on foreign sales. Criticism service only offered to agency's clients. "I offer evaluation of the strength of the book's development and execution of its potential given my experience for more than a decade as an editor at Macmillan Publishing, Basic Books, Avon Books and Crown Publishers." 100% of business derived from commission on ms sales.

**Tips:** "The children's and juvenile market is one of the most healthy and expanding sectors of the publishing industry. I expect it to remain so."

**MARTHA CASSELMAN, LITERARY AGENT,** Box 342, Calistoga CA 94515-0342. (707)942-4341. "Regret we cannot return long-distance phone queries; please query by mail with SASE." Estab. 1978. Member of ILAA. Represents 6 clients in juvenile and young adults. 2 clients specialize in picture books, 2 in young adults, 2 illustrators specialize in juvenile art. 80% of clients are new/unpublished writers. Qualifications for representation: "Authors should be familiar with the field." Commission: 15% domestic

 *The asterisk before a listing indicates that the listing is new in this edition.*

sales, plus 10% foreign sales. Charges for copying, overnight mailing services. "I have made a cautious entry into the juvenile and young adult market. Sales have been to reputable publishers."

**\*SJ CLARK LITERARY AGENCY,** 101 Randall St., San Francisco CA 94131. (415)285-7401. Owner: Sue Clark. Estab. 1982. Represents 15 clients. 1 client specializes in picture books, 2 in young adults/teens, 1 writer also illustrates own manuscript. 95% of clients are new/unpublished writers. Prefers to review new material via query then entire ms; Ms/illustration packages: send "copy of final art." Reports in 1-2 months on a query, 2-3 months on a ms, 2-3 months on a ms/illustration package. Handles 100% fiction, 10% young readers, 30% middle readers, 59% young adults. Commission: 20% on domestic sales. 100% of business derived from commission on ms sales.

**RUTH COHEN, INC.,** Box 7626, Menlo Park CA 94025. (415)854-2054. President: Ruth Cohen. Estab. 1982. Member of ILAA. Represents 60-70 clients. 7 clients specialize in picture books, 20 in young readers, 10 in young adult books, 5 writers illustrate own books, 5 clients specialize in juvenile art. 50% of clients are new/unpublished writers. Qualifications for representation: "Submission of quality material in the form of a partial ms and illustrations (if illustrator has been published before) or a partial ms for older children if author has not been published before; plus list of credits and SASE." Prefers to review new material via an outline plus 3 sample chapters; ms/illustration packages (must include SASE). Reports in 14 days on a query, 21 days on a ms or ms/illustration package, 14 days on illustrations. Has sold *Jase the Ace*, by Joanne Rocklen (ages 7-10, short novel); *Melba the Brain*, by Ivy Ruckman (ages 8-12, novel); *Animal Tracks*, by Arthur Dorros (ages 5-10, picture science book). Commission: 15% domestic sales; 20% foreign sales. Charges for foreign/telex or phone calls and overseas mailing.

**CRAVEN DESIGN STUDIOS, INC.,** 234 Fifth Ave., 4th Floor, New York NY 10001. (212)696-4680. President: Tema Siegel. Estab. 1981. Represents 20 illustrators. Qualifications for representation: "Illustrators should have a few years experience and have some published pieces. How many pieces published does not matter as much as how good they are and how well they represent a specific style." Ms/illustrations packages: submit samples—photocopies that do not have to be returned—or a self addressed mailer. I will call for portfolio if interested. Reports in 2 weeks on illustrations. Handles 100% illustrations (10% picture books, 10% young readers, 3% middle readers, 2% young adults); also 85% textbooks. Commission: 25% domestic sales; 25% foreign sales. 100% of business derived from commission on illustrations.

**\*EDUCATIONAL DESIGN SERVICES, INC.,** Box 253, Wantagh NY 11793. (718)-539-4107 or (516)221-0995. President: B. Linder. Estab. 1979. Represents 12 clients; young adult/teen, writers of textual material for education market only. Prefers to review new material via query, entire ms, outline/proposal, outline plus sample chapters and/or portfolio. Reports in 4-6 weeks on query or ms. Recently sold *American History w/N.Y. State* (Amsco); *Economics* (Modern Curriculum Press), *Nueva Historia de los Estados Unidos* (Minerva). Commission: 15% on domestic sales, 25% on foreign sales. Other fees: "long-distance phone calls and handling costs." No response without SASE.

**PETER ELEK ASSOCIATES,** Box 223, Canal St. Station, New York NY 10013. (212)431-9368. Executive Assistant: Liza Lagunoff. Estab. 1979. Represents 30 clients. 8 clients specialize in picture books, 8 in young readers, 2 in middle readers, 1 in young adult books, 5 clients specialize in juvenile art. 20% of clients are new/unpublished writers; 50% new/unpublished illustrators. Accepting new clients "very selectively." Qualifications for representation: "intent on making a career as a professional writer; experience writing for children (not simply a teacher, librarian or parent)." Prefers to review new material via a query; with outline proposal. Reports in 14 days on a query, 21 days on a ms or ms/illustration package. Handles 30% nonfiction (60% picture books, 40% middle readers); 50% fiction (60% picture books, 20% young readers, 20% middle readers); 20% ms/illustration package (80% picture books, 10% young readers, 10% middle readers). Has sold *Esmerelda & the Pet Parade*, by Cecile Schoberle (picture book, Simon & Schuster); *The Rosy Fat Magenta Radish*, by Janet Wolf (picture book, Joy Street Books/Little, Brown & Company); *Jason Quest*, by R.D. Ballard (middle reader, Scholastic). Commission: 15% domestic sales; 20% foreign sales. If required, charges for ms copying, courier charges. 100% of business derived from commission on ms sales.

**Tips:** "Sadly too many individuals are encouraged by 'schools' and writing courses to believe that they are innovative and have the ability to write for children. Few have studied publishers' catalogs and bookstore/library shelves to see what is already there."

**ETHAN ELLENBERG/LITERARY AGENT**, #5-C, 548 Broadway, New York NY 10012. (212)431-4554. President: Ethan Ellenberg. Estab. 1984. Represents 35 clients. 3 clients specialize in picture books, 1 in young readers, 1 writer illustrates own books. 100% of clients (in children's books) are new/unpublished writers; 100% new/unpublished illustrators. (In adult books 50% of clientele published before.) Qualifications for representation: a professionally prepared manuscript and/or illustrations ready for submission to publishers. "Query, sample chapters or entire ms are all acceptable to submit as long as they include SASE. No preference." Reports in 2-3 weeks for all submissions, no matter what. Handles 50% fiction, 50% ms/illustration package. Has sold *The Devil Ate My Blintzes*, by Ben Hillman (age 0-8, Waterfront Press). Commission: 15% domestic sales; 20% foreign sales. "The only expense I charge is a photocopying fee for duplication of ms for submission."

**Tips:** "I am actively seeking new clients and I look forward to hearing from anyone serious about children's books. Before opening my own agency I was in charge of the contracts for juvenile publishing at Bantam, so I know the field well. I enjoy children's books and I'm excited about the opportunities the field has."

**\*HEACOCK LITERARY AGENCY, INC.**, Suite #14, 1523 6th St., Santa Monica CA 90401. (213)393-6227. President: Jim Heacock. Vice President: Rosalie Heacock. Estab. 1978. "We'll send free brochure on our services if writers will request and enclose SASE." Member of ILAA (Independent Literary Agents Association); Association of Talent Agents. Represents 50 clients. 5 clients specialize in picture books, 5 in young readers. Qualifications for representation: "Each must have been published by a *major* house at least four times in the recent past." Prefers to review new material via query, outline/proposal and/or outline plus sample chapters. Reports in 2 weeks on query, 4 weeks on ms/illustration package. Handles 15% nonfiction, 15% young adults; 25% fiction, 25% young readers; 60% ms/illustration package, 30% picture books, 30% young readers. Recently sold titles: *My Little Piggies*, by Don and Audrey Wood (Harcourt Brace Jovanovich); *Tom Thumb*, by Richard Jesse Watson (Harcourt Brace Jovanovich); *Cory Coleman Grade Two*, by Larry D. Brimner (Henry, Holt, Inc.). Commission: 15% on domestic sales (on first $50,00 earnings each year, then 10% for balance of year); 25% on foreign sales (if sold direct 15% — if agent used 25%). Other fees: "Our out-of-pocket actual costs for postage, telephone, packing, photocopies, etc." 95% of business derived from commission on ms sales; 5% from consultant contracts in advising authors or negotiating contracts for them. "This charge is $125 per hour plus expenses. We do not have time for criticisms."

**Tips:** "We prefer to restrict our efforts to a small and select group of highly talented writers and offer a maximum personal service. Equally so for illustrators with national award-winning potential."

**J. KELLOCK & ASSOCIATES LTD.**, 11017-80 Ave., Edmonton Alberta T6G 0R2 Canada. (403)433-0274. President: Joanne Kellock. Estab. 1981. Represents approximately 70 clients. 5 clients specialize in picture books, 10 in young adult books, 10 writers illustrate own books, some clients specialize in juvenile art. 30% of clients are new/unpublished writers; 1% new/unpublished illustrators. Qualifications for representation: "It is always preferable to acquire a writer who has one or two books on the market, but new talent must be looked at providing any project is well thought out, professionally written, competition studied, and required age group carefully considered. Helpful if illustrators have a reputation as an artist, and are VERY serious about becoming an illustrator for children's material. They must love such children's books." Prefers to review new material via a query; outline/proposal; outline plus 3 complete sample chapters; or one finished piece of art work, 3 b&w sketches. Reports in 1 week on a query, 3-4 weeks on a ms, 2 weeks on a ms/illustration package, 1 week on illustrations. Handles 2% nonfiction picture books, and 5% middle readers; 3% fiction picture books, 15% young readers and 12% young adults; 4% ms/illustration package picture books, 2% young readers, 15% middle readers, 9% young adults; 3% illustration only picture books, 15% middle readers, 9% young adult books. Has sold *A Promise to the Sun*, by Tololwa Marti Mollet (pre-school, Little, Brown & Company); *I Spent My Summer Vacation Kidnapped Into Space*, by Martyn Godfrey (juvenile, Scholastic Inc.); *Holy Joe*, by Mary Blakeslee (young adult, Stoddart Publishing/Toronto). Commission: 15% English language sales; 20% foreign sales. Reading/criticism service fee fiction and nonfiction: no fee under 2,000 words; $40 for three chapters juvenile or young adult work, balance read free of charge if the work shows publishing possibility. SASE required for return of material. "I basically concern myself with style working with subject/whether or not work fits into the right age group; character development, action, point of view/voice. My reader sometimes deals with ms from new writers. Require a SASE with all submissions. Charges for postage and long distance calls." 70% of business derived from commission on ms sales and 30% from reading fees/criticism service. "I do not charge for reading three chapters, and that is usually enough to tell me if a ms works. I do not request complete ms if ms not working."
**Tips:** "I do very well with sales of children's work, and consequently more and more writers of this material seek me out. I fight hard for my children's writers, particularly if sale is to Canadian publisher, as here children's writers are still somehow considered second class. I also sell TV/film."

**BARBARA S. KOUTS, LITERARY AGENT**, 788 Ninth Ave., New York NY 10019. (212)265-6003. Literary Agent: Barbara Kouts. Estab. 1980. Member of ILAA. Represents 22 clients. 4 clients specialize in picture books, 8 in young readers, 10 in young adult books, 2 writers illustrate own books. 60% of clients are new/unpublished writers. Qualifications for representation: "I am looking for writers with some background in writing (i.e., published stories or articles). But I will look at new material, too." Prefers to review new material via a query. Reports in 1-2 weeks on query, 3-4 weeks on ms. Handles 40% nonfiction (10% picture books, 45% middle readers, 45% young adult books); 60% fiction (25% picture books, 25% young readers, 25% middle readers, 25% young adult books). Has sold *A Man Named Thoreau*, Robert Burleigh (middle readers, Atheneum); *The Makeover*, Jane Parks-McKay (young adult book, Morrow Junior Books); *The Enchanted Tapestry*, Robert San Souci (picture book, Dial). Commission: 10% domestic sales; 20% foreign sales. Charges photocopying fee. 100% of business derived from commission on ms sales.

**LIGHTHOUSE LITERARY AGENCY**, 1112 Solana Ave., Box 2105, Winter Park FL 32790. (407)647-2385. Director: Sandy Kangas. Estab. 1988. Member of Authors Guild. Represents 68 clients. 8 clients specialize in picture books, 6 in young readers, 6 in young adult books. 35% of clients are new/unpublished writers. Qualifications for representation:

"Some prior success is a plus, but not a requirement. More important is a professional work attitude. We enjoy working with authors who are receptive to criticism, those who realize that good writing is the art of rewriting." Prefers to review entire ms. "Do not send your only copy." Ms/illustration packages: send quality copies of artwork. Do not send original artwork until requested to do so. Reports in 2 weeks on a query, ms, ms/illustration package or illustrations. Handles 30% nonfiction (50% picture books, 25% young readers, 25% middle readers); 70% fiction (50% picture books, 25% young readers, 25% middle readers). Commission: 15% domestic sales; 20% foreign sales. Offers criticism service. 93% of business derived from commission on ms sales; 7% criticism service.

**Tips:** "Due to the large volume of submissions received, we are more apt to accept for marketing work by writers with a track record. We will still read unsolicited material from new writers."

**\*RAY LINCOLN LITERARY AGENCY**, Elkins Park House, #107-B, 7900 Old York Road, Elkins Park PA 19117. (215)635-0827. CEO: Mrs. Ray Lincoln. Estab. 1974. Represents 33 adult and 20 children's book authors. 2 clients specialize in picture books, 5 in young readers, 5 in middle readers, 8 in young adults/teens. 20% of clients are new/unpublished writers. Qualifications for representation: "must have a fresh, appealing style. I handle nonfiction as well as fiction in both juvenile and adult categories." Prefers to review new material via query (first); sample chapters later, if sample is of interest. "I then request the full manuscript." Reports in 1-2 weeks on a query, 3-4 weeks on a ms. Handles 25% nonfiction (10% middle readers, 15% young adults); 75% fiction (10% picture books, 25% young readers, 15% middle readers, 25% young adults). Recently sold titles: *Maniac Magee*, by Jerry Spinelli (Little Brown), *Upchuck Summer's Revenge*, by Joel Schwartz (Dell), *Dragon Flies*, by Molly McLaughlin (middle and YA, Walker). Offers criticism service. 100% of business derived from commission on ms sales.

**Tips:** "I particularly like the 5 and up categories, including young adult, and plan to expand."

**LITERARY MARKETING CONSULTANTS**, Ste. 701, One Hallidie Plaza, San Francisco CA 94102. (415)391-7508. Director: Barbara Hargrave. Estab. 1984. Represents 18 clients. 1 client specializes in picture books, 1 in young readers, 5 in young adult books, 1 client specializes in juvenile art. "We welcome queries from new writers. However, these must be excellent quality to interest us enough to show further curiosity about the author's project. The query must be original, neatly typed, contain a SASE, and 1) a paragraph about the author, 2) a paragraph about the story, 3) any plans for illustrations/format, and 4) advise regarding target age group and approximate word count." Prefers to review new material via a query. "Do not submit ms/illustrations at all! Advise us of them in the query. We will not be responsible for any unsolicited material we receive." Reports in 1 month on a query, 2 months on a ms. Handles 75% fiction (25% nonfiction juvenile and YA). Commission: 15% domestic sales; 20% foreign sales. Offers a criticism service "for our clients—no fee. Criticism is done by experienced writers in the particular genre, but only for our clients in any case." Charges a handling fee, "so we don't have to charge for extras like criticism or necessaries like expenses." 95% of business derived from commission on ms sales. "We only critique work that we agree to market for the writer."

**Tips:** "Look at what is already out there before sending us a query. A new focus in 1990 will be on juvenile and YA religious books; also we look at teachers' supplements, activity books and parenting material, as well as fresh ideas for fiction."

**\*SCOTT MEREDITH LITERARY AGENCY, INC.**, 845 Third Ave., New York NY 10022. (212)245-5500. FAX: (212)755-2972. Vice-President and Editorial Director: Jack Scovil. Estab. 1946. Represents 2,000 clients. 25 clients specialize in picture books, 35 in young readers, 35 in middle readers, 50 in young adults/teens, 5 writers also illustrate their own manuscripts. "The 2,000 (represented) are established authors, though we also work with new writers." Qualifications for representation: "if an author has sold a book to a major publisher, or three to lesser publishers, we'll read a new script without charge, and take on the author for commission representation if we find the script salable and consider the author generally promising." Prefers to review new material via entire ms or "at least one" sample chapter; ms/illustration packages: send "final text but rough sketches, since different publishers have different size requirements, etc., for finished art." Reports in a day or two on a query, 2 weeks on a ms, 2 weeks on a ms/illustration package; "We guarantee decision on all submissions within 2 weeks." Handles 35% nonfiction (20% picture books, 20% young readers, 30% middle readers, 30% young adults); 45% fiction (20% picture books, 20% young readers, 30% middle readers, 30 % adults); 20% ms/illustration package (70% picture books, 20% young readers, 25% middle readers, 5% young adults). "We don't represent illustrators: only writers who also illustrate. However, we'll sometimes accept a straight illustration assignment for a client." Recently sold *Barney's Horse*, by Syd Hoff (Harper and Row, picture book); *Harvey's Wacky Parrot Adventure*, by Eth Clifford (Houghton-Mifflin, middle readers); *The Young Astronauts*, by Jack Anderson and Shariann Lewitt (Zebra Books, YA). Commission: 10% on domestic sales, 20% on foreign sales. Reading/criticism service: "we don't call it a 'reading' fee since the single fee covers a detailed response on why we've determined that the material is salable or unsalable, and assistance in revisions (without further charge) where we consider revisions necessary to make a script salable." Critiques range "anywhere from 2 single-spaced pages to as many as a dozen or more. Reports are based on multi-readings by staff and written by Scott Meredith personally with staff assistance." Other fees: "No charge for local calls and ordinary mail; we charge long distance calls (such as a rare call to foreign publishers) or shipments by FedEx at our cost only." 90% of business derived from commission on ms sales, 10% from reading/criticism services. "If we find a script salable, or it becomes salable following our suggested revisions, we will represent the author; but we won't take on a script and represent its author if the submission is irreparably unsalable."
**Tips:** The juvenile publishing market is "very strong now. It was weak for a while when government subsidies slowed down and school systems decreased buying, but that's rectified itself. And juvenile publishers in most cases are starting to pay higher advances. We used to tell potential juvenile writers, rather apologetically, that advances were absurdly low buy royalties often went on forever and added up nicely; but now even advances are pretty respectable. They're not the lottery-winner advances paid for some adult books, but at least they're well into the thousands rather than the hundreds."

**MEWS BOOKS LTD.**, 20 Bluewater Hill, Westport CT 06880. (203)227-1836. President: Sidney B. Kramer. Estab. 1975. Represents 50 "active at one time" clients. 10 picture books; 20 young readers; 30 writers illustrating own mss; 1 client specializes in juvenile art. 20% of clients are new/unpublished writers. Qualifications for representation: "We look for professional handling of material presented. If material calls for illustration, send very rough sketches so that the ultimate work can be visualized. Recommendation by published author or expert is useful. Work should have clear purpose and age delineation. Previously published authors (in any category) have greater credibility with publishers." Prefers to review new material via query; character and plot outline/proposal. No original illustrations are accepted by us. "We try to process material within 30 days." SASE. Have sold to Simon & Schuster, Western Publishing, Crown, *Parents*. Commission: 15% domestic sales (10% for authors previously published extensively); 20% foreign sales. 100% of business derived from commission on ms sales.

Tips: "President offers individual, domestic and international legal service to authors in need of negotiating assistance (as an attorney and former publisher). The agency offers extensive foreign representation."

**\*MULTIMEDIA PRODUCT DEVELOPMENT, INC.**, 410 S. Michigan Ave., Chicago IL 60605. (312)922-3063. President: Jane Jordan Browne. Estab. 1971. Represents 100 clients of whom 12 write juveniles. 4 clients specialize in picture books, 4 in young readers, 2 in middle readers, 2 in young adults/teens. 5% of clients are new/unpublished writers. Qualifications for representation: "They must be published authors." Prefers to review new material via a query with SASE required for reply. Handles 25% nonfiction (30% picture books, 15% young readers, 15% middle readers, 15% young adults — 100% of 25%); 75% fiction (30% picture books, 15% young readers, 15% middle readers, 15% young adults — 100% of 75%). Recently sold *Eagle Bait*, by Susan Coryell (middle readers — Harcourt, Brace); *Big Friend, Little Friend*, by Susan Sussman (young readers — Houghton-Mifflin); *Me and My Name*, by Mary Jane Miller (middle readers — Viking). Commission: 15% on domestic sales, 20% on foreign sales. Additional fees charged for "photocopies, foreign postage and phone/fax." 100% of commission derived from commission on ms sales.

**PAMELA NEAIL ASSOCIATES**, 27 Bleecker St., New York NY 10012. (212)673-1600. FAX: (212)673-7687. Contact: Lisa Allyn Worth. Estab. 1982. Member of SPAR, Society of Illustrators. Represents 15 clients. 5 clients specialize in picture books, 5 in young readers, 5 in young adult books, 5 clients specialize in juvenile art. Qualifications for representation: "We represent illustrators and are willing to review work. Artists should send promos and slides — NO ORIGINALS, and if they wish the materials returned, must include a SASE." Prefers to review printed promos, no originals.

**THE NORMA-LEWIS AGENCY**, 521 Fifth Ave., New York NY 10175. (212)751-4955. Partner: Norma Liebert. Estab. 1980. Qualifications for representation: "he/she must write a ms that we think is marketable." Prefers to review new material via a query; ms/illustration packages: do not send any original artwork, send reproductions only. Reports in 2 weeks on a query, 4 weeks on a ms. Handles 50% nonfiction, 50% fiction. Commission: 15% domestic sales; 20% foreign sales. 100% of business derived from commission on ms sales.

**\*SIDNEY E. PORCELAIN AGENCY**, Box 1229, Milford PA 18337. (717)296-6420. Manager: Sidney Porcelain. Estab. 1951-2. Represents 20 clients. 3 clients specialize in picture books, 1 in young adults/teens, 1 writer also illustrates own manuscripts. 80% of clients are new/unpublished writers. Prefers to review new material via query and portfolio. Reports in 1 week on a query, 2 weeks on a ms, 2 weeks on a ms/illustration package. Handles 50% fiction (40% middle readers, 10% young adults). Commission: 10% on domestic sales, 20% on foreign sales. 100% of business derived from commission on ms sales.

**S.I. INTERNATIONAL**, 43 E. 19th St., New York NY 10003. (212)254-4996. FAX: (212)995-0911. Children's Director: Mr. Don Bruckstein. Estab. 1958. Member of Graphic Artists Guild. Represents 25 clients. 5 clients specialize in picture books, 5 in young readers, 6 in young adult books, 2 writers illustrate own books, 17 clients specialize in juvenile art. Qualifications for representation: "previous illustration work published." Prefers to review new material via a portfolio. Reports in 2 weeks on ms/illustration package, 1 week on illustrations. Commission: 25% domestic sales; 35% foreign sales.

**\*RICHARD W. SALZMAN ARTIST REPRESENTATIVE,** 1352 Hornblend St., San Diego CA 92109. (619)272-8147. Associate: Greg Kaiser. Estab. 1982. Member of Society of Photo & Artist Representatives, GAG, AIGA. Represents 28 clients. 18 clients specialize in picture books, 18 in young readers, 18 in middle readers 18 in young adults/teens, 12 illustrators specialize in juvenile art. Qualifications for representation: "design based solely on portfolio." Prefers to review new material via "mailed samples — try to include some for us to keep on file. Slides are acceptable." Handles 20% nonfiction; 20% fiction; 20% ms/illustration package; 30% illustrations only. Commission: 25% on domestic sales, 30% on foreign sales. Criticism service fee: "$75 per hour — illustration & photo only"; verbal criticism service. Additional fees: "cost of portfolio and 75% of any advance cost." 75% of business derived from commission on ms sales; 5% from criticism services.

**\*SCHLESSINGER-VAN DYCK AGENCY,** 12 S. 12th St., 2814 P.S.C.F.S. Building, Philadelphia PA 19107. (215)627-4665. Partner/Agent: Barrie Van Dyck. Estab. 1987. Represents 40 clients. 2 clients specialize in picture books, 2 in middle readers, 3 in young adults/teens. 50% of clients are new/unpublished writers. Qualifications for representation: "we prefer authors with publishing credentials but it is not mandatory. We are selecting authors carefully according to quality of writing, in both fiction and nonfiction." Prefers to review new material via query (for fiction); outline/proposal for nonfiction. Reports in 2 weeks on a query, 4 weeks on a ms. Handles 50% nonfiction, 50% fiction. Recently sold *The Bread Sister of Sinking Creek*, by Robin Moore (Harper & Row, ages 9-14); *Maggie Among the Seneca*, by Robin Moore (Harper & Row, age 9-14); *Amazing Lizards*, by Jayne Pettit (Scholastic, age 8-12). Commission: 15% on domestic sales, 20% on foreign sales. Other fees: office expense fee, long distance phone, UPS mailing, duplicating of manuscripts. 100% of business derived from commission on ms sales.

**\*SINGER MEDIA, CORP.,** 3164 Tyler Ave., Anaheim CA 92801. Associate Editor: Dorothy Rosati. Estab. 1940. Represents 100+ clients. 20 clients specialize in picture books, 10 in young readers, 40 in young adults/teens. 20% of clients are new/unpublished writers, 20% cartoonists. Qualifications for representation: "We syndicate to foreign markets and like to obtain reprint rights." Prefers to review new material via query and entire ms; ms/illustration: send final text. Reports in 3 weeks. Recently sold titles: *Juvenile Activity Books* (PSI, Ottenheimer University). Commission: 20% on domestic sales, 25% on foreign sales, 50% on syndication. Reading fee: "We charge $250 which is minimal when compared with the fees of other professionals. If we succeed in placing the manuscript with a publisher, this fee is refunded in full. This is only a one-time payment." Critiques are comprised of "professional evaluation by published authors." 98% of business derived from commission on ms sales; 2% from reading/criticism services."
**Tips:** "We like books and scripts of interest to the international market."

**SANDRA WATT & ASSOCIATES,** Ste. 4053, 8033 Sunset Blvd., Los Angeles CA 90046. (213)653-2339. Agent: Robert Drake. Estab. 1976. Member of ILAA, WGAW, SAG, AFTRA. Represents 50 clients. 5 clients specialize in young adult books. 75% of clients are new/unpublished writers. Qualifications for representation: "be talented, competent and professional." Prefers to review new material via a query. Reports on a query in 1 week, 8 weeks on a ms. Handles 80% fiction (10% young adult books). Recently sold *The Voice*, by Cynthia Labrum (upper YA, teen suicide); *I'll See You Forever*, by Naomi Feldman (middle YA, juvenile diabetes); *Wise Acres*, by Raymond Obstfeld (upper YA, coming-of-age). Commission: 15% domestic sales; 25% foreign sales. Charges marketing fee: $50-100. 100% of business derived from commission on ms sales.

WRITERS HOUSE, 21 W. 26 St., New York NY 10010. (212)685-2400. Executive Vice President: Amy Burkower; Director: Susan Cohen. Contact: Sheila Callahan, Megan Howard. Estab. 1973. Member of ILAA. Represents 300 clients. Clients specialize in picture books, young readers, young adult books, writers illustrating own book. Small percent of clients are new/unpublished writers. Accepting new clients "on a limited basis." Qualifications for representation: "material we think we can sell and a person we'd like to work with." Prefers to review new material via a query or outline plus 2 sample chapters. Reports on a query in 2-3 weeks, 6-8 weeks on a ms, 2-3 weeks on ms/illustration package. Handles mostly fiction books; smaller % of nonfiction as ms/ illustration packages. Susan Cohen has sold *Fortune*, by Diane Stanley (picture book, Morrow); *Whitney Cousins*, trilogy, by Jean Thesman (middle grade, Avon); *Borgel*, by Daniel Pinkwater (YA, Macmillan). Amy Berkower has sold *Rookie Stars*, by Dean Hughes (middle grade, series, Knopf); *Hollywood Daughters*, by Joan Lowery Nixon (YA, 4 book series, Bantam); *Naked in Winter*, by Jeroke Brooks (YA novel, Franklin Watts). Commission: 15% domestic sales; 20% foreign sales. Charges for extraordinary expenses (big photocopying jobs, telexes, messengers) deducted from disbursements to writers. Most of business % derived from commission on ms sales; some from foreign and performance rights sales, and agency also represents submission rights for some small publishers.

TOM ZELASKY LITERARY AGENCY, 3138 Parkridge Crescent, Chamblee GA 30341. (404)458-0391. Agent: Tom Zelasky. Estab. 1986. Represents 7 clients. All clients are new/unpublished writers. Qualifications for representation: "A writer's work must be professional in quality, i.e., has the subject matter been researched from psychological background meaningful to the growth of the written age category. Is the material written in an applicable form for the reader; it should not be written because the writer emotionally and stubbornly wants to impose his own, narrow approach." Prefers to review new material via a query and outline proposal. Reports in 2 weeks on a query, 6-8 weeks on a ms. Handles 10-15% each on nonfiction, fiction, ms/illustration package and illustrations only. Commission: 10-15% domestic sales; 15-25% foreign sales. Reading fee is $75. "Reader and agent" write the critiques. "Additional costs, after reading fee is used up, is deducted from royalties earned." Payment of criticism fee ensures writer's representation by agency.
Tips: "If you send us a manuscript, please include a self-addressed envelope (SASE) large enough to contain the work in case it is returned to you. Also, provide postage, but do not affix the stamps to the envelope."

# WOULD YOU USE THE SAME CALENDAR YEAR AFTER YEAR?

Of course not! If you scheduled your appointments using last year's calendar, you'd risk missing important meetings and deadlines, so you keep up-to-date with a new calendar each year. Just like your calendar, *Children's Writer's & Illustrator's Market* changes every year, too. Many of the editors move or get promoted, rates of pay increase, and even editorial needs change from the previous year. You can't afford to use an out-of-date book to plan your marketing efforts!

So save yourself the frustration of getting manuscripts returned in the mail, stamped MOVED: ADDRESS UNKNOWN. And of NOT submitting your work to new listings because you don't know they exist. Make sure you have the most current writing and marketing information by ordering *1991 Children's Writer's & Illustrator's Market* today. All you have to do is complete the attached post card and return it with your payment or charge card information. Order now, and there's one thing that won't change from your *1990 Children's Writer's & Illustrator's Market* - the price! That's right, we'll send you the 1991 edition for just $15.95. *1991 Children's Writer's & Illustrator's Market* will be published and ready for shipment in February 1991.

Let an old acquaintance be forgot, and toast the new edition of *Children's Writer's & Illustrator's Market*. Order today!

*(See other side for more helpful children's writing books)*

---

## To order, drop this postpaid card in the mail.

☐ **Yes!** I want the most current edition of *Children's Writer's & Illustrators Market*. Please send me the 1991 edition at the 1990 price - $15.95.* (NOTE: *1991 Children's Writer's & Illustrators Market* will be ready for shipment in February 1991.) #10190

Also send me these books to help me get published:

____(#10101) Writing for Children & Teenagers, $12.95,* paper
____(#1121) The Children's Picture Book, $16.95,* paper
____(#30082) How to Write & Illustrate Children's Books $22.50*

*Plus postage and handling: $3.00 for one book, 50c for each additional book. Ohio residents add 5 1/2% sales tax.

☐ Payment enclosed (Slip this card and your payment into an envelope)
☐ Please charge my: ☐ Visa ☐ MasterCard

Account # _____ Exp. Date _____

Signature _____

Name _____

Address _____

City _____ State _____ Zip _____

(This offer expires August 1, 1991)

**Writer's Digest Books**
Writer's Digest Books
1507 Dana Avenue
Cincinnati, OH 45207

Credit card orders call toll-free 1-800-289-0963

5619

# More Books to Help You Get Published!

## Writing for Children & Teenagers
*by Lee Wyndham/revised by Arnold Madison*
Filled with practical know-how and step-by-step instruction, including how to hold a young reader's attention, where to find ideas, and vocabulary lists based on age level, this third edition provides all the tips you need to flourish in today's children's literature market.
208 pages/$12.95, paperback

## The Children's Picture Book: How to Write It, How to Sell It
*by Ellen E. M. Roberts*
If you'd like to try your hand at writing children's picture books, this guide is for you. It answers virtually every question about the writing and selling process: how to choose a subject, plot a story, work with artists and editors, and market your book. Includes advice from professional picture book writers and editors, plus a list of agents who handle picture books.
189 pages/$16.95, paperback

## How to Write & Illustrate Children's Books
*Edited by Treld Pelkey Bicknell & Felicity Trotman*
A truly comprehensive guide that demonstrates how to bring freshness and vitality to children's text and pictures. Numerous illustrators, writers, and editors contribute their expert advice.
160 pages/$22.50

*Use coupon on other side to order today!*

---

# *Clubs/Organizations*

Professional organizations provide a writer or artist with a multitude of educational, business and legal services. Much of these services come in the form of newsletters, workshops or seminars that provide tips about how to be a better writer or artist, types of business records to keep, health and life insurance coverage you should carry or organizational competitions to be aware of.

As you read through the listings included here you will notice that some are open to professionals only, some are geared for amateurs and still others have different membership levels. Feel free to write for more information regarding any group that sounds interesting to ascertain its membership qualifications as well as services offered to members.

In addition to the educational benefits of belonging to a professional organization is the added "social" aspect of learning from peers and having a support system to help you through "dry" creative or financial periods. Membership in a writer's or artist's group also presents to a publisher an image of being serious about your craft. Of course, this provides no guarantee that your work will be published, but it offers an added dimension of credibility.

**\*ACTION FOR CHILDREN'S TELEVISION (ACT),** 20 University Rd., Cambridge MA 02138. (617)876-6620. President: Peggy Charren. Purpose of organization: "ACT is a national nonprofit children's television advocacy organization working to encourage diversity in children's television and to eliminate commercial abuses targeted to young children." Qualifications for membership: "payment of $20 yearly membership dues." Membership cost: "Membership begins at $20. Members may contribute more if they wish." Sponsors workshops/conferences; open to non-members. "ACT sponsors annual Achievement in Children's Television Awards for children's television series, home videos and public service campaigns." Awards a certificate. Contest open to non-members.

**AMERICAN SOCIETY OF JOURNALISTS AND AUTHORS,** 1501 Broadway, New York NY 10036. (212)997-0947. Executive Director: Alexandra Coator. Qualifications for membership: "Need to be a professional nonfiction writer published 8-10 times in general circulation publications." Cost of membership: Initiation fee—$50; annual dues—$120. Group sponsors annual conference May 5th, 1990; monthly workshops in NYC. Workshops/conferences open to non-members. Publishes a newsletter for members that provides confidential information for nonfiction writers. Sponsors contests that are open to non-members.

**THE AUTHORS GUILD,** 234 W. 44th St., New York NY 10036. (212)398-0838. Assistant Director: Peggy Randall. Purpose of organization: membership organization of 6,700 members that offers services and information materials intended to help authors with the business and legal aspects of their work, including contract problems, copyright matters, freedom of expression and taxation. Qualifications for membership: book author published by an established American publisher within 7 years or any author who has had three works, fiction or nonfiction, published by a magazine or magazines of general circulation in the last 18 months. Associate membership also available. Annual dues-$90. Different levels of membership include: associate membership with all rights except voting available to an author who has work in progress but who has not yet met the qualifications for active membership. This normally involves a firm contract offer from a publisher. Workshops/conferences: "The Guild and Authors League of America conduct several symposia each year at which experts provide information, offer advice, and answer questions on subjects of interest and concern to authors. Typical subjects have been the rights of privacy and publicity, libel, wills and estates, taxation, copyright, editors and editing, the art of interviewing, standards of criticism and book reviewing. Transcripts of these symposia are published and circulated to members." Symposia open to members only. "The *Author's Guild Bulletin*, a quarterly journal, contains articles on matters of interest to writers, reports of Guild activities, contract surveys, advice on problem clauses in contracts, transcripts of Guild and League symposia, and information on a variety of professional topics. Subscription included in the cost of the annual dues."

**THE AUTHORS RESOURCE CENTER,** Box 64785, Tucson AZ 85740-1785. (602)325-4733. Executive Director: Martha R. Gore; Associate Director: Diane C. Gore. Purpose of organization: to help writers, graphic artists and illustrators understand the business and professional realities of the publishing world—also have literary agency (opened March 1, 1987) and artists agency (opened January 1990) that markets members' books and illustrations to publishers. Qualifications for membership: serious interest in writing or illustrating. Membership cost: $50 per year for aspiring and published members. "Professional development workshops are open to members at a discount and to the general public. TARC instructors are actively publishing and often have academic credentials. The *Tarc Report* is published bimonthly and includes information about markets, resources, legal matters, writers workshops, reference sources, announcement of members' new books, reviews and other news important to members. Sample copy is $3. Subscription included in membership fee. *TARC* was established in 1984."

**\*CALIFORNIA WRITERS' CLUB,** 2214 Derby St., Berkeley CA 94705. (415)841-1217. Secretary: Dorothy V. Benson. Purpose of organization: "We are a nonprofit professional organization open to writers to provide writing and market information and to promote fellowship among writers." Qualifications for membership: "publication for active members; expected publication in five years for associate members." Membership cost: entry fee, $20; annual dues $25. (Entry fee is paid once.) Workshops/conferences: "Biennial summer conference, July 12-14, 1991, at Asilomar, Pacific Grove, CA; other conferences are held by local branches as they see fit." Conferences open to nonmembers. "Newsletter, which goes out to all CWC members, to newspapers and libraries, publishes the monthly meetings upcoming in the seven branches, plus the achievements of members, and market and contest opportunities." Sponsors contest. CWC's "major contest is for non-members, every two years, and first prizes in 5 categories is free tuition to the biennial conference; second prize is cash; and third prize a certificate."

**CANADIAN AUTHORS ASSOCIATION,** Ste. 104, 121 Avenue Rd., Toronto ON M5R 2G3 Canada. (416)926-8084. Contact: Executive Director. Purpose of organization: to help "emerging" writers and provide assistance to professional writers. Membership is

**The asterisk before a listing indicates that the listing is new in this edition.**

divided into three categories for individuals: Active (voting): Persons engaged in writing in any genre who have produced a sufficient body of work; Associate (non-voting): Persons interested in writing who have not yet produced sufficient material to qualify for Active membership, or those who, though not writers, have a sincere interest in Canadian literature; Apprentice (non-voting): Persons interested in learning to write who may join the Association as apprentices for a period not exceeding two years, unless they are bona fide students. Membership cost: $90-active members, $75-associates, $50-apprentice. Workshops/conferences: 69th Annual Conference, June 21-25, 1990 in Edmonton AB. "The conference draws writers, editors and publishers together in a congenial atmosphere providing seminars, workshops, panel discussions, readings by award-winning authors, and many social events." Open to non-members. Publishes a newsletter for members only. Also publishes a quarterly journal and a bienniel writer's guide available to non-members. "The Association created a major literary award program in 1975 to honor writing that achieves literary excellence without sacrificing popular appeal. The awards are in four categories—fiction, (for a full-length novel); nonfiction (excluding works of an instructional nature); poetry (for a volume of the works of one poet); and drama (for a single play published or staged). The awards consist of a handsome silver medal and $5,000 in cash; they are funded by Harlequin Enterprises, the Toronto-based international publisher." Contest open to nonmembers. Also contests for writing by students and for young readers (see Vicky Metcalf and Canadian Author & Bookman Awards).

**\*CHILDREN'S READING ROUND TABLE OF CHICAGO,** #1507, 3930 N. Pine Grove, Chicago IL 60613. (312)477-2271. Information Chairperson: Marilyn Singer. Purpose of organization: "to support activities which foster and enlarge children and young adults' interest in reading and to promote good fellowship among persons actively interested in the field of children's books." Qualifications for membership: "membership is open to anyone interested in children's books. There are no professional qualifications; however, the majority of our members are authors, freelance writers, illustrators, librarians, educators, editors, publishers and booksellers." Membership cost: $12 for year (June 1 through May 31), applicable to members within our Chicago meeting area; Associate Membership, $8, limited to persons outside the Metropolican Chicago Area or who are retired. "All members have same privileges, which include attendance at meetings; newsletter, *CRTT Bulletin*; yearbook published biennially; and access to information about CRRT special activities." Workshops/conferences: Children's Reading Round Table Summer Seminar for Writers & Illustrators, given in odd-numbered years. The 3-day seminar, at a Chicago college campus, usually in August, features guest speakers and a variety of profession-level workshops, manuscript critiquing and portfolio appraisal. Enrollment is open members and nonmembers; one fee applicable to all. Meals included, housing extra. Also, Children's Reading Round Table Children's Literature Conference, given in even-numbered years. One-day program, at a Chicago college campus, usually in early September. Program includes guest authors and educators, variety of workshops, exhibits, bookstore, lunch. Enrollment open to members and nonmembers; one fee applicable to all. *CRRT Bulletin, Children's Reading Round Table of Chicago* is published seven times a year, in advance of dinner meetings, and contains articles; book reviews; special sections of news about authors and artists; librarians and educators; publishers and booksellers. An Opportunity Column provides information about professional meetings, workshops, conferences, generally in the Midwest area. The *Bulletin* is available to members on payment of dues. Sample copies may be requested. Awards: "We do give an honorary award, the Children's Reading Round Table Annual Award, *not* for a single book or accomplishment but for long-term commitment to children's literature. Award includes check, lifetime membership, plaque. Nominations can be made *only* by CRRT members; nominees are not limited to membership."

INTERNATIONAL BLACK WRITERS, Box 1030, Chicago IL 60690. (312)995-5195. Executive Director: Mable Terrell. Purpose of organization: to encourage, develop and display writing talent. Qualifications for membership: the desire to write and willingness to work to excel in the craft. Membership cost: $15/year. Different levels of membership include: senior citizens and youth. Workshops/conferences: 1990 conference, June 8-10, Chicago IL. Open to nonmembers. Publishes a newsletter detailing issues of importance to writers, competitions. Nonmembers subscription: $15/year. Sponsors an annual writing competition in poetry, fiction and nonfiction. Deadline: May 30th. Awards include plaque and certificates. Contest open to nonmembers.

NEBRASKA WRITERS GUILD, 4111 Gertie, Lincoln NE 68516. (402)488-9263. President: Harry A. Dolphin. Purpose of organization: to assist regional writers in their professional development. Qualifications for membership: active members qualify by having marketed some of their production. Prose writers must have sold a minimum of 5,000 words published in media with minimum 2,500 circulation. Poets' requirements are established on a different basis. Associate members accepted. Membership cost: no initiation fees, current annual dues are $10. Different levels of membership include: very special writers (currently, 3) are honorary members; 30-year members are life members; active members (explained above). Associates submit material for evaluation. Workshops/conferences: 1990 conferences will be April 21 in Wayne, Nebraska, with the October 20 site to be announced at the April meeting. Open to nonmembers. Publishes news pertaining to members and information of assistance to members.

SAN DIEGO WRITERS/EDITORS GUILD, 3235 Homer Street, San Diego CA 92106. (619)223-5235. Treasurer: Elizabeth W. Smith. "The Guild was formed January, 1979 to meet the local writers' needs for assignments and editors who seek writers. The use of the Guild as a power to publicize poor editorial practices has evolved. We hope to meet writers' needs as we become aware of them and as members are willing to provide services." Activities include: monthly social meetings with a speaker, monthly newsletter, membership directory, workshops and conferences, other social activities. Qualifications for membership: published book; three published, paid pieces (nonfiction, fiction, prose, poetry), paid editor, produced screenplay or play, paid and published translations, public relations, publicity or advertising. "All professional members must submit clear evidence of work and a brief résumé. After acceptance, member need not requalify unless membership lapses." Membership cost: $25 annual fees, $40 member and spouse, $12.50 full-time student and out-of-state or county member. Different levels of membership include: associate and professional. Workshops/conferences: Fiesta/Siesta Conference, Murrieta Hot Springs and Spa, Murrieta, CA 92362, April 20, 21, 22, 1990. Open to nonmembers. Publishes a newsletter giving notice of meetings, conferences, contests.

SCIENCE FICTION WRITERS OF AMERICA, INC., Box 4236, West Columbia SC 29171. (803)791-5942. Executive Secretary: Peter Dennis Pautz. Purpose of organization: to encourage public interest in science fiction literature and provide organization format for writers/editors/artists within the genre. Qualifications for membership: at least one professional sale or other professional involvement within the field. Membership cost: annual active dues—$56; affiliate—$39; one-time installation fee of $10; dues year begins July 1. Different levels of membership include: affiliate requires one professional sale or professional involvement; active requires three professional short stories or one novel published. Workshops/conferences: annual awards banquet, usually in April or May. Open to nonmembers. Publishes newsletter. Nonmember subscription: $12.50 in U.S. Sponsors SFWA Nebula® Awards for best published SF in the categories of novel, novella, novelette, and short story. Awards trophy. Contest open to nonmembers.

**SOCIETY OF CHILDREN'S BOOK WRITERS**, Box 296, Mar Vista Station, Los Angeles CA 90066. (818)347-2849. Chairperson, Board of Directors: Sue Alexander. Purpose of organization: to assist writers and illustrators working or interested in the field. Qualifications for membership: an interest in children's literature and illustration. Membership cost: $35/year. Different levels of membership include: full membership — published authors/illustrators; associate membership — unpublished writers/illustrators. Workshops/conferences: 30-40 events around the country each year. Open to nonmembers. Publishes a newsletter focusing on writing and illustrating children's books. Sponsors Don Freeman Award for illustrators, 2 grants in aid.

**SOCIETY OF SOUTHWESTERN AUTHORS**, Box 3522, Tucson AZ 85740. Purpose of organization: to promote mutually supportive fellowship, recognition of achievement, stimulation and encouragement of professional writers. Qualifications for membership: professional authorship of books, articles, plays, movie and TV scripts. Membership cost: $10/year. Different levels of membership include: regular members, associate members. Workshops/conferences: we hold a writer's seminar the last week of each January at the University of Arizona to raise funds for scholarship awards for promising young writers. Open to nonmembers. "The Write Word" keeps members up-to-date on the activities and achievements of fellow members." Sponsors yearly scholarship awards for nonprofessional writers of short stories and articles. Awards $500 for winners in each category. Contest open to nonmembers.

No professional can ever know all he needs to know about his craft or the business aspects involved in maintaining a profit. Keeping up with trends in publishing, as well as changes in tax and copyright law, are only some of the topics covered by writing and illustration workshops.

Be aware that not every workshop included here relates specifically to juvenile writing or illustrating. Special courses for mystery, science fiction, western and romance writing are genres which transfer nicely to middle- and young adult readers plus general workshops in watercolors and oils for illustrators to enhance technique.

These listings will provide you with information describing what courses are offered, where and when, and the costs. Some of the national writing and art organizations also offer regional workshops throughout the year. Write for information.

**COUNCIL OF AUTHORS AND JOURNALISTS, INC.**, (formerly Dixie Council of Authors and Journalists, Inc.), % Ann Ritter, 1214 Laurel Hill Dr., Decatur GA 30033. (404)320-1076. Writer workshops geared toward beginner, intermediate, advanced, professional levels. Emphasizes general fiction, nonfiction, marketing, agents, editors. Classes/courses offered: 6-8 class periods each of 5 days. Guest speaker each evening. Workshops held: each June, usually beginning on Father's Day; one week, daily classes. Length of each session: 5 days. Maximum class size: averages 30. Writing facilities: comfortable motel rooms, acres of moss-draped oaks, beach. Cost of workshop: estimated at $195. Cost includes classes, individual conference/evaluation with instructor, contests (more than $1,000 in awards). Write for more information. "1990 is the 30th annual writing conference sponsored by CAJ."

**DRURY COLLEGE/SCBW WRITING FOR CHILDREN WORKSHOP**, Drury College, Springfield MO 65802. (417)865-8731. Assistant Director, Continuing Education: Lynn Doke. Writer and illustrator workshop geared toward beginner, intermediate, advanced, professional levels. Emphasizes all aspects of writing for children and teenagers. Classes/courses offered include: "A Picture Book from Idea to Publication," "What Makes Children Laugh," "Nuts and Bolts for Beginners," "Writing from Personal Experience." Workshop held in November. Length of each session: 1 hour. Maximum class size: 25-30. Cost of workshop: varies, includes sessions, refreshments. Send SASE for more information.

**HIGHLIGHTS FOUNDATION WRITERS WORKSHOP AT CHAUTAUQUA**, 711 Court St., Honesdale PA 18431. (717)253-1192. Conference Director: Jan Keen. Writer workshops geared toward beginner, intermediate, advanced levels. Classes/courses offered include: "Children's Interests," "Writing Dialogue," "Beginnings and Endings," "Science Writing," "My Stories for Young Readers." Workshops held July 14-21, 1990, Chautauqua Institution, Chautauqua, NY. Length of each session: 1½ hrs. Maximum class size: 100. Cost of workshop: $1,500 (if registered before April 25, early bird rate is $985); includes registration fee, gate ticket fee, workshop supplies and all meals. Write for more information.

**\*ROBERT QUACKENBUSH'S CHILDREN'S BOOK WRITING AND ILLUSTRATING WORKSHOP,** 460 East 79th St., New York NY 10021. (212)744-3822. Contact: Robert Quackenbush. Writer and illustrator workshops geared toward beginner, intermediate, advanced, professional levels. Emphasizes picture books from start to finish. Classes/ courses offered include: fall and winter courses, extend 10 weeks each—1½ hour/week; July workshop is a full five day (9 a.m.-4 p.m.) extensive course. Workshops held fall, winter and summer. Maximum class size: 8. Writing and/or art facilities available: work on the premises; art supply store nearby. Cost of workshop: $450 for instruction. Write for more information.

**SEMINARS FOR WRITERS,** (formerly Self-Publishing Children's Books), % Writers Connection, Ste. 180, 1601 Saratoga-Sunnyvale Rd., Cupertino CA 95014. (408)973-0227. FAX: (408)973-1219. Program Director: Meera Lester. Writer's workshops geared toward beginner, intermediate levels. Length of each session: six-hour session usually offered on a Saturday. Maximum class size: 35-40. Occasional seminars on writing for children (approximately 2-3 per year). Bookstore of 200 titles of writing, reference and how-to books. Write for more information.

**SIXTH ANNUAL CHILDREN'S LITERATURE CONFERENCE,** Hofstra University, 232 Memorial Hall, Hempstead NY 11550. (516)560-5997. Writers/Illustrators Contact: Lewis Shena, director, Liberal Arts Studies. Writer and illustrator workshops geared toward beginner, intermediate, advanced, professional levels. Emphasizes: fiction, non-fiction, poetry, submission procedures, picture books. Workshops held April 28, Saturday, 9:30 a.m. - 4:00 p.m. Length of each session: 2 hours. Maximum class size: 20. Cost of workshop includes: workshop, reception, lunch, panel discussions with guest speakers, e.g. "What An Editor Looks For." Write for more information. Co-sponsored by Society of Children's Book Writers.

**SOUTHERN CALIFORNIA SOCIETY OF CHILDREN'S BOOK WRITERS ILLUSTRATORS DAY,** 11943 Montana Ave. #105, Los Angeles CA 90049. (213)820-5601, 457-3501. Illustrator Regional Advisor: Judith Enderle. Illustrator workshops geared toward beginner, intermediate, advanced, professional levels. Emphasizes illustration and illustration markets. Classes/courses offered include: presentations by art director, children's book editor, and panel of artists/author-illustrators. Workshops held annually—this year's (90) Illustrator's day is Nov. 11. Length of each session: full day. Maximum class size: 100. "Editors and art directors will view portfolios. We want to know if each conferee is bringing a portfolio or not." Cost of workshop: $80 members, $90 nonmembers, includes lunch, handouts.
**Tips:** "This is a chance for illustrators to meet editors/art directors and each other."

**SUMMER WRITERS CONFERENCE,** Hofstra U - U.C.C.E. - Memorial 232, Hempstead NY 11550. (516)560-5997. Writers/Illustrators Contact: Lewis Shena, director, Liberal Arts Studies. Writer and illustrator workshops geared toward beginner, intermediate, advanced, professional levels. Emphasizes fiction, nonfiction, poetry, children's literature, stage/screen. Classes/courses offered: "Besides workshops, we arrange a series of

 **The asterisk before a listing indicates that the listing is new in this edition.**

readings and discussions." Workshops held Monday-Friday—2 weeks—July 9-20, 1990. Length of each session: daily, approximately 2½ hours of workshop and 1-2 hours of informal meetings. Maximum class size: 20. Writing/art facilities available: lecture room, tables, any media required will be gotten. Cost of workshop: noncredit, approximately $486; includes 1 workshop per day—special readings—special speakers. Dorm rooms available at additional cost. Write for more information.

**VASSAR INSTITUTE OF PUBLISHING AND WRITING: CHILDREN'S BOOKS IN THE MARKETPLACE**, Box 300, Vassar College, Poughkeepsie NY 12601. (914)437-5900. Program Coordinator: Claudia Duffy. Director: Barbara Lucas. Writer and illustrator workshops geared toward beginner, intermediate, advanced, professional levels. Emphasizes "the editorial, production, marketing and reviewing processes, on writing fiction and nonfiction for all ages, creating the picture book, understanding the markets and selling your work." Classes/courses offered include: "Writing Fiction," "The Editorial Process," "How to Write a Children's Book and Get It Published." Workshop held in 1989—June 18-25 (normally the 2nd or 3rd week in June). Length of each session: 3½-hour morning critique sessions, afternoon and evening lectures. Maximum class size: 55 (with three instructors). Cost of workshop: approximately $600, includes room, board and tuition for all critique sessions, lectures and social activities. "Proposals are pre-prepared and discussed at morning critique sessions. Art portfolio review given on pre-prepared works." Write for more information.
**Tips:** "This conference gives a comprehensive look at the publishing industry as well as offering critiques of creative writing and portfolio review."

**Advance.** A sum of money that a publisher pays a writer prior to the publication of a book. It is usually paid in installments, such as one-half on signing the contract; one half on delivery of a complete and satisfactory manuscript. The advance is paid against the royalty money that will be earned by the book.

**All rights.** The rights contracted to a publisher permitting a manuscript's use anywhere and in any form, including movie and book-club sales, without additional payment to the writer.

**ASAP.** Abbreviation for as soon as possible.

**B&W.** Abbreviation for black and white artwork or photographs.

**Backlist.** A publisher's list of books not published during the current season but still in print.

**Biennially.** Once every two years.

**Bimonthly.** Once every two months.

**Biweekly.** Once every two weeks.

**Bleed.** Area of a plate or print that extends beyond the actual trimmed sheet to be printed.

**Book packager.** Draws all elements of a book together, from the initial concept to writing and marketing strategies, then sells the book package to a book publisher and/or movie producer. Also known as book producer or book developer.

**Business-size envelope.** Also known as a #10 envelope, it is the standard size used in sending business correspondence.

**Camera-ready.** Art that is completely prepared for copy camera platemaking.

**Caption.** A description of the subject matter of an illustration or photograph; photo captions include names of people where appropriate. Also called cutline.

**Clean-copy.** A manuscript free of errors and needing no editing; it is ready for typesetting.

**Contract.** A written agreement stating the rights to be purchased by an editor or art director and the amount of payment the writer or illustrator will receive for that sale.

**Contributor's copies.** Copies of the issues of magazines sent to the author or illustrator in which his/her work appears.

**Copy.** Refers to the actual written material of a manuscript.

**Copyediting.** Editing a manuscript for grammar usage, spelling, punctuation, and general style.

**Copyright.** A means to legally protect an author's/illustrator's work. This can be shown by writing ©, your name, and year of work's creation.

**Cover letter.** A brief letter, accompanying a complete manuscript, especially useful if responding to an editor's request for a manuscript. A cover letter may also accompany a book proposal. A cover letter is not a query letter.

**Cutline.** See caption.

**Disk.** A round, flat magnetic plate on which computer data is stored.

**Division.** An unincorporated branch of a company.

**Dot-matrix.** Printed type in which individual characters are composed of a matrix or pattern of tiny dots.

**Final draft.** The last version of a "polished" manuscript ready for submission to the editor.

**First North American serial rights.** The right to publish material in a periodical before it appears in book form, for the first time, in the United States or Canada.

**Flat fee.** A one-time payment.

**GAG.** Graphic Artists Guild.

**Galleys.** The first typeset version of a manuscript that has not yet been divided into pages.

**Gatefold.** A page larger than the trim size of a book which is folded so as not to extend beyond the edges.

**Genre.** A formulaic type of fiction, such as adventure, mystery, romance, science fiction or western.

**Glossy.** A black and white photograph with a shiny surface as opposed to one with a non-shiny matte finish.

**Gouache.** Opaque watercolor with an appreciable film thickness and an actual paint layer.

**Halftone.** Reproduction of a continuous tone illustration with the image formed by dots produced by a camera lens screen.

**Hard copy.** The printed copy of a computer's output.

**ILAA.** Independent Literary Agents Association, Inc.

**Illustrations.** May be artwork, photographs, old engravings. Usually paid for separately from the manuscript.

**Imprint.** Name applied to a publisher's specific line or lines of books.

**IRC.** International Reply Coupon; purchased at the post office to enclose with text or artwork sent to a foreign buyer to cover his postage cost when replying or returning work.

**Keyline.** Identification, through signs and symbols, of the positions of illustrations and copy for the printer.

**Kill fee.** Portion of the agreed-upon price the author or artist receives for a job that was assigned, worked on, but then canceled.

**Layout.** Arrangement of illustrations, photographs, text and headlines for printed material.

**Letter-quality submission.** Computer printout that looks like a typewritten manuscript.

**Line drawing.** Illustration done with pencil or ink using no wash or other shading.

**Mechanicals.** Paste-up or preparation of work for printing.

**Middle reader.** The general classification of books written for readers 9-11 years of age.

**Modem.** A small electrical box that plugs into the serial card of a computer, used to transmit data from one computer to another, usually via telephone lines.

**Ms, mss.** Abbreviation for manuscript(s).

**One-time rights.** Permission to publish a story in periodical or book form one time only.

**Outline.** A summary of a book's contents in 5-15 double spaced pages; often in the form of chapter headings with a descriptive sentence or two under each one to show the scope of the book.

**Package sale.** The editor buys manuscript and illustrations/photos as a "package" and pays for them with one check.

**Payment on acceptance.** The writer or artist is paid for his work at the time the editor or art director decides to buy it.

**Payment on publication.** The writer or artist is paid for his work when it is published.

**Photocopied submissions.** Submitting photocopies of an original manuscript instead of sending the original. Do not assume that an editor who accepts photocopies will also accept multiple or simultaneous submissions.

**Photostat.** Black-and-white copies produced by an inexpensive photographic process using paper negatives; only line values are held with accuracy. Also called stat.

**Picture book.** A type of book aimed at the preschool to 8-year-old that tells the story primarily or entirely with artwork.

**PMT.** Photostat produced without a negative, somewhat like the Polaroid process.

**Print.** An impression pulled from an original plate, stone, block, screen or negative; also a positive made from a photographic negative.

**Proofreading.** Reading a manuscript to correct typographical errors.

**Query.** A letter to an editor designed to capture his/her interest in an article you purpose to write.

**Reading fee.** An arbitrary amount of money charged by some agents and publishers to read a submitted manuscript.

**Reporting time.** The time it takes for an editor to report to the author on his/her query or manuscript.

**Reprint rights.** Permission to print an already published work whose rights have been sold to another magazine or book publisher.

**Response time.** The average length of time it takes an editor or art director to accept or reject a manuscript or artwork and inform you of the decision.

**Rights.** What you offer to an editor or art director in exchange for printing your manuscripts or artwork.

**Rough draft.** A manuscript which has been written but not checked for errors in grammar, punctuation, spelling or content. It usually needs revision and rewriting.

**Roughs.** Preliminary sketches or drawings.

**Royalty.** An agreed percentage paid by the publisher to the writer or illustrator for each copy of his work sold.

**SAR.** Society of Author's Representatives.

**SASE.** Abbreviation for self-addressed, stamped envelope.

**SCBW.** Society of Children's Book Writers.

**Second serial rights.** Permission for the reprinting of a work in another periodical after its first publication in book or magazine form.

**Semiannual.** Once every six months.

**Semimonthly.** Twice a month.

**Semiweekly.** Twice a week.

**Serial rights.** The rights given by an author to a publisher to print a piece in one or more periodicals.

**Simultaneous submissions.** Sending the same article, story, poem or illustration to several publishers at the same time. Some publishers refuse to consider such submissions. No simultaneous submissions should be made without stating the fact in your letter.

**Slant.** The approach to a story or piece of artwork that will appeal to readers of a particular publication.

**Slush pile.** What editors call the collection of submitted manuscripts which have not been specifically asked for.

**Software.** Programs and related documentation for use with a particular computer system.

**Solicited manuscript.** Material which an editor has asked for or agreed to consider before being sent by the writer.

**SPAR.** Society of Photographers and Artists Representatives, Inc.

**Speculation (Spec).** Writing or drawing a piece with no assurance from the editor or art director that it will be purchased or any reimbursements for material or labor paid.

**Subsidiary rights.** All rights other than book publishing rights included in a book contract, such as paperback, book club and movie rights.

**Subsidy publisher.** A book publisher who charges the author for the cost of typesetting, printing and promoting a book. Also vanity publisher.

**Synopsis.** A brief summary of a story or novel. If part of a book proposal, it should be a page to a page and a half, single-spaced.

**Tabloid.** Publication printed on an ordinary newspaper page turned sideways.

**Tear sheet.** Page from a magazine or newspaper containing your printed story, article, poem or ad.

**Thumbnail.** A rough layout in miniature.

**Transparencies.** Positive color slides; not color prints.

**Unsolicited manuscript.** A story, article, poem, book or artwork sent without the editor's or art director's knowledge or consent.

**Vanity publisher.** See subsidy publisher.

**Word length.** The maximum number of words a manuscript should contain as determined by the editor or guidelines sheet.

**Word processor.** A computer that produces typewritten copy via automated typing, text-editing, and storage and transmission capabilities.

**Young adult.** The general classification of books written for readers ages 12-18.

**Young reader.** The general classification of books written for readers 5-8 years old. Here artwork supports the text as opposed to picture books.

The age-level index is set up to help you more quickly locate book markets geared to the age group(s) for which you write or illustrate. Read each listing carefully and follow the publisher's specific information about the type(s) of manuscript(s) each prefers to read and the style(s) of artwork each wishes to review.

## Picture books
## (preschool-8-year-olds)

Accent Books
Advocacy Press
Aegina Press/University Editions
African American Images
Aladdin Books/Collier Books for Young Adults
Albatross Books Pty. Ltd.
Alegra House Publishers
American Bible Society
Arcade Publishing
Atheneum Publishers
Barrons Educational Series
Beacon Press
Bradbury Press
Bright Ring Publishing
Carnival Enterprises
Carolina Wren Press/Lollipop Power Books
Carolrhoda Books, Inc.
Charlesbridge
Child's World, Inc., The
Chronicle Books
Clarion Books
Cobblehill Books
Coteau Books Ltd.
Council for Indian Education
Crocodile Books, USA
Crowell Junior Books, Thomas Y.
Davenport, Publishers, May
Dial Books for Young Readers
Doubleday
Dutton Children's Books
Eakin Publications
Exposition Phoenix Press
Farrar, Straus & Giroux
Four Winds Press
Godine, Publisher, David R.

Green Tiger Press
Harbinger House, Inc.
Harcourt Brace Jovanovich
Harvest House Publishers
Holiday House Inc.
Holt and Co., Inc., Henry
Homestead Publishing
Houghton Mifflin Co.
Humanics Children's House
Ideals Publishing Corporation
Jalmar Press
JB Lippincott Junior Books
Jewish Publication Society
Joy Street Books
Just Us Books, Inc.
Kar-Ben Copies, Inc.
Kendall Green Publications
Kingsway Publications
Knopf Books for Young Readers, Alfred A.
Kruza Kaleidoscopix, Inc.
Lion Books, Publisher
Lion Publishing Corporation
Little, Brown and Company
Lodestar Books
Lothrop, Lee & Shepard Books
McElderry Books, Margaret K.
Mage Publishers Inc.
Maryland Historical Press
Metamorphous Press
Morehouse Publishing Co.
Multnomah Press
National Press Inc.
New Seed Press
Oddo Publishing, Inc.
Odyssey Press
Orchard Books
Parenting Press, Inc.
Paulist Press

Perspectives Press
Philomel Books
Pippin Press
Potter, Clarkson N.
Price Stern Sloan
Random House Books for Young
   Readers
Rosebrier Publishing Co.
St. Paul Books and Media
Scholastic Hardcover
Scholastic, Inc.
Scojtia, Publishing Co., Inc.
Scribner's Sons, Charles
Standard Publishing
Stemmer House Publishers, Inc.
Sterling Publishing Co., Inc.
Trillium Press
TSM Books, Inc.
Tyndale House Publishers
Volcano Press
Walker and Co.
Warner Juvenile Books
Weekly Reader Books
Winston-Derek Publishers, Inc.

## Young readers
## (5-8-year-olds)

Accent Books
Advocacy Press
Aegina Press/University Editions
African American Images
Aladdin Books/Collier Books for
   Young Adults
Albatross Books Pty. Ltd.
Alegra House Publishers
American Bible Society
Atheneum Publishers
Barrons Educational Series
Beacon Press
Behrman House Inc.
Bookmaker's Guild, Inc.
Bradbury Press
Bright Ring Publishing
Carnival Enterprises
Carolina Wren Press/Lollipop Power
   Books
Carolrhoda Books, Inc.
China Books
Chronicle Books
Clarion Books
Cobblehill Books
Council for Indian Education
Crowell Junior Books, Thomas Y.

Dial Books for Young Readers
Dillon Press, Inc.
Double M Press
Doubleday
Dutton Children's Books
Eakin Publications
Exposition Phoenix Press
Farrar, Straus & Giroux
Friendship Press, Inc.
Godine, Publisher, David R.
Harbinger House, Inc.
Harvest House Publishers
Herald Press
Holiday House Inc.
Holt and Co., Inc., Henry
Homestead Publishing
Houghton Mifflin Co.
Humanics Children's House
Ideals Publishing Corporation
Incentive Publications, Inc.
Jalmar Press
JB Lippincott Junior Books
Jewish Publication Society
Joy Street Books
Just Us Books, Inc.
Kendall Green Publications
Kingsway Publications
Knopf Books for Young Readers, Al-
   fred A.
Kruza Kaleidoscopix, Inc.
Lerner Publications Co.
Lion Publishing Corporation
Little, Brown and Company
Lothrop, Lee & Shepard Books
McElderry Books, Margaret K.
March Media, Inc.
Maryland Historical Press
Meadowbrook Press
Messner, Julian
Metamorphous Press
Morehouse Publishing Co.
Multnomah Press
National Press Inc.
New Seed Press
Oddo Publishing, Inc.
Orchard Books
Parenting Press, Inc.
Paulist Press
Perspectives Press
Philomel Books
Pippin Press
Players Press, Inc.
Potter, Clarkson N.
Price Stern Sloan

Proforma Books
Random House Books for Young
   Readers
Rockrimmon Press, Inc., The
St. Anthony Messenger Press
St. Paul Books and Media
Scholastic Hardcover
Scholastic, Inc.
Scojtia, Publishing Co., Inc.
Scribner's Sons, Charles
Shoe Tree Press
Sri Rama Publishing
Standard Publishing
Stemmer House Publishers, Inc.
Trillium Press
Volcano Press
Walker and Co.
Warner Juvenile Books
Waterfront Books
Weigl Educational Publishers
Winston-Derek Publishers Inc.

## Middle readers
## (9-11-year-olds)

Aegina Press/University Editions
African American Images
Aladdin Books/Collier Books for
   Young Adults
Alegra House Publishers
American Bible Society
Arcade Publishing
Archway/Minstrel Books
Atheneum Publishers
Avon Books
Barrons Educational Series
Beacon Press
Behrman House Inc.
Bookmaker's Guild, Inc.
Bradbury Press
Breakwater Books
Bright Ring Publishing
Carnival Enterprises
Carolrhoda Books, Inc.
China Books
Chronicle Books
Clarion Books
Cobblehill Books
Council for Indian Education
Crowell Junior Books, Thomas Y.
Dial Books for Young Readers
Dillon Press, Inc.
Double M Press
Doubleday

Dutton Children's Books
Eakin Publications
Enslow Publishers Inc.
Exposition Phoenix Press
Faber and Faber, Inc.
Facts on File
Farrar, Straus & Giroux
Fiesta City Publishers
Four Winds Press
Free Spirit Publishing
Friendship Press, Inc.
Godine, Publisher, David R.
Greenhaven Press
Harbinger House, Inc.
Harcourt Brace Jovanovich
Herald Press
Holiday House Inc.
Holt and Co., Inc., Henry
Homestead Publishing
Houghton Mifflin Co.
Incentive Publications, Inc.
JB Lippincott Junior Books
Jewish Publication Society
Joy Street Books
Just Us Books, Inc.
Kendall Green Publications
Kingsway Publications
Knopf Books for Young Readers, Al-
   fred A.
Kruza Kaleidoscopix, Inc.
Lerner Publications Co.
Liguori Publications
Lion Books, Publisher
Lion Publishing Corporation
Little, Brown and Company
Lodestar Books
Lothrop, Lee & Shepard Books
Lucent Books
McElderry Books, Margaret K.
March Media, Inc.
Maryland Historical Press
Meadowbrook Press
Messner, Julian
Metamorphous Press
Misty Hill Press
Morehouse Publishing Co.
Mosaic Press
Multnomah Press
National Press Inc.
New Day Press
New Seed Press
Oddo Publishing, Inc.
Orchard Books
Pando Publications

## Young adults
## (12 and up)

Proforma Books
Rosen Publishing Group, The
St. Anthony Messenger Press
St. Paul Books and Media
Sandlapper Publishing Co., Inc.
Scholastic Hardcover
Scholastic, Inc.
Scojtia, Publishing Co., Inc.
Scribner's Sons, Charles
Shaw Publishers, Harold
Shoe Tree Press

Standard Publishing
Starfire
Stemmer House Publishers, Inc.
Trillium Press
Walker and Co.
Waterfront Books
Weekly Reader Books
Weigl Educational Publishers
Western Producer Prairie Books
Winston-Derek Publishers Inc.

# _____ *Age-Level Index*
# *Magazine Publishers*

The age-level index is set up to help you more quickly locate magazine markets geared to the age group(s) for which you write or illustrate. Read each listing carefully and follow the publisher's specific information about the type(s) of manuscript(s) each prefers to read and the style(s) of artwork each wishes to review.

## Picture books
## (preschool-8-year-olds)

Brilliant Star
Chickadee
Cochran's Corner
Day Care and Early Education
Dolphin Log
Highlights for Children
Hobo Stew Review
Humpty Dumpty's Magazine
Lighthouse
Mad Magazine
My Friend
National Geographic World
Nature Friend Magazine
Pennywhistle Press
Scienceland
Sing Out!
Skylark
Together Time

Turtle Magazine
Tyro Magazine
Wee Wisdom Magazine
Young Salvationist
Your Big Backyard

## Young readers
## (5-8-year-olds)

Atalantik
Brilliant Star
Calli's Tales
Chickadee
Child Life
Children's Playmate
Cochran's Corner
Day Care and Early Education
Equilibrium
Friend
Friend Magazine, The
Highlights for Children

Hob-Nob
Hobo Stew Review
Humpty Dumpty's Magazine
In-Between
Jack and Jill
Kid City
Lighthouse
Nature Friend Magazine
My Friend
Noah's Ark
Pockets
School Magazine, Blast Off!, Count-
    down, Orbit, Touchdown
Scienceland
Sing Out!
Single Parent, The
Skylark
Tyro Magazine
*U*S*Kids®
Wee Wisdom Magazine
Wonder Time
Young American
Young Judaean
Your Big Backyard

**Middle readers
(9-11-year-olds)**

Atalantik
Boys' Life
Brilliant Star
Child Life
Children's Digest
Clubhouse
Cobblestone
Cochran's Corner
Cricket Magazine
Crusader
Discoveries
Dolphin Log
Equilibrium
Faces
Friend Magazine, The
Highlights for Children
Hob-Nob
Hobo Stew Review
In-Between
Jack and Jill
Junior Trails
Lighthouse
Mad Magazine
My Friend
National Geographic World
Nature Friend Magazine

Noah's Ark
Odyssey
On The Line
Owl Magazine
Pennywhistle Press
Pockets
Radar
Ranger Rick
School Magazine, Blast Off!, Count-
    down, Orbit, Touchdown
Scope
Shofar
Sing Out!
Single Parent, The
Skylark
3-2-1 Contact
Touch
Tyro Magazine
*U*S*Kids®
Venture
Wee Wisdom Magazine
World of Busines$ Kids, The
Young American
Young Crusader, The
Young Judaean

**Young adults
(12 and up)**

Aim Magazine
Animal Tales
Atalantik
Boys' Life
Careers
Class Act
Clubhouse
Cobblestone
Cochran's Corner
Equilibrium
Exploring
Faces
Group
Guide Magazine
HiCall
Hob-Nob
Hobo Stew Review
In-Between
Insights
Jackie
Keynoter
Lighthouse
Listen
Mad Magazine
My Friend

National Geographic World
Nature Friend Magazine
Odyssey
Owl Magazine
Pennywhistle Press
Pioneer
Scholastic Math Magazine
Scope
Seventeen Magazine
Sing Out!
Single Parent, The
Skylark
Starwind
Straight
'TEEN Magazine

Teenage
3-2-1 Contact
Tiger Beat
Tiger Beat Star
TQ
Tyro Magazine
Venture
Voice
With
World of Busines$ Kids, The
Young American
Young Judaean
Young Salvationist
Youth Update

# Q

# R

# S

# Other Books of Interest
# for Children's Writers and Illustrators

**Annual Market Books**

Artist's Market, edited by Susan Conner $19.95

Humor & Cartoon Markets, edited by Bob Staake (paper) $15.95

Novel & Short Story Writer's Market, edited by Robin Gee (paper) $18.95

Photographer's Market, edited by Sam Marshall $19.95

Poet's Market, by Judson Jerome $18.95

Songwriter's Market, edited by Mark Garvey $18.95

Writer's Market, edited by Glenda Neff $23.95

**Writing for Children**

The Children's Picture Book: How to Write It, How to Sell It, by Ellen E. M. Roberts (paper) $16.95

Families Writing, by Peter R. Stillman $15.95

How to Write & Illustrate Children's Books, by Treld Pelkey Bicknell & Felicity Trotman $22.50

Nonfiction for Children: How to Write It, How to Sell It, by Ellen E. M. Roberts $16.95

Writing for Children & Teenagers, 3rd Edition, by Lee Wyndham/Revised by Arnold Madison (paper) $12.95

Writing Young Adult Novels, by Hadley Irwin & Jeannette Eyerly $14.95

**Illustration**

Drawing & Painting with Ink, by Fritz Henning $24.95

Fantasy Art, by Bruce Robertson $24.95

Illustration & Drawing: Styles & Techniques, by Terry R. Presnell $22.95

Painting Watercolor Portraits that Glow, by Jan Kunz $27.95

People Painting Scrapbook, by J. Everett Draper $26.95

Putting People in Your Paintings, by J. Everett Draper $22.50

**Reference Books**

Beginning Writer's Answer Book, edited by Kirk Polking (paper)$13.95

The Complete Guide to Self-Publishing, by Tom & Marilyn Ross (paper) $16.95

How to Write a Book Proposal, by Michael Larsen $10.95

How to Write with a Collaborator, by Hal Bennett with Michael Larsen $11.95

Knowing Where to Look: The Ultimate Guide to Research, by Lois Horowitz (paper) $15.95

Literary Agents: How to Get & Work with the Right One for You, by Michael Larsen $9.95

Time Management for Writers, by Ted Schwarz $10.95

12 Keys to Writing Books that Sell, by Kathleen Krull (paper) $12.95

The 29 Most Common Writing Mistakes & How to Avoid Them,by Judy Delton $9.95

Word Processing Secrets for Writers, by Michael A. Banks & Ansen Dibell (paper) $14.95

The Writer's Digest Guide to Manuscript Formats, by Dian Dincin Buchman & Seli Groves $16.95

How to Sell Your Photographs & Illustrations, by Elliot & Barbara Gordon (paper) $16.95

Business & Legal Forms for Authors & Self Publishers, by Tad Crawford (paper) $15.95

**Graphics/Business of Art**

Airbrushing the Human Form, by Andy Charlesworth (cloth) $27.95

Artist's Friendly Legal Guide, by Conner, Karlen, Perwin & Spatt (paper) $15.95

Basic Graphic Design & Paste-Up, by Jack Warren (paper) $13.95

Color Harmony: A Guide to Creative Color Combinations, by Hideaki Chijiiwa (paper) $15.95

Complete Airbrush & Photoretouching Manual, by Peter Owen & John Sutcliffe (cloth) $24.95

The Complete Guide to Greeting Card Design & Illustration, by Eva Szela (cloth) $27.95

Creative Ad Design & Illustration, by Dick Ward (cloth) $32.95

Design Rendering Techniques, by Dick Powell (cloth) $29.95

Dynamic Airbrush, by David Miller & James Effler (cloth) $29.95

Getting It Printed, by Beach, Shepro & Russon (paper) $29.50

The Graphic Artist's Guide to Marketing & Self Promotion, by Sally Prince Davis (paper) $15.95

How to Design Trademarks & Logos, by Murphy & Rowe (cloth) $24.95

How to Draw Charts & Diagrams, by Bruce Robertson (cloth) $24.95

How to Draw & Sell Cartoons, by Ross Thomson & Bill Hewison (cloth) $17.95

How to Draw & Sell Comic Strips, by Alan McKenzie (cloth) $18.95

How to Understand & Use Design & Layout, by Alan Swann (cloth) $24.95
The Creative Artist, by Nita Leland (cloth) $27.95
Business & Legal Forms for Fine Artists, by Tad Crawford (paper) $12.95
Business & Legal Forms for Illustrators, by Tad Crawford (paper) $15.95
Marker Rendering Techniques, by Dick Powell & Patricia Monahan (cloth) $32.95
Presentation Techniques for the Graphic Artist, by Jenny Mulherin (cloth) $24.95
Studio Secrets for the Graphic Artist, by Jack Buchan (cloth) $29.95
Type: Design, Color, Character & Use, by Michael Beaumont (cloth) $24.95

## Watercolor

Getting Started in Watercolor, by John Blockley (paper) $19.95
Painting Nature's Details in Watercolor, by Cathy Johnson (cloth) $24.95
Watercolor Interpretations, by John Blockley (paper) $19.95
Watercolor Painter's Solution Book, by Angela Gair (cloth) $24.95
Watercolor Fast & Loose, by Ron Ranson (cloth) $21.95
Watercolor—The Creative Experience, by Barbara Nechis (paper) $16.95
Watercolor Tricks & Techniques, by Cathy Johnson (cloth) $24.95
Watercolor Workbook, by Bud Biggs & Lois Marshall (paper) $19.95
Watercolor: You Can Do It!, by Tony Couch (cloth) $26.95

## Mixed Media

Catching Light in Your Paintings, by Charles Sovek (paper) $18.95
Colored Pencil Drawing Techniques, by Iain Hutton-Jamieson (cloth) $24.95
Exploring Color, by Nita Leland (cloth) $26.95
Keys to Drawing, by Bert Dodson (cloth) $21.95
The North Light Illustrated Book of Painting Techniques, by Elizabeth Tate (cloth) $27.95
Oil Painting: A Direct Approach, by Joyce Pike (cloth) $26.95
Painting Seascapes in Sharp Focus, by Lin Seslar (cloth) $24.95
Pastel Painting Techniques, by Guy Roddon (cloth) $24.95
The Pencil, by Paul Calle (paper) $17.95
Tonal Values: How to See Them, How to Paint Them, by Angela Gair (cloth) $24.95
Decorative Painting for Children's Rooms, by Rosie Fisher (cloth) $29.95

A complete catalog of Writer's Digest Books and North Light Books is available
**FREE** by writing to the address shown below. To order books directly from the
publisher, include $3.00 postage and handling for 1 book, 50¢ for each additional
book. Allow 30 days for delivery.

**Writer's Digest Books/North Light Books**
**1507 Dana Avenue, Cincinnati, Ohio 45207**
Credit card orders call TOLL-FREE
1-800-289-0963

Write to this same address for information on *Writer's Digest* magazine, Writer's
Digest Book Club, Writer's Digest School, Writer's Digest Criticism Service, North
Light Book Club, Graphic Artist's Book Club, *The Artist's Magazine*, HOW Magazine
and *Story* Magazine.

Prices subject to change without notice.

# Notes

# Notes